Linguistic Culture and Language Policy

The language policies and rules that nations draw up dictate which form of language will be taught in schools and used as the official tongue of the nation. The focus of this book will be to look at language policy in three very different nations and to examine how their policies are grounded in each of their own unique cultures.

By looking closely at the multilingual democracies of India, France and the USA, Harold Schiffman examines how their policies evolved. The author shows how language policy is primarily a social construct that rests on other conceptual elements such as belief systems, attitudes and myths. It is these elements that the author presents as the *linguistic culture* of a society. Contrary to viewing language policy as the specific, overt and explicit embodiment of rules, this book examines how these policies are formed within a broader framework and are heavily influenced by the covert and implicit grass-roots of its own linguistic culture. By seeing language policy as culture-specific we can understand why language policies evolve the way they do, why they work, or not, and how people's lives are affected by them. In addition, the author also focuses on one linguistic minority region of each of his chosen nations, to show how linguistic minorities in these areas have been dealt with over the centuries, and how policies have evolved to deal with these challenges to the 'official' language.

This book will be of interest to linguists specialising in multilingual/ multicultural societies, bilingual educationalists, curriculum planners and teachers.

Harold F. Schiffman is Professor of South Asian Regional Studies and Luce Professor of Language Learning at the University of Pennsylvania.

The Politics of Language

Series editors: Tony Crowley,
University of Manchester

Talbot J. Taylor,
College of William and Mary,
Williamsburg, Virginia

In the lives of individuals and societies, language is a factor of greater importance than any other. For the study of language to remain solely the business of a handful of specialists would be a quite unacceptable state of affairs.

Saussure

The Politics of Language series covers the field of language and cultural theory and will publish radical and innovative texts in this area. In recent years the developments and advances in the study of language and cultural criticism have brought to the fore a new set of questions. The shift from purely formal, analytical approaches has created an interest in the role of language in the social, political and ideological realms and the series will seek to address these problems with a clear and informed approach. The intention is to gain recognition for the central role of language in individual and public life.

Other books in the series include:

Broken English
Dialects and the Politics of Language in Renaissance Writings
Paula Blank

Verbal Hygiene
Deborah Cameron

Linguistic Ecology
Language Change and Linguistic Imperialism in the Pacific Region
Peter Mühlhäusler

Language as Ideology
Gunther Kress and Robert Hodge

Language in History
Theories and Texts
Tony Crowley

Researching Language
Issues of Power and Method
Kay Richardson, Deborah Cameron, Penelope Harvey, Ben Rampton and Elizabeth Frazer

Linguistic Culture and Language Policy

Harold F. Schiffman

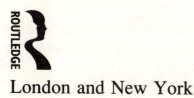

London and New York

First published 1996
by Routledge
11 New Fetter Lane, London EC4P 4EE

Simultaneously published in the USA and Canada
by Routledge
29 West 35th Street, New York, NY 10001

First published in paperback 1998

Typeset in Times by
J&L Composition Ltd, Filey, North Yorkshire
Printed in Great Britain by
Redwood Books, Trowbridge, Wiltshire

'Language, linguistics, and politics in Tamilnad' by Harold F. Schiffman in
Edwin Gerow and Margery D. Lang (eds) *Studies in the Language
and Culture of South Asia* (1974): by permission of University of
Washington Press; 'S büchnawele' by André Weckmann from
schàng d sunn schint schun làng (1975): by permission of the author

British Library Cataloguing in Publication Data
A catalogue record for this book is available from the British Library

Library of Congress Cataloguing in Publication Data
A catalogue record for this book is available from the Library of Congress

ISBN 0–415–12875–7 (hbk)
ISBN 0–415–18406–1 (pbk)

Contents

List of figures and tables

Figures

Tables

Preface

This book has had a very long gestation. After a sabbatical in which I spent a month in Strasbourg in 1987, I began to write a long article about language policy in three 'multilingual democracies'. Before I knew it, other concerns began to make themselves felt, and the end result is this book. In a sense, however, my interest in language policy goes back to my first period of study in India in 1965–6, where universities and schools had just reopened after riots over the Official Language issue. At a meeting of the fellows of the American Institute of Indian Studies in Pune in early 1966, I was asked several times what it was like doing research among those 'fanatical' Tamil 'chauvinists'. I had not until then thought about policy issues, since I was working on the syntax of aspectual verbs, but a germ was planted, and I began to see sociolinguistic connections that I had previously ignored.

In the early 1970s I discovered the work of the German sociologist of language Heinz Kloss, and began to teach a course on language policy through the Anthropology and Linguistics departments at the University of Washington. Kloss's work focused strongly on the German experience in America, and this led me to explore certain issues of German-American linguistic assimilation using sources available to me through family connections.

In the mid-1970s my colleague Michael Shapiro and I published a book on the sociolinguistics of South Asia (Shapiro and Schiffman 1981), for which we originally had planned for a chapter on language and politics. Various constraints, mostly time and money, prevented its inclusion, but some preliminary thinking about it did occupy a corner of my mind. What concerned me most about most treatments of language policy by social scientists was that there was little attention paid to humanistic concerns. Political scientists and sociologists of language (with some notable exceptions) have concentrated on quantifiable, empirically verifiable data, and have little patience with such things as the power of a poem to move another human being, or the love of one's language that might impel someone to give up one's life for it. Such expressions are usually dismissed as 'primordialism', or are explained away with such axioms as 'every man has his price', meaning that primordialism can usually be bought off.

The other area that I always found lacking in social-scientific treatments of language policy was language itself. Though 'language' is obviously a factor in a 'language and politics' situation, it is usually treated as a kind of 'black box', that is, its internal workings, the interface between language and social behaviour is either ignored or dealt with only mechanistically. Furthermore, one gets the impression that many social-scientific accounts would differ not at all if the particular language in the context being investigated were any other language of the world. That is, all languages are treated as being the same, or all linguistic cultures are treated as interchangeable. Since I see French linguistic culture as very different from Tamil linguistic culture or Japanese linguistic culture, I am interested in the particularities of these differences, rather than boiling everything down to fit a theoretical framework popular at the moment in one or another social-science discipline. Nor can I see the differences between French linguistic culture and Japanese linguistic culture as merely differences in the French and Japanese political systems.

For these reasons this book eschews theoretical constructs of a formalist, post-modern, or neo-Marxist kind, but insists instead on the primacy of linguistic culture as the locus of language policy. In other words, it puts language, and everything associated with language, at the centre of language policy, both in terms of its formation and the study of it.

Many people have helped me with various tasks associated with this project, and I very much want to acknowledge the contributions and help of the following persons: Roland Breton, William Bright, Nina Catach, John Joseph, Penelope Gardner-Chloros, Pierre-Yves Connan, Heles Contreras, Marie-Noelle Deseilligny, François Grin, Eugene Hunn, Jurgen Klausenburger, Alain Howiller, A. G. Menon, Jonathan Pool, Sumathi Ramaswamy, David Rothel, Richard Salomon, Ken Taylor, Talbot Taylor, Michael Toolan, Henriette Walter and Linda Ward. I am indebted to the Graduate School, University of Washington, for support of research on German-Americans in 1976, and for sabbatical quarters in 1976, 1987 and 1993–4 that enabled me to carry out the work, and to the J. William Fulbright Foundation for a Fulbright/CIES grant for research among Tamils in Singapore and Malaysia in 1994.

I also thank my wife Marilyn and my son Timothy for being willing to be dragged along on these overseas stints, and my students in my language policy course for requiring me to focus my ideas more sharply.

Harold Schiffman
May 1995

1 Introduction: language policy and linguistic culture

1.1 TYPOLOGIZING LANGUAGE POLICY

The original plan for this book was that it be a study of different kinds of language policies, to be exemplified by a selection of typical kinds of policies exhibited by a small number of nation states (and other polities) in the modern and pre-modern world. I had originally intended to contrast the policies of the USA, France and India, since those are familiar to me from personal research, and because they are in some ways very typical. French language policy represents *centrist* policy par excellence, that is, a unilingual policy decreed from above, handed down and strictly controlled by a highly centralized state (multilingual, but refusing to recognize it). US language policy was to exemplify *laissez-faire* policy as applied to a supposedly mono-lingual state that is actually multilingual; Indian language policy was to represent an admittedly multilingual nation to which the Soviet policy model has been transplanted, but with unhappy results.

There are other models that fit somewhere in between these, but these three elegantly represent a *continuum* of policies, from the autocratic centrist policy of France to the multilingual accommodationist (even then limited) policy of India, with the USA somewhere in between. They also represent three kinds of historical development – the autocratic, monarchic European centrist type that has its roots in the nation-building period of sixteenth-century France, which the French Revolution simply carried to its logical extreme; the 'democratic' separation of powers development seen in the USA two centuries ago, and the post-modern, post-colonial striving of newly emerging nations (India).

But there are a number of problems with the notion that one can easily typologize language policies and arrange them along a conti-nuum. One is that things never quite fit in a linear order in typologies, but beyond that, even in a given polity, the policy rarely fits the situation without problems of various sorts. For one thing, there is usually a difference between the policy as stated (the official, *de jure* or overt policy) and the policy as it actually works at the practical level (the covert, *de facto* or grass-roots policy). This may result from some historical change, for example, increase in numbers or political power of a formerly insignificant minority, such as by immigration, demographics (birth rate), or conquest of territory. But alas, the 'fit' between language policies and the polities for which they have been devised are rarely appropriate, and in actual practice a typology of policies would look very different from a typology of the multilingual states that they have been applied to. This led me to consider whether there were good reasons why policies were often poorly selected, or whether this was in some way an 'accident' of history (if there is such a thing), or perhaps even misguided or wrongheaded (for some reason). I began to wonder whether language policy can in fact be managed by human beings in an explicit interventionary way.

1.2 POLICIES AND POLITIES

Another problem with the typological approach to language policies is that the possession of one or another kind of language policy is not only a characteristic of nation states, but also of smaller administrative or territorial divisions within them, such as states or provinces in federalized polities (e.g. the cantons of Switzerland, the provinces of Canada, the states of India and the USA, the republics of the Soviet Union, etc.). Beyond that, we may find differing policies exhibited at the municipal level, in educational institutions of all sorts (school districts, universities), in libraries, in the judiciary, in different levels of state bureaucracy,[1] as well as in non-governmental bodies such as churches (temple, mosques, . . .), labour unions, fraternal lodges and so on. Furthermore, though overt policy may be guaranteed at the federal or central level, the 'trickle-down' effect of these policies may be minimal at the local level, or the resources to defend these rights may be inadequate. With these levels of complexity, it would seem almost futile to attempt to establish types of language policies, and even if it could be done, many generalizations would be lacking. In typologies that have been attempted, we often see a confusion between societal multilingualism and policies *about* multilingualism, that is, we see an assumption that what is *de jure* the case is also *de facto* the case, and vice versa.[2]

It is of course true that multilingualism is often to some extent the *product* of certain language policies, just as it seems also verifiable that certain policies have come about in order to deal with the multilingualism of the citizenry. Which comes first (the chicken or the egg) is not *a priori* obvious.

1.3 INPUTS AND OUTCOMES: CAUSES AND EFFECTS

Another problem with some approaches to questions of language policy, language planning, language loyalty, and other sociolinguistic issues, is that that some researchers seem to interpret reasons for various developments as *outcomes* of policy when it is clear that they are elements *underlying* the policy. That is, conclusions are drawn about supposedly causal relationships between language and policy that seem to me totally turned around.

It is also an unfortunate fact that in the literature on language policy and language planning these two topics are treated as one. In study after study containing the term 'language policy' in the title one finds in fact that the topic is really language planning; this is fine, of course, if language planning is the main thrust of the policy in question. For my purposes, I prefer to distinguish the two. For the time being, let us use as a working definition of language policy and language planning the following:

> The term *language policy* here refers, briefly, to the policy of a society in the area of linguistic communication – that is, the set of positions, principles and decisions reflecting that community's relationships to its verbal repertoire and communicative potential. *Language planning* is understood as a set of concrete measures taken within language policy to act on linguistic communication in a community, typically by directing the development of its languages.
>
> (Bugarski 1992: 18, emphasis in original)

Another view of this dichotomy is presented in an article by Cloonan and Strine (1991: 268ff.) who characterize the language planning approach to that policy development as *deliberate*, *rational*, *prospective* and *institutional*. (By prospective is meant that it is future-oriented, and planning precedes implementation; by institutional is meant that it is organized by planning bodies or institutions.) But Cloonan and Strine demonstrate that a great deal of policy formulation in the USA, for example, is none of these – it tends to be decentralized, lacks formal fact-finding, is reactive and *ad hoc*. Because of the lack of federally mandated language planning, in other words, policy formulation is carried on at state and local levels, and in response to client demands. The result is, of course, a hodge-podge of rules, regulations and policies that may be in conflict with other state, local, or even federal rules, regulations and policies; thus a state like California may have an official policy on English (arrived at by referendum) requiring one approach, and simultaneously have statutory laws (codes, rules) mandated or arrived at by other avenues. We will examine this in detail in Chapter 9; my point is to show that it is futile to look for overt policies where none exists, and a waste of time always to focus on explicit planning, or to consider something to *be* the policy simply because it is written.

I shall build on this distinction to broaden the notion of policy even further, and restrict the notion of planning to deliberate, explicit or concrete activities on behalf of language. In the process we shall see that much more happens at the covert level, especially in polities like the USA, than at the overt level.

1.3.1 Need for broader scope

As an example of the need for a broader scope to the notion of policy, consider the sociolinguistic situation we find in South Asia, where the existence of sharply differentiated spoken and written varieties of a given language (*diglossia*) has profound effects on language policy.[3] In diglossic linguistic cultures, typically, overt policies specify the rights and domains of specific languages, but only to the literary or standard language – they ignore the existence of a broad spectrum of verbal repertoires that are employed by people in various ways. As various researchers have pointed out (Ferguson 1959a; Hudson 1991b), diglossia arises under certain social conditions, and once established, becomes a social construct that governs the uses and functions of different varieties; there is widespread agreement in the society about the cultural legitimacy and differentiation of these codes and their uses. Essentially diglossia controls both the 'corpus' of all varieties in use[4] and the status of each variety. Any attempt by policy-planners to change this situation will encounter widespread resistance from many if not all segments of society.

Overt language policy in South Asia is therefore neither causative nor resultative with regard to diglossia: the policy ignores spoken repertoires, which are thought of as 'broken', corrupt', low', vulgar', etc., almost in the hope that this will cause them to disappear. But diglossia in such areas persists, and has persisted perhaps for millennia. The *persistence* of diglossia in an area like India is not so much an overt *policy* issue as it is a deep-seated cultural behaviour towards language. That is, diglossia has to be considered to be a *given*, an underlying assumption, an input to the decision-making process, even an underlying *cultural policy* if you will, not a result of it, and not something that can be ignored.[5] Since it is not part of the explicit policy, it is not amenable to change in the same way that more explicit aspects of policy might be. In some parts of the world, diglossia might perhaps be eliminated by a stroke of some ruler's pen, but it is clear in India that no ruler would even contemplate it, let alone attempt it. Were such a peremptory attempt to be made, it would certainly fail.

As we shall see in other ways as well, certain issues that might seem to be policy issues (in the overt understanding of the term), and therefore subject to manipulation and planning, are not amenable to political intervention or manipulation, and diglossia in South Asia is one of these.[6]

When we consider such complexities, it becomes obvious that if we are to search for explanations of why certain polities have the kinds of language policies they have, we must look more deeply into their linguistic histories, in particular those aspects of language that I have come to refer to as 'linguistic culture'.[7]

1.4 THE LOCUS OF LANGUAGE POLICY

It should be clear by now that the basic tenet of this book is that language policy is ultimately grounded in *linguistic culture*, that is, the set of behaviours, assumptions, cultural forms, prejudices, folk belief systems, attitudes, stereotypes, ways of thinking about language, and religio-historical circumstances associated with a particular language. That is, the beliefs (one might even use the term myths) that a speech community has about language (and this includes literacy) in general and its language in particular (from which it usually derives its attitudes towards other languages) are part of the social conditions that affect the maintenance and transmission of its language.[8] Therefore, typologizing language policies without looking at the background in which they arise is probably futile, if not simply trivial. In this light, works like that of Falch (1973), a dry catalogue of types of language policy in Europe, tell us nothing about why a particular polity exhibits a particular policy. It is as if the choice of language policies was totally *random*, from 'off the shelf' as it were, without any relationship to the historical, social, cultural, educational or religious conditions extant in a particular area. There may indeed be such an appearance of randomness in certain polities – certainly there have been autocratic rulers and megalomaniacs who made single-minded decisions, but even so, we can demonstrate that such autocrats are usually the products of their own culture; they are deeply embedded in some sort of cultural tradition. These traditions may be part of the 'great tradition' of the culture, or may be less highly respected, or even officially or internationally despised aspects of culture, such as widespread anti-semitism, racism, or chauvinism of any sort. These policy-makers may be simply responding to certain conditions in their background that they may be unaware of, or consider perfectly natural and appropriate. This is particularly true when inappropriate policies are handed down with the expectation that they will be implemented without regard for local conditions.

In nineteenth-century Tsarist Russia, for example, the *de jure* policy was one of Russian only, and on the surface, this is what prevailed. In actuality, deviations from this policy occurred, such as in those portions of partitioned Poland occupied by Russia. We know from anecdotal evidence, however, such as the autobiographies of Polish speakers like Maria Skłodowska Curie, that teachers in the schools she attended covertly taught in Polish, all the while paying lip-service to Russian, and parading the best students (that is those knowing Russian best) before the school inspectors, who visited occasionally to see if various aspects of school policy (including language policy) were being carried out. We also know that in the same Russian Empire, exceptions were made for Finnish and Swedish that were not allowed for Slavic languages, and yet other more restrictive rules applied to non-Indo-European languages spoken in various areas of the Russian Empire, such as the Turkic languages of central Asia, the Caucasian languages of the Caucasus, Armenian, etc. I am tempted to refer to such policies as 'Potemkin' policies, since they resemble another aspect of Tsarist rule, the Potemkin village. This was the habit of constructing false-front villages, with actors costumed as peasants, smiling and waving to Tsarina Catherine the Great as she passed by. Catherine was happy that her peasants were happy, and could return to other pursuits. Language policies with a false front, publicly declaring that only one language may be used, but concealing another reality, sometimes even colluding with that reality, probably exist in many places in the world. It is danger-ous, I think, to act as if the Potemkin policy is the reality.

Other examples of 'Potemkin' policies are the case of Catalan in many 'Castilian-medium' schools in Catalonia during the Franco period in Spain; the case of primary schools language medium in Nagaland (northeast India), where teachers use Nagamese (Naga Pidgin) for much of the oral communication, while the textbooks and all overt signs of language policy perpetuate the notion that the school is in 'English-medium' (Sreedhar 1974), and German-American parochial schools in nineteenth-century America.

Thus, to return to the example of diglossia, the fact that a language is diglossic is in actuality a feature of the linguistic culture of the area where that language is used, rather than of the language or of the overt language policy *per se*. To speak of a particular language as diglossic or not, is at best imprecise, since a language (e.g. English) as spoken in one part of the world may exhibit no diglossia, while the same language (again using English as an example) as used in a creole community (or in African-American speech communities in the USA) would have to be considered to constitute a diglossic situation. Nor can *speakers* of a particular language be characterized as diglossic; only their behaviour, or the behaviour of the speech *community*. And, I think it can be shown, beliefs and attitudes about the language determine and condition the maintenance of diglossia as a fact of linguistic culture. In the case of the Tamils, for example, it is the set of beliefs about the antiquity and purity of Tamil that unites all members of the linguistic culture (irrespective of religion, caste or nationality) in its resistance to any change in the corpus or status of Tamil, by which of course is meant H-variety Tamil (Schiffman 1974: 127).

1.4.1 Empirical bases for the study of linguistic culture

In all linguistic cultures that I know of there are certain understandings that culture-bearers have about what makes language polite, and what constitutes lack of politeness. Though these rules are not hard and fast – people make exceptions for small children, for example – and there are different understandings of what is polite among older people than among younger people (and between men and women, people with power and people without, etc.), there is a certain amount of commonality in the understandings about how language is to be used to get certain things done.

The study of how language is used, and how members of the culture acquire and display knowledge of usage, has been approached in different ways by philosophers, anthropologists, sociologists of language, social psychologists, and so on. Notwithstanding, these approaches to the cultural context of language all recognize that the formal study of linguistic codes is necessary but not sufficient to our understanding of how people communicate. In the case of a diglossic language like Arabic or Tamil, one may understand and perfectly control the various codes involved in the diglossic complex (that is the rules of Qur'anic Arabic, of modern literary standard Arabic, or colloquial Egyptian Arabic) but may not be able to communicate in many situations in the Arab world because of an inadequate understanding of when which form is used for what and with whom.

This knowledge of sociolinguistic rules is not recognized by theoretical formal linguists as part of grammatical knowledge; typically, theoretical linguistics treats the different codes as totally different systems with their own grammatical rules. Knowledge of when to use which form has often been dismissed as a matter of mere 'performance', when in fact this knowledge, though implicit in particular linguistic cultures, can be empirically described and codified. Ground-rules seem to exist, and the study of pragmatics, or of communicative competence, or the ethnography of communication[9] (various terms have been proposed by different disciplines) has already given us much insight into these behaviours.

For my purposes, this kind of rule-making about language is part of linguistic culture; it is as important to know how politeness rules affect different age groups, gender groups and ethnic groups within a society as it is to study overt rules about the use or form of entire codes.

1.4.1.1 Cultural determinism?

It is probably important at this point to discuss what is known in anthropology as *cultural determinism* and how the study of linguistic culture differs. Cultural determinism is the term for the notion that different cultures cause or determine certain behaviours in their members, and that these cultural rules bind or constrain people, allowing them no alternative but to act in a certain way. In fact in a growing number of legal disputes involving members of different subcultures, litigants have been known to claim that they were simply acting by their own cultural rules, and could not be expected to act any differently. Many anthropologists now warn us to avoid cultural determinism and not 'incarcerate' people in their cultures; some even advocate abandonment of the notion of 'culture' completely.

My use of the notion that there is such a thing as linguistic culture does not rest on the premise that it is deterministic. I do not claim that certain cultural/linguistic values predetermine that certain language policies will evolve. I do not give strong credence to the Whorfian hypothesis, and am aware of all of the problems of claiming that 'language structures determine ways of thinking'. I do however believe that if we throw out the notion of culture, in particular the idea that there is a complex of values, beliefs, myths etc. concerned with language, we have thrown out the baby with the bath water. Language itself is a cultural construct; it is not inherited genetically from one's parents. But neither is it reconstituted and reconstructed by every speaker anew in every generation. Language is transmitted to each generation with little change; language acquisition proceeds in much the same pattern in all societies we know of.[10] And much of culture (if we still accept the notion that there is such a thing) is transmitted through language. Most ethnic minorities that are threatened with extinction would (and do) claim that without language, their culture is lost.

The notion of linguistic culture might be problematical for culture critics, but it is indispensable for scholars in such disciplines as sociolinguistics and the sociology of language. In fact, there already exist large amounts of scholarship devoted to the study of linguistic culture, even if this has not been the term employed.

1.4.1.2 Sociolinguistic research

Since the 1950s and 1960s there has been much research done by sociolinguists and sociologists of language in the field of 'language and culture'. Susan Ervin-Tripp's work on address systems (1969); work by others on naming practices (including no-naming); Haugen's work on folk orientation in Iceland (1957), etc. Some overlap here with work in linguistic pragmatics (although pragmatics persists in claiming that it is culture-free and therefore universal, which is not borne out by the facts).

1.4.1.3 Pragmatics

There is a large and growing body of literature on linguistic *pragmatics*, dealing with such questions as why people say what they do, why things often mean something different from what they appear to mean, and how people actually *use* language, for example, to express politeness, to be evasive, to 'do things with words'. Such questions as why a particular combination of morphemes seems polite in one language but not in another are shown to be questions of linguistic culture, not of linguistic structure.

1.4.1.4 Anthropological linguistics and ethnoscience

Anthropologists have long been interested in how speakers of various languages construct nomenclatures for kinship, for colour terminology, and many other kinds of folk classificatory schemes that are now known under the rubric of ethnoscience, folk science, or cognitive anthropology. Plant classificatory schemes among the Koya (folk botany), how to ask for a drink in Subanun (Lounsbury) etc.: attempts to sort out where the Whorfian hypothesis might be valid, and where not.

1.4.1.5 Folk attitudes about language: folk linguistics

Perhaps the pioneering work in this area is the Hoenigswald article (1966) which lays the groundwork and proposes a number of questions for further study. He suggests we consider such questions as:

- What do people think about language?

- What do they think about their own versus other languages?

- Is their language part of or intelligible with languages in another language family?

- What do they think of multilingualism?

- What do they know about (or think about) language differences that are correlated with social differences (age, sex, race, etc.)?

- Where do names come from, and what power derives from naming people or things?

- What do bilingual communities think about each other?[11]

- Where does language come from? This brings in origin myths, linguistic divinity myths, ideas such as the 'Bow-wow' theory, and religious conceptions of language.[12]

1.4.1.6 Attitudes about literacy

It seems to be established that attitudes about literacy can be directly correlated with the literary tradition of a particular linguistic culture. Cultures with long literary histories tend to have high respect if not reverence for literacy and literature; cultures with oral traditions may have less or no respect for writing, or see written language as an attempt to control them (by magic), or as corrupting to language (Aryans and Sanskrit). Attitudes can be transferred to another language and linguistic culture through immigration – American immigrant groups from linguistic cultures with long literary histories (e.g. Jews, Chinese) transfer their attitudes to the new language, and perform well in school, even if the members of the immigrant group were themselves illiterate at the time of immigration.

1.4.1.7 Study of language and religion

In a later chapter we examine the kinds of ideas about language found in the Bible, the Qur'an, and other texts of 'peoples of the Book'. There we find such notions as 'Shibboleths', taboos, and the Tower of Babel as God's punishment.

1.4.1.8 Autobiographical and anecdotal evidence

Attention to autobiographies of well-known bilingual individuals or products of multilingual environments will reveal information about schooling practice, about covert language policy, and about linguistic culture. Marie Skłodowska Curie (Poland under the Tsars); Albert Schweitzer (Alsace in the German Empire); Brittany (Hélias 1975); Ireland.

1.4.1.9 Propaganda studies

There exists a body of literature on propaganda, and its analysis reveals ideas about linguistic culture within certain totalitarian states, for example, Nazi Germany, where language was equated with 'blood', and territory occupied by German speakers was captured as 'German' territory (*Blut und Boden*); Marxist and Stalinist theories about language (Marxist theory etc.).

1.4.1.10 Particular linguistic cultures: language as a 'core' value

There is a number of linguistic cultures where both the speakers and outsiders who know the culture speak of the strong bond between language and culture. In these cultures language seems to be what Smolicz (1979) calls a 'core value', that is, a defining characteristic of the culture. According to this model:

> [E]ach culture possesses a number of basic characteristics which are essential for the transmission and the maintenance of that culture; these core values identify a given culture. For example, in the Italian community in Australia, family religion and language (dialect) appear to be three relevant core values, whereas for the Jewish community they are religion, cultural patrimony and

historicity. . . . When language is the core value of a cultural group, it may be an important factor in determining the members' cultural identity. In extreme cases it might even appear as the sole cultural value, as is evidenced by the Flemings in Belgium or the Québécois in Canada, who built their national identity almost exclusively on the defence of their linguistic rights.

(quoted in Hamers and Blanc 1989: 117)

In a little-quoted monograph on the problems of language in Wales, Saer *et al.* (1924) describe Welsh linguistic culture and the necessity of knowing Welsh to participate in it. They consider that monolingual English-speaking Welsh children are culturally disadvantaged by not knowing Welsh. Following Smolicz, one might say that knowledge of Welsh is a defining core value for the Welsh, and that lack of access to the language cuts Welsh children off from powerful sources of identity.

> The English-speaking child in Wales . . . cannot obtain the full satisfaction of free functioning as in the case of the bilinguist, for the established customs and conventions of Wales require the use of the Welsh language for their natural and traditional expression. The English-speaking monoglot, therefore, living in Welsh-speaking Wales, is deprived of an important part of the stimulus of his social life.
>
> The institutions native to a country that have persisted for many generations best express the people's genius. The institutions of Wales that have established themselves effectively in the habits of the people are of such a nature that their enjoyment, as well as their efficiency, is diminished when they are conducted in any language but Welsh. The Eisteddfod – national, provincial, and local; nights with the harp, when impromptu stanzas are composed and sung by the composers as their turn comes round; preaching meetings, literary meetings, lectures, concerts, singing schools, adult Sunday-schools, evening social gatherings for relating folk-tales, dramatic performances – these and other institutions are so dependent on the use of Welsh that they lose much of their appeal when attempted in another language. The Welsh tongue is a 'social passport' which alone ensures participation in these many cultural amenities. It is also necessary for everyday social intercourse: anyone who uses the language in conversation with a Welsh-speaking Welshman is immediately accepted as a comrade, and is welcomed into a democracy of peers.

(Saer *et al.* 1924: 68–9)

1.5 OVERT POLICIES AND COVERT POLICIES: POLICY IN CONFLICT WITH REALITY

It is not a difficult task to show that researchers of language policy have often confused language policies with multilingualism itself, and have often attempted to map both on to the same symbolic representation, with the result that neither the policy nor the facts of multilingualism emerge clearly. In the case of polities such as Switzerland, Belgium and some others, it is clear that some people assume that if the polity of the state is one of bi- or multilingualism, then the population or citizenry is also bi- or multilingual. Such notions of a 'bilingual' or 'multilingual' citizenry are probably mostly unproven and unprovable, as an examination of such polities will show. What we have in Belgium, Switzerland, India, etc. are a few bilinguals, many monolinguals, but more importantly perhaps, many speakers whose linguistic repertoires exhibit characteristics of extended diglossia, that is, with varying proficiencies in the registers of different linguistic codes, usually as a result of schooling in some language other than the mother tongue. Furthermore, this feature of multilingual but limited repertoires is a feature of the linguistic culture in question. It is supported and transmitted by the culture, irrespective of the overt policy with regard to the various codes in question. If we remember that diglossia is a community feature, that is, is characteristic of a linguistic *group* rather than of an individual, we can better understand how it operates at times in defiance of the explicit policy of the area. (Were it an individual feature, that is, a set of unrelated clusters of proficiencies in various codes, we would be dealing with sets of individual bilinguals whose bilingualism was not a cultural feature.)

Perhaps the best way of looking at this problem is to consider that language policy seems to be dichotomized into *overt* (explicit, formalized, *de jure,* codified, manifest) policies and *covert* (implicit, informal, unstated, *de facto,* grass-roots, latent) aspects of the policy; what usually gets ignored, of course, are the covert aspects of the policy.[13] That is, many researchers (and policy-makers) believe or have taken at face value the overt and explicit formulations of and statements about the status of linguistic varieties, and ignore what actually happens down on the ground, in the field, at the grass-roots level, etc. Fortunately there is recognition in some quarters that some kind of dichotomy must be recognized; Gessinger (1980) posits a difference between explicit and implicit policy in the following way:

The narrower and broader meaning of the term language policy should not be confused, however, as they are different in one essential point: language policy in a narrow sense – I call it *explicit* language policy – is social decision-making that is directly geared toward those contexts of the lives of the speakers that are transmitted by language, whereas *structural* language policy denotes those actions of social groups or state administrations which incorporate those contexts of life (that are demonstrably linguistically conveyed), into the all-encompassing context of general political practice.

(Gessinger 1980: 22–3)

That is, Gessinger distinguishes between *explicit* and *structural*, the latter being a kind of incorporation of linguistic conditions into the basic assumptions of the political fabric and *modus operandi* of the state.[14] This is slightly different from what I am calling linguistic culture, but certainly his *structural* language policy would be one component of what linguistic culture would entail.

1.5.1   Overt and covert policy in the USA

Let us illustrate this with an example from language policy in the USA. The USA as is well known has no overt stated policy regarding the English language, so one might assume, as some students do, that the statement that the USA 'has no official policy' is equivalent to 'has no policy' or is 'neutral' with regard to English or any other language. Having no overt policy with regard to the English language (or any other language) does not mean, however, that there is not a *covert* policy with regard to the *English* language (and other languages).

It does not take sharp powers of observation to be able to perceive that English is the dominant language in the life of the citizens of the USA (or indeed in North America as a whole, as our French-Canadian neighbours readily note). It is the primary (in some cases exclusive) language used in schools, colleges, business, in state, federal and local administration, in health-care delivery, in the media, in sports, in entertainment, etc. etc. Outsiders to US anglophone culture (e.g. francophone Canadians) see English as an irresistible force, a vibrant, powerful linguistic culture that overpowers all other languages.[15] The fact that English is not legally protected, guaranteed, promoted etc. does not mean automatically that some other language might be able to mount a strong challenge to it, that is, that there is a level playing field when it comes to competing for any of the domains now dominated by English.

To take a hypothetical example, let a politician address his constituents in some language other than English, or let some parents demand public schooling in a language other than English, for the furore to erupt. One could list many more examples of what might happen if American citizens were to attempt to carry on various kinds of public business – applying for a job, registering for unemployment, enrolling in school, applying for a driver's licence – and were to insist on the 'right' to do it in some language other than English. Then we would hear something about the (covert) policy of the USA; we would hear that 'everybody knows' that the default language is English, and attempts to use another language are illegitimate in some way. In other words, the *covert* language policy of the USA is not neutral, it *favours* the English language. No statute or constitutional amendment or regulatory law is necessary to maintain this covert policy[16] – its strength lies in the basic assumptions that American society has about language. We will examine what these assumptions are in detail in the chapter on US language policy.

Another example of the 'cleavage' between overt and covert policy gained credence for me when I first contemplated the question of linguistic assimilation in the German-American Church (Schiffman 1987). It became gradually obvious to me that most previous research on the subject of language shift among German-Americans had looked only at the official documents, statistics and policies of German-American religious bodies. They had ignored grass-roots developments of various sorts[17] that in fact laid the groundwork for the later 'abrupt' shift (or what was perceived to be an abrupt policy shift, but what was actually a *de jure* recognition of the *de facto* shift that had occurred much earlier).

This ignorance was made possible by the diglossic nature (Ferguson 1959a) of German at the time of emigration as well as by the extended diglossic relationship (Fishman 1967) between German and English in the Church bodies. As we shall see, diglossic linguistic situations often mask the true nature of linguistic repertoires (and therefore of language policies) by presenting a view of language that is skewed in favour of the 'high' language, ignoring the actual domains of the 'low' language. As was evident in the German case, this had disastrous results for the German language in America, since policy-makers in the German-American churches were blind to the reality of actual (multilingual) linguistic use within the (monolingual) policy they had established.

1.5.2 Register and repertoire

Another distinction that is often missing in language policy studies is the recognition that there is a difference between 'linguistic register(s)'[18] (based on functional differentiation of different linguistic codes), linguistic repertoire (based on the proficiencies of language users) and the *functional load*[19] of a register in the linguistic culture in question.

This can again be illustrated by comparing official language policy in India with the actual linguistic behaviour of groups, especially socioprofessional groups, and individuals' proficiencies to use different codes. As is well known, despite the paucity of officially sanctioned domains for English in post-Independence India, use of this language continues to predominate in business, higher education, Western professions (medicine, science, technology), and some other domains. Attempts to legislate the use of indigenous languages in these domains fails for a number of reasons. The primary one is that there are no indigenous *registers* for Marathi, Tamil, Bengali, etc. in these domains, despite attempts to create them artificially by translating English terminology into these languages. This failure persists because:

1 Registers are not simply lists of vocabulary, but also involve the existence of preferred rhetorical devices, abbreviatory conventions, and are developed primarily by a community of language users using them to solve a particular task; they must be an integral yet separate part of a recognized standard language, most of which have registers for literature, philosophy, *belles-lettres* and some other humanistic disciplines, but are often monopolized and controlled by pundits whose priorities (e.g. purism) are often an impediment to the development of other registers.[20]

2 People knowing English are loath to cut themselves off from international developments in their fields, which flourish primarily in English; that is, there is an internationally recognized English *register* for these disciplines and one cannot participate in the work of the discipline without doing so in English.[21]

3 Professionals who have a linguistic repertoire that consists of proficiency in English in a professional register do not see the utility of adding to their repertoire knowledge of a register whose usefulness has not been proven. Essentially they see this as coming about only through extra *cost* (Pool 1991). Researchers who fail to distinguish between these also fail to understand how policy

decisions made at the central level tend to have no appreciable effect on the use of English.

Thus, in diglossic situations such as that of the German-American Church, or as in diglossic linguistic cultures such as India, overt policy may favour one variety (code, language, lect) and disfavour another, but speakers may exhibit highly developed repertoires in certain languages (in both cases English) that may be out of proportion to the legal status accorded this variety in the official policy. Often this is because the code in question possesses a highly marked register (e.g. English for science, business, medicine, technology in India) that has made difficult the task of developing indigenous registers for Tamil, Gujarati, Bengali, etc. Or, conversely, the German-American Church regulated the status of which language would be used for school religious subjects (that is, the religious register), but allowed English *de facto* to dominate other school subjects, thinking that this policy would produce stable bilinguals who would remain loyal to German in religious domains, rather than become compartmentalized bilinguals with different repertoires, in particular English competence, in the practical registers such as business etc. No attention was or is given in these polities to the *functional load* of English in the repertoires in question, nor to the fact that English dominated the L-domains (non-prestigious, usually spoken language domains) of the younger and better-educated generations. That is, the policy-makers of the German-American Church ignored the fact that its pupils were predominantly English speakers, as if this could have no effect on the outcome of the policy. Steeped deeply in their own loyalty to German, they could not see how attached these so-called bilinguals had become to the English language, and the appropriateness of certain codes for certain tasks. Policies that ignore such aspects of language *use* 'down the road' as it were, that are not specified in their overt policies, do so at their peril.[22] When transplanted to American soil, where an overtly *laissez-faire* policy prevails (within a covertly assimilationist linguistic culture),[23] such policies are doomed to failure.

1.5.3 The congruence of policy and polity

While policy and reality must be kept separate (since they do not represent the same thing) attempts to typologize language policy necessarily reflect many of the same dimensions and factors used to symbolize users' competencies. The closer the representation of policy comes to the representation of users' competencies, the better the congruence or 'fit' of the policy to the linguistic reality, and the less tension (and social strife) we should be able to predict there will be between the two. That is, if users have diglossic or triglossic repertoires, a policy that takes these into account and legitimizes the status of these varieties will be more congruent with the reality than one that ignores these repertoires. As we shall see, except for polities such as Luxembourg (Hoffmann 1981) and Malta, few policies ever explicitly mirror the multiglossic reality; in particular, few policies ever take any cognizance of the existence of L-variety language, let alone establish guarantees of its domains and registers.[24]

Later, in the chapter devoted to the question of typologies of policies, we will consider attempting to establish a typology of policies, beginning with a catalogue of the types of 'fit' or congruence (or lack of them) between the policy and the reality.

1.5.4 Overt and covert policy in Switzerland

Another example of a lack of fit between the overt and covert policy is that of Switzerland, that is, Swiss language policy and linguistic reality. In the Swiss Federal Constitution of 1874 (revised to 1953), Article 116 specifies which languages are official and national:

> German, French, Italian and Romanche are the national languages of Switzerland.

> German, French and Italian shall be deemed the official languages of the Confederation.[25]

(quoted in Hughes 1954: 128)

This is the text of the Swiss Federal Constitution that refers to language, *in its entirety*. From this statement it is quite difficult to visualize what Swiss citizens actually do with language, since it totally ignores the reality of language use or of the repertoires of language users in Switzerland – the constitutional language says nothing about the extensive domains of *Schwyzertüütsch* and the very restricted domains of *Schriftdeutsch* among 'German' Swiss; it fails to recognize that Italian has few if any domains at the federal level, and it fails to recognize the extensive *extended* (Fishman 1967) diglossic relationship between Romansch and German (of various varieties).[26] One must look to cantonal regulations of various sorts, as well as at decisions of the Swiss Supreme Court, to see what local conditions (policies) are imposed on language. And when one does[27] it becomes clear that language policy in Switzerland is totally dependent on educational policy, which is exclusively a cantonal responsibility.[28] This is in fact a problem in many federated polities – in India, in Switzerland, and in the former Soviet Union the federal policies are explicit to varying degrees, but what happens at local levels, for example, in various states of India, Soviet republics, or Swiss cantons often is or was severely at variance with federal stipulations.

1.5.5 Overt and covert in other polities

In another polity where policy is supposedly very explicit and overt, that of post-Independence India, for example, there are few guarantees of linguistic minority rights at the state level. In Tamilnāḍu, Karnataka and Maharashtra, the rights of various linguistic minorities (e.g. Telugus in Tamilnāḍu, Tamils and Marathis in Karnataka, and Gujaratis and Kannaḍigas in Maharashtra) are protected (as are all minorities in all states), not by any constitutional provisions, but by an agreement of chief ministers of the states (1961), according to which if in any area 15 per cent of the population belong to minority groups, official documents must be published in minority languages. Since this is so vague, many interpretations of how it should be implemented can be entertained.[29] Unlike European polities, where bilateral agreements between Germany and Denmark, for example, guarantee the rights of linguistic minorities in each other's country, no agreements exist between states in India to guarantee the rights of Telugus in Tamilnāḍu or Tamils in Andhra Pradesh, for example.[30] These varieties are in effect relegated to L-variety status, though as mentioned, this domain is not recognized as a legitimate one.[31] Or as we have seen exploding in the news in recent years, Soviet policy has not succeeded in working out a solution for Armenian minorities within Azerbaidjan, Mizkhetian minorities in Kirgizia, or Gagauz minorities in Moldavia, etc. (though until recently the rights of Russian minorities in all non-Russian areas seemed secure). Now with the break-up of the USSR, rights for minorities of all sorts seem to be in question everywhere.

In fact in Switzerland, the territorial principle is guaranteed to the letter, so French speakers in a German-Swiss canton have *no rights* except to L-variety use *chez soi*. The same pertains in Belgium and in many other supposedly 'bilingual' polities – the policy actually mitigates against bilingualism in favour of enforced territorial monolingualism. We will examine further examples of the disparity between policy and linguistic reality in a later chapter.

1.5.6 Overt and covert policy in Africa

In an article dealing with language planning in Cameroon, Tadadjeu (1975) uses the terms 'formal' to characterize the legacy of language policy established by the colonial powers in Africa, and 'informal' to refer to missionary policy regarding religious goals:

> However, these [colonial policies] were formal policies as distinct from informal language policies which were carried on by Missionaries. William Welmers[32] has shown that, although the missionaries did not overtly claim to have their own language policy, they did actually have one for religious purposes. This consisted in developing vernacular language programs as means for reaching their spiritual goals . . .
>
> From the practical point of view, the missionary policy, which was tolerated to some extent in countries under the French rule, has been consistently extended beyond their purely religious borders to cover educational purposes.
>
> (1975: 55)

From being a covert and tacit policy of missionary schools during the colonial period, this policy has now devolved into one where secular community support of vernacular schools is now the rule in post-colonial Cameroon.

1.6 SOME MYTHS ABOUT LANGUAGE

The notion that language policy might be grounded in mythology may seem too bizarre to warrant any serious attention whatsoever. Lest it seem that myths about language are too vague and unspecified to have any effect on language use, let alone language policy, let me quote from a number of sources where this aspect of linguistic culture has been dealt with directly – in the study of attitudes about the Japanese, Arabic and French languages.

1.6.1 Myths about Arabic

The idea that the Arabic language is deeply imbued with myth has been dealt with squarely by Ferguson (1959b) in an unambiguously entitled article. Since much of what Ferguson says about the mythologizing of Arabic is also applicable to other languages, I will quote him rather extensively.[33]

In every speech community attitudes and beliefs are probably current about the language of the community as well as about other languages and language in general. Some of these are true, i.e. correspond very well to objective reality, others are involved with esthetic or religious notions the validity of which cannot be investigated empirically, and still others which purport to deal with facts are partly or wholly false. All these attitudes and beliefs, regardless of their truth-value, will be called here 'myths'. . . . This paper deals with the set of myths about Arabic current in the Arabic speech community today.

(1959b: 375)

Ferguson states that myths about Arabic are fairly uniform in the speech community, even though the language is spread over a vast territory. The myths may be summarized under four headings: the superiority of Arabic; the classical–colloquial diglossia; dialect rating; and the future of Arabic. We will go into greater detail about these aspects of the myth of Arabic in the chapter on linguistic culture, and in particular in the discussion about language and religion.

1.6.2 Myths about Japanese

Another compelling study of mythologizing about language is a work by Roy Andrew Miller entitled *Japan's Modern Myth: The Language and Beyond* (1982). The modern myth Miller is referring to is, not surprisingly, the Japanese language, as the title indicates.[34]

For modern Japan, the Japanese language is a way of life, and the enormous amount of speculation, writing, and talking about it that goes on at every level of Japanese life constitutes an entirely distinctive and marvelously self-contained way of looking at life.

In modern Japan, the Japanese language is never allowed to be taken for granted, not by anyone, not for a single moment. . . . The language not only serves the society as a vehicle for daily communication, but it also manages, as we shall see, to be a cult and myth as well. . . . To the Japanese today, the Japanese language is not simply the way they talk and write. For them, it has assumed the dimensions of a national myth of vast proportions.

(1982: 4–5)

Miller then goes on to describe the many ways and the wide variety of expression that are involved in creating and sustaining the myth of the Japanese language.

We have already emphasized that the modern myth of Nihongo is, in all its essentials, nonscientific and antiscientific. Though it has been erected, like all myths, around a hard inner kernel of truth, its special sociolinguistic function within contemporary Japanese society is to conceal and obfuscate those same tiny elements of fact behind an elaborate facade of mythic fiction. One searches in vain throughout the myth of Nihongo for anything that will correlate with the linguistic facts of the Japanese language as it is actually spoken and used by the Japanese people.

(1982: 65)

One could quote at length from Miller's study; in the chapter on linguistic culture I will do so extensively to illustrate how myths about language are part of linguistic culture and how they influence language policy in Japan. Where the myth of *Nihongo* affects the world at large is its conception of languages other than Japanese, for example, languages like English.

1.6.3 Myths about French

Another part of the world where Anglo-Saxons readily note a difference in attitudes about language is the world of *la francophonie*, the French-speaking world, especially France. In France, attitudes about language (both French and other languages, particularly English) can be observed with little or no deep searching; they are overt and widely disseminated. This has been observed and discussed in monograph-length studies such as those of Gordon (1978) and Flaitz (1988). Many observers have noted that the French see their language as having a mission in the world; it is seen as universal, pure and lucid, the proper and appropriate medium of the values of humanism – the language of civilization *par excellence*. We will also deal with French myth-making in more detail later, and we will see how mythologizing about French is an ongoing enterprise.

In short, language policies do not evolve *ex nihilo*; they are not taken off a shelf, dusted off, and plugged into a particular polity; rather, they are *cultural constructs*, and are rooted in and evolve from historical elements of many kinds, some explicit and overt, some implicit and covert.[35] It is in the covert areas that we need to seek the origins of the overt facets of a policy, not vice versa. The task of this study will be to expose the linguistic cultures of three societies – the USA, France and India – to scrutiny, and to see how overt policy in these polities functions within the linguistic culture, where it came from and where it is going.

1.7 RELIGION, LINGUISTIC CULTURE AND LANGUAGE POLICY

Much could and has been written about religion and language; what we are concerned with are the effects of religion on language policy, especially as an aspect of linguistic culture. Some of the work on language and religion has focused on the language policy of particular religious bodies, especially when the goal is language maintenance by ethnic minorities in immigrant societies etc. (Kloss 1977a; Fishman 1966). Other studies are devoted to the study of the effect of religious languages on the development of national languages and/or competing standards. For the purpose of illustration I will focus on this element, though the former is just as important in the long run and constitutes a neglected area of study in many polities. The effect of religion on the maintenance of diglossia and the compartmentalization of domains also has repercussions for policy studies that should not be minimized.[36]

In a later chapter, we will examine in detail some facts of language policy that seem strongly correlated with religion in various parts of the world.

- India: In India there exist differently named speech varieties whose speakers classify them as different *languages*, but which linguists can find almost mutually indistinguishable. Hindi is the 'language' declared by Hindus; Urdu is declared (in the Indian census) by Muslims (Khubchandani 1983).

- Former Yugoslavia: A similar dichotomy exists in the former Yugoslavia between the Serbian and Croatian literary 'languages', maintained primarily by the identification of Serbian with Eastern Orthodoxy and the Cyrillic script, while Croatian is written with the roman alphabet and is associated with Roman Catholicism.

- Poland: Poland is a Roman Catholic 'island' wedged between Protestant Germany and Orthodox Russia, and to some Poles, the Roman Catholic Church is credited with helping to 'overthrow' the Communist regime through its strong support of Solidarność.

- Korea: Under Japanese occupation, American missionaries used Korean language and Hangkul writing in their schools; schools under Japanese control used Japanese. Today Korea has the highest percentage of Christians in any Asian country.

- France and the Suisse Romande: In France and French Switzerland, Protestantism is correlated with standard French. In Protestant Swiss-French cantons, dialect (*patois*) has declined; *patois* has survived only in Catholic areas (Breton 1991).

- Sri Lanka: The Tamil/Sinhala conflict is reinforced by Hindu/ Buddhist animosity. Tamils see no way to remain Hindu without Tamil; Sinhalese see Tamils as a beachhead for penetration by numerically superior, predominantly Hindu India.

- Britain: Welsh language and non-conformism combined to resist Anglicization and spread of Church of England.

- Former Soviet Union: Much linguistic nationalism was supported by religious differences: the Baltic states are non-Orthodox (Lutheran or Roman Catholic); Orthodox/Muslim conflict exacerbated (and still exacerbates) certain ethnic conflicts in the Caucasus; other Islamic republics resist domination of 'Orthodox' Russia.

- Belgium: The first *raison d'être* of Belgium was to carve off the Catholic provinces from Protestant Holland; later a linguistic split between Flemish and French Walloons developed.

- Pakistan: Religion (Islam) was paramount in the establishment of Islamic Pakistan, but once established, the linguistic split between East (Bengali-speaking) Pakistan and West Pakistan (Panjabi, Urdu) led to split that resulted in the independence of Bangladesh.

- Canada: French/English differences are exacerbated by the Roman Catholic/Protestant split; the Roman Catholic French clergy see language differences as an ally of Catholicism.

- The Arabic world and the Arabic language: As we have already seen in our discussion of myths about language, myths about Arabic and the purity and beauty of Classical Arabic have a strong effect on language policy in the Arab world.

We will deal with these aspects of religion and language policy in the chapter on religion and myth; suffice it to say here that many supposedly linguistic conflicts in the world often are exacerbated by religious associations of various sorts; conversely, religious strife may be strengthened by linguistic animosities, though of course the two can exist completely independently, as we have seen in Northern Ireland.

1.8 THE STRUCTURE OF THIS BOOK

As mentioned earlier, the focus of this book will be to look at language policy in three different polities – France, India, the USA – and to see how their policies are grounded in linguistic culture. To do this we will need to examine linguistic culture in general and its manifestations in those three cultures. The book contains the following chapters:

- A chapter that will examine extant typologies of language policy to see how they might be improved for our purposes.

- A chapter to examine the workings of religion and myth in the development of language policy.

- A chapter to delineate the various aspects of linguistic culture in France, and its overt language policy in general.

- A chapter to see how this is manifested in overt (and covert) policy with regard to one region, in this case Alsace.

- A chapter to delineate the various aspects of linguistic culture in India, and its overt language policy in general.

- A chapter to see how this is manifested in overt (and covert) policy with regard to one region, in this case the Dravidian south in general and the state of Tamilnāḍu in particular.

- A chapter to delineate the various aspects of linguistic culture in the USA, and its overt language policy in general.

- A chapter to see how this is manifested in overt (and covert) policy with regard to one region, in this case the state of California and its policies toward linguistic minorities, especially the Native-American languages and Spanish.

- Conclusion.

2 Typologies of multilingualism and typologies of language policy

2.1 INTRODUCTION

The original plan of this book was to be an attempt at a typology of language policies, analysing their main characteristics and arranging them in some sort of schema that would elucidate and explain why certain types prevail, how they work in principle and in practice, and be a contribution to the disciplines of sociolinguistics, the sociology of language, politico-linguistics, and all the other disciplines that have attempted to categorize language policy. These may be grouped under the general rubric of 'social linguistics' (Grillo 1989).

It soon became clear that this attempt would have to be abandoned, and for a number of reasons. The data were not comparable, the theoretical frameworks that various people had worked in were not congruent, and when all was said and done, there were almost as many variables to factor in as there were polities and policies. But there were other reasons why taxonomies of this sort are impossible, as we will see below.[1]

This is not to say that there have been some valiant attempts to contribute to our knowledge of this area, and I will acknowledge these as they arise in the discussion.[2] But one of the main problems that arises in the study of language policy – namely the lack of congruence between policy and the sociolinguistic conditions of the group in question – is rarely adequately dealt with in many analyses, despite the best efforts of talented researchers.

In fact there is a tendency, especially for lay analysts of language policy, to confuse language policies with societal multilingualism itself, and to map both on to the same symbolic representation. It is perhaps natural for decision-makers to assume that their policy fits the facts of multilingualism, and if it does not, to blame the facts rather than the policy. Thus popular accounts of language policy in

France praise the monolingual policy, assuming almost that France is monolingual, when this is far from the case. Multilingualism is thus perceived as a pesky problem that would go away if people would only see the beauty of the policy. The result of such analyses is that neither the policy nor the facts of multilingualism emerge clearly. As we are concerned here to describe language policy in three distinct nation states, both in terms of overt explicit policy and in terms of how the overt policy is rooted in the linguistic culture of the language/area in question, we need to look at a much broader range of variables than are usually taken into account when discussing both multilingualism and language policies. For starters I would say that just to come up with adequate descriptive typologies of the two, we will need to consider the following:

1 Religio-confessional aspects of the use of certain languages.
2 Existence of strongly *diglossic* tendencies in the linguistic code of any or all varieties in question.
3 Existence in a multilingual state of competing standard varieties of some minority codes in adjacent states.[3]
4 The effects of the *functional load* of register(s) on the policy.
5 Implications of linguistic *repertoire* in the policy (especially focusing on degrees of proficiency in various skill-areas, both active and passive, of various codes).
6 Implications of linguistic *register* in the policy (in particular, implications of the existence of a dominant exocentric register for science and technology from an internationally dominant and prestigious language).

We have already seen that it is misleading and perhaps even dangerous to take overt statements about language policy at face value, since the way a policy *operates* or *functions* in a society is strongly conditioned by the covert aspects of its linguistic culture. That is, *overt* (explicit, formalized, codified) forms of policy are meaningless without taking into consideration those aspects that are essentially *covert* (implicit, informal, unstated, grass-roots *reality*) since most researchers who study language policy are not interested merely in typologizing them (except as a prelude to further analysis) but are interested in how they operate. That is, they are interested in whether the policy that promotes Hindi as the 'national language' in India, for example, has actually had any effect, and if not, why not? The *why not*, I believe, will be explained by looking at India's linguistic culture, not at overt policy.[4]

2.1.1 Previous typologies

Let us examine some of the previously proposed typologies in order to see how they have or have not been adequate.

2.1.1.1 Typologies of policy

When the focus is on typologies of language policy, the important literature can be summarized on the fingers of one hand. This may result from the fact that a focus on language *policies* of multilingual states (polities etc.) reveals that policies are usually designed to minimize many complex aspects of societal multilingualism because such complexity is inconvenient for the workings of the modern post-industrial state. As an instrument of political integration (or whatever else language policies are used for), complexity is inefficient, even in linguistically 'tolerant' polities such as Switzerland. What is lacking is a conceptual framework that recognizes the complexity of societal multilingualism even when language policies, and typologies thereof, do not. In this chapter I review the typologies of language policy proposed by Kloss (1966a), Stewart (1972) [1968] and Ferguson (1966) (as well as the critique of them by Fasold (1984)) but expand upon them to include other notions, such as linguistic 'register', verbal 'repertoire' (Trudgill 1983: 100–1; Shapiro and Schiffman 1981: 177), and a more sophisticated appreciation for the role of diglossia (Ferguson 1959a; Fishman 1967) than has often been the case. There is a need to go beyond the narrow typologies of language policy because such typologies are often based on a study of overt and *de jure* policies, which may differ radically from actual grass-roots (*de facto*, covert) implementation of the policies.

2.1.1.2 Policy and policies

We can also distinguish here a difference between *features* of policies and *kinds* of policies. Under the former, the best description of what features different kinds of policies exhibit is the work of Kloss (1940, 1977a). He delineates a number of features of language policies that are useful descriptors.

A. PROMOTIVE VERSUS TOLERANCE POLICIES

- *Promotive* policies encourage the use of particular language(s) by constitutional, administrative and legal (statutory) guarantees; devote and/or guarantee resources (money, personnel, space) for a language; specify and reserve domains of use (school, courts, administration) for a language; may be non-explicit, promoting one (or more) languages without explicitly mentioning them. Overt promotion policies name the language or languages in legal code, constitution, etc. and what the rights and territories of the language or languages (or of the speakers) shall be, etc.

- *Tolerance* policies allow the use of language usually without explicitly devoting resources, time, space etc. to them; no domains are reserved; can also be covert (not mentioning anything) or overt (openly stating and naming which language will be tolerated, perhaps with a time-limit).

- *Mixed* policy may still tolerate language(s) of a minority, to ensure smooth functioning of polity/burocracy: for example, danger signs in four languages in the Singapore rapid transit system; drivers' licensing (written) tests in various minority languages in Washington State; social security information in many languages in the USA; translation provided in court cases; schools using minority languages for transitional 'bilingual' education at their own expense, or paid for by parents. Few or no public resources are used to *promote* these languages, only to tolerate them, or make the state run more smoothly.

B. EGALITARIAN VERSUS RESTRICTED

Policy may treat languages even of a small minority as totally equal, always placing both/all languages on equal footing, addressing all citizens as if bilingual, etc.

C. JURISDICTIONAL LIMITATIONS

Polity may tolerate/promote certain languages only in restricted areas or domains.[5] Right to use a language may be reserved for, or restricted to a particular function within the polity, for example, religious, military, bureaucratic, data-gathering. Or the right may be guaranteed only for a segment of the population, for example adults (but not children).

- *Personal Rights.* State may allow (even *guarantee*) individuals the right to use the minority language in certain situations or territories. The right is portable and belongs to the person wherever he or she goes and interacts with organs of the state.

- *Territorial Rights.* Right to use a particular language may be restricted to a particular territory within the polity, or even certain domains within a restricted territory.

D. OTHER CHARACTERISTICS NOT DEFINED BY KLOSS

- De facto *versus* de jure policies. Related to overt/covert distinction. Policies may *de jure* pertain to one language, but *de facto*, tolerate or even encourage use of some other language. School policy may *de jure* reserve domain for Language 1, but *de facto* Language 2 is widely used, or understood to be mandatory.

- *Covert versus overt policies. Covert* policies make no mention of *any* language in any legal document, administrative code, etc. Guarantees of linguistic rights must be inferred from other policies, constitutional provisions, 'the spirit of the law', or just the fact that the legal code is composed in a certain language and not another, etc. We may also use the terms implicit, unstated, common law, *de facto*, traditional, customary, grass-roots, etc. Covert policies may be subversive or collusive.

    Overt policies state explicitly the rights of *any or all* linguistic groups to the use of their language in whatever domains they specify. Overt policies strongly guarantee the freest tolerance policy, since they overtly state what is tolerated. We may also use the terms explicit, specific, *de jure*, constitutional, and statutory.

2.2 DISCUSSION OF TYPOLOGIES OF MULTILINGUALISM: LINGUISTIC REGISTERS AND REPERTOIRES

The sociolinguistic literature is rife with descriptions of many different cases of multilingualism, often in excruciating detail. There are few attempts to categorize societal multilingualism into an overall general framework, and basically only three have focused on the types of language policy and how they deal with societal multilingualism. This section will begin with a reprise of these three attempts (Kloss 1966a; Stewart 1972 [1968]; Ferguson 1966 as well as the critique of them by Fasold 1984).[6]

2.2.1 Kloss 1966a

One of the more valiant attempts to categorize multilingualism and relate it to typologies of language policy is that of H. Kloss, in an article entitled 'Types of multilingual communities: a discussion of ten variables' (Kloss 1966a). The following is an attempt to summarize his main points.

1 *Types of speech communities* Speech community: all the citizens in a given state but excluding those whose mother tongue is spoken natively by less than 3 per cent: National Core Community (NCC).

2 *Mother tongue: major types*

  (a) Monolingual type A: Iceland, Portugal, Japan.

  (b) Bi/trilingual type B: consists of two or 3 linguistic communities *each* of which comprises at least 4 per cent of the population. Three seems to be the maximum that can be put on an equal par (e.g. Switzerland, or India's three-language formula). More than three seems to overtax, tangle, render inefficient the state's administrative and legislation etc. Equality of two in Canada, Belgium, Finland and three in Switzerland (India's three is fictitious); even in Switzerland the third (Italian) gets short-changed.

  (c) Multilingual type C: more than three languages: usually a four-plus language situation is neutralized by one foreign language for example English/French etc. Even in many B and C countries, multilingualism is restricted to the federal level, while in the states/cantons etc. monolingualism reigns (Belgium, Switzerland etc.).

3 *Number of languages used by individuals* There is no correlation between state and individual on this.

  (a) Fully monolingual citizenry: examples of an NCC A1 – Portugal, Iceland, Japan.

  (b) Diglossic citizenry: examples of an NCC A2 – Greece, Egypt, Haiti: diglossic language, two varieties.

  (c) Bilingual citizenry: examples of NCC A3 – citizenry may be monolingual but is faced with another language (second) in school, cultural setting, etc. Nagaland?

  (d) Tri/multilingual citizenry: examples of NCC A4 – monolingual Maltese are faced with Italian and English as second/third (diglossic?) languages; monolingual Luxembourgers are faced with French and German as second/third languages.[7]

In NCCs of 3 and 4, the second or third tongue is characterized by:

  (a) Voluntarism: no compulsion by external factors to adopt second tongue as own.

(b) Permanence: long-term stability in relationship between two languages.
(c) Functional diversification: different domains of different languages.[8]

While NCCs of type A are common, type B (bilingual) may be monolingual or bilingual. Usually widespread B NCCs are very rare: even where they may be equal by law, widespread bilingual citizenry is usually not: Switzerland, Belgium remain monolingual; Canada exhibits bilingualism mostly among French; South African bilingualism mostly among Afrikaners, etc.

Often the international reputation of a language may have some influence on tendency of other tongue speakers to learn it, but this has no effect in the case of English speakers in Canada learning French.

NCC B – various types:

(a) Bilingual, but only one language official: nineteenth-century Belgium (Dutch were backward).
(b) One community is numerically inferior.
(c) One pursues a policy of linguistic oppression at all costs. (nineteenth-century Russia; Sri Lanka 1958–present, Iraq towards Kurds, etc.).

NCCs of type C (more than three languages of sizeable population):

(a) Enthrone one indigenous and one foreign: Pakistan.
(b) Use two imported ones (Italian and English in Somalia, French and English in Cameroon).

4   *Types of personal and impersonal bilingualism*

Personal bilingualism:

(a) Natural bilingualism: result of mixed marriages, mixed neighbourhood, etc.
(b) Voluntary bilingualism: result of strictly private endeavour, or is matched by efforts of the state to encourage it (language is not only taught, but *used*).
(c) Decreed bilingualism: backed by state but against wishes of population (Poland pre-1914, Ukraine under Tsars, etc.).
(d) Impersonal bilingualism: official blanks (census forms, social-security application forms, IRS forms), postage stamps/currency, official public notices (posters), etc. (People are not bilingual, things are.)

5 *Legal status* Is the language 'official/national':
   (a) For the whole state?
   (b) For part of territory only?
   (c) Promoted in schools or elsewhere?
   (d) Tolerated by authorities only?
   (e) Prohibited by authorities?
6 *Segments of population involved*
   (a) All adult males?
   (b) All literate males/adults?
   (c) All secondary school graduates?
   (d) (India) all breadwinners?
7 *Type and degree of individual bilingualism* From full co-ordinate bilingualism to marginal knowledge.
8 *Prestige of languages*
   (a) Rich literature?
   (b) Modernization?
   (c) International standing?
   (d) Prestigeful speakers?
9 *Enthusiasm of authorities* Is it *bilinguisme de promotion* or *bilinguisme de concession/resignation* as in Belgium.
10 *Degree of distance* Are languages related or distant?
11 *Indigenousness of languages* (versus relic-imported under colonialism) Hawaii: Japanese 'latecomers' versus Hawaiian 'natives'; Malays in Malaysia (versus Tamils, Chinese).
12 *Attitude toward linguistic stability* In immigrant societies, attitude is that language shift is natural; in older societies attitude is that language loyalty is natural.

2.2.1.1 Problems with Kloss's typology

The problem with this schema is that although Kloss enumerates and describes most of the factors that are operative in multilingual polities and are sometimes recognized in multilingual policies, situations like the di- and triglossic polities exhibited by Cameroon, Luxembourg, Malta, Somalia and large parts of India are not adequately handled by a binary or two-dimensional cross-classification. I have attempted to illustrate some combinations of his factors by placing a number of well-known linguistic situations (polities, communities) shown in Table 2.1, but in fact a number of important kinds of bi- and multilingual polities cannot be easily placed here.

Table 2.2, and the list of variables that are used in it, assumes that there are three 'national types' of multilingualism, and that most

Table 2.1 Kloss's typology: types of communities and types of individual bilingualism

	Number of languages used by individuals			
	1: Monolingual citizenry	*2: Diglossic citizenry*	*3: Bilingual citizenry*	*4: Tri- or multilingual citizenry*
A. MONOLINGUAL COMMUNITY	Portugal Japan, Iceland	Greece, Egypt, Haiti	Pre- and post-colonial societies in Africa, S. Asia	Malta, Luxembourg
B. BI-TRILINGUAL COMMUNITY/POLITY	n/a	?	Rare, but some Switzerland, Belgian, Canadian, S. Africa, Paraguay	Some India; some USSR some Swiss
C. MULTILINGUAL COMMUNITY/POLITY			Pakistan?	Somalia Cameroon South Asia

known multilingual situations can be fitted into it. It seems to assume that the monopaedoglossic types are different from the others, and that the bilingual 1, 3 pattern (such as Belgium) does not begin as monopaedoglossia, that is, it seems to presume that bilingual Belgians (presumably mostly Flemish speakers) do not spend their pre-school years as monolinguals. It also does not distinguish whether a community is multilingual *as a result* of language policy or *despite* it. That is, is multilingualism an *outcome* of the policy, or does it develop or persist contrary to or independently of the policy? Diglossic and multiglossic communities, such as India, are also difficult to represent on such a scheme, since Greek diglossia is only one type; Swiss (German) diglossia is usually not mentioned in any *policy* discussion of Swiss multilingualism, but is certainly a factor that cannot be ignored. When bilingualism and multilingualism are introduced, the assumption seems to be that much personal bilingualism is the norm, when in fact we are more likely to find diglossia and triglossia – only certain domains are the reserve of one or another variety. What seems to be happening in Kloss's taxonomy is that he does not systematically distinguish between the policy type and the multilingualism type; mapping one system on to another is indeed a daunting task (and difficult to keep separate), since, as he points out, multilingualism may come about because of the language policy, such that if it were absent or different, the community might be monolingual. In other instances the multilingual policy has little effect on the linguistic habits of the citizens – the populace remains predominantly monolingual, so that the goal of the policy is a multilingual *state*, but not necessarily a multilingual populace.

Kloss is to be commended for trying, at least, to reconcile the two. The areas where his taxonomy falls short are in its failure to distinguish register and repertoire; its failure to distinguish between diglossia and bilingualism; and to distinguish between passive and active command of a particular variety in both register and/or repertoire.

Table 2.2 Some combinations yielded by number of languages in NCC and number used by individuals

National type	Use pattern	Example
A. MONOPAIDOGLOSSIC	1 Complete monolingualism	Iceland
	2 Diglossic (vernacular with prestige language studied later)	Greece
	3 Bilingualism	Paraguay
	4 Trilingualism	Malta
B. BILINGUAL	1 'Impersonal bilingualism' (government bilingual, citizens monolingual)	Parts of Switzerland
	2 Bilingualism in government and in *both* speech communities	(Hypothetical)
	1, 3 Government and one speech community bilingual, other monolingual	Belgium
	1, 3 Government and one speech community monolingual, other bilingual	Spain (Catalunya) Peru, Morocco
C. MULTILINGUAL	All regional languages considered national	(Hypothetical)
	One regional language considered national	Ethiopia
	National language imported	Guinea

Table 1 from Kloss (1966a)

2.2.1.2 Stewart 1972 [1968]

Stewart's attempt at a typology begins with a tentative definition:

> National multilingualism – . . . the use within a single policy [*sic*] of more than one language.
>
> (1968:531)[9]

Stewart then goes on to describe how post-colonial societies have attempted to deal with multilingualism, stating that his goal is:

> intended to contribute to the development of a comparative framework for describing national multilingualism by suggesting a technique for describing national sociolinguistic situations. In particular it will emphasize the kinds of social, functional, and distributional relationships which different linguistic systems may have within . . . national boundaries, and it will develop both a conceptual framework and a system of notation for identifying these.
>
> (1968:532–3)

Stewart's attempt to typologize multilingualism is based on the establishment of four *attributes* (Standardization; Autonomy; Historicity; Vitality), seven language *types* (Standard (S); Classical (C); Artificial (A); Vernacular (V); Dialect (D); Creole (K); Pidgin (P)), and ten *functions* (Official (o); Provincial (p); Wider communication (w); International (i); Capital (c); Group (g); Educational (e); School (s); Literary (l); Religious (r)). A final factor of importance is the specification of the degree of use of each of the linguistic systems within the national communities, based on the percentage of speakers: the highest is Class I (75 per cent or more of the population) down to Class VI (below 5 per cent of the population).

Stewart then (wrongly, I think) moves to narrow his definition by the exclusion of some of the functions he has just established:

> The most obvious modification which should be made in the earlier definition of national multilingualism is the exclusion from it of linguistic systems having highly restricted functions of a kind which makes them marginal to the patterns of communication within the polity. The i, e, s, l, and r functions are of this nature. . . . With this modification, national multilingualism can be defined as *the established use within a single polity of more than one linguistic system with an o, p, w, c, or g function.* In some cases, it may prove more practical to list only those linguistic systems belonging to class V or higher [that is, above 5 per cent of the population].
>
> (1968:542–3, emphasis in original)

The problem with this exclusion is that in a polity such as India, the 'o' status of English is legally very marginal, and has a built-in 'sunset clause'; the 'p' function is non-existent; the 'w' function is officially restricted (Hindi is supposed to dominate this function); there is no 'c' function, and the 'g' function is limited to the community of Anglo-Indians, who constitute less than 1 per cent of the population. Yet no-one can deny that English plays an important role in the linguistic life of that polity; the main functions of English in India are for higher education (specifically excluded from his 'e' function), and as the language of business. Since the best jobs are in businesses and professions requiring a knowledge of English, there is a strong push for proficiency in this language that exceeds all attempts to stifle and control it, that is, to restrict its functions or domains. Furthermore, since higher education is constitutionally reserved for the states, and they have had little success in restricting English in higher education, overt and *de jure* controls on English do not work. If English is required for higher education, time will have to be spent in secondary and elementary school learning it, so *de facto* English dominates domains where it has no 'legal' status. In other words, English has a higher 'functional load' than its explicit legal status in a state like India would predict.[10]

2.2.1.3 Ferguson 1966

Ferguson's approach follows somewhat in the vein of Stewart's, since it is an attempt to establish whether sociolinguistic profile *formulae* can be used to succinctly characterize types of policy for the purposes of comparison.

Ferguson begins by distinguishing between major languages (Lmaj), minor languages (Lmin) and languages of special status (Lspec).

1 A major language (Lmaj) is characterized as follows:
- Being spoken as a native language by more than 25 per cent of the population or more than 1 million people.
- Being official in the nation.
- Being the language of education of more than half of secondary-school graduates of the nation.
2 A minor language (Lmin) is characterized by:
- Being spoken natively by no more than 25 per cent of the population but by no less than 5 per cent or 100,000 speakers.

- Being used as a medium of instruction above the first years of primary school.
3 Languages of special status (Lspec) are characterized by:
  - Not falling into above categories.
  - Being used widely for religious purposes.
  - Being used widely for literary purposes.
  - Being used widely as a lingua franca.
  - Being used widely by an age-sector of the population.

Given the above, Ferguson states that the formula for Spain would be as follows:

$$5L = 2Lmaj + 1Lmin + 2Lspec$$

This means that there are five languages: two major (Castillian and Catalan), 1 minor (Basque), and two special (Latin and French, which at the time of writing were widely studied in secondary school).

But as Ferguson pointed out, this formula does not give any information about the type and function of the languages in question. He therefore proposed to adapt portions of Stewart's typology (see above), that is, the five basic types:

1 Vernacular (V): Non-standard native language of a speech community.
2 Standard (S): A vernacular which has been standardized.
3 Classical (C): A standard which has died out as a native language.
4 Pidgin (P): A hybrid language combining the lexicon of one language with the grammar of another.
5 Creole (K): A pidgin which has become nativized.

Thus the previous formula can now be expanded as follows:

$$5L = 2Lmaj(2S) + 1Lmin(V) + 2Lspec(C, S)$$

This means that the major languages are standardized, the minor language is a vernacular, and of the two specialized, one is classical and the other standard.

Furthermore, the basic *functions* of Stewart's taxonomy also need to be incorporated:

1 g: used principally by one particular speech community, which marks its users identifably to others in the larger speech community;

2 o: used officially, either by law, or administratively, at the national level;

3 w: used as a lingua franca or lwc (language of wider communication) within the polity;

4 e: used for education beyond primary school; textbooks are published in it;

5 r: religious purposes;

6 i: international language, used to communicate beyond national borders;

7 s: studied as a subject in schools.

The previous formula can now be expanded again to:

$$5L = 2Lmaj(So, Sg) + 1Lmin(Vg) + 2Lspec(Cr, Ss)$$

To accommodate diglossia in this formula, Stewart had proposed the diacritic of a colon with C or S followed by V or K, so that C:V means 'Classical/Vernacular' and S:K means 'Standard/Creole'. Ferguson also proposes to indicate a nationally dominant language (spoken by over 75 per cent of the population) by bold-facing the **S**. Another factor which is difficult to represent is the fact that there may be a cluster of minority languages that comprise a high percentage of the population, but the individual languages are not spoken by large numbers. Ferguson proposes to lump these together enclosed by braces, with a raised plus sign after the number of major languages, that is $5^+\{V\}$. Ferguson also notes a number of other kinds of information that might be useful to note in a linguistic situation, but are hard to symbolize without unnecessary complexity. One would be the extent of dialect diversity:[11] the amount of bilingualism or multilingualism, the difference between indigenous and immigrant languages, and information about literacy rates and writing systems.

The formula for a polity such as Mexico can now be given as follows:

$$10^+ = 1(\mathbf{So}) + 6^+(6Vg, \{V\}) + 3(Cr, 2Ss)$$

This means that there are 10-plus languages; one standard and official spoken by the majority of the population; six-plus minor languages, six of which are vernaculars used for general purposes by a segment of the population, and a bloc of other vernaculars; and three special-purpose languages, one classical used for religion (Latin), and two standards studied in school. As is obvious, the formulae cannot be interpreted without an added textual exegesis.

2.2.2 Fasold's critique

Fasold's 1984 critique of the foregoing focuses on the essential fact that neither language policy types nor types of societal multilingualism are discrete, either–or kinds of phenomena. Instead, bilingualism can be variable, language competence can be gradient, the degree of standardization of a language can vary, and the amount of bi- or multilingualism seems to vary from community to community and individual to individual.[12] When an attempt is made to say that this community's multilingual repertoire is minus this or plus that, qualities are confused with quantities. Furthermore, language policies are *constructs*, and they change over time.[13] Social constructs consist of different elements, and elements that were important at one point (e.g. an origin myth) may lose validity or currency at a later point.[14] A policy that might have been developed for a decentralized, rural citizenry may no longer be viable in the twentieth century, with an urbanized literate population. Demographic factors may change, making the former minority the *de facto* majority. The policy that seemed so glorious at the moment of independence may turn sour as the independence heroes retire to their rocking chairs. It is for these reasons that proposals to taxonomize multilingualism and language policy always fail in some way: they force binary distinctions on to variable, gradient phenomena; they ignore or minimize diglossia (especially extended diglossia in the Fishman 1967 sense), and they minimize the factors of repertoire and register – what *uses* language is put to in a society, and what kinds of proficiency *users* have in the various codes that are available to them. It is to these deficiencies that I now turn.

2.3 REGISTER AND REPERTOIRE

2.3.1 Linguistic register

The concept of linguistic register has been described by Trudgill as follows:

> Linguistic varieties that are linked . . . to occupations, professions or topics have been termed *registers*. The register of law, for example, is different from the register of medicine, which in turn is different from the language of engineering – and so on. Registers are usually characterized solely by vocabulary differences; either by the use of particular words, or by the use of words

in a particular sense.

Registers are simply a rather special case of a particular kind of language being produced by the social situation.

(1983: 101)

Halliday *et al.* devote a long section to register in their 1964 work. They also refer to register as 'distinguished by use'.

I would suggest an improvement on Trudgill's definition by expanding the definition of register to include, in many cases, a preference (or even a dispreference) for particular *syntactic patterns* or *rhetorical devices.* In reality many different kinds of registers tend to prefer or eschew the passive voice, metaphors, imperative verbs, short sentences, as well as having a preference for certain lexical *devices* (such as acronyms or blends) as well as certain more established lexical items and resources (such as Graeco-Latin vocabulary).[15]

Let us tentatively propose the following definition of *Register*:

A set of specialized vocabulary and preferred syntactic and rhetorical devices/structures, used by specific socioprofessional groups for special purposes. A register is a property or characteristic of a *language*, and not of an individual or a class of speakers.

Crucial for our discussion of register in the context of multilingualism and language policy is the fact that some languages *lack* certain registers: in Western industrial societies they may lack ethnoscientific registers (folk taxonomies for classifying plants, animals or natural phenomena), or specialized poetic registers, specialized politeness systems, or registers for speaking in a trance.[16] In pre-industrial societies the languages lack legal, technical, scientific and medical registers and subvarieties of these (e.g. the register that airline pilots use to communicate with air-traffic controllers). Such languages either function without such registers, which relegates them to a marginal status within a larger multilingual society (Stewart's 'g' [group] function), or the members of such linguistic cultures acquire proficiency in these registers in other languages. In many post-colonial societies, of course, the registers they acquire proficiency in are registers of English or another ex-colonial language.

What this illustrates, of course, is that registers for a particular language may be *di-* or even *tri*glossic: certain registers are in the domain of the H-variety (religion, literature, ethnohistory), some in the domain of the L-variety (conversation, jokes/stories, intimacy/

courtship, automotive/mechanical, building/construction trades, etc.) and certain registers (high-tech, higher-education) may be in the domain of a totally different language.

2.3.2 Repertoire

Another useful concept that focuses on the *user* rather than on the *use* of special registers is that of linguistic or *verbal repertoire* (Gumperz 1964: 137). Trudgill defines this as the 'totality of linguistic varieties used [in different social contexts] . . . by a particular community of speakers'.

Since different speakers may have repertoires different from the set of varieties shared by the group as a whole, I would define repertoire as an *individual's* particular set of skills (or levels of proficiency) that permit him or her to function within various registers of (a) language(s). Different individuals' repertoires will vary (plus or minus, active or passive) and will be gradient (scaled from low to high proficiency).

This claim is based on certain observable phenomena:

- No individual (even highly educated) controls *all* registers of a language; each individual's repertoires *vary* when compared to other people's, both in domain and proficiency.

- A person's individual repertoires may be *diglossic* and/or *multilingual*: she or he may be able to function in the H- and L-domains of her or his language and the registers assigned to those domains, but also perhaps in a 'foreign' (or classical, etc.) specialized register (e.g. for medical/technical/scientific usage, or religious usage).

- Certain members of the linguistic community may lack active proficiency in certain registers but may passively understand them; this passive knowledge is culturally appropriate and not to be considered in any way aberrant.[17]

- Despite the appearance of multilingualism, even of fluency in the manipulation of a particular register, particular individuals may not have communicative competence in other registers of the same language. This is particularly true in the case of so-called 'bilinguals' who have learned a particular register in a non-native situation.[18]

Examples of preferred syntactic patterns/rhetorical devices of a particular register:

- *Legalese* Prefers redundancy, long sentences: 'The party of the first part did willingly and knowingly will, bequeath, convey, impart, and transfer said property (described in Exhibit A) to party of the second part . . . '; 'Plaintiff alleged that the defendant did slash, hold, beat, punch, kick, strike, stomp, pummel and beat (the plaintiff) . . . '.

- *Medicalese* Prefers acronyms and abbreviations, Graeco-Latin vocabulary: 'Let's run a CAT-scan and then also check her SGOT's; take a look at that haematoma near the right-lateral tibia. Oh, and check the beta-quants in her lipids.'

- *Psychology* The *APA Publication Manual*, the style-book of the American Psychological Association, sets policy for 16 member journals and over 200 non-member journals. In over 200 pages, it specifies that psychological writing should be clear and maximally informative, writers should use short sentences, the active voice of verbs, and eschew metaphors and figurative writing (Rhodes and Thompson 1990).

- *Linguistics* Specialized jargon, lots of abbreviations ('LP', 'GPSG', 'GB'), rhetorical preferences (e.g. certain imperative verbs): 'Consider the following data from Madurese . . . '; 'Observe that daughter-adjacency is more common in . . . '; 'Recall that lenition must precede palatalization . . . ', but not '*Think about the fact that . . . '; '*Remember that there is an ordering paradox if . . . ' or '*Take a gander at these data from Okeefenokee . . . '.

- *Financial/stock-market* Inanimate objects (commodities) are anthropomorphized: 'Silver suffered today, gold took a beating, but oil futures and aerospace are looking hopeful.'

- *Other registers* May prefer the active voice or the passive voice; multisyllabic words to monosyllabic ('An ornithological specimen in digital captivity is more valuable than double that number concealed in the umbrageous foliage' for 'A bird in the hand is worth two in the bush'); rhyming slang (Cockney), alliteration ('nattering nabobs of negativism'), etc.

It may be instructive to compare linguistic registers and repertoires in a way that shows both the properties of registers (as characteristics of a particular language) and individual linguistic repertoires that may be diglossic or multilingual (but not fluently multilingual, only controlling a particular set of registers). Table 2.3 attempts to display a wide range of possible registers that might be found in a selection of

Table 2.3 Particular registers, general registers and one individual's diglossic repertoire

Registers of a diglossic language		Registers in general (most languages?)	Particular repertoire Active	Passive
	L	Argots, slangs, jargons	+	+
H		*Belles-lettres*		+
H		Bureaucratic		
		Clinical		
		Computer science		
	L	Construction trades	+	
	L	Conversational	+	+
H		Dramatic/stage/media	−	+
H	L	(public speaking)	−	+
	L	(folk taxonomies)	−	+
		Fashion, design	−	−
	L	Intimacy, courtship	+	+
	L	Jokes, story-telling	+	+
H		Legal, juridical	−	
		Maths/science		
	L	Automotive/mechanical	+	
		Medical		
H		Ordinary prose/	+	+
	L	letter-writing	+	+
H		Religious, prayer,	−	+
H		trance language	−	+
		Technical/scientific		
	L	Sports	+	
		Motherese		
		∞		

languages; it also shows that particular inventories of registers of particular languages are a subset of all the possible registers, and that an individual's repertoire may show mastery of some registers in one variety of a language, some in another variety, and some in a totally distinct language.

2.3.3 Examples of complex real situations

Lest it appear that this is too finely tuned for any natural language situation, this list may be compared with that shown in Rubin (1972 [1968]: 518–20), where she attempts to distinguish in what contexts citizens of Paraguay use their repertoires of Spanish and Guaraní, or the careful distinctions made by triglossic Luxembourg, whose citizens' differential use of Lëtzebuergesch, German and French is described by Hoffmann (1981).

To make the contrast between repertoire and register clearer, let us examine what a particular speaker's repertoire might be like if a speaker had a repertoire commanding registers that involved two levels of a diglossic language plus socioprofessional registers from another (third) variety, in this case an international language. To be specific, this woman is a Tamil speaker and has a BSc. in Mathematics and Computer Science.

In the schema in Table 2.4, the repertoires of this speaker are divided up among two varieties of a diglossic language (Tamil), and English (in fact Indian English, since there are lexical, syntactic, intonational, and phonological differences between IE and American or RP varieties). The speaker controls some repertoires actively and some only passively; the technical/mathematical registers are actively controlled in (Indian) English, and it is safe to say that the

Table 2.4 A diglossic and multilingual linguistic repertoire; the speaker is female, Tamil-speaking, with higher degrees in mathematics

Registers in general	H-variety Tamil	L-variety Spoken Tamil (P = Passive)	(Indian) English Active	Passive
Argots, slangs, jargons		?		
Belles-lettres	+			P
Bureaucratic	+			P
Clinical				P
Computer science			A	
Construction trades		P		
Conversational		+	+	
Dramatic/stage/media	+	+		P
(public speaking)	+			P
Ethnoscientific				
(folk taxonomies)		+		
Fashion, design				P
Intimacy, courtship		+		
Jokes, story-telling		+		
Legal, juridical				P
Maths/science			A	
Automotive/mechanical		P		
Medical				P
Motherese		+		
Ordinary prose/	+		A	
letter-writing		+		
Religious, prayer	+			
Technical/scientific			A	
Sports		P		
∞				

speaker would not be able to function in Tamil in these modes except to do low-level arithmetical calculation. In some cases the speaker may actively control a Tamil register and passively control an English register, such as in *belles-lettres*, meaning that such a person is capable of doing creative writing in Tamil but would probably not exhibit high proficiency in the English register, except passively, that is to read and enjoy a novel. For ordinary prose, the speaker would have an active command of both L-variety Tamil and English, but no prose register exists for L-variety Tamil. A male speaker of Tamil with a similar professional background would probably have a similar repertoire, except that his control of 'Motherese' would be passive, rather than active, his control of 'Automotive/mechanical' might be active, his control of 'folk taxonomies' would more likely be passive and his control of 'sports' would perhaps be active.

Useful though these squared-off tables may be, I prefer to propose another type of diagram, one that represents linguistic repertoires as a set of *concentric circles* rather than as parallel columns. The reason for preferring a diagram such as that shown in Figure 2.1 is that the nested circles can better demonstrate a number of factors not indicated by the parallel columns.

First, all speakers of a diglossic language share the innermost circle, which also represents early childhood and nuclear-family intimacy. This is the domain of family life, story-telling, jokes, folk wisdom, conversation, food, street life and intimacy. With schooling, speakers begin to acquire domains associated with education in the L-variety language. As Tamil speakers approach the end of secondary education, where they have mastered the H-variety of their language, proficiency in English increases, and certain registers are reserved for the domain of English – technical subjects, mathematics, social sciences, etc. Higher education expands these repertoires further, but they will only be acquired after the acquisition of H-variety Tamil repertoires. The circles can be understood as a progression from the centre outward, with thresholds at the H-variety Tamil 'boundary' and at the English 'boundary'. Different speakers will have different repertoires, represented by different sectors or segments within each circle, but the *sequence of acquisition* will be similar for all speakers.[19]

Second, the concentric circle model emphasizes that the L-variety language is the basis of and at the centre of one's linguistic repertoire – it is the native language, the language one dreams in, the first learned and the last forgotten. All other repertoires are added on, but do not replace the L-variety. This is the repertoire that is taken for granted, and typically is given no protection in language policy – domains and reserves are usually only specified for H-variety languages and/or foreign imports, with exceptions in a few polities such as Luxembourg.

Third, the concentric circle model allows us to account for *gradience* and variability in proficiency, something that few policies seem to want to deal with. The line that begins at the centre and moves toward the edge can represent gradient ability, since proficiency usually increases with time.

Fourth, the concentricity of the circles also shows that if domains shift,[20] it is usually from one adjacent circle to another, not hopping over one band to penetrate a non-adjacent circle. A passive competence is possible within any circle, of course, but the largest number of passive competencies is most likely to be in the language learned last, in this case English. The circle might also contain a small 'passive' segment for yet another language, since in India it is quite common for speakers who claim no active command of Hindi to watch and enjoy Hindi movies, or to understand a bazaar language associated with marketing and shopping. In the concentric circle model, a niche for passive Hindi (cinema) is shared with Tamil and English.

Fifth, the circles also show what happens when attempts are made (such as have been in India and Sri Lanka) to restructure the repertoire with demands for reserved segments for another language (e.g. as Hindi or Sinhala, respectively). English then functions as the *buffer* language, the neutral territory that keeps the invasive languages at bay. Under Indian language policy, the attempt to capture domains of languages not reserved for Hindi has so far been restricted to those registers associated with English, whereas in Sri Lanka, the perception (among Tamils) was that Sinhala intended to invade and replace not only English sectors, but sectors that had been the reserve of H-variety Tamil, such as entrance examinations to university. English, under that policy, was to be stripped away, or reduced severely. It is perhaps the disparity between the levels of penetration that explains the intensity of Tamil resistance in Sri Lanka, compared with that seen in India, where Hindi made claims only to the registers in the outer band of sectors.

Sixth, the concentric circle model also depicts language registers and repertoires as an integrated, natural continuum – something akin to a living organism, rather than just a list of disparate proficiencies. As such, the threat of another language is seen as an invasive *virus* seeking to penetrate the cell, displace certain repertoires, alter its make-up so as to replicate itself, and perhaps even kill the original cell. One could carry this virological analogy too far, but it could help explain something of the emotional reaction to language spread and policies that seek to bring it about.

Finally, the concentric circle model allows us to depict diglossia as a feature of registers and repertoires. As such it is not a deficit or a disfunctionality, but a natural part of the repertoire of a speaker. Diglossia is, after all, a kind of language *policy*, since it is the result of decision-making of some sort, cumulatively over time.

2.3.4 Policy in conflict with observable reality

We have seen that researchers tend to confuse language policies with multilingualism itself, and have often attempted to map both on to the same symbolic representation, with the result that neither the policy nor the facts of multilingualism emerge clearly. In particular we have seen that what is often missing is the distinction between 'linguistic register(s)' (based on language use) and linguistic repertoire (based

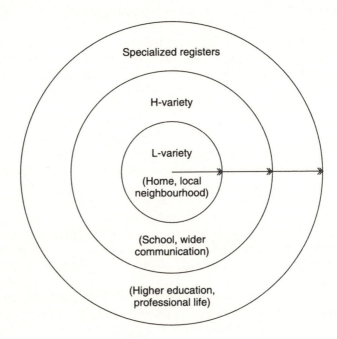

Figure 2.1 Concentric repertoires as a function of age and life experience

on the proficiencies of language users). And as Fasold has pointed out, linguistic continua with variable or gradient functions are too often forced into discrete either/or cells.

While policy and sociolinguistic reality must be kept separate (since they do not represent the same thing) attempts to typologize language policy must reflect some of the same dimensions and factors used to symbolize users' competencies. The closer the representation of policy comes to the representation of users' competencies, and allowing for differing proficiency and gradient-ranking of ability, as well as gradience in the expectations the policy makes of the citizenry, the better the 'fit' of the policy to the linguistic reality, and the less tension there will be between the two.[21] That is, if users have diglossic or triglossic repertoires, a policy that takes these into account and legitimizes the status of these varieties will be more congruent with the reality than one that ignores these repertoires. As we have already noted, except for polities such as Luxembourg and Malta, few policies ever explicitly mirror the multiglossic reality; in particular, few policies ever take any cognizance of the existence of L-variety language, let alone establish guarantees of its domains and registers.[22]

If one were to try to establish a typology of policies, one might begin with a catalogue of the types of 'fit' or congruence (or lack of them) between the policy and the sociolinguistic reality. That is, a list might look like the following:

- Policies with a (near) perfect fit: *Japan, Portugal, Iceland.* (These turn out to be monolingual speech communities that also have a monolingual policy.)

- Policies that ignore diglossic repertoires (particularly L-variety) and concentrate only on the registers of the H-variety: *Singapore.*

- Policies that establish rights for varieties that few users have any proficiency in: *Finland* (for Swedish).

- Policies that divide the H-registers between a 'local' language and a 'foreign' language, the latter having long-standing dominion over its registers by virtue of local consensuality: *India.*

- Policies that place two (or more) H-variety codes on an equal basis, but ignore L-variety repertoires: *Belgium* (for Flemish); *Canada* (federally, for French).

- Policies that recognize territorial rights for certain languages, with gradience in the distribution of registers (and assumed repertoires) based on the size of the populations: the *former Soviet Union* (and other polities using the Soviet policy model); *Switzerland (de facto*, but not *de jure)*.

* Policies that establish a monopoly on all registers for one variety, ignoring the registers and repertoires of L-varieties and their speakers, and thwarting the development of H-variety registers in competition with the monopolistic language: *France.*

In terms of how these policies might be then symbolized, let us continue with the concentric circle model, keeping policies distinct from realities. To represent language policy in India and how it lines up with the reality of the repertoires of many of its citizens, I propose the model shown in Figure 2.2.

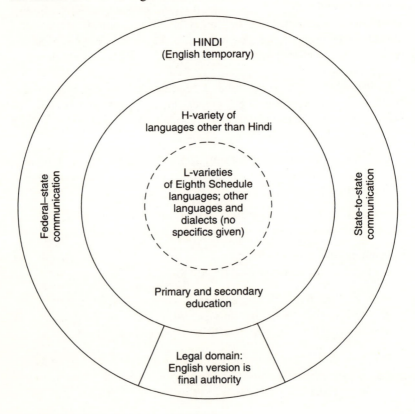

Figure 2.2 Language policy in India

Figure 2.2 shows a policy that makes no statements about domains of L-variety language; for the space occupied by H-variety Tamil in Table 2.4, this policy allows any language mentioned in the Eighth Schedule (Article) of the Indian Constitution. In the outer ring the policy reserves most segments for Hindi, but allows temporary domains for English; in one case it reserves a domain for English (ultimate authority of English versions of laws). It takes no cognizance of the *de facto* control of higher education, medical/technical/ scientific and business domains by English. This policy also makes no mention of all the other linguistic varieties (languages, dialects, etc.) spoken natively by millions of Indian citizens that are not recognized by the Eighth Schedule.[23] These varieties are in effect relegated to L-variety status, though as mentioned, this domain is not recognized as a legitimate one.[24]

Another situation, illustrated in Figure 2.3, shows that lack of fit between Swiss language policy and sociolinguistic reality. In the Swiss Federal Constitution of 1874 (revised to 1953), section 116 specifies what languages are official and national:

German, French, Italian and Romansch are the national languages of Switzerland.
German, French and Italian shall be deemed the official languages of the Confederation.

(Hughes 1954: 128)[25]

This is the text of the constitution that refers to language, in its entirety. From this statement it is in fact difficult to make any kind of symbolization that recognizes either registers or repertoires, except to distinguish between 'official' and 'national', but I would propose either separate circles or one circle segmented into four, with the outer circle adjacent to Romansch left blank.[26]

Neither of these symbolizations reflects the reality of language use or the repertoires of language users in Switzerland – it fails to recognize the extensive domains of *Schwyzertüütsch* and the very restricted domains of *Schriftdeutsch* among 'German' Swiss; it overlooks the fact that Italian has few if any domains at the federal level, and it ignores the extensive *extended* (Fishman 1967) diglossic relationship between Romansch and German (of various varieties). One must look to cantonal regulations (Falch 1973: 37–40) to see what local conditions (policies) are imposed on language; this is in fact a problem in many federated polities – in India, in Switzerland, and in the former Soviet Union the federal policies are explicit to varying degrees, but what happens at local levels, for example in

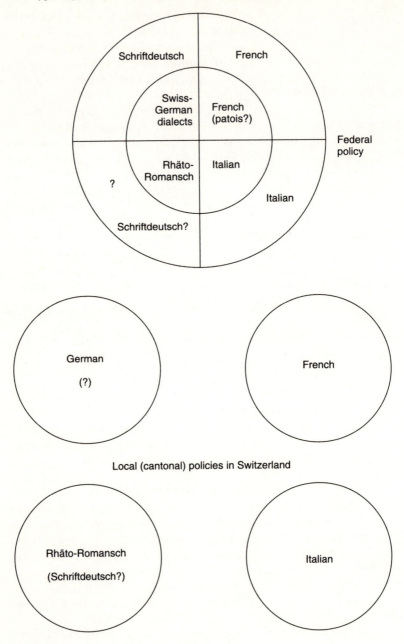

Figure 2.3 Language policy in Switzerland

various states of India, Soviet republics, or Swiss cantons is (or was) often severely at variance with federal stipulations. In India, for example, there are few guarantees of linguistic minority rights at the state level – in Tamilnāḍu, Karnataka and Maharashtra, the rights of various linguistic minorities (e.g. Telugus in Tamilnāḍu, Tamils and Marathis in Karnataka, and Gujaratis in Maharashtra) are rather tenuous, and groups that are quick to protest linguistic chauvinism at the federal level are themselves guilty of it at the state or local level. In Switzerland the territorial principle is guaranteed to the letter, so French speakers in a German-Swiss canton have in fact no rights except to L-variety use *chez soi*.

Further examples of the disparity between policy and sociolinguistic reality could be adduced, but my point is not to catalogue all the major types, only to show the disparities. My proposal is to use a symbolization scheme that:

1 Recognizes the difference between register and repertoire (the former being the jurisdiction of policies, the latter representing the reality of use and users).
2 Notes the centrality of L-variety domains at the core of a user's reality, and as the first variety acquired.
3 Recognizes the gradual acquisition of other varieties, usually segmented into repertoires appropriate for different registers, and recognizes that control of repertoires is gradient or variable along a continuum.
4 Recognizes the reality that policies typically ignore certain facts of linguistic use and users' repertoires; 'multilingual' policies are in fact rarely congruent with the linguistic reality of *any* of its users, except perhaps that of the dominant linguistic community;
5 Recognizes that policies that stake out domains for H-varieties and ignore the domains of L-varieties may in fact be doing the least contentious thing, as long as there is a perception of equality.
6 Recognizes that language 'strife' should perhaps best be characterized, not as 'the language of a majority being imposed on a minority' but as the question of WHICH LANGUAGE WILL LEGITIMATELY OCCUPY (DOMINATE) WHICH DOMAIN OR FUNCTION in the society, and how this can be regulated with a perception of fairness.
7 Recognizes that policies may have contradictions built into them, or may be deliberately vague and/or ambiguous, often because of stalemated conflict. The choice of a 'neutral' (perhaps foreign, ex-colonial) language to dominate certain (usually) H-variety registers may be a compromise that pleases no one; the lack of an

explicit reserve for L-variety language may be a deliberate loop-hole that allows non-prestigious varieties to be tolerated.

Obviously, no diagram and no description can take into account all the factors that enter into the decision-making which results in the variety of language policies that could possibly be enumerated, nor can all the even larger variety of multilinguistic situations known to us be easily catalogued. In the post-colonial era following the end of World War II, when attention first turned to the language policies of many newly independent nations, the idea of using the taxonomy, a symbolic classificatory system known to anthropologists, seemed appropriate. Policy-planners and language-planners wished to know how their country compared with others, and how to develop a policy that fitted their own circumstances. But in the ensuing period, pri-orities have perhaps changed. There is more of a concern with dynamic systems and a recognition of the fluidity of categories. The Soviet Union, long a model for other multilingual polities, has collapsed, and its much-vaunted language policy seems to have been less successful (and less tolerant) than it once appeared. Concerns with pragmatics have turned our attention to such issues as what language is used for and who uses what in what situation. Ideally, symbolizations of policy and symbolizations of multilingualism should always be paired, so that the 'fit' of the policy to the obser-vable sociolinguistic reality can always be seen clearly. And since the boundaries between languages (and their dialects) are often perme-able, and because proficiency in them is variable, we will never be able to provide neat pigeon-holes for everything. This may not make language policy makers happy, but perhaps in the meantime language policy-makers have come to accept that language policy cannot be handed down from above.

3 Religion, myth and linguistic culture

One of the most basic issues where language and religion intersect is the existence, in many cultures, of *sacred texts*, sometimes composed in *hieratic* (or sacred) languages that are used for religious purposes only.[1] For cultures where certain texts are so revered, there is often almost an identity of language and religion, such that the *language* of the texts also becomes sacred, and must be controlled, kept pure, kept out of the wrong hands (or wrong ears), and may even become the monopoly and source of livelihood for a hereditary priesthood.

3.1 WHAT IS MEANT BY LANGUAGE?

In discussions of this sort, I find it necessary to begin by attempting to establish some guidelines about what is meant by 'language'. That is, we can talk about:

- Language as a rule-governed human communicative system.

- Languages proper, that is, individually named varieties and their subvarieties (dialect, jargon, lingo, slang, patois, argot, . . .).

- Language as a cultural system.

- Language as the *functions* that it performs – symbolic, ritual, instrumental, phatic, lingua franca, (Language of Wider Communication), etc.

These distinctions are often, but tragically not always, differentiated when policies about language are formulated. If we do not maintain these distinctions we will find that what is meant by *language* may become confused; when this confusion occurs in the real world, it may eventually become conflictual.

3.1.1 Language as code

For a structural or theoretical linguist, language is the *code*, meaning it is the sets of phonological, morphological, syntactic and semantic rules that together with the lexicon, can be used to construct (or characterize) any or all sentences of the language; when these sentences are combined into larger units, we get *texts*, but neither the sentences nor the texts are part of the code. They are rather the *output* of the code – what the grammar generates or produces.

This is a somewhat narrow interpretation of the notion of language, but many linguists would agree with the Chomskyan notion that since the sentences of a language are in fact infinite in number, there is no way we can characterize or list them all, and we would not want to say that a language consists only of the sentences that have already been produced (or recorded), to the exclusion of all the possible sentences that have not yet been uttered, or were never recorded.

Formal linguists, especially those who follow *autonomous* theories of linguistics, would also hold that languages *per se* are culture-free; the code, in other words, expresses nothing of the culture or the *Weltanschauung* of its speakers, nor are the grammatical categories, phonological rules, or syntactic constructs amenable to manipulation by the speakers or culture-bearers in general. By excluding texts and sentences from language, of course, it is easier to substantiate this view. This notion is known as 'linguistic relativity' and it holds that every linguistic group has at its disposal a perfectly adequate vehicle for its everyday linguistic needs – no language, therefore, is any better or more sophisticated (or, for that matter, more primitive) than any other.

The idea that linguists would exclude sentences or texts from what they think of as a language probably seems strange to scholars in other disciplines, and is therefore responsible for constituting a source of confusion, if not downright scorn, for this theoretical focus.

3.1.2 Language as text or discourse

Much more common among humanists is the notion that when we think of language, we mean primarily the *texts* or *discourses* that have already been produced, and traditionally this has meant written ones, rather than 'mere' oral conversational discourses. This body of texts constitutes the literature of the linguistic culture in question, of course, and since literatures differ in quantity (some are voluminous, some scanty or non-existent) languages are thought, in this view, to differ in quality. It is here that we begin to hear things about 'the beauty, the grandeur' of a particular language, or of the 'impoverished state' of some other language. It is also here that we might encounter the opinion that a particular language which has never been used as a medium of education, or has never been standardized, or is not anyone's national language, is therefore *inadequate* for these purposes. Such a language might be deemed inadequate because of lack of vocabulary (lexicon) or because it has no social or political prestige, or because it is associated with a particular group of people.

To take a concrete example, the French, as we shall see in a later chapter, are often heard expressing themselves about the superiority of their own language, and complaining about the crudity of other languages, or the threat of other languages (and their cultures) to French. Some writers even attribute 'imperialistic' behaviour to particular languages, especially the English language. Such judgements of course usually focus on the supposed beauty, superiority, crudity or whatever of the *literature* (or lack of it) of a particular language, or on certain *ideas* that have come to be associated with particular linguistic cultures, or malevolent forms of them. Sometimes people can even get rhapsodic about the code itself, though the basis for their judgement is often not obvious to others; Rona gives some interesting examples from speakers of Guaraní, a language spoken in South America:

> Guaraní, by the richness of its lexicon, by the perfection of its grammatical structure, by the superabundance of the words it possesses for the expression of abstract concepts and by the beauty and diversity of its forms of diction, is on a par with the lineages of languages of countries of the highest culture.
>
> (1966: 278)[2]

3.1.3 Language as culture

Here we must make a further distinction, between texts in a particular language, and the ideas and beliefs contained in those texts, or expressed by them. Very often this distinction is not made; instead, we hear that there is an identity of language and thought, indeed of language and culture, or that a particular language is best suited to express certain thoughts or ideals. This notion, known as the (Sapir–) Whorf(ian) hypothesis, or *linguistic determinism,* is associated with the American linguist Benjamin Lee Whorf, who not only believed that language influenced thought, but that language *determined* thought. To Whorf, a language like Hopi, because of the structure of the Hopi verb, had a far superior conceptual apparatus for talking about the theory of relativity.[3]

French linguistic culture is forthright about this, but Americans can also be heard in various parts of their history using the inseparability of the English language and the American notions of justice, freedom and liberty to justify certain laws and language-policy regulations. It is because of these confusions that I insist on the idea that *linguistic culture* is separate from both language and text, but inseparable from language and politics. After all, the most 'beautiful' language can also be used to express humble or even repugnant thoughts or ideas, and not just noble ones.

My own training as a theoretical linguist predisposed me to an autonomist view of language early in my career, but my exposure to sociolinguistically complex linguistic cultures, such as those found in India, gradually drew me to the theoretical standpoint that these distinctions must be maintained. I see these as *nested* relationships: language as code is nested in language-as-text; there can be no texts without the code, after all. Language-as-text is nested in linguistic culture, but is not identical to it – the ideas, beliefs, myths, attitudes and prejudices found in a text, though seen as inherent in the text, may have been current in the culture before that text ever was composed. And since language is the most elaborate cultural *construct* that we have, it is tempting to dismiss some aspects of its constructedness, for example its grammar, as being as ephemeral as its discourses. But language is also the primary *vehicle* of acculturation, of learning one's culture, constructed though it may be.

When a child 'learns a language' a number of things happen: the child acquires the code, and learns to manipulate it. But the child does not acquire the code by observing the code, but by observing and hearing texts (sentences, discourses) in the language. Embedded in those texts are meanings, values, beliefs, attitudes, myths; some would even say *discourses*. In other words, language acquisition also involves the acquisition of ideas about language (and many other phenomena in the world). The generative-transformational notion of language acquisition is that the child *constructs* a grammar based on the input available (texts, utterances) and that grammar is for the most part identical to the grammar of the language of the child's forebears; any differences in the code will reflect the minor differences between the language of its peers and that of the child's parents. Here confusion again reigns in many minds, since language changes very slowly in its history, and what may appear to be a 'mere construct' may be something that is the product of centuries of 'construction'.

Finally, the main thesis of this book is that if language policy is not deeply rooted in the linguistic culture of a language group, it is not going to *fit* the needs of its speakers very well. Language policy is therefore not just a text, a sentence or two in the legal code, it is a belief system, a collection of ideas and decisions and attitudes about language. It is of course a *cultural construct*, but it is either in tune with the values of the linguistic culture or it is in serious trouble. And it is in this chapter that we will see how different religious beliefs can find their expression in linguistic culture, and thereby in language policy.

3.2 RELIGIOUS BELIEFS AND LINGUISTIC CULTURE

3.2.1 The Judaeo-Christian tradition

Let us begin at the beginning, with myths about the origin of language, to see how various conceptions about language are embodied in important religious texts in the Western world. Most of the world's great religions which have textual traditions (the so-called 'Peoples of the Book') have at some point in their canon a story, myth or parable about the origin of language, and the role of the deity for it.

In Genesis, the first book of the Judaeo-Christian Bible, there is an account of how language began. Adam, still the only human on earth (Eve had not yet appeared) was directed by God to name things, specifically, to name the birds and beasts.

> And out of the ground the Lord God formed every beast of the field, and every fowl of the air; and brought them unto Adam to see what he would call them; and whatsoever Adam called every living creature, that was the name thereof. And Adam gave names to all the cattle, and to the fowl of the air, and to every beast of the field.
>
> (Genesis ii, 19–20)

As Harris points out (Harris and Taylor 1989: 35) Adam named things before there was any need to have language as a communicative device, since Eve had not yet been created. Note that in this tradition, God did not create language; humans, following God's direction, created language, or at least a nomenclature.[4] Later on, in response to human arrogance, God created linguistic *diversity*, in the story of the creation of the Tower of Babel in Genesis ii 1–9. In the process, God also dispersed the peoples of the earth in many directions.[5]

Despite this rather mundane view of language (one in which language is not at first associated with communication, since Adam is still the only human, followed by the deliberate creation of linguistic diversity as a sort of punishment for man's arrogance) there is still leeway in the interpretation of these texts for the development of a tendency, in both Judaism and Christianity, for *fundamentalism.* That is, though we are told at first that language was not created by God, God's Word must be obeyed, God's Word is law. God told Adam and Eve not to eat of the fruit of the tree of the knowledge of good and evil, but they disobeyed Him (misled by a snake) and were expelled from the Garden of Eden. God was communicating with them, therefore, in some way other than *language*, since Adam had made up the nomenclature, the language he used with Eve. God's Word, however, tended to be recorded (by humans) in some particular form or in a particular *language* thereafter, so that the tendency to obey the Word of God became wedded to a particular human recording of it.

In the New Testament, in the book of the apostle John, we find another view of the Word of God:

> In the beginning was the Word, and the Word was with God, and the Word was God.
>
> (John i, 1)

In this version (which many people think comes from Genesis, since it sounds primeval) we are told that the Word was identical to God; it was there in the Beginning, God controlled it, and it was holy. It is this version of biblical thinking about language that authorizes and underlies fundamentalism, and supports the notion that the Bible is *God's Word* – it is true, it contains only truths, and nothing may change or contradict it.

The way this may then get expressed in language policy is by the following progression:

• Every word of the Bible is true; you cannot change a word of it.

• There are Christian languages and heathen languages.

• God spoke Hebrew (or German, or English, etc.).

• Only languages for which there are translations of the Bible are worth knowing.

- If the King James version of the Bible was good enough for God, it is good enough for me.

- The way words are written in the Bible is the only correct way to write and spell them.

One quickly discovers that logical arguments and factual explanations have little weight with belief systems based on the above. In classes where I teach about language policy, I often have to remind students that the English version of the Bible is a *translation* and that the original text was in Hebrew/Aramaic and Greek; it also comes as as a surprise to some that certain texts were taken into the Bible while others were excluded by human agency. But devotion to the sanctity of text and the truth of God seems easily to be confused, and the idea that the 'King James' Bible is a translation, the product of human effort, and therefore subject to error (in translation, in interpretation) can just as easily get lost.[6]

3.2.2 Other traditions

We shall become familiar with other cultural notions about language that are deeply rooted in the religions of India in the chapters on India and Tamilnāḍu. In a later section we will also deal with myths about Arabic, which are strongly influenced by notions current in Islam about what language Allah spoke, how the Prophet Muhammad recorded what God said to him, and how this affects Muslims' attitudes about the Arabic language.[7]

3.2.3 Linguistic purism

In many linguistic cultures there exist movements that have as their goal linguistic *purism*. This has been defined in a number of different ways, but often involves religious fundamentalism and a return to (or a search for) linguistic authenticity; it often takes the form of removing from the language elements (usually lexical) that appear to be foreign, or corrupt, or lacking in true authenticity in the linguistic culture in question.[8] Annamalai's definition is widely used:

> Purism is the opening of the native sources and closure of the non-native sources for the enrichment of the language. Though the native sources are open in general, the dialectal and literary sources are often treated differently. The opening and closure can be seen as applied to materials and to models. Models are

the derivational, compounding and syntactic patterns. . . . The factors which lead to purism may be, theoretically, internal or external to the language. . . . More important than any structural consideration is the attitude of speakers toward native and non-native elements. . . . The attitude . . . is determined by socio-cultural, political and historical factors which are external to language. There are certain conditions some or all of which must be present for the puristic regulations to emerge in any language . . . [such as when the] social order is undergoing change with power relations redefined.

(Annamalai 1979b: 3–5)

3.2.3.1 Purism as language policy

As we can see, devotion to linguistic purism is a kind of language policy – there is an attempt to control where vocabulary comes from, what sources (external or internal) it will draw from, what syntactic and derivational process it will utilize. Central to all of this is a *belief system*, consisting of some or all of the following:

- A belief that there exists somewhere, perhaps in the past, or in a particular textual tradition, a state of 'purity' that the language can aspire to, or return to.

- A belief that there are people with special knowledge, capable of making decisions about what is pure and what is not.

- A belief that purity is a good thing, capable of renewing or strengthening the moral fibre of the language, its linguistic culture, or its speakers.

- There may also be a belief that purity is associated with a religious state, that is by keeping the language pure we keep religion pure, which helps keep the world from disintegrating.

- Purism may be associated with religious fundamentalism and fundamentalist movements, with political movements, national-ism, national integration, millennialism, and many other kinds of social, political and cultural phenomena.

Puristic movements in linguistic cultures come and go, they wax and wane. As Annamalai points out, they are often associated with changes in the social order or when power relations are being redefined. They are often very unscientific, relying on dubious ideas about what is native and what is not, and as a result many aspects of the movement get 'fudged' because of ignorance of the history of various words, or because it becomes too complicated to remain consistent.

3.2.3.2 Loan translation

For example, many puristic movements allow 'loan translation' of borrowed elements, which means that if a word can be coined that effectively translates the pieces of the borrowed word, the concept can be kept. Thus German, which went through a period of purism (but has now emerged from it) consciously coined terms like *Fernsprecher* for 'telephone' and *Fernsehen* for 'television' but in recent years has abandoned attempts to *calque* foreign words and now simply borrows, mostly from English. In Tamil (as we shall see more extensively in another chapter), borrowed words from Sanskrit, Hindi, English and other languages were (and are) consciously expunged in an attempt to return to the purity of Old Tamil; when television broadcasting came to South India, Tamil too had to find a Tamil word, and resorted to a loan translation – *tolaikaaṭci* (*tolai* means 'distant' and *kaaṭci* means 'show') in lieu of using the English word or the all-India Sanskritic *dūrdarṣan*, which is itself a loan translation from 'tele-vision'. Even Old Tamil contains some loan words (from Sanskrit) – but when it was pointed out that the word *aracu* 'government' was originally from Sanskrit *rāj*, the solution was to declare quite simply that Sanskrit had borrowed the word from Tamil, rather than the opposite. Purism may rely on philology and 'scientific' linguistics for arguments it finds useful, but if the arguments reveal inconsistency and error, they can be twisted to suit the goals of the puristic movement.

3.3 RELIGION, LINGUISTIC CULTURE AND LANGUAGE POLICY

Much could and has been written about religion and language; what we are concerned with are the effects of religion on language policy, especially as a deep-seated expression of linguistic culture. Some of the work on language and religion has focused on the language policy of particular religious bodies, especially when the goal is language maintenance by ethnic minorities in immigrant societies etc. (Kloss 1977a; Fishman 1966). Other studies are devoted to the study of the effect of religious languages on the development of national languages and/or competing standards. For the purpose of illustration I will emphasize this element, though the former is just as important in the long run and constitutes a neglected area of study in many polities. The effect of religion on the maintenance of diglossia and the compartmentalization of domains also has repercussions for policy studies that should not be minimized.[9]

To get an idea of the breadth of policy-related religious issues, consider the following facets of language policy in various parts of the world.

- *Belgium* The first *raison d'être* of Belgium was to create a buffer state across the English Channel, and second to carve off the Catholic provinces from Protestant Holland; once the religious safety was assured, a linguistic split (hitherto ignored) between Flemish and French Walloons began to grow, and continues to be a problem even today.

- *Britain* Welsh language and non-conformism combined to resist Anglicization and the spread of the Church of England. Welsh temperament took to Methodism and the Methodist hymns, but rejected an established Church of Wales, which eventually had to be disestablished.

- *Canada* French/English differences are exacerbated by the Roman Catholic/Protestant split; the Roman Catholic French clergy see language differences as an ally of the Roman Catholic Church.

- *France and the Suisse Romande* In France, French Protestantism is credited with spreading standard French into southern France (at the expense of Occitan) and Switzerland (Breton 1991). In Protestant Swiss-French cantons, dialect (*patois*) has declined; *patois* has survived only in Catholic areas (Breton 1991). French first penetrated into (German-speaking) Alsace as Huguenot refugees from France fled into Alsace, at the time not yet under French hegemony, but tolerant of Protestants; but Strasbourg, being oriented strongly to the Lutheran cause, forbade the French *Calvinists* to settle in Strasbourg; they therefore went to smaller towns (Colmar, Sélestat, Wissembourg, etc.), bringing French with them, and helping to establish beachheads and inroads of French in an originally monolingual German-speaking area, and helping to legitimize the claim that Alsace is *deeply* French.

- *India* There exist differently named speech varieties in India whose speakers will classify them as different *languages*, that is

Urdu, Hindi and Panjabi. But scholars familiar with the area know that the linguistic differences between these codes are minimal, if perceptible at all. The differences are less linguistic than religious, but the misconception is exacerbated by the existence of different writing systems – Hindi is written with the *dēvanāgari* writing system and borrows its learned vocabulary from Sanskrit; Urdu is written in Perso-Arabic script and has borrowed its learned vocabulary from Persian and Arabic. As for Panjabi, it is the 'language' that most recently obtained language status under the constitution of India, bolstered by the fact that sacred writings of Sikhism were in Panjabi written in *Gurumukhi* script. This led (in 1966) to the establishment of a Panjabi language state; Hindus then had to have a non-Panjabi state (Hariana). Other dialects of Hindi (Rajasthani, Maithili, Bhojpuri, Bihari) have tried to obtain this status but have yet to succeed. Hindi is of course the language variety declared by Hindus; Urdu is declared (in the Indian census) by Muslims, even by some whose mother tongue is probably something totally different (Khubchandani 1983). In other words, declaring in the Indian census to be a speaker of one of these three languages is more a declaration of ethnicity, or of religious faith, and less a linguistic declaration.

- *Korea* Under Japanese occupation, American missionary groups were allowed to use Korean language and *Hangkul* writing in their schools; other schools under Japanese control had to use Japanese. The result was the greatest success in Christian missionizing in any Asian country. This successful identification of Korean with Christianity means now that in emigration, for example in the USA, Korean-language churches draw in non-Christian Koreans as well, since churches help preserve Korean ethnicity, as well as being useful for brokering marriages.

- *Pakistan* Similar to Belgium, religion (Islam) was paramount in the establishment of Islamic Pakistan, but once established, the linguistic split between East (Bengali-speaking) Pakistan and West Pakistan (Panjabi, Urdu) loomed larger and led to a split that resulted in the independence of Bangladesh.

- *Poland* Dismembered by (Protestant) Germany, Austria and (Orthodox) Russia, Poland was left with the Roman Catholic Church as the chief defender of its ethnicity and language; the Church's primary goal was, of course, to insure that Roman Catholicism would survive as well. The Polish Catholic Church therefore assured its own survival by linking it with issues of language loyalty, and strengthened it with special dispensation by Rome to use Polish in all domains (not just the homily during the otherwise Latin mass). Today the Roman Catholic Church is credited with helping to 'overthrow' the Communist regime through its strong support of Solidarność, and can still be said to play a definitive role in politics. According to some estimates, 93 per cent of Polish population claims membership of the Polish Catholic Church, the highest in Europe. Having a pope of Polish origin has certainly also been of some use.

- *Former Soviet Union* Much linguistic nationalism is supported by religious differences: the Baltic states are non-Orthodox (Lutheran or Roman Catholic); the Armenian/Azerbaijani split is rooted in the Orthodox/Muslim conflict; other Islamic republics resisted the domination of 'Orthodox' Russia, and have opted out of the Soviet Union and its successor, the Commonwealth of Independent States.

- *Sri Lanka* The Tamil/Sinhala conflict is reinforced by the Hindu/Buddhist conflict. Tamils see no way to remain Hindu without Tamil versions of their Saivite texts; Sinhalese see Tamils as a beachhead for penetration by numerically superior, predominantly Hindu India.

- *Switzerland* Language differences and religious differences (Protestant/Catholic) crosscut each other, rather than intensify each other. There are predominantly Protestant and predominantly Roman Catholic cantons in both German-speaking and French-speaking Switzerland. (Ticino (Italian-speaking) is itself a Protestant refuge from predominantly Roman Catholic Italy.)

- *Former Yugoslavia* A similar dichotomy between the Serbian and Croatian literary 'languages' is maintained primarily by the identification of Serbian with Eastern Orthodoxy and the Cyrillic script, while Croatian is written with the roman alphabet and is associated with Roman Catholicism. Any actual differences between these varieties rest on lexical peculiarities only; the situation is complicated by the existence of Bosnian varieties associated with Islam, which have their own lexical borrowings from Arabic or Turkish. Actual linguistic differences in phonology, morphology or syntax are not correlated with the religious differences (Brabec *et al.* 1954; Ivić 1958; Kohn 1960). The situation is further confused when we learn that most so-called Muslims are not believers; being a Bosnian or a Muslim in this tragic area means being descended from people who once adhered to Islam; the same can be said of 'Orthodox' Serbs and 'Catholic' Croatians. The differences are not linguistic (the isoglosses follow different configurations than the political boundaries), so in the current tension, identity is ascertained by determining a person's name.

• *The Arabic world and the Arabic language* We shall consider this later in this chapter, especially the way myths about Arabic and the purity and beauty of Classical Arabic have a strong effect on language policy in the Arab world.

We will deal with some of these aspects of religion and language policy in some of the later chapters dealing with particular linguistic cultures. Suffice it to say that many supposedly linguistic conflicts in the world are often complicated by religious associations of various sorts; conversely, religious strife may be strengthened by linguistic animosities, though of course the two can exist completely independently, as we see in Northern Ireland, where no linguistic differences exacerbate the communal conflict there. In the popular press, conflicts such as the ongoing civil war in Sri Lanka are usually presented as primarily religious in nature, whereas I see it as primarily linguistic, with religious underpinnings.

3.4 SOME MYTHS ABOUT LANGUAGE

As we have already noted, it may seem strange in this day and age to seek the origin of language policy in 'deep dark' myths from the past. But in fact many linguistic cultures have myths about language and these beliefs are often strongly cherished by members of the linguistic culture. Where they affect policy is in the area of attitudes toward the language, attitudes about other languages (and their speakers), the rights of other language speakers, and in challenges to the established policy. Let us look briefly at some examples from languages as disparate as Afrikaans, Arabic, French, Japanese, Karen and Navajo.

3.4.1 The victory of Afrikaans: from L-variety to H-variety

The history of the Afrikaans language in South Africa is of a despised L-variety of Dutch, thought by some to have passed through a stage of creolization, managing to expel standard Dutch from dominance of the H-domains in Afrikaner linguistic culture, becoming itself the H-variety.[10]

The 'triumph' of Afrikaans over various obstacles, and against such formidable enemies as English is shown by Roberge (1992) to have involved a considerable amount of myth-making about the language, its ontogeny (origins), and its association with other aspects of Afrikaner ethnicity.

Since English is also part of the linguistic picture in South Africa, one may also see this as an uneasy kind of triglossia that has since devolved into a diglossic situation when it was recognized as a *fait accompli* that Dutch was no longer viable in the linguistic culture. Since 1948 (as is the case with Belgium) there has resulted a kind of linguistic apartheid with English and Afrikaans occupying separate linguistic cultures. English of course still manages to predominate because of its immense international prestige and power, and because of the concentration of English-speaking people in the upper and middle classes, that is in the professions, but because Afrikaners constitute the majority of those of European descent, they have managed to carve out a space for their language that restricts English much more than it is restricted in, for example, francophone Canada. How this will fare in the newly constituted multiracial South Africa is another question, since the myths that supposedly helped the language to survive may now work against it.

3.4.2 Myths about Arabic

The idea that the Arabic language is deeply imbued with myth has been dealt with squarely by Ferguson (1959b) in an eponymously entitled article. Since much of what Ferguson says about mythologizing about Arabic is also applicable to other languages, I will quote him rather extensively.[11]

> In every speech community attitudes and beliefs are probably current about the language of the community as well as about other languages and language in general. Some of these are true, i.e. correspond very well to objective reality, others are involved with esthetic or religious notions the validity of which cannot be investigated empirically, and still others which purport to deal with facts are partly or wholly false. All these attitudes and beliefs, regardless of their truth-value, will be called here 'myths'. . . . This paper deals with the set of myths about Arabic current in the Arabic speech community today.
>
> (Ferguson 1959b: 375)

Ferguson goes on to reveal that myths about Arabic are fairly uniform in the speech community, even though the language is spread over a vast territory. The myths may be subsumed under four headings:

1 The superiority of Arabic.
2 The classical-colloquial diglossia.
3 Thoughts about the ranking of various dialects.
4 The future of Arabic.

Aside from myths about the language, one can also discern in Arabic linguistic culture, indeed throughout the Islamic world, a strong belief in the *sacredness* of Arabic:

> Muslims consider the Koran to be holy scripture only in the original Arabic of its revelation. The Koran, while it may be translated, is only ritually valid in Arabic. This is connected with the notion of Arabic as a 'sacred language'. Language itself is sacred, because of its miraculous power to communicate and to externalize thought. In this sense, language is essentially the same as the Divine power of creation. In order to create, God speaks a Word in the Spirit; similarly, man externalizes what is within his mind by formulating words with the breath, by giving breath 'form' in sound. The power of words to transmit to another consciousness the knowledge of the speaker lies in the fact that true words *are* themselves what they mean, or were at their origin; they are the object itself in sound. . . . 'Sacred' languages preserve this original power of language to an eminent degree; liturgical languages like Latin, the older forms of Greek, and Church Slavonic, have also preserved this power to a lesser degree.
>
> (Glassé 1989: 46)

This account goes on to describe how modern languages have, on the whole, lost this 'sacred' quality; the identity of word and the object named is no longer direct, it has become obscure, as a result of the sin of Cain.[12] Glassé also seems to be of the opinion that Arabic, though originally a desert nomadic dialect, has maintained a fresh directness that makes it a more suitable vehicle than many others:

> Thanks to the relationship of words to their roots, as if to a supraformal archetype, a deeper and more universal sense often superimposes itself upon a particular meaning in a phrase in classical Arabic. Simple statements, which are the rule in the Koran, open, under the right conditions of receptivity, into astonishing and vast horizons; the world is reduced to ripples in

consciousness. These and other qualities make Arabic an incomparable medium for dialogue between man and God in prayer.

(Glassé 1989: 47)

Our interest here is not to argue about the properties of Arabic, its beauty, its timelessness, but to examine the attitudes displayed by those who so describe it, and in particular, how those attitudes affect language policy-making in the Arab world, and in the Islamic world in general. To take one example (Mead 1988), language policy-making in Malaysia is complicated by an underlyingly Islamic notion of the meanings of words. When policy-makers began implementing the changeover from English to Malay in Malaysia's courts, those translating English legal terminology into Malay assumed that legal terminology is like terminology for chemistry or for anatomy – if the word 'atom' can be unambiguously translated into Malay, then so can the term for *'nolo contendere'*:

> The reformers appeared to hold, first, that meaning was fixed by the linguistic item that carried it, and second, that an equivalent item could be formulated in a second language and be applicable to precisely the same range of referents. We may hypothesize that the reformers' backgrounds reinforced this view. Islamic culture teaches that language has divine origins, is precise, and hence no useful distinction can be drawn between the dictionary definition of a word and its significance. . . . Secondly, Malay schools rely heavily on rote learning . . . and pupils are not encouraged to question the conventional meaning of a text. The lawyer, on the other hand, had learnt to distinguish meaning as object (or artifact) and meaning as act. . . . Meaning is created by the interactional process, and the appropriate connotation denoted by a specific term derives from the situational and linguistic contexts within which it is used.

(Mead 1988: 73)

Thus the notion of the 'fixedness' of meanings of words is carried over from Arabic, where this attitude is not surprising, to Malay, which is not a 'sacred' language, but is immersed in a culture where Islam is given strong emphasis; here again we see that many of the beliefs of one linguistic culture may be transferred to another, and affect the status of a totally different language. Legal language, of course, has a long tradition in Arabic, and though Malaysia's legal system is a remnant of British colonialism, and its legal language is now a translation of English legal language, the attitude towards words and their meanings inherent in the Islamic tradition affects the way law will be practised in Malaysian courts.

Later, in our analysis of French linguistic policy, we will see that 'fixedness' (French *fixisme*) is itself a kind of myth that crops up in puristic movements; the idea is that language was 'fixed' once and for all in the past, and cannot be changed now by mere mortals. Or, that attempts to change things are corrupting, and weaken the language, making it vulnerable to attack from its enemies.

3.4.3 Myths about Japanese

Another compelling study of mythologizing about language is a work by Roy Andrew Miller entitled *Japan's Modern Myth: The Language and Beyond.* The modern myth Miller is referring to is, not surprisingly, the Japanese language, as the title indicates.[13]

> For modern Japan, the Japanese language is a way of life, and the enormous amount of speculation, writing, and talking about it that goes on at every level of Japanese life constitutes an entirely distinctive and marvelously self-contained way of looking at life.
>
> In modern Japan, the Japanese language is never allowed to be taken for granted, not by anyone, not for a single moment. . . . The language not only serves the society as a vehicle for daily communication, but it also manages, as we shall see, to be a cult and myth as well. . . . To the Japanese today, the Japanese language is not simply the way they talk and write. For them, it has assumed the dimensions of a national myth of vast proportions.
>
> (Miller 1982: 4–5)

Miller then goes on to describe the many ways and the wide variety of expression that are involved in creating and sustaining the myth of the Japanese language:

> We have already emphasized that the modern myth of Nihongo is, in all its essentials, nonscientific and antiscientific. Though it has been erected, like all myths, around a hard inner kernel of truth, its special sociolinguistic function within contemporary Japanese society is to conceal and obfuscate those same tiny elements of fact behind an elaborate facade of mythic fiction. One searches in vain throughout the myth of Nihongo for anything that will correlate with the linguistic facts of the Japanese

language as it is actually spoken and used by the Japanese people.

(Miller 1982: 65)

One could quote at length from Miller's study; it would be for us a mere curiosity, were not myths about Japanese relevant for the rest of the world precisely in the way the myth of *Nihongo* affects the way the Japanese are taught to conceive of languages other than Japanese, languages like English for example. It also affects the whole enterprise of teaching Japanese as a second language, and even has a foreign-policy effect – specifically the occasional references to the supposed superiority of the Japanese, their language, and the inferiority of other cultures, whose languages, like their gene pools, are corrupted by mixtures of all sorts. When these pronouncements, often made by high officials of the Japanese government, are publicized in the West, international relations often are jeopardized.

3.4.4 Myths about French

Another part of the world where Anglo-Saxons readily note a difference in attitudes about language is the world of *la francophonie*, the French-speaking world, especially France. We will deal with this in some detail in the next chapter, devoted to the subject of French language policy. As we shall see there, French language policy is a construct that rests on many assumptions, including the superiority of the French 'language', however defined. Many French scholars have tried to demythologize this construct, but the French themselves remained unmoved by such efforts. What we will also see is that the myths about French are not simply hoary legends from the past, but are constantly being reconstructed. Mythologizing about the French language is an ongoing process, though few within French society recognize it.

3.4.5 Myths about Navajo

A New World culture in which language is strongly intertwined with myth is that of the Navajo. In their world-view, the world was created by thinking, speaking, or singing about it:

> Words, like thoughts, are considered to have creative power. In mythology things came into being or happened as people thought or talked about them. Repeating something four times will cause it

to occur. A request made four times cannot be easily denied.

(Witherspoon 1977: 22)

To the Navajo, man can think only with symbols, so some symbols must have existed before thought. The first few sentences of the first paragraph of the emergence myth read: 'The one that is called "water everywhere". The one that is called "black earth". The one that is called "first language." . . .' These phrases are significant in that they indicate that in the beginning were the word and the thing, the symbol and the object. . . . Symbol is word, and word is the means by which substance is organized and transformed. Both substance and symbol are primordial, for in the beginning were the word and the element, the symbol and the symbolized.

(1977: 46)

For the Navajo the world was actually created or organized by means of language. The form of the world was first conceived in thought, and then this form was projected on to primordial unordered substance through the compulsive power of speech and song.

(1977: 47)

The Navajo, as is well known, are the most language-loyal Amerindian culture in North America; some of this may have to do with the demographic size of the group, but much of it may be related to their world-view about language, and its importance in their universe, without which there can be no human life. For the Navajo, death of their language would obviously mean not only the death of Navajo culture but the destruction of the world. For the Navajo, language maintenance is equivalent to holding the world together and avoiding utter chaos.

3.4.6 Divine power and language in Southeast Asia

In Myanmar and Thailand there is an important minority linguistic group, the Karen, who have a myth about Y'wa, the divine power who creates nature, that strongly influences their loyalty to their language:

Y'wa is said to have given books to his various children, sometimes said to number seven, who are the ancestors of the major ethnic groups in the world known to the Karen. This gift of a book was, of course, the gift of literacy. The Karen, however, are negligent with the book given to them and it is eaten by animals. . . .

Y'wa offers the Karen the consolation that at some future date, 'foreign brothers' will bring the gift of literacy – in the form of a golden book – back to them.

(Keyes 1977: 52)

When American Baptist missionaries began to work among the Karen in the early nineteenth century, they found a fertile field for their missionizing, and the Karen, for their part, found the gift of the Christian Bible (a golden book) to be the fulfilment of a promise told in a myth. It should not be hard to imagine what resistance to the implementation of Burmese and Thai national language policies might be like among the Karen and other peoples of this area, where similar myths are widespread. The implications of this for the workings of language policy in the area can not be minimized.

3.5 CONCLUSION

When all is said and done, we must conclude that language policies do not evolve *ex nihilo*; they are not taken off a shelf, dusted off and plugged into a particular polity.[14] In linguistic cultures with ancient religious traditions, especially textual traditions, there are often ideas about language and its origin, its purpose, and its sanctity embodied in the religious tradition. And just as these textual traditions often consist of accretions of earlier and later material, and just as different portions of the text may contradict each other, we may find that language policies themselves consist of many parts, some explicit and overt, some implicit and covert. Often the overt policy is a later attempt to make sense of earlier cultural rule-making about language, but I would hold that it never succeeds in superseding the underlying ideas about language. It is therefore in the covert areas that we need to seek the origins of the overt facets of a policy, not vice versa.

4 Language policy and linguistic culture in France

Another part of the world where language and linguistic culture constitute a core value is France and the rest of the French-speaking world – *la francophonie*. As one eminent writer puts it:

> France is today the only nation in the world with legislation requiring (since 1794) the exclusive use of the national language in all public and private acts, from the drafting of laws to the language of commercial transactions and even a private citizen's last will and testament, etc. . . . . France is the most extreme case [*le cas limite*] of a nation totally identified with one language, but which goes beyond this to defend the integrity of this linguistic personality in all aspects of social life against the claims and encroachments of any and all languages from inside or outside its borders. . . .
>
> Certain international observers consider this policy aberrant in the age of computers and mass-media which is already upon us. . . . But French public opinion, perhaps anaesthetized by its poorly-understood monolingualism, is not sensitive to the urgency of language problems.
>
> (Balibar 1985: 9)

4.1 EPITOMIZING FRENCH LINGUISTIC CULTURE

4.1.1 The law of *8 pluviose an II*

On 27 January, 1994, France attained the bicentennial anniversary of an explicit policy regarding its national language.[1] In some ways, the law enacted on this date, that of *8 pluviose an II*, accurately epitomizes French official language policy, because, according to Balibar

(1985: 9), this law makes it the oldest (explicit) language policy in the world. As we shall see, the adoption of the policy of *8 pluviose*, though it was part of many revolutionary policies adopted in the fervour of the times, remained in force after the Revolution: while many other policies and laws were abrogated, repealed or fell into disuse, this one was so much a product of its times that there was never any thought of changing it. When we examine the effects of this law in detail, however, we will see that it did not enforce the kind of linguistic rigidity that is attributed to it. As we shall see, its strength lies in what it is perceived or remembered as having required, rather than in what it actually required.[2] On the other hand, I will try to show that the law of *8 pluviose* has come to typify French linguistic culture so well that even as we pass its two-hundredth birthday, it shows few signs of being out of touch with what French people seem to think about language.[3] There is a risk here, of course, of confusing the chicken with the egg. Has France pursued a relentless monolingual policy because the law of *8 pluviose* enabled it to do so, or is the law of *8 pluviose* a manifestation of deeper impulses of French culture? To answer this question, we must look at what happened during the eighteenth century and, in particular, in the last two decades before 1789. Many claims have been made for the revolutionary changes which happened to the French language during the French Revolution: what we need to establish is what the sociolinguistic situation was in the years preceding the Revolution, so as to be able to evaluate what effect the language law of 27 January, 1794 (*8 pluviose*) actually had.

4.1.2 The 'radiance' of French

As is obvious to any Anglo-Saxon visitor to France, French language policy is overt and self-confident; it has exerted an effect on other polities and policies for centuries, owing largely to the prestige of the French court and to the firm conviction of its speakers of the superiority of French language and culture. The wide dissemination of French loan words in many languages of Europe attests to the prestige and *rayonnement*[4] of French language and culture, beaming out like a bright beacon, signalling to other languages and cultures to take note of *la gloire* of France and French. Since this policy and the attitudes underlying it are so strong and noticeable, and have been so consistent through royal and republican regimes alike, we cannot fail to take note of French language policy as a type to be reckoned with. Such a policy is self-assuredly centrist and all powerful: it recognizes no equals for the language (or culture, which are equated) on French territory; it brooks no opposition. Given the continued centralization of French power in Paris, with little regional autonomy or authority (including school policy), it is no wonder that regional languages in France feel trampled under the weight of *la langue nationale*. Furthermore, there is today a new variable to be taken into the equation – languages brought by guest-workers and other immigrants to France in the decades since the collapse of the French colonial empire. Speakers of these languages are in some cases even more demanding than the speakers of France's traditional national minorities, who have perhaps learned more effectively to sublimate their feelings through centuries of disapprobation. Today, there is widespread concern in France about the loss of the international status French had acquired during the Enlightenment, and as anglophone visitors to France are well aware, much of the blame for this loss is laid at the feet of Anglo-American culture and the English language. What we will try to do in this chapter is trace the rise of French to its most 'glorious' zenith and then attempt to contextualize the apparent decline, both internationally and nationally, in the way that French culture views this decline, that is, as due to external forces. As we will see, this decline is viewed both as beyond the control of French, but at the same time within the control of The French, should they wish to resist it, that is, it is seen as a failure of will, the will to resist a malicious and relentless linguistic juggernaut imposed from without.[5]

4.2 HISTORICAL BACKGROUND

As we have already noted, there is no clear and discernible moment in the history of any linguistic culture when the origins of language policy are revealed. Myths about language origins do not seem to involve imagery of a burning bush, a pillar of fire, an epiphany on the road to Damascus. Origin myths may have as an important element a divine revelation to a certain worthy human, but overt policies about language are not usually ascribed such origins. Certainly in the case of French, there never was any doubt about the origin of French as a daughter of Latin. In the development of French linguistic culture, however, one has to look for signs of the beginnings of French consciousness as being more than, or no longer just, a daughter of Latin. One of these is certainly the point at which French acquires its own name (*françois*, later *français*) instead of *la langue romane*. The rise of a French cultural policy on language parallels the rise of

France as a power in Europe, expanding into territory previously controlled by the dukes of Burgundy, the English throne, the Hapsburgs (Alsace), and so on, radiating out (that metaphor again) from Paris in all directions, and rolling over the regional languages in its path. Many descriptions of language policy in France start with the *ordonnance* of *Villers-Cotterêts* in 1539. I prefer, none the less, to start with the oath signed by the grandsons of Charlemagne, the *Serment de Strasbourg*.[6] Ironically, or perhaps not so, this text is associated with Strasbourg, a city which at the time was far from being French speaking, but eventually acquired the status of a symbol for both France and Germany and their 'right' to claim this city and its hinterland.

4.2.1 French attitudes about language

As we have already noted, the French-speaking world (*la francophonie*) is a linguistic culture with markedly obvious attitudes about language in general and the French language in particular. In France, as has been noted, attitudes about language are overt and readily observable.[7] This has been observed and discussed in monograph-length studies such as those of Gordon (1978) and Flaitz (1988). Harmer, in a book totally devoted to the subject of *Uncertainties in French Grammar*, describes the French nation as:

> deeply and passionately interested in its own language, and is rarely, if ever, tired of proclaiming the fact. '*La grammaire est une institution nationale*', affirms M. Arland in *Cinq propos sur la langue française* . . . ; Mr. Galliot, writing in *Vie et language* . . . describes the Frenchman as 'homo grammaticus, in the heart of whom slumbers . . . a miniature Vaugelas, always ready to get worked up about a point of semantics or of syntax, and always superciliously censorious of inexactitudes and gibberish.' . . . It is certain that the concern shown for their mother tongue by the French . . . is not a recently developed characteristic. It has existed for four centuries or considerably more.
>
> (Harmer 1979: 3)

Gordon has noted that the French see their language as having a mission in the world; it is seen as universal, pure and lucid, the proper and appropriate medium of the values of humanism:

> As characteristic as the concern of many Frenchmen for the purity of their language – and their concern lest it become corrupt – is a

widely held conviction that in teaching French they are both serving a *mission civilisatrice*, however much in recent times this term might evoke smiles or scorn, and, at the same time, strengthening France's political role in the world at large. . . . The French *mission civilisatrice* is related to a subconscious faith that France is bearer of the universal idea that human nature is everywhere and at all times basically the same, that its laws have been most fully realized by France and that, therefore, one does not speak of 'French civilization', but of civilization simply.

(Gordon 1978: 5–6)

On 31 December, 1975, the president of France, Valéry Giscard d'Estaing signed into law an act (Law No. 75-1349) to protect the French language from encroachments from (in particular) English, and to guarantee its status in certain commercial and other domains in France itself. During the debates that led to the passage of this legislation, a wide spectrum of political parties expressed support for the law. One, M. Georges Cogniot, speaking for the French Communist Party, expressed himself before the *Sénat* (on 23 October, 1975) in words that could have come from almost any part of the political spectrum:

Language is a powerful factor of national consciousness, the vehicle par excellence of that national heritage, of which the school cannot fail to be the principal organ of transmission. We are not in agreement with those who resign themselves to the decline of the French language, to a superficial and impoverished picture of its grammar, its lexicon, its stylistics, or to the elimination of the teaching of the national literature.

(HCLF 1975: 121)[8]

And, as Flaitz notes:

French has been observed to function and to be consciously promoted as a symbol of French political, cultural, and ideological preeminence in the sixteenth–nineteenth centuries. Today many French people allegedly believe that . . . English . . . is similarly imbued with value-laden features often found to conflict with French values and norms.

(Flaitz 1988: 9)

In other words, French speakers have strong positive attitudes toward the French language; they think of it as characterized by rationality, lucidity and clarity, and they see it as strongly linked to aspects of French culture that they value highly. They think of the French language not just as a vehicle of French culture, but as its highest embodiment. And since they see language and culture as strongly linked, they also fear that the spread of English will bring with it cultural values that they dislike: their attitudes toward English are therefore supposedly influenced by their dislike of certain aspects of Anglo-American culture. Flaitz's work, a detailed examination of French attitudes about English in general, is also a study of basic French assumptions about language, which are in effect attitudes about French. Flaitz attempts early in her work to establish whether there is such a thing as 'language ideology' and what its relationship to culture might be: she bases her definition of ideology on the work of David Smith (1973):

> In looking more closely at culture, we find ideology which is seen to include a set of beliefs concerning how things are, how they should be, and how to relate both to each other and to behavior. Language, too, to Smith constitutes a subsystem of culture.
>
> (Flaitz 1988: 14)

As Flaitz notes, Smith eventually also defines ideology in the same terms as he defines culture: her point is to establish whether Fishman's notion (Fishman 1977) of 'ideological encumberedness' of a particular language is the same as 'culturally marked', 'value-laden', 'culturally loaded', 'ideologically-charged' or whatever. That is, she wishes to determine whether there is any empirical reality to the notion that languages have cultural values associated with them (since most such assertions are simply that, and have not been empirically demonstrated). My approach will be not to debate whether French pronouncements about the role of the French language are an 'ideology' or merely an aspect of its culture: I will take these pronouncements at face value, and treat them as *prima facie* expressions of commonly held beliefs, currents of thought, and basic cultural assumptions that underlie and form the basis for French language policy, both historically and in the present.[9] As with any other linguistic culture, many aspects of French linguistic culture are rooted deeply in the past, and no clear point of origin can be determined. Nevertheless some prominent features of French linguistic culture can be observed, and my point will be to show how French language policy has its origin in its linguistic culture.

4.3 THE ORIGIN OF FRENCH, THE ORIGIN OF FRANCE

When one asks oneself where the French language comes from, one easy answer is that Julius Caesar brought Latin to Gaul during the expansion of the Roman Empire, and by some gradual process not fully understood, Latin became French.[10] The people that Caesar encountered in Gaul were Celts, and some words of Celtic origin are found in modern French: Brittany is also a region where a Celtic language (Breton) is still spoken. Few French people know however that Breton speakers began to arrive from Britain in the fourth century, and that Brittany was not united with France until the marriage of Charles VIII with Anne of Bretagne in 1491, and annexed by François I in the Edict of Union in 1532. What may be ignored in all of this is another group of speakers, *les Francs*, the Franks, a Germanic-speaking tribe[11] who moved west from Germany proper around the fifth century, that is in the Merovingian and Carolingian periods. Clovis, a Merovingian king of the Franks, was baptized in 496 at Reims, furthering the spread of Christianity among his people, and instigating the tradition that true legitimate kings of France would have their coronations at the cathedral in Reims, and nowhere else. French speakers of today remember Charlemagne, but forget that he was a German speaker. Two generations after Charlemagne, however, one of his grandsons, Charles the Bald, opted to speak publicly in the *lingua romana* (Old) French, while his brother spoke *teudesca lingua*, (Old High) German.[12] In other words, there was a language shift going on at this point, and the daughter dialects of Latin spoken on French soil were moving east and north from their original home-land,[13] eventually to spread as far as southeastern Belgium in the north, and the Vosges mountains in the east (and on into Switzerland), where the eastern boundary of French remains today.

Thus the first evidence we have of the emergence of a French language distinct from Latin is the text of the 'French' version of the oath in the Strasbourg Oaths of 842, even though it was still referred to by the term *lingua romana* instead of by the yet to come *françois* or *la langue françoise*. As we will see in the next chapter as well, it is ironic (but perhaps telling) that the first notice of this language, and the first recording of it (the oath itself) took place in Strasbourg, a city that was to be much contested by French and German rulers for over a millenium. At this time this dialect was still referred to as a 'Roman language', but as it was spreading among the western Franks, it eventually became known as *le françois* and later, *le français*, but the connection between Frank and *franc* is undeniable.[14] Apparently, the French language was being codified by the clerics as a language of administration, and by 842, was deemed worthy to be used instead of Latin in the Strasbourg Oaths. The account of the oath-taking (memorialized by Nithard, yet another grandson of Charlemagne), is still in Latin however, but the texts of the oaths themselves are cited in the two vernacular tongues (von Steinmeyer 1963: 82–4). There are several interesting questions to ask here:

1 Why did Charles and Ludwig swear oaths in vernacular languages rather than in Latin?
2 Why did they do it in the language of the other brother's kingdom?
3 Why did the chronicler, Nithard, record the oath-taking verbatim, instead of paraphrasing it or reporting it in Latin?[15]

One theory would be that an oath, being a performative act, requires, for the sake of sincerity, to be sworn in an actual language that one has some connection to: thus the choice of two 'rude' tongues instead of Latin.[16] This act also represents the reciprocity of their vows, setting the two languages on an equal footing. As for why Nithard chose to report the actual words, this may mean that a cognitive shift of some sort had occurred, such that the two languages, French certainly, are somehow legitimized by this act, or had already been legitimized by their use by the clerics at this time. The other, more ironic, if not tragic aspect of this situation is that the grandsons of Charlemagne met to forge an alliance against their third brother, Lothaire, who, when the Carolingian Empire had been divided among them, had been granted the territory between those of Charles and Ludwig. His territory, Lothringen/Lorraine, was to be carved up by Charles and Ludwig as a result of the oath. Lothaire was weak, and was unable to resist his brothers' encroachments. The rest, as they say, is history – Lorraine, Alsace and other parts of the kingdom of Lothaire were the bones of contention between France and Germany for the next 11 centuries, that is until the end of World War II, 1, 103 years after Charles and Ludwig uttered their oath. Here we must confront one of the most crucial aspects of a linguistic culture: its origins. As with family genealogies, linguistic cultures like to have illustrious forebears. They like to think of their births as legitimate, even divinely ordained. What French linguistic culture has to face is that the first documented use of (some kind of) French involved a king of France swearing an oath of complicity with another king in order for the two of them to steal their brother's territory. The subsequent history of French political expansion into this territory, which represents France's present eastern borders, is hardly ennobled by this beginning, though the French view has always been to see it as a natural expansion to its 'natural' borders.

Another aspect of the situation that has been submerged is that the first documented use of French was in a situation of bilingualism,[17] in fact of reciprocal bilingualism, such that the French king spoke German, and the German king spoke French. Today this might be seen as a politically correct and noble thing to do, but that original bilingual act has been nullified by the subsequent attempts of both Germany and France, throughout their troubled contention over this region, to stamp out the natural bilingualism of the area. We will deal with this in more detail later, but note how the mythology about the French language and Strasbourg contains layers and layers of contradictions (not the least of which concerns the birth of *La Marseillaise*, not in Marseilles as many assume, but in Strasbourg during the Revolution). What is clear is that while it may have been irrelevant what languages people spoke in the France, Lorraine and Germany of the time, eventually as the doctrine of *cujus regio, ejus lingua* was promulgated by the modern nation state, language(s) eventually *became* the issue, and bilingualism became the casualty. One might rephrase this and say that the Strasbourg Oaths came back to haunt both France and Germany in another form, that is, as a conspiracy in which the French and German linguistic cultures determined to exterminate that which lay between them – bilingualism and dialectophone speakers of whatever was not French and not German.

4.4 THE *ORDONNANCE* OF *VILLERS-COTTERÊTS,* 1539 (FRANÇOIS I)

The next great milestone in French language policy occurred in 1539. The village of Villers-Cotterêts, a cantonal *chef-lieu* in the *département* of Aisne, was the place from which François I issued the edict of the same name in 1539, ordaining the use of the French language for the administration of justice, the establishment of the civil state and the compilation of notarized laws.[18] The standard view of this edict is that it was designed to remove Latin, once and for all, from such domains, but many have noted that it was a double-edged sword: implicitly, it was used to annihilate languages other than French as well.

Much of what we know about the spread of French and the sociolinguistic situation at various points of French history is found in

Brunot (1967), an encyclopaedic 13-volume study of the history of the French language, in the form of a *philologie sociologique* (Brunot's own term) which concentrates on social conditions much more than on the internal historical dynamics of French. It is impossible to deal with the issues of language policy and the French Revolution without coming to terms with Brunot, because of both his exhaustive study of the subject, and his strong opinions and interpretations of events. On the one hand one is grateful that he has sifted through immense amounts of primary sources to catalogue for us the history of the language – and especially the events of the Revolution as they pertain to language – but his process leaves us with an interpretation that we may not wish to accept. Brunot's work took more than three decades to complete, was 'subcontracted' in part to other writers, and one of them, Bruneau, actually finished the editing task.[19]

4.4.1 From 1539 to *8 pluviose*

As Brunot and others note, France had a weaker central government in 1539 than it does now, and no universal literacy, so the effect of the *ordonnance* of *Villers-Cotterêts* was practically nil in terms of its application to regional languages. Speakers of most regional varieties of French[20] were illiterate in all the languages of their environments, so whether some people wrote things in French or in other languages had little effect on them. Each time some new territory was added to France (and the history of France from at least 1539 to the French revolutionary wars is of gradual territorial expansion) a feeble effort was made to announce that henceforward the *ordonnance* of *Villers-Cotterêts* was to be obeyed in the new territories. But in fact this edict was largely ignored, even for written purposes, and we will need to examine just exactly what was the linguistic situation in various border territories at the time of the Revolution in order to understand why it was deemed necessary to have new laws that rectified the ineffectiveness of the *ordonnance* of *Villers-Cotterêts*.

But before we do this, we should examine one effect that has been largely ignored during this period, and that is the connection between the Reformation and the French language, in particular the use of standard French by French Protestants who had to flee persecution after the revocation of the Edict of Nantes. The Edict of Nantes was issued by Henri IV in 1598, establishing religious and political rights for Protestants. Gradually, however, these rights were abrogated and were then totally revoked by Louis XIV in 1685, causing the massive expatriation of French Protestants (known in exile as Huguenots), who fled to Protestant lands in Europe (Germany, the Netherlands, Alsace[21] and Switzerland), to America and South Africa, but also into internal exile in isolated areas of the centre and south of France,[22] bringing standard French with them. As Breton has shown (1991: 39), in Occitan-speaking parts of France and in French Switzerland there is a correlation on the one hand between the use of standard French and Protestantism, and on the other with Roman Catholicism and the retention of *patois*. Wherever French Protestants went, they helped spread standard French, and local dialects tended to die out. As for Alsace, as we shall see, it was the arrival of Huguenots that brought the first major incursions of French. Ironically, since the free city of Strasbourg was a strong supporter of Luther and Lutheranism, Calvinist Huguenots were not welcome, so they were diverted to the cities of the *Décapole*, a group of smaller towns in Alsace, thereby helping French to penetrate this territory even more deeply.

4.5 THE FRENCH LANGUAGE AND THE ENLIGHTENMENT

4.5.1 The establishment of the *Académie française*

It was of course during the Enlightenment that the French language came into its own, coming to be viewed as the most refined, elegant and civilized tongue in creation, and was adopted by foreigners such as Frederick the Great of Prussia and the whole of Tsarist Russian aristocracy, who preferred it to their own cradle languages. Few outside France realize that earlier, in the Renaissance and on into the sixteenth century, French intellectuals feared that French was in danger of being overwhelmed by Italian (and even Spanish), and that strong promotional measures were taken to help the French language resist this incursion. But it is to this period that we owe the birth and development of the *Académie française*, founded in 1635 originally as a private endeavour, but eventually becoming an organ of the regime when it was chartered by Parlement in 1637 (under pressure from Richelieu). There are those who consider the French Revolution to have been a victory for status planning in France, allowing the French language finally to establish its status as the language of all education, administration, journalism, commerce, etc., and the founding of the *Académie française* as a milestone for corpus planning. It enabled and encouraged the development of new vocabulary, a standardized grammar, and a consensus about spelling[23] that brought French from the situation where French intellectuals despaired of

French ever being able to compete with Latin, Italian or Spanish, to a point where French was seen as the most brilliant language in Europe, one that could claim that it was indeed a new 'classical' language.

4.5.1.1 What did the Académie française actually accomplish?

It is when one looks at the *Académie française* as an instrument of corpus planning that it becomes apparent that the *Académie* was actually a body which gave its imprimatur to new vocabulary and to certain new locutions (mainly syntactic constructions). It did not itself innovate – in fact after its initial successes of raising the prestige of French letters of the seventeenth century, it quickly became a conservative body that inhibited innovations of any sort. In the matter of straightening out and regularizing the morass of French orthography, the *Académie* was largely useless, and often had to delegate matters to a small committee or even one person, in order to be able to proceed with periodic reprintings and/or new editions of its dictionary. Article 26 of its charter (Gordon 1978: 26) gave it the authority to publish a dictionary, a grammar, a rhetoric and a 'poetic' (rules for poetry), but it was not authorized to regularize French orthography, and the history of attempts to do so, both within the Academy and outside it, is a rocky road indeed: this has surfaced again in the attempted reform of 1989–90.

Let us review some of these issues, because many of them, still unresolved, plague French spelling to this day. The Enlightenment was supposedly the age of reason, and reason dictated that the French language should operate according to rational principles. In one sense, the French *savants* and *philosophes* could declare French to be a rational language by just pronouncing it to be so. To an outsider, the notion that French is rational, pure, clear and lucid is not obvious, but it seems to be an article of French linguistic culture that this is so. What seemed to be more difficult was to rationalize French spelling, and this may have had something to do with the fact that there was no adequate theory of phonology to base French orthography on, and because the direction of phonological change in France had been reductionist – many sounds found in Latin were lost, and a Latinate (or for that matter, Greek-faithful) orthography was difficult to learn for anyone who had never studied classical languages. The notion that writing systems should be 'phonetic', and not, for example, morpho-phonemic, was a basic assumption of the 'rationalist' approach, even though it unleashed other problems. That is, a radically phonetic orthography, one which only represented the sounds actually spoken, would reduce many French words to homonyms.[24] Elimination of double letters (which of course are never phonetically double) would have resulted in simplicity, but might have then required the use of diacritics to distinguish phonetic differences such as [e] from [ɛ], for example *été* '(has) been', is not distinguished from *était* '(it) was' in modern popular pronunciations, but if they are both written, for example, <ete>, they cannot then be distinguished grammatically, and therefore semantically. In other words, simplification and phoneticization of orthography engendered other problems, because, to put it rather too simply, French may have had fewer consonants than Latin, but it seemed to compensate for this loss by adding vowel contrasts that had previously been predictable from the old spellings. Eliminating double consonants and the silent letters would result in certain letters varying according to which accent they carried when one form of the root was suffixed in some other way.

For example, if the feminine adjective *bonne* ([bɔn]) 'good', were deprived of its doubled letters, the resulting spelling <bone> would tempt most speakers to pronounce it [bon] instead of [bɔn]; and a diacritic would have to be added to prevent this. Similarly, if the silent <e> were removed, the result would be <bon>, but this is already the masculine form, pronounced [bõ]. Many similar problems arise with variously marked <e>s; the second vowel of the verb 'to celebrate', *célébrer* changes in certain derivatives, such as *célèbre,* 'famous'. Until the reform of 1989–90, the future singular of this verb was written *célébrera* 'will celebrate' even though it was pronounced as if spelled *célèbrera* [selɛbrɜra]. One can see that you can either have a regular system (and ignore pronunciation) or have a phonetic system (and have many irregularities); Catach (1991) lists many of the French verbs (and other forms) that are problematical in this manner, plaguing the French learner and the foreigner alike. Similarly, the two vowels of a word like *enfant* 'child' are pronounced identically, that is [ãfã]; the choice of many reformers was to use only the <an> version. The tendency then, as now, is to retain the same spelling of the vowel in any word that undergoes changes of pronunciation when complexities of morphology (suffixes and prefixes) are taken into account. This mitigates against simplification of doubling and silent letters: the principle is known as preserving the form of the root, no matter what happens grammatically. Thus compounds involving *terre,* 'earth', continue to have doubled <rr> (e.g. *terrestre,* 'terrestrial') despite the fact that there is no phonetic doubling; otherwise one must either change the spelling of *terre* itself, presumably to something like <tere, tère> or even <ter>; or, *terrestre* would have to be spelled <terestre> or even <terèstre>. All these solutions are unpalatable, so the non-phonetic doubling of consonants is retained, in many cases, to this day.[25]

At the time there was a widespread notion that the academicians had 'fixed' the language with its grammars and dictionaries, but almost as soon as the first editions appeared in print, they seemed outmoded and in need of revision. Sound change was proceeding quite rapidly here, and the archaicity of the academic orthography, if based on the dictionary, was obvious. Furthermore, the academicians themselves tended to ignore the orthography that their authoritative works dictated the use of, and spelled words any way they liked. Printers tore their hair out when faced with the manuscripts of Voltaire, for example, who refused to be of any help to them. Some writers (e.g. Saint-Pierre), known as *néographes d'avant-garde*, 'avant-garde spellers', went overboard with their new systems. In 1740 the *Académie* gave d'Olivet plenipotentiary powers to carry out a reform, since it was obvious that a committee of 40 could make no decisions. He eliminated many internal 'silent' <s>s, many double and silent letters, but still left many exceptions. Even some reforms such as the deletion of <t> but not of final silent <s> from *parents* (→ *parens*, pronounced [parã]) went through, only to be reintroduced in the so-called 'reform' of 1835. D'Olivet really only modified what he could not justify maintaining, but in many respects present-day French spelling is in worse shape than it was in the dictionary of Richelet (1680) as far as retention of silent letters is concerned.

As French speakers themselves know, and second-language learners of French also know only too painfully, the retention of silent letters such as <s> to mark plurals, along with non-phonetic <e> to mark feminine nouns leads to many traps, since this often requires a knowledge of grammar that for native and foreigner alike may be shaky at best, especially when it comes to the notorious past participles. Reformers such as de Wailly, whom Brunot characterizes as the last word in the application of philosophical grammar to spelling, were well intentioned, but would have required radical changes, including new kinds of diacritics (e.g. an undotted <ı> replaces <y>, <ġ> replaces <j>, double <ss> is replaced by <ʃ>, in order to prevent its being pronounced voiced; <x> is replaced by <s>, which may be voiced, as in *aus animaus* [ozanimo] for *aux animaux* 'to the animals'. And de Wailly is himself inconsistent, writing *nous anploîrons* 'we use' in the same paragraph as *on emploie* 'one uses'. The battle was between the adherents of usage and the defenders of rationality, that is whether to try to control usage, or to follow usage and allow it free rein, since, as everyone knew, usage was itself inconsistent.[26] Should one try to capture usage, and then fix it for all time, or should one 'go with the flow', as it were? Or should one perhaps ask *whose* usage is being given as a standard? (Obviously, the same questions still get asked today in many another linguistic culture.) In the end, the reformers were not victorious. The *Encyclopédists*, academicians and *savants* fell back on older usage – not quite early *Académie* spelling, but a compromise of the early seventeenth century. As Diderot put it:

> You pronounce one language, and you write another; and for the rest of your life you are so used to this craziness, which brought on so many tears in your childhood, that if you gave up the bad spelling for one closer to pronunciation, you would not recognize the spoken language with this new combination of characters.[27]
>
> (quoted in Brunot, vol. 6(2): 953)

4.5.1.2 French/Latin diglossia

One of the battles French intellectuals and writers had to fight during the seventeenth and eighteenth centuries was to establish French as a literary language, as the language of creative writing, and the language of science. It becomes clear in retrospect that Latin was no longer a language that intellectuals relied on for any real purposes, but it was still the language of almost all education, from elementary school through to university. The only clear victory of this period is that Latin ceases to be a language of poetry, and begins to disappear from all *belles-lettristic* activity. The great *philosophes* and writers of this period – Montesquieu, Voltaire, Diderot, Descartes, Racine, Moliere, etc. – all wrote in French. Those who were eloquent expressed their eloquence in French, not Latin. Here we begin to see the classic confrontation between two languages locked in a diglossic relationship, and what happens when one attempts to shift into the domains dominated by another. French was claiming the domain of creative writing: at the same time it became the language of science writing – something of a new genre – as experimentation in science expanded outside the traditional domains. Science experimentation therefore diffused through French, and French became well known outside France, to the consternation of many who felt that it had less freedom inside France than outside. Latin had represented tradition and universality: from the point of view of word-formation rules it had recognized derivational processes that served science well – scientists everywhere in Europe knew what was meant when a new word was formed. In the late seventeenth century some works were still written in Latin, but more and more was being written in French, and then translated into Latin. Science was practical and innovative: it was very popular and courses were attended by a broad spectrum of people, many of whom did not know Latin.

Much of the scientific revolution took place, then, outside the established institutions of learning (which were focused on humanistic study) and therefore was outside the grip of Latin. Latin died, therefore, domain by domain: language shift, from Latin to French, occurred domain by domain, first in *belle-lettres*, then in the sciences, and last (much later) in ecclesiastical domains. Simultaneously, dialect literature was dying out: it happened faster in *langue d'oui* than in *langue d'oc*. As the dialects died, some people took a scientific interest in them, as objects rather than as passions. The passion returned in the nineteenth century, in the age of romanticism, but not in the eighteenth. The *patois* lost domains as well, retaining only the spoken domain. They were adapted to use in daily life: terminology was appropriate for rural agricultural life, but they certainly had no future as languages of higher education, science, etc. Another development of this era was that of journalism, and French captured it, as a new domain, with no competition from any other language. During the Revolution, *feuilles villageoises* or village newspapers were founded to bring revolutionary news to the people, and these were without exception in French. So French expanded into domains that had previously belonged to *patois*, as well.

4.5.1.3 Latin and the Church

Religion remained the last domain of Latin, but there was still some use of *patois* in sermons, since peasants did not understand French or Latin: but of course some priests were not locally born to the region they served, and did not know *patois*. The bishops knew *patois* was best if they were to communicate anything: in *langue d'oui* more French was known and used, but in *langue d'oc* this was not so. But if the priests did not speak *patois*, they knew the peasants understood their French better than their bad *patois*. In sum, the Church's policy was to use whatever language served their purposes best, with Latin reserved for the mass and certain liturgical uses. If French was what had to be used to understand the people, French would be used: if *patois* was more useful, *patois* it would be. There was therefore a diglossia but not a uniform one. The Church tried to conserve Latin, but not French. In *langue d'oui, patois* begins to cede to French in church. In *langue d'oc* (south of the Loire), there is much *patois* and no French.[28]

4.5.1.4 French in les collèges

During this period what we would call secondary education was dominated by *collèges*,[29] but these were institutions teaching all subjects through Latin. Reformers were therefore not to be found inside the *collèges*: Rollin published a landmark plan in 1726, the first plan for the study of the *langue nationale*.[30] Voltaire, Diderot, *les philosophes*, etc. condemn Latin, but the teaching hierarchy in the *collèges* are opposed to dropping it. Only the Benedictines started education without Latin (other schools began literacy with Latin, maybe taught no French at all), not to abolish the old order but to suppress its monopoly. 1762 was a watershed year for the old pedagogy – because of fear of the Jesuits, their *collèges* were closed by Parlement. Some 113 Jesuit *collèges* closed their doors, and Latin-based education went out with them.

4.5.2 Summing up the pre-revolutionary era

In the 20 years preceding the Revolution the educational system shows a confused picture, a *mêlée*, and many conflicts of interest. Experimental sciences pushed for abandonment of Latin, but philosophy professors and humanists in general pushed to retain the classics. Brunot quotes an interesting argument by Roland namely that the argument that French is not rich enough to use is not a good argument, since 'languages enrich themselves by practice, and argumentation makes them clearer and more precise' (quoted in Brunot, vol. 7(4): 110). This reinforces my own argument (in Chapter 2) that new registers develop their vocabularies by trial and error, and that intellectual ferment will generate the vocabulary to fill the needs of the users. At this time we begin to see people writing books for provincials to save them from the embarrassment of making mistakes in French due to the influence of their *patois*. In discussions of pedagogy, some began to advocate that children should learn French first, that is, there should be no Latin immersion without some French. They advocated putting French and Latin on an equal footing, and began to argue that French was itself a classical language on a par with Latin, known from Dublin to the Volga, but respected more outside France than within. In the last quarter of the eighteenth century, in all new sciences and schools devoted to them, only French was taught. The *Collège de France* was timid, changing slowly: at the eve of revolution, there was still no chair for French at the *Collège de France*, thought by some to be the premier institution of higher learning in France. In summary, on the eve of revolution, the clergy were opposed to French; 'liberals' and reformers felt that French, like Latin, was now a universal language, and the French people themselves were the most opposed to this notion. One reformer, Nicolas Adam, even proposed a policy:

1 It should be necessary to pass a test in order to be a teacher.
2 Someone should get organized and compose an official grammar.
3 No one should learn Latin until they pass a test in French grammar.

But many realized that there was a need for the reform of education, with new sciences and new knowledge expanding in the Enlightenment. Reform meant learning vernacular languages: but the traditionalists did not give up easily. As Daumon put it, the *malheur* of French schools was never to be at the level of their century. Brunot makes a revealing statement here about how a policy developed:

> There was no directing policy, no general ordinance that consecrated the changes, nor imposed them. The monarchy had no pedagogical system whatsoever. The royal power was present at the struggle, but did not get involved in it.[31]

(quoted in Brunot, vol. 7(4): 130)

4.5.2.1 French in elementary schools

It is useful at this point to recall that eighteenth century *philosophes* were not in favour of universal mass education: they did not think it would be useful to the peasant, and utilitarianism was in vogue. Primary schools, therefore, were not doing anything to spread French, because they were non-existent for the masses. But from the seventeenth century on growing attention was paid to spelling (orthography). It became a thing of social value (good graces, good breeding) to exhibit good spelling, especially for women. Recall that even at this time, because of the diglossia established by the *Académie française*, people would make many spelling errors, if they wrote as they spoke. As we have already seen, many of the 'silent letters' of the current orthographic system still in use today were already not pronounced two centuries ago, and because many spelling rules preserve distinctions that are marks of grammatical gender or number, proper spelling required some knowledge of grammar.[32] There was a sort of gender segregation: good orthography became a mark of good finishing-school, manners for young ladies, while Latin was still needed by men for a traditional career in law, medicine, etc. Knowing French was not necessary for men in these professions. But in the end, ignorance of French gradually became a barrier and a danger especially in the business world. Conclusion: with some exceptions elementary education did not play much of a role in the diffusion of French throughout the country.

4.5.2.2 A last gasp: 25 June 1778

Finally, on the eve of the Revolution, a regulation of the 25 June 1787 established municipal councils in all *les pays d'èlection*[33] where none had existed before. This established the municipal governments still known today, delegating the administration of towns and villages to appointed or elected officials. Village and community councils had to discuss things and keep records of all sorts, deal with all sorts of parties, and answer petitions and requests. They appointed school-teachers, tax-collectors, and recorded taxes. A person could not make a contract, write a will, register a birth, get married or die without having it done in French. From this moment on,[34] the rule was to keep records in French, not in *patois* or Latin. The villagers elected to these councils had to learn French fast, and maybe they learned it from the bailiffs or sergeants at arms rather than from school. The *ordonnance* of *Villers-Cotterêts* finally took effect, but this time to exclude *patois*. Naturally oral discussions may have been in *patois* or French *patoisé*,[35] but records were in French. In the end even a small village having only 3,000 inhabitants might have a bailiff, a provost, a lieutenant and fiscal procurer, six notaries, four sergeants, twelve procurers, and four town clerks (*greffiers*). This brought with it demands that schools be established to train such people. The monarchy had until now always centralized power around itself, and disenfranchised the *patois*. The new devolution of power to village councils required new structures and ways of administration, and it was by the French language that it arrived in the villages. And this meant, too, that outsiders may have had to be brought in to do this work: the effect was of a French 'garrison' occupying the village. Brunot, among others, does not wish to convey the impression that this new devolution of power inspired linguistic particularism however. He claims that though the edict of 1787 gave the provinces some power, and consecrated some notions of particularism, they were not based on any linguistic notions. He claims that among all the demands that came from the provinces, such as during the writing of the *cahiers de doléances*, no demands based on linguistic particularism ever surfaced, and though the grievances are often written in poor French, they are almost all in French.[36] Brunot is anxious to show that there is no such thing as an idea of linguistic provinces before the Revolution: apart from speakers of other *idiomes* such as German and Bas-Breton, Basque, Flemish and Italian, the speakers of romance-derived language (French, Occitan, Catalan and their *patois*) were uninterested in defending their rights, he claims. But other factors were involved in the spread of French. One was the network of roads constructed in the eighteenth century – a comparable effort had not been made since Roman times. New roads came in where there had been none before, and they all radiated out from Paris, helping to spread French. Another factor was that of seasonal work and migratory professions: many professions had their own argots, which may have been based on regional speech forms, but became jargons or pidgins, which outsiders could not easily understand. These had an effect on local *patois*, as these trade jargons tended to be fairly uniform across the territory. But seasonal migration may have helped to spread French, too. Brunot feels that the one effective thing the monarchy did to vanquish local speech forms was to order the use of French for local administration and to create a system of roads radiating out from Paris.

4.5.2.3 The linguistic situation in the marginal territories

The linguistic situation in the parts of France where standard French is not the dominant speech form could be the subject of a separate study (Slone 1989; Tabouret-Keller 1972 [1968]). We deal with this in part in the next chapter, by focusing on Alsace in particular, and other regions briefly.

4.6 THE FRENCH REVOLUTION AND FRENCH LANGUAGE POLICY

In today's mode of political thinking,[37] it is revolutionaries and partisans of the Left that are usually the champions of small disenfranchised groups, and partisans of the Right that wish to allow no rights for minorities. It may come as a surprise to some, therefore, that in the French Revolution the speakers of non-standard French dialects and other languages and dialects were seen as counter-revolutionary, as enemies of the Revolution, and that therefore these languages needed to be stamped out, annihilated, destroyed. Some of these enemies of non-standard language were persons of good will, who saw the dialects as barriers to communication, as obstacles to the spread of the ideas of the Revolution which, once made available to every citizen, would enlighten and liberate them. Others saw advocates of 'federalism' (especially linguistic federalists who championed the dialects) as nefarious enemies of the republic: these were people who stood to benefit from the monarchy and lose their benefits in a republic, and chief among these were priests and former nobles. For their part the champions of the republic were like religious evangelists, who wished to save ignorant citizens from perdition. Their revolutionary zeal was a missionary zeal, and some of their efforts degenerated into fanaticism, persecution, and even execution of their enemies on the dreaded guillotine.

4.6.1 Personalities, milestones, legislation

We cannot summarize various 'reforms' of the French Revolution without saying something about who was making policy, how it was to be carried out, and what effects policies had hundreds of miles away in territories where few people actually knew French. It was, after all, a time of chaos and great upheaval and the revolutionaries were 'making things up as they went along', so they were not always sure what the outcome of their decrees and decisions would be. For students of language policy and for readers who have not studied French history thoroughly, it is instructive to understand the different forces that were demanding different things, and were often working at cross purposes. Legislative bodies came into existence, committees were formed, and they made recommendations: then these bodies were disbanded, their leaders perhaps sent to the guillotine (or into exile), their powers abrogated or usurped by other bodies, which themselves were then perhaps overthrown. To make matters more complex, a new calendar was introduced, and the names of its months are often used to mark certain milestones of the French Revolution. Let us note the following framework of events, actors, and consultative bodies:

1 January–May, 1789: elections held for *Etats-Généraux*.[38]
2 Beginning of the compilation of the *cahiers de doléances*, or lists

of grievances on the part of various members of society, especially members of the Third Estate (that is ordinary people).

3   5 May, 1789: *Etats-Généraux* meets, begins to make decisions.

4   The king rejects the decisions of the *Etats-Généraux*.

5   9 July, 1789: the *Assemblée nationale* declares itself to be the *Assemblée nationale constituante*.[39]

6   14 July, 1789 storming of the Bastille.

7   4 August, 1789: royal and noble privileges are abolished.

8   26 August, 1789: Declaration of the Rights of Man and the Citizen.

9   December, 1789–January, 1790: Protestants receive political rights, Jews become citizens.

10   14 January, 1790: decision to translate decrees into the *idiomes* of the country (but not into *patois*).

11   11 August, 1790: Grégoire, shocked by what he sees being written in the *cahiers de doléances*, sends out his linguistic survey.

12   1790–1: upheavals, shortages, hunger, civil disturbance. Counter-revolutionary forces gain strength, emigration increases.

13   3 September, 1791: *Assemblée nationale* approves the constitution for a constitutional monarchy.

14   30 September, 1791: the *Assemblée nationale constituante* disbands (unable to succeed itself, its members are ineligible to stand for election for the *Assemblée législative*).

15   1 October, 1791: *Assemblée législative* convenes and begins to plan legislation. Seeing need for committees, establishes several, such as a *Comité d'instruction public* (Committee on Public Instruction) and others. (Note that the CPI, established on 14 October, 1791, and consisting of 24 members, continued in a similar form, but with some different members, after the *Assemblée législative* was disbanded, as a committee of the *Convention*, in 1792.)

16   1791: *Assemblée législative* hears proposals, such as the seminal one of Condorcet, to teach citizens to read and write (French?), but passes no legislation. Meanwhile in various provincial cities (Colmar, Toulon, Marseille), provincial and municipal councils establish (or recommend the establishment of) schools to teach *la langue française*.

17   17 August, 1792: creation of the first Revolutionary Tribunal.

18   22 September, 1792: proclamation of the (First) Republic, and establishment of the *Convention*.

19 7 October, 1792: *Convention* orders the acceleration of translations, appoints a committee to oversee it.

20 10 October, 1792: CPI made recommendations on what to do for citizens not knowing French, became Title III of a later decree.

21 18 October, 1792: CPI publishes the report of Lanthenas – to destroy the *patois*, but to tolerate the *idiomes* held in common with neighbours.

22 24 October, 1792: adoption of the revolutionary calendar, which was proclaimed to be in effect retroactively to 21 September, 1791, but dates for which are counted only from the point of proclamation. Thus 21 September, 1792 begins the second year (*an II*) of the Revolution.

23 6 April, 1793: creation of *Comité du salut publique* (Committee of Public Safety), under the *Convention:* the Committee of Public Safety proceeds gradually to usurp power, remove its enemies and establish a dictatorship.

24 July, 1793: debates of July 1793 – the former abbot, Grégoire, gets his chance to present his ideas.

25 27 July, 1793: Maximilien de Robespierre becomes a member of the Committee of Public Safety. A man of personal integrity and probity, he is viewed by many as an extremist. His base of support was in the Paris Commune (the *sans-culottes*) and among the intellectuals and *philosophes*, rather than among the more conservative deputies from the provinces. Acting from the Committee of Public Safety, he declares language issues to be affecting the public safety (insurrection and treason are associated with other languages, etc.), and starts to formulate policy that conflicts with policy coming from the Committee of Public Instruction.

26 30 September, 1793: Grégoire makes his report to the Committee of Public Instruction, which then goes to the *Convention*.

27 21 October, 1793: law of *30 vendémiaire an II*: decree establishing state schools, teaching children to speak, read and write the French language.

28 October 1793–January 1794: *la terreur* (the Terror): dictatorship of Robespierre, acting through the Committee of Public Safety.

29 27 January, 1794: proposal of *8 pluviose an II* at the Committee of Public Safety, enacted by decree of same date: *French shall be taught in every commune where the local people do not speak French.* (Note that this is cast as a public safety issue, not an

issue of public instruction, and the Committee of Public Safety is
now running the government, not the *Convention.*)

30   25 February, 1794: creation of *écoles centrales* (central government schools), to replace the universities closed by the Revolution.

31   1 April, 1794: suppression of the Provisional Executive Council:
Committee of Public Safety becomes preponderant.

32   16 April, 1794: decree strengthening the Terror.

33   20 July, 1794: (*2 thermidor an II*) – the decree of *8 pluviose* has
teeth added to it: sanctions are decreed for failure to use French.

34   26–28 July, 1794: (*8–10 thermidor an II*): fall and execution of
Robespierre. End of the Terror. This marks the end of one major
phase of the French revolution, and this milestone is often
referred to simply as *thermidor,* that is 'before' (and/or) 'after'
thermidor.

35   31 May, 1795: Revolutionary Tribunal is done away with.

36   27 August, 1795: vote of the Constitution of 1795 (*an III*) ratified
by referendum.

37   26 October, 1795: end of the *Convention,* replaced by *Directoire,*
a five-person council elected by the *Conseil des Anciens* and the
Conseil des Cinq-Cents ('the Five Hundred'). End of major
'reforms' of the French Revolution, including language legislation.

4.6.1.1 The Abbé Grégoire

One of the most ardent proponents of a policy of *francisation* was
Grégoire, a former abbot who defrocked himself as part of the policy
of throwing off privileges of the *ancien régime*. He proposed a plan in
the first months of 1790, and sent out questionnaires to the remotest
areas to find out more about the linguistic situation there. Grégoire's
concern was aroused by the things he read in the *cahiers de
doléances,* the lists of grievances that people sent in to the convention of the *Etats-Généraux*. Many of these grievances were written in
a form that was remote from any kind of standard French, that is they
were written in the language customary in their area at the time –
often it was in 'French', but not, in Grégoire's opinion, very good
French. In the opinion of people like Grégoire, of course, there was
no notion that French should be adapted to the needs of ordinary
people: what they needed was to be taught (good) French so that they
could benefit from the ideas of the Revolution, since the language was
just in the state it needed to be to act as a vehicle for the Revolution.

As for the desires of the Third Estate, many simply stated that they would like to have schools established, and this became a recurring issue in subsequent constitutions and legislation about schools and language. Grégoire decided to survey all of France to determine how and when *les patois* were still being used, and once this information could be gathered, to take action. Grégoire was a man who planned carefully and held to his goal of spreading French throughout France. Eventually he was appointed to the Committee of Public Instruction, where he was able to propound his ideas about *francisation*, based on his own survey of the dialect situation. He predicted somewhat later (on 30 September, 1793 to the *Convention*) that:

> thus will disappear little by little the local jargon and dialects of six million Frenchmen who do not speak the national language, for, as I may not repeat too often, it is more important to extirpate politically this diversity of vulgar tongues than to prolong the infancy of reason and the senility of prejudice.[40]
>
> (quoted in Brunot, vol. 7: 142)

While Grégoire did not perhaps invent revolutionary language policy, he certainly came to personify it. But others were also working on language policy on other committees and before other forums.[41]

4.6.1.2 Talleyrand

On 10 September, 1791, Talleyrand, another important revolutionary figure, had expounded his own *politique de la langue*. In the *Assemblée nationale* (*Assemblée constituante*), Charles-Maurice de Talleyrand-Périgord, the former bishop of Autun, presented his idea of popular instruction: schools were, he said 'an idea that has become inevitable'.[42] Until now, from the convocation of the *Etats-Généraux* onward, the policy has been translation.[43] There was a need to keep in contact and rapport with the people – this is what the Revolution is about, after all. But many people were opposed: they saw it as a return to pre-1539 (*Villers-Cotterêts*) and 'linguistic federalism' (federalism is a naughty word in the French Revolution), because it was linguistic differences that had divided them, and they wanted now to be united. But the translation policy began to lose steam.

4.6.1.3 Various muddled efforts

There had been some translations of the constitution – into southern dialects (20 January, 1791) and into Italian (29 February, 1791). On 4 March, 1792 a circular was sent to several southern *départements* to see if the translations were good. On 2 June, 1792 it was reported that there were not enough translations, they were not good enough, and some demanded a 'Central Bureau of Translation': but then it was revealed that the law of translation had not been promulgated, and laws that are not promulgated are as good as dead. The translation effort muddled along: some areas set up departmental bureaux, but it was hard to find good help. The output was meagre. The constitutional clubs supported the work but it was a losing battle – they could not keep up with the decrees and laws coming out. In Breton a number of good things happened: the Bretons were avid for the use of their language, and there are many manuscripts and publications extant from this period. In Alsace, the situation was special – we will examine this in detail in the next chapter.[44]

4.6.1.4 The battle of words

People began to debate the question of what language or *patois* was used for. One begins to note a diglossia, or a new form of it: the use of German (in Alsace) or *patois* for local events, but French for national celebrations (*fêtes nationales*), especially revolutionary holidays, etc. Some revolutionaries noted at this time that the clergy who were opposed to the Revolution used their pulpits to speak (in *patois*) against the Revolution. This meant that *patois* became identified in some people's minds as anti-revolutionary. One of the features of the Revolution was the creation of popular societies, or 'clubs' to further the Revolution. A *Société populaire de Strasbourg* decided on 26 June, 1790, that its discussions would be in both French and German, and minutes taken in both. Later (23 June, 1791) they decided to alternate languages, French at one meeting, German at another.

By 1792 France was at war with Austria, and fervour for the Revolution and for France was at its peak. The revolutionary war hymn, *La Marseillaise*, which eventually became France's national anthem, was born on the eve of the war on 20 April, 1792. Many revolutionary slogans had been circulating: Rouget de l'Isle spent a feverish night dashing off this *chant de guerre de l'armée du Rhin*. Taken up by volunteers from Marseille, it spread across France like wildfire, now associated with Marseille, and was accepted with a kind of religious zeal. Brunot feels that the *hymne nationale* gave the peasants the will to comprehend the Pater of the new faith, and converted them to the idea that they could learn. Whatever it did, it was accepted with a fervour and spontaneity that seemed to unite ordinary people under an idea and a banner they could understand.

4.6.1.5 Other measures and their effect on language

On 22 December, 1789, the old political divisions (duchies, etc.) were abolished and replaced by new, smaller administrative units called *départements*. Some have claimed that the abolition of old political divisions had an effect on the languages/*patois*. Brunot for one denies this: he points out that the term *province* was not used until June, 1787, creating the *Assemblée de provinces*. Some deputies however did object to the divisions that broke up linguistic areas (e.g. *pays basque*) into various subdivisions, that is that this was a divide-and-conquer kind of rule – Alsace and Lorraine became Moselle, Bas-Rhin, and Haut-Rhin. Brunot calls this 'first rank measures' (vol. 6(1): 75), which did not have the specific goal of spreading French, but of making everything equal. But one way or another the new divisions helped spread French, because the new subdivisions of the *départements* had to interact with Paris in French, so indirectly they contributed to the demise of *patois*. Brunot indicates that most of the assembly members wanted to get rid of the divisions that helped retain regional special interests and prevented the emergence of a new spirit and new national interests.

Linguistic 'federation' (a *bête noire*) was therefore shelved: translation hindered the work of making France one and indivisible – one nation, one law, one king (and one language?). According to Brunot, the creation of *départments* did not destroy anything but a 'fictitious imagining of old philologists'(vol. 6(1): 75). There never were dialect families, there is no hierarchy of dialects, family trees, or whatever, according to Brunot.[45]

4.6.1.6 What did the first stage of the revolution accomplish?

To summarize: the first *assemblées* did not innovate with regard to the language of the acts, they did not forbid anything, and did not impose anything. There is much translation from French to German, and much bilingual usage, both written and spoken, but translation does not advance the cause of the progress of French.[46] Therefore, like the revolutionaries themselves, Brunot sees the next step as inevitable: the abandonment of translation, the need for a way to spread the French language.

4.6.1.7 Alsace and the linguistic terror

The end of the translation policy meant the unleashing of negative campaigns of various sorts against those who benefited from and preferred translation, such as the Alsatians. The justification for the end of the translation policy is the rise of counter-revolution, the 'hate of the republic', and other politically incorrect behaviours. Brunot chastises the Alsatians for reacting too soon to perceptions of persecution – there were already many examples of bilingual usage which had not been proscribed, so why were they getting hot and bothered? Perhaps they knew what was coming, because in the end, Brunot himself describes a *terreur linguistique* in Alsace.

4.7 STAGE TWO: IMPATIENT FORCES

Grégoire and Talleyrand were not the only advocates of *francisation* at work in the legislative bodies. Bertrand Barère de Vieuzac (1755–1841) was impatient with the progress of the Revolution, especially the spread of French into border territories and the residue there of other loyalties. Barère acted as the spokesman of the Committee of Public Safety to the *Convention*. Thus it was Barère, speaking before the *Convention* on 27 January, 1794 (*8 pluviose*), who asserted that:

> federalism and superstition speak Breton; emigration and hate of the Republic speak German; the counter-revolution speaks Italian and fanaticism speaks Basque. Let us smash these faulty and harmful instruments. It is better to instruct than to translate; it is not up to us to maintain these barbarous jargons and crude dialects which can only be of further service to fanatics and counter-revolutionaries.[47]

> (quoted in Brunot, vol. 9(1): 181)

4.7.1 The *cahiers de doléance* and the survey of Grégoire

As we have noted, Grégoire[48] was disturbed by what he had read in the *cahiers de doléances*, and devised a survey with 43 questions about *patois* and customs that he began to send out on 11 August, 1790, to many correspondents in all parts of France.[49] Here we have what is probably the first sociolinguistic survey in history, even if flawed in its motivations (i.e. to annihilate the *patois*). There are a number of problems with the survey:

1 Though some of the questions are quite appropriate as questions about sociolinguistic issues, some others are the questions of a politician, that is, they are 'loaded' questions.

2 Not all regions of France were surveyed.

3 Grégoire did not publish or retain some responses, that is, not all questions were understood in the spirit Grégoire intended, and some responses may have been contrary to what Grégoire wanted.

4 Grégoire's organization of the questions was strange, for example question (1) about the universality of French should have been followed by questions (17) about use in the towns, (18) what was the territorial limit, and (29) do country people speak it.

5 Many answers cannot be taken at face value, that is, respondents themselves are giving impressionistic answers even if they think they are being accurate.

It is curious that Brunot does not directly connect Grégoire's survey with the *cahiers des doléances*, which arrived in Paris in a state that showed, to Grégoire at least, that there was a great need for *francisation*. Today we would say that what existed in many parts of French was a diglossic situation (Brunot calls it bilingualism, but it is clear he means what we would today term diglossia). French was the language of parade, ceremony, Sundays. Women (without good education) were embarrassed by their inability to speak. One acquired French, the language of civilization, but one practised *patois*. The French language had its effect on *patois*, and the *patois* had a counter-reaction on French, affecting it in various ways, one of which led to the publication of dictionaries of *gasconismes*, etc. – nobody wanted to sound like a country hick.

4.8 WHAT *DID NOT* HAPPEN DURING THE FRENCH REVOLUTION?

So far we have concentrated on trying to present the 'facts' of the French Revolution as if events moved forward in a rational and systematic way. In fact, things moved, not surprisingly, in fits and starts, and the chaos of the Revolution made things much more confusing than what we have presented. In retrospect, many scholars of the period now debate what the actual effects of the Revolution were, since there was much backtracking, revocation of previous legislation, and reactionary attempts *ex post facto* to return to the stability of the *ancien régime*. When Brunot looks back on the revolution, he sees French language policy as essentially fixed from the revolution onward – no matter which regime, monarch, empire, restoration or republic – the picture of language policy that emerges is strongly consistent with the notion that standard French expresses *liberté, egalité, fraternité,* and all other dialects (usually denigrated as *patois*), are lesser instruments. This notion is a pre-revolutionary notion, and as Gordon puts it, there was no break between monarchical language policy and revolutionary language policy: the Revolution actually achieved what had been set in motion during the *ancien régime*, and in a much more efficient manner.[50] And writers like Brunot are products of this policy, as they are products of its schools. He reveals his biases quite frankly – he is happy when French 'progresses' in various parts of France, and is unhappy when certain policies fail during the Revolution. When the latter is the case, he usually consoles himself by saying that even failed policies still remained 'on the books' as it were, and were eventually successful decades later. Thus as universal education developed and spread during the nineteenth century, and was directed centrally from Paris, the language policies of the French Revolution became educational policy as well. It was allied with anti-clericalism, and since the Roman Church had always championed regional dialects and languages, French speakers of non-standard languages had to choose: would they be good *républicains* or would they ally themselves with 'ignorance' and 'prejudice'?[51]

4.8.1 Language policy failures of the Revolution: orthography reform

Where the French Revolution significantly failed to have any effect was on the way French was spelled. There were proposals (e.g. Daunou, during the discussions of July, 1793) to reform the orthography, since it was a century or more since the appearance of the first dictionary of the *Académie française*, and there were many things preserved in writing that were no longer used in the spoken language, which created (and still create) serious problems for *native* speakers. But other reformers did not wish to cloud the issue by adding complexities to the legislation, and French remained stuck with an orthographic system that better reflected, and still reflects, the state of affairs of 250 years ago.[52]

4.8.2 First period: from the *Etats-Généraux* to the *réunion de la Convention*

4.8.2.1 Nation and national language

Brunot, quoting Vaublanc (1806), says that the French Revolution gave us the notion that language makes the nation. He quotes Merlin de Douai as having claimed (on 31 October, 1790) that the 'Alsatian people became one with the French people because it wanted to, not because of the Treaty of Münster. Its *volonté* legitimized the union (quoted in Brunot, vol. 9(1): 4)' Since there was no expression of will involved in the union under the Treaty of Westphalia, Douai is referring to the will of the Alsatians to become part of France by voluntarily adopting the French language. Thus the language became the cement that bonded various kinds of Frenchmen together, and in this view, the French Revolution was really a revolution about language. The Revolution went through various phrases – patriotism took on a religious aspect, with evangelical overtones and cultic fervour associated with *la patrie*. And like evangelistic movements, it had elements of superstition, fanaticism, persecution and martyrdom. National unity meant 'unity of hearts' which meant 'unity of language'. The idea that 'each nation must have one language', followed by the notion that 'each nation must have only one language' (monolingualism?), spread across Europe, and a century later (i.e. by 1918) was still forming the basis for new nation states. Let us use Brunot's three-stage division of the French Revolution as a prism to examine a number of things.

1 *Etats-Généraux* to *Convention*: decisive, but no laws specifically about language.
2 The Terror: rigorous decrees ordaining use of language. Few lasting results, but some 'forward' motion.
3 *9 thermidor* to *18 brumaire*: back-tracking, but some institutions are created, and *francisation* proceeds.

From the *Consulat* onward, through the (Napoleonic) Empire and into the nineteenth century, what was set in motion gains momentum. The groundwork is laid, the policies begin to take root. For Brunot and others, the national language was a product of the national unity but also became a factor in *creating* national unity. Once anti-revolutionary reaction re-established itself, the principle of linguistic unity did not get dropped: unity of language meant from then on the most rapid vehicle of communication to make people more intelligent, spread reason, increase morals, comfort the people and assure the goals of *liberté, égalité* and *fraternité.*

4.8.2.2 Assemblée nationale *and the schools*

There is relative silence in the *cahiers de doléances* about language: people want public education, including language instruction. Various plans for public instruction are brought forward – to teach people in their own language; to no longer use Latin in schools – but were often silent on whether schooling should be in French or local languages – opinions varied.

4.8.2.3 The report of Talleyrand: the first explicit language policy

Talleyrand made a report to the *Assemblée* on 10, 11 and 19 September, 1791. He recommended to the *Assemblée constituante*, near the end of its session, that there be public instruction in French (and not in dialect), to be taught by example and not by principle at first, with the goal of making people able to speak purely and write the national language correctly. When the *Assemblée constituante* adjourned, nothing had been done with Talleyrand's proposal: they were left where they had been with the Constitution (Article I), which specified that 'there be created and organized public instruction, free and common to all citizens . . . '.[53]

4.8.2.4 Committee of Public Instruction

The next important event was the creation on 14 October, 1791, by decree, of a Committee of Public Instruction, composed of 24 members. There were many discussions that year, ending in a very important report by Antoine Caritat, Marquis de Condorcet – the *philosophe* who was also president of the *Assemblée législative*. His main points were:

1 It must be decided what language to use in elementary school.[54]
2 Latin was to be banned, once and for all.
3 It was important, for real equality, that language cease to separate people into two classes.

With all this talk about *instruction publique*, what effect did it have on schools in reality? In fact many revolutionary decrees had already destroyed what schools there were, by the abolition of tithing, the requirement of oaths for religious teachers, and the general turmoil. Some people dreamed of wonderful new schools: some only regretted the old schools, bad as they were, since they had not yet been replaced by anything. As the Germans in Alsace noted, if the new pedagogy recommended that one not teach Latin because no one understood it, and that incomprehension damaged the minds of children, and if one should use French because it would be understood, then why teach French to children who only understood German? Would not that damage their minds as well? All the reformers agreed that Latin must go: many felt that French should replace it, especially in *les collèges*. Talleyrand wanted this, Condorcet wanted it, but the universities were still operating mostly in Latin, though all sciences and arts were by now taught in French. Now the attack on Latin really began, and there was a shift to French as the language of instruction and as an object of instruction, even in *collèges* and universities, from 1790 on. Condorcet carried his campaign for French and against Latin in an important speech before the *Assemblée nationale*, but by this time the debate was largely won. As we have already noted, one easy way to weaken the power of Latin in universities was to close them down, and found other institutions of higher learning.

4.8.2.5 French as a religious language

One battle that was long and drawn out, continuing even after the main language legislation had either been passed or had fallen into disuse, was the question of the language of Catholic Mass. Grégoire for one wanted to make Mass be in French: his idea was that people should pray in French. This intrusion into the private belief systems of French citizens, inconceivable under the American notion of separation of church and state, was carried on in earnest because of the perception that the priests were preaching against the Revolution, and were keeping people ignorant by the use of Latin and/or *patois*. There were even attempts to create a revolutionary cult, with worship of supreme reason, the Supreme Being, revolutionary hymns, and the like. Could the *Assemblée nationale* make this happen? Some, including Grégoire, believed that it could: a minority wanted a change of liturgical language, perhaps in the manner of the Reformation, but only a minority. The *Assemblée nationale* did not attempt to fix this.

4.8.2.6 *Third stage: from the convening of* la Convention *to 9* thermidor

On 22 October, 1792, the Committee of Public Instruction made its recommendations for citizens not knowing French: the text became Title III of a decree. On 18 October, 1792, Lanthenas had reported[55] to the Committee that the *patois* should be destroyed, but the *idiomes*, held in common with neighbouring countries, be tolerated. 'The people' (*les sans-culottes*) seemed to be ahead of the Committee and the *Convention* however – they wanted to be good republicans and they continued to write, demanding the Committee of Public Instruction and the Convention do something about the language and education issue. The measures adopted so far, depending on translation of decrees and hypothesizing about the language of instruction were seen as too tolerant. Lanthenas (18 December, 1792) proclaimed the need to destroy *les patois*, but to preserve *les idiomes*. A proposed decree of November, 1792 would have promoted the French language, and used other languages (e.g. German) in areas where French was not spoken – what one would call today 'transitional bilingualism' – and would have used other *idiomes* as needed. Only Title I was voted on however: other titles were dropped, though Title IV, stipulating paying bilingual instructors 200 *livres* more per year, did get passed. But no sooner was one decree passed than the debate started all over again. There was confusion and heated debate during spring and summer of 1793 in the *Convention*. Grégoire makes a speech on 30 July, 1793; various other people express themselves too – Daunou for one wanted to reform the orthography.

4.8.2.7 *Law of* 30 vendémiaire an II

Finally, the law of *30 vendémiaire an II* (21 October, 1793) was passed. It decrees setting up state primary schools, teaching people to speak, read and write the French language. Some applications of the law took place right away, for example at Strasbourg. But the *Convention* was not finished: it began to amend the law of *30 vendémiaire* almost immediately. On *5 brumaire* the Committee proposed additional articles (6 and 7). On *14 brumaire*, the law was *en question*; on the 19th, there were more revisions; on the 24th, they added the phrase 'Instruction shall be in the French language *partout* (everywhere)'. In November/December, more discussion: a counter-plan (Bouquier) with everything 'freer'. The *Convention*[56] preferred Bouquier, voted, then left it hanging. Certain sections of Bouquier's proposals were voted on, others left unresolved. At the same time people began to complain about the problem of the lack of books for school use, and the lack of a pedagogical grammar.[57] Someone proposed a national republican catechism, others proposed a national grammar, an idea that had come through in the *cahiers*. It was decided to have a contest for a grammar; a jury was nominated (but not until the *18 messidor an II*/6 July, 1794), and contestants had until 21 December, 1794 to submit their works. Note that this takes us to late 1794; Robespierre and the Terror are finished, and other important legislation has already been voted in.

4.8.2.8 Failure of the translation policy

Meanwhile, the *Convention* had continued the tradition of preceding bodies, of translating laws and decrees into German, Italian and (with less success) into other languages. This proceeded slowly because of the many problems. Some people (e.g. Roussel) were opposed all along, and vehemently so. On 7 October, 1792, the *Convention* created a commission to accelerate translation, and named a set of commissioners, among them Rul, Dentzel, Grégoire and Bourdon to carry this out. Those who were opposed to continued translation said that it was wrong to bargain with 'jargons' – what was needed was to stamp them out. Meanwhile the Committee of Public Safety had made its own decree[58] about translation, on 20 June, 1792, with modifications on 27 July. But it is not clear whether this was carried out. They were still deliberating about translation on 4 December, 1793 (*14 frimaire an II*).

4.8.2.9 Robespierre

The period during which translations were allowed (from 7 November, 1792, by a decree of the *Convention)* and encouraged, coincides by chance with the rise of Robespierre, a lawyer from a northern region (Pas-de-Calais) who was respected by many as a man of honour, thought to be personally incorruptible, but also dangerous because of his fanaticism, his charisma and his unrelenting pursuit of certain policies to the detriment of his political enemies. The Committee of Public Safety was created in April, 1793: on 20 June, 1793 the Committee gets into the linguistic act and tries to simplify the translation process, but it is not clear whether this decree was executed: on 4 December, 1793 (*14 frimaire an II*) they were still quibbling about translations. Robespierre is elected to the Committee of Public Safety on 27 July, 1793 and becomes the Committee's driving force and leading voice, instituting the Terror (law of *22 prairial*/June 1794). He destroyed his enemies on the Left and Right, judging, punishing and sometimes executing people with minimal trial, closing churches and substituting a *culte de la raison*, until he finally overstepped himself, and was deposed (and executed) almost exactly a year later, on *9 thermidor an II* (2–8 July, 1794), a victim of his own excesses. After this the pendulum swung back; there was a return to a semblance of tolerance and more acceptance of human limitations. Robespierre and his policies have left us with the terms 'Terror' and 'terrorism', the latter still very much with us two centuries later, though Robespierre often sounds moderate when compared with some of his henchmen. His power base was the 'people' – *les sans-culottes* – especially the *commune de Paris*. As a public prosecutor of the Paris criminal court he condemned people to death. These are the well-known excesses of the French Revolution which to many people *are* the French Revolution. During his time in the Committee of Public Safety Robespierre made it the power-centre in the revolution, and his 'agents', such as Rousseville, made scathing denunciations and proposals for the treatment of counter-revolutionaries, enemies of the people, etc. who encouraged secession and emigration and sedition in frontier areas.[59] Though the Committee of Public Safety was originally a committee of the *Convention,* the tail was wagging the dog, and the Committee came to wield power that it had usurped from the *Convention*. In what is referred to as a *coup d'état*, Robespierre, the most powerful figure in the Committee was ganged up on by his enemies at both ends of the political spectrum, and on 27 July, 1794 (*9 thermidor*) was deposed, to suffer the same fate as people suffered under him – execution by guillotine. Thus, during, this period certain questions of language, supposedly the concern of the Committee of Public Instruction, are taken over by Robespierre and others, and Barère's denunciation of *les idiomes* – leading to the decree of *8 pluviose an II* (27 January, 1794) before the Committee of Public Safety, not the *Convention*. But it is the *Convention* that votes the Decree of *8 pluviose* (27 January, 1794), according to which French-speaking school-teachers were to be appointed within ten days in all areas where French was not spoken hitherto. Some sources refer to January, 1794 as the beginning of the dictatorship of Robespierre: this coincides of course with the Committee hearings on language questions of *8 pluviose*.

4.8.2.10 Break with les idiomes and les patois

The representatives and translation commissioners who visited the marginal areas were now campaigning against the policy of translation, and Barère continued the floor fight against them in January, 1794 (*pluviose an II*). The *idiomes* are now in danger, but not the *patois*. In the marginal areas lurked fanatical priests (Basque, Breton), foreign influences, emigration and danger. 'The shadows are too thick to penetrate' (by the light of the revolution).[60] Also, the *idiomes* were likely to be influenced by counter-propaganda, from inside and outside. There was no way to know what was going on, no way to control them. Barère felt that this was a matter of public safety, and so in speaking for the Committee of Public Safety on *8 pluviose an II* (27 January, 1794) Barère denounced the dangers that '*les idiomes anciens, welches, gascons, celtiques, wisigots, phocéens et orientaux*' represented for the republic. Based on the testimony of representatives, these old[61] languages had prevented the revolution from penetrating into nine important *départements*. In Bretagne, with the help of Bas-Breton, the priests were supposedly directing the consciences of the peasants, preventing them from knowing the laws. In Haut- and Bas-Rhin it was the identity of language which summoned the Prussian and Austrian military incursions which led to emigration. Meanwhile the Basques were under the domination of priests, while in Corsica, Paoli was perverting the public spirit. Thus Barère, speaking as if language was a matter of public safety, made his famous declaration about smashing the faulty instruments, the superstitious and hateful fanatics who speak Breton, German, Italian and Basque.

4.8.2.11 8 pluviose/27 January, 1794

Discussion of the decree of *8 pluviose* was brief. Barère did not want it to be watered down by too many extensions, while Grégoire wanted to extend it to dialects. It was decided that teachers of French language would be nominated in a period of ten days, in all the *départements* where the inhabitants spoke Breton, Italian, Basque and German.[62] This is the decree that according to Balibar makes French language policy the oldest (explicit) language policy of any polity in the world. Brunot notes how relaxed the application of the old ordinances had been over the centuries in the introduction of the use of French language for all public acts. The *Convention* had the choice between a rigorous doctrine and the maintenance of the prevailing temperament. They chose the former. So the decree of *8 pluviose* took effect: what was discovered immediately was that there were no teachers who were perfectly bilingual in both the local languages and French – if there were such people, they were already engaged in other enterprises. Precious few applicants applied for these positions, and even with the best of intentions, the decree could not be carried out. So the next solution was to start an *école normale* or teacher training institute. This would be a kind of 'crash course' held in Paris, and the trainees would then be sent to the provinces to teach others. By decree of 27 September, 1794 (*6 vendémiaire an III*) the *école normale* was instituted. But this, too, turned out to be poorly thought out. Few candidates presented themselves, and in the meantime the original old schools were closed with nothing to substitute for them. Remember that we are now in the period known as the Reign of Terror, so what there was, was a *terreur linguistique*, with much persecution and impugning the reputations of people of good will. It resulted in emigration (to Germany, with the attendant anxiety that emigrants would return with armies to fight against the revolution), and in threats of deportation (to move all the Alsatians to the interior of France, or resettle people from the interior in Alsace). Eventually, of course, everything returned to the old ways – both languages used on an equal basis; translations continued, with the *Convention,* the Committee of Public Safety and the Committee of Public Instruction collabourating on translating decrees, realizing that the *decrét Barère* was not going anywhere. As Brunot puts it, what reasonable policy is there that would not have allowed these concessions and would not have subordinated the advantages of *francisation* to other pressing needs?

Brunot feels he has to apologize for the failure of the *Convention,* the Committee of Public Safety and the Committee of Public Instruction to carry out their own wonderful policies, but it is also true that these bodies were faced with staggering problems, with new ones arising every day: war, inflation, invasion, insurrection, intrigues, etc. One thing that the decree of *8 pluviose* did do, with unintended consequences, was finally to eliminate Latin for good: a decree of 22 February, 1793 decided that Latin would no longer figure as a major aspect of secondary education. Some local ordinances also banned Latin, at least with the effect of making it a subject of instruction, not a language of instruction. Another policy of this period was to ban (i.e. close down) many *collèges* (secondary institutions) and universities. Many did not reopen for years, after which point Latin was long gone. The decree of *25 messidor an III* (13 July, 1795) had this effect: the *Collège de France* was allowed to stay open; the University of Strasbourg (a hotbed of *germanitude*) was closed, not to reopen until 1871. Another reason for the failure of *8 pluviose* was the lack of books, especially an easily understood and agreed-upon grammar of French. They did agree (much later) to have a contest to get one written, but this was easier said than done. The grammar which eventually won had in fact been written before the revolution.

4.8.2.12 Decision on the école normale

The plan for a teacher training college did not meet anybody's needs. It did not produce a methodology to teach teachers: the *école normale* actually became an *école normale superieure*. The only useful thing it produced was a debate about orthography. The *école normale* was condemned by the *Convention* on *27 germinal an III* (16 April, 1795), and it closed down even before the end of the school year.

4.8.2.13 One more attempt

On 19 and 20 October, 1794 the Committee of Public Instruction adopted a new project: to teach French, spoken and written, to everybody, that is to include adult education. Further, in parts of the country with a special *idiome*, Article 3 provided that they would teach in two languages so that French would eventually become familiar to everyone in the republic. Accordingly, bilingual education was allowed, but only as a transitional measure. The *Convention* took this up on *27 brumaire an III*. Article 3 was adopted with an amendment: teaching would be in French, and the *idiomes* would be used only as an auxiliary language[63] but this last part was not explicitly stated, only understood. Brunot calls this a break with *8 pluviose*. Tolerance could be interpreted here as authorization to use the *idiomes* for whatever purposes one wanted. For Brunot this was disastrous because it did not mention the reason for using the *idiomes*, and opened the door to a return to linguistic pluralism, linguistic federalism, and all the other evils of the pre-revolutionary era. Further to this, there was a law passed in the month of *brumaire an IV*, which eviscerated *8 pluviose an II* even further – it deleted state-funded salaries for teachers, and discontinued provisions for the inclusions of girls. The Committee of Public Instruction deliberated with the Commission of the Eleven, and came up with a 'conference committee' version, saying (in Article 4) that in every primary school, pupils will be taught reading, writing, counting and the elements of morals. A proposed Article 5 stipulated that the teaching be done in French, but it did not survive legislation. Brunot's assessment is that nobody had the necessary convictions to defend the law of *8 pluviose*.

To Brunot, this was not a retreat, this was an abdication. The language policy was abandoned![64] In late 1795 (on 26 October) the *Convention* was disbanded, and was replaced in early November by a five-man *Directoire* elected by various councils. Under the *Directoire* there was not much progress for the *école primaire*. It was the same old story – wonderful ideas, nice plans, but not much action. There was a slow increase in attendance in publicly supported schools in various places. The one good thing that happened, says Brunot, was that French did take possession of higher and middle education. The *Convention* did kill off Latin, and French alone was authorized in all new schools, various *grandes écoles*, science schools, polytechniques, etc. – all the new institutions created by the revolution as a counter-weight to the old ones, which were shut down. When the old schools reopened, if they were able to at all, they then had to fit themselves into the new language policy, which they did. And at last there was a contest for a national grammar, won by L'Homond. On *14 brumaire an VII*, Lakanal reported to 'The Five Hundred' that Lhomond's *élémens de la grammaire française* had been selected by a jury, and that it should be published at government expense. It was tailored to the bare necessities of a child's comprehension and age: Lhomond was a student of Brunot's hero, Rollin, who was the voice crying in the wilderness for so long about the need for a standard French grammar. This grammar was then pedagogically and grammatically sound, and set the standard for other, later works that eventually claimed a monopoly in all French schools.

4.9 FRENCH IN THE NINETEENTH CENTURY

The import of Brunot's analysis of the revolution is that the most lasting affects of language policy, described above, are that certain principles are established – such as what language will be used in schools, and what kind of French will be taught, following what model of grammar. In and of itself, the French Revolution did not effect many changes at the grass-roots level. But later reformers and educational pioneers found the fields ploughed for them, and France was able to develop the uniform system that has held sway until today: all educational policy set in Paris, all schools controlled by Paris, all teachers employees of the French state, and assignable at will to any school in France.[65] The main reason that language policy set during the Revolution did not take effect until 80 years later, of course, was that France did not have a compulsory educational system until the Third Republic, which came into being after the defeat of 1871 in the Franco-Prussian War. There were, of course, revolutionary and early nineteenth-century attempts to set up schools, but many of these efforts came to naught, as we have seen. When the new system was finally in place,[66] with teachers trained at *écoles normales* founded and financed by the state, the revolutionary and Napoleonic policies that were to govern the schools were already in place, and an extremely centralized, élitist educational system was the result. The Third Republic harked back to the rhetoric of the First Republic, and implemented its decrees: it was anti-clerical, anti-monarchical, anti-*patois*, and it picked up where Grégoire and Barère had left off. But what kind of French language did it privilege, and how rigid was the legal system that supposedly protected it?

4.9.1 French language policy in the nineteenth century: myths and facts

One of the most vexatious factors in dealing with language policy in France today is that many notions that the French have about their language, especially its orthography, are based on myths that appear to have arisen in the nineteenth century, and concern the legal status of the orthography and the role of the *Académie française* in setting rules. That is, there seems to be a popular understanding in France that language policy was set in stone sometime in the nineteenth century, or during the Revolution.[67] The various components of this understanding may vary, but here are some of the possible elements or variant readings of this myth.

- French language policy was ordained during the French Revolution by the law of *8 pluviose*, and like it or not, is therefore sacrosanct, because 'the people' delegated this authority to the revolutionary policy-makers (*la Convention*).

- French language policy, especially corpus policy, is the domain of the *Académie française*, which makes the rules (especially about spelling): this power has been delegated to it by the state.

- There were laws passed in about 1835 (opinions vary) that required schools to teach the kind of French defined (in some vague manner) according to whatever principles the *Académie française* uses. French orthography is the language, warts and all: though it may sometimes be illogical, that is its beauty, and to learn its rules imparts a kind of discipline that is good for people. One submits oneself to it for the greater glory of France. (This view may be held by the same people who claim that the French language is inherently logical.) This 'love of spelling' above all else is attacked by reformers as *le fétichisme de l'orthographe.*

- Phoneticism, or writing things the way they 'sound' is tantamount to chaos, disorder, *le déluge*, and will bring forth anarchy, riots, the breakdown of society, morals, and the end of civilization. Not one change must be allowed in this direction.

- Attempts to change orthography, modernize or simplify spelling, are linked (inexplicably) to another bugaboo, the dangers of *franglais*. Defence of orthography and defence of the French language from pressures *outre-Manche*, that is from Anglo-America, are one and the same.

4.9.1.1 The myth of 1835 and the orthography reform of 1989–90

Let us examine these myths in the context of a recent attempt to modernize and simplify, if only minimally, French orthography. This was the attempt made in 1989–90, and promulgated after hefty debate in a French government publication entitled 'Les Rectifications de l'orthographe' published on 6 December, 1990.[68] French corpus policy was placed in the hands of an organ of the government called the *Conseil supérieur de la langue française,* which was 'installed' in October 1989, and given the mission, among others, of formulating clear and precise propositions about French spelling: of bringing to it useful corrections and adjustments in order to resolve, as much as one can, problems of how to write; to eliminate uncertainties or contradictions, and to permit some rules for the correct formation of new words demanded by science and technology:

> I only wanted to underline that [something of] *permanence*[69] appears and imposes itself as soon as one undertakes to act on the structures of French, and that this *permanence* expresses itself in such words as certitude, clarity, precision, purity, all qualities that make our language supreme in the domains of ethics, of law, of [international diplomatic] agreements and negotiations and, more generally, in the art of exposition and of definition.
>
> If it were to lose these characteristics that have made it uni-

versal, our language would lose adherents and experience a reduction in use in the world.

(Druon 1990: 36)[70]

M. Druon goes on, in predictable fashion (as we can already see in his words quoted above) to praise the French language, praise the *Académie*, praise all the people who have worked on the proposals and who care about the French language, and to suggest that the proposals for spelling reform in this report are minor – they have been arrived at after hard work by experts, and they only make '*rectifications*', that is minor corrections, where there are inconsistencies that plague its users and add nothing to the beauty and grandeur of the edifice.[71] No great fundamental earth-shaking reform is proposed: no one is required to adopt them, they are utilitarian and useful and no one is pretending to make French spelling simple and rational (which might be a *desideratum* for some, but will not be for others). Changes will be based on what is already happening in the genius of the language, that is in the ways people already write (in letters, etc.) even though they are not 'correct'.[72] As we have already noted above, one cannot master French spelling without mastering a particular concept of grammar, namely, one that embodies in the spelling certain coding conventions that tell us something about grammatical relations in the sentence. Words are spelled in a certain way so that we can always tell what the root of the word is, despite morphological accretions that might distort it. We always know when a word is borrowed from Greek, also, because of Greek spellings retained (e.g. <ph> for [f]). We must be always mindful in French spelling whether words are plural or singular, and how adjectives and past participles are marked for number and gender, even if no trace of this remains in pronunciation.

A famous example of this problem occurred in the early 1960s, when France was struggling with the issue of Algerian independence, and a dissident group of generals, known later as the *Organisation de l'armée sécrete*, or OAS, attempted a coup d'état. Troops loyal to the *putschistes* were thought to be about to land at Orly airport, from where it was feared they would then advance on Paris. General Charles de Gaulle, then President of the Republic, went on television to exhort the French people to resist this illegal putsch: '*Je m'adresse aux Français!*', he declared. (phonetically, [žmadrɛs o frāsɛ].) Then, realizing that his exhortation was ambiguous, and could either be interpreted as 'I address myself to the French (man)' or 'I address myself to the French (people)', he added ' . . . *au pluriel!*' to make it explicitly plural. In this, as in many other cases in the spoken language, there is no way to indicate this difference without circumlocutions such as the one de Gaulle employed. In written French, the difference is clear: *au français* is singular, *aux français* is plural (even here the plural is not marked on a word ending in /s/.) Thus only written French is capable of maintaining the *certitude, clarté, précision* and *pureté* that the French consider to be inherent qualities of their language, and thus French spelling must not be allowed to descend into phoneticism. Note how de Gaulle, who was without a doubt deeply imbued with the notion of the primacy of the written language, was trapped by the situation. He went on television and radio to have as immediate an effect as his words could, but the electronic media only conveyed his spoken pronunciation, not the force of the written, and he had to spell it out.[73]

4.9.1.2 *The furore over the orthography reform of 1989–90*

Despite M. Druon's attempt to legitimize the reform by invoking the names of all the people who had authorized it, including the members of the *Académie française* who had approved the project unanimously, the announcement of this reform evoked a storm of protest.[74] In fact, most attempts at reform of French spelling in the last two centuries have drawn protests, and many well-meaning attempts have failed.[75] Chief among these may be mentioned an attempt in 1901, the *arrêtés ministériels* of G. Leygues, which introduced 'tolerances' for the past participles.[76] Another attempt of 1939–40, proposed by Dauzat and Damourette, failed perhaps because France was preoccupied by war. Dauzat was involved again in 1953. Commissions of ministers, of teachers, the *Académie des Sciences*, etc. have all made proposals, to no avail. The proposal of 1989–90 contained another imperative – the demands of the information revolution, that is, the increased use of computers, which have little tolerance for minute mistakes, and in any case cannot yet be programmed to assure that past participles agree with their antecedents in number and gender. One might call it the 'spell-checker' reform, since it was designed to help French science and French *informatique* compete in a world dominated by English-speaking computers.[77]

4.9.2 Construction of the modern myth

Nina Catach (1991) has written a useful review of some of these attempts. She focuses on a part of the mythology, the 'imaginary decree of 1832'. When many of the opponents of reform want to defend their opposition to reform, they invoke this *décret*, which has supposedly never been abrogated, and which supposedly authorized the spelling norms of the *Académie française* as a 'state orthography' (p.115), which alone is valid. When questioned in detail about this decree, respondents state that it dates from some time between 1832 and 1835, when two actual related events did occur:

• The Guizot law regarding elementary education (28 June, 1833).

• The appearance of the sixth edition of the *Dictionnaire de l'Académie française* (1832–5).

As Catch points out, the myth of the imaginary decree is recent – it does not receive explicit mention before about 1970. It has been abundantly repeated by the press during the recent furor (e.g. *Figaro* of 30 November, 1988, citing 'the official birth act of the orthography, dating to a decree of Louis-Philippe . . . requiring all officials to bring their spelling into line with that of the Academy's dictionary' (p.113)). Catch outlines a number of assumptions contained in this myth:

• Spelling can be 'fixed' once and for all. She refers to this as *fixisme*.

• It is forbidden for anyone other than the *Académie française* to meddle with French spelling (judicial argument).

• Any attack on this state (of the language), which is taken as definitive and untouchable, whether it concerns spelling errors or attempts to let the language evolve, is scandalous.

No denial of the factual errors involved in this myth, nor of what Catch calls the 'moral' errors (because the language is usually thought of as belonging to 'the people'), have ever been undertaken by competent authorities, but rather are accepted and reproduced, more or less as follows:

'Since the middle of the nineteenth century, the spelling system of the Academy is the only official one in France.' . . . (To this is sometimes added:) 'for entrance into public employment.'
(Catch 1991: 114)

As Catch points out, various authors and authorities, from Thimonnier to Brunot to Marcel Cohen, have participated in the perpetuation of these notions, and believe them to be true. Some attribute the decree to Louis-Philippe, the *roi-citoyen*: others insert words like 'authorized' and 'obligatory' and *exigé aux emplois* (required of public employees). Later writers insert the word 'decree' and everyone else takes it from there – both conservatives and reformers seem to accept that a certain spelling was 'official' and 'required'. The former feel that *fixisme* should carry the day, and that no changes are permissible; the latter claim that if Louis-Philippe could decree a particular form, then latter-day reformers can decree some changes, too. Even the *Académie française* seems to be unable to convince the public that it has never been charged with defining a particular orthography, despite numerous denials. It reminds people that it is only supposed to 'build on usage' (*greffer l'usage*) and not ordain usage. And never did it demand the exclusive right to make such decisions. Catach attributes the origins of this myth to the history of education in the nineteenth century. The education establishment, as it existed in the early part of the century, grappled with the problem, but grammar (in French co-terminous with spelling, as we have seen) was in any event not taught until the sixth grade. As we saw earlier, there was a long-standing lack of agreement about what kind of grammar to teach, when to teach it, and whom to teach it to:

- Should one teach Latin grammar to young children, who do not as yet know Latin?

- Should one teach a kind of French grammar that was highly Latinate, and thus based on Latin grammar, not French?

- If one should teach French in its most pure, lucid and eloquent form, as exemplified in the grammars of the academicians – then which academician's grammar should one use?

As Catach points out, the actual directives to teachers in the 1830s give alternatives – at least 12 different grammars are authorized (i.e. recommended) for primary schools, 11 different grammars are authorized (i.e. recommended) for superior primary schools, and three dictionaries, that of the *Académie française* last. Yet a myth has evolved, according to which there is an ordained standard, and everyone must learn it. As anyone who has ever studied French can recall, an inordinate amount of time is spent on dictations (*dictées*) where sentences are read to students who must write them down without error. These *dictées*, of course, are full of traps – exceptional words, phrases requiring the 'accord' of the noun with the past participle (taking special note of number and gender), and all the irregular verbs of the language in their full morphological panoply. A mere spelling test, with words spelled in isolation as in English-medium schools, will not do, of course, since it is the *syntax* of words that must agree in various ways that determines the spelling. Catach blames on the one hand the conservatives – for their adherence to the notion that the system can never change, and on the other hand the reformers – for seeing the nineteenth-century norm as a vicious, oppressive plot, when it was in fact accepted as a boon by those elements of society that had never been offered it before. Thus the reformers have accepted the idea of decrees and laws as just more evidence of brutal state dogmatism, and cannot understand why the masses did not rise up in revolt and reject it.

4.9.3 Rights for regional languages: *la Loi deixonne*

As we will be discussing the question of regional languages in the chapter on Alsace, we reserve until then a discussion of the so-called *Loi deixonne*, passed in 1951, which allowed regional languages to be studied in French schools for the first time since the eighteenth century.

4.9.4 *Franglais* and the Anglo-Saxon menace

Much has been written about modern France and its ferocious resistance to the spread of English, and the pernicious version of anglicized French, known as *franglais*, that is current in many domains in France. Much of French public opinion can be galvanized over this issue, and in fact much overt policy-making in post-war France has been directed at preserving French from the incursions of English. English speakers of course notice this stuff as soon as they arrive in the country: language learners, even those earnestly desiring to practise their French, experience the shock of having their English-accented French rejected, reviled and sneered at. Tourist magazines warn against this mania, and daily newspapers in the English-speaking world carry articles reporting the latest silliness. We have now come full circle in this chapter since we earlier discussed the debates about French ideology. What strikes one most vividly in the debates on this issue is that the French are not only willing to have their government intervene to defend the French language, they demand that it do so, and there seems to be unanimity in this area from one end of the political spectrum to the other, as we have seen in the case of the 1975 law. But when the government attempts to touch the spelling rules, there are screams of protest. Some even blame *franglais* for the spelling débâcle.

Weinstein (1989) has detailed the development of various methods for dealing with threats to French, one of which, *la francophonie*, is an international organization devoted to co-ordination of various efforts of French-speaking countries and other areas where French is used, even as a subsidiary language. France has taken the lead in some of these efforts, but Canadian French, feeling more threatened, have also taken initiatives. President de Gaulle and his prime minister Pompidou created the *Haut comité pour la défense et l'expansion de la langue française* in 1966, with the goal of purifying French within France. In 1972 terminology commissions in various ministries were created to help prepare vocabulary and avoid reliance on other languages. Some of these terminology lists were ordained for use within the civil service, others were merely suggestions, but the idea was that schools and governmental agencies would lead here.

In 1975 the law mentioned earlier (No. 75-1349), now referred to as the *Bas-Lauriol* law was signed by President Giscard d'Estaing. This law contained sanctions for use of impure words in civil life, especially in business. Various ministries then published lists of acceptable substitutes for *franglais* or English terms.

In 1984 President Mitterrand replaced the *Haut comité* with a General Commissariat and an advisory comittee of the French language, attached to the prime minister's office. Their goals are to encourage, co-ordinate, disseminate and publish all activities related to the spread and defence of the French language. Then in 1986 a new terminology commission was created, to accelerate work where there was otherwise nothing happening, and co-ordinate work of various ministries. Mitterrand also created another organization, the *Haut conseil de la francophonie,* to help involve and co-ordinate efforts with other French-speaking countries (previously France had resisted creating a Commonwealth/*Communauté* because it did not wish to appear to be neo-colonial, and the status of Québec in this Commonwealth/*Communauté* could not be resolved to the satisfaction of the Canadian government).

Part of the problem with French purism is that users of French in other places, such as Canadians or Belgians, Haitians or Senegalese, sometimes prefer their own norms, which may not exactly involve foreign words, but contain locutions not used in France. French speakers from the Hexagon, they claim, look down on these regional features when they should be acting together to fight other dangers. Another problem is that even French speakers find some of the puristic efforts simply ludicrous, and jokes of all sorts abound. Nevertheless a certain infrastructure now exists that can be useful in various ways: it is this *permanence* that M. Druon referred to earlier in the discussion of orthography reform.

4.10 CONCLUSION

As we have seen, there are two high water marks for French linguistic culture and policy development – the development of the *Académie française* and the French Revolution. We have noted that the founding of the *Académie française* was a victory for corpus planning. It enabled and encouraged the development of new vocabulary, a standardized grammar, and a more or less fixed orthography.[78] Where the French language was once seen as being in such a desperate situation that members of French linguistic culture despaired of it ever being able to compete with Latin, Italian or Spanish, it acquired the status of the most brilliant language in Europe, one that could claim that it was a new 'classic' language. The French revolution, for its part, was a victory for status planning in France, firmly establishing French as the language of all education, administration, journalism, commerce, etc., leaving only the religious domain still in the clutches of Latin. Corpus planning was not affected by the revolution, and when French acquired the status it did, it was the corpus of the pre-revolutionary élite that was deemed to be the kind of French that was needed. Looking back, we can see that nineteenth- and twentieth-century French people conflate the notions of status and corpus planning. They assume that because status planning was ordained by the Revolution, the corpus that was given that status was also somehow ordained, and is protected rigidly by laws, constitutional provisions, or whatever. This belief is now difficult to shake. What the French Revolution also seems to have done is to ordain and legitimize certain myths, such that those surrounding the law of *8 pluviose* (and what it supposedly set in motion), and the myth of the Fixed Orthography of 1835, most recently invoked during the last two decades. We see that French language policy, believed by some (e.g. Balibar 1985) to be the most explicit and restrictive in the world, is more of a cultural construct than an explicit policy. Its power rests in what people imagine it to consist of, rather than on actual statutes or rigid codes. In other words, policy is not as explicit as French people think it is – but it is every bit as restrictive as they believe it is, as long as they think it is.

5 French in the marginal areas: Alsace and the other regions

5.1 CORE AND PERIPHERY

As we have seen in the previous chapter, France has a history of policy-making about language, both overt and covert, that has involved the construction of a myth about the French language. The myth involves such metaphors as 'brilliance' and 'radiance', and the French language is supposed to be seen radiating its brilliance out from the centre, illuminating other languages, *idiomes*, *patois* and so on, both within France and in other nations. The history of France has been one of expansion from this core around Paris (the region known as Ile de France) to the marginal areas, by which is meant the territories lying between the core and the 'natural' boundaries: the Atlantic, the Rhine, the Pyrenees, the Alps. In areas where the boundaries are not notably 'natural', such as the north of France, the political boundary almost (but not quite) corresponds to the linguistic boundary between French, Netherlandic, and various Germanic dialects. What is left over constitutes *la Wallonie*, the French-speaking part of Belgium, and *la Suisse romande* the French-speaking part of Switzerland.

Ignored, reviled and despised in all of this, of course, are the regional languages of France, and as we have seen, the French are inconsistent in how they deal with these speech forms.[1]

Though the general policy has been to try to extirpate all forms of language spoken in France that are not standard French (irrespective of whether the speech forms are languages, dialects, *patois*, or whatever), there have been moments when this agenda has been relaxed, and the *idiomes* and *patois* have been given a breathing space. Despite the relentless juggernaut of the French language[2] the regional languages today show signs of survival, and even revival: rumours of their death seem greatly exaggerated.

5.2 HISTORY OF A REGION

In this chapter we examine the regions of France, and in particular *one* region of France where the ancestral language of most people is not French, and where linguistic varieties other than French have never had any explicit rights under French hegemony. The particular region we will focus on is Alsace,[3] which has had a troubled linguistic history for much of recorded time, and for reasons, in my estimation, that have more to do with a clash of linguistic cultures than for geopolitical reasons. Alsace and Strasbourg represent something of deep cultural significance to both Germany and France – as we noted in the last chapter, the earliest example of a text in French (that is Old French as distinct from some forms of late Latin) is the *Serment de Strasbourg*, known in English as the 'Strasbourg Oaths' and in German as *die Strassburger Eide*. This was, significantly, a bilingual document. Ludwig (Ludhuvicus) the German and Charles the Bald, grandsons of Charlemagne, met to swear oaths and create an alliance against their third brother Lothaire. They did this in Old French and in the *teudesca lingua* – Old High German – but the German king said his oath in French and the French king swore in German.

Thus the stamp of bilingualism is associated with Strasbourg from the very first 'official use' of the 'French' language (whether or not this is remembered in the rest of France), and furthermore the bilingualism of the two brothers was (at least in the telling of it) *reciprocal*. The other thing of moment associated with this act is that it was a political pact mounted against their own brother to deprive him of his inheritance, the territory subsequently known as Lorraine/ Lothringen, so the strife that endured over that issue was thus written into the first bilingual document, and sworn in the city of Strasbourg. Eventually, of course, Strasbourg and all of Alsace also became a pawn of the two realms, and as we know, France and Germany fought over the combined spoils, Alsace-Lorraine, for the next eleven hundred years: the *Serment de Strasbourg* was sworn on 14 February, 842. The linguistic boundary, at that time, seems to have been the Vosges mountains, as it continues to be today (though as we shall see, the number of young speakers of Alsatian continues to diminish).

5.2.1 The cathedral of Notre Dame de Strasbourg

Another deeply cherished symbol for both France and for Germany is the cathedral of Notre Dame de Strasbourg. It is as dear to the hearts of the French as it is deeply embedded in the imaginations of

German-speakers, many of whom have probably read Johann Wolf-gang Goethe's paeans to the cathedral written when he was a student there. The sight of the facade of the cathedral draped with an enormous Nazi flag during the occupation of 1940–5 was profoundly offensive to the French (and to most Alsatians, I might add). Alsa-tians were continually forced to choose between being French or German, when what they would have liked would have been a cultural identity that was bilingual and bicultural. The search for an identity that could include at least Alsatian dialect (if not *Hoch-deutsch* as well) along with French has not ended in Alsace, though the French government is content with the fact that most Alsatians now know French (again).

The poem by André Weckmann, *s büchnawele*, 'The Navel', expresses this desire simply and eloquently:

> . . .
> elsasser sen haisst
> d fanschter gross ufrisse
> fer dàss de wénd bi uns inkehre kànn
> der vun oscht wi der vun wescht
> elsasser sen
> haisst e bruck offe halte
> vun volik ze volik

> 'To be Alsatian means
> to throw open the windows wide
> so that the wind can come in to us
> the one from the East and the one from the West
> To be Alsatian
> means to hold open a bridge
> from people to people.'
> . . .

Alsatian intellectuals, however, though they are disturbed by many aspects of French policy in Alsace (and in the other linguistic minority territories in general), are also frustrated by their inability to inspire their compatriots to get involved in any of the solutions they propose, such as bi- or trilingual education. They would also like to build upon the notion that Alsace once was a region that repre-sented a bridge between two cultures, but has rarely been allowed to serve that function in recent centuries. They emphasize too the growing importance of the German language (especially after the reunification in the early 1990s) in a more 'united' Europe after

1992, and the fact that dialect speakers are a resource for France, since they can learn German easily.

After each shift in German or French power, the region has always had to deny its most recent past, that is, it has had to deny what was required of it by the previous regime, and atone for its lack of loyalty to a regime (either one) that it accepted only half-heartedly. It has to deny its own cultural identity, in other words, its identity as a bilingual area that has attempted to blend the best of both cultures but has always had to then deny one or the other. Each of the 'parent' cultures (*la mère patrie* and *das Vaterland*) has emphasized only those elements of Alsace's culture that it valorizes – the French emphasize that *La Marseillaise* was composed in Strasbourg, the Germans emphasize that Gutenberg worked in Strasbourg and Goethe was a student there and in effect launched a literary move-ment (the *Sturm und Drang*) with his ode to the Strasbourg cathedral (*Von deutscher Baukunst*) composed in 1771 at Sesenheim. His love affair with Frederike Brion was later transformed into the 'Gretchen' character in *Faust*. In short, Germany's greatest poet had an attach-ment to Strasbourg that he has passed on to subsequent generations. Whether Strasbourg is on French territory or on German soil is almost irrelevant – it lives in the German literary imagination, and on a clear day (i.e. before the advent of modern industrial air pollution) the cathedral could be seen from great distances on the German side of the Rhine, which was, of course, partly the reason for building cathedrals so high.

Figure 5.1 is from a poster entitled *L'attente*, 'The Wait', published in France during the last years of German occupation of Alsace that ended in 1918. In it a young Alsatian woman, identifiable by her *coiffe*, the large black bow and ribbon, sits dreaming of her redemp-tion by France from the sinister clutches of Germany. A dim outline of the cathedral of Strasbourg is visible through the window behind her. In her hand she clutches a red, white and blue *cocarde*.[4]

It is perhaps no exaggeration to say that Strasbourg and Alsace play a part in the mythologizing of their languages and their linguistic culture by both the French and the Germans, and it is perhaps this depth of feeling that has made the region a political and cultural plum that both have had to fight over.

5.2.2 Lévy on the linguistic history of Alsace

The best source of the linguistic history of Alsace, together with clear statements about the actual distribution of dialect forms, isoglosses

Figure 5.1 L'attente: Alsace patiently awaits her rescuer

(subdialectal boundaries) and other interesting facts of linguistic practice in Alsace is to be found in the two-volume work of Lévy (1929). A more succinct version of the linguistic history of the area can be found in Philipps (1975). Hartweg in a number of articles (1981, 1983, 1986) summarizes both the linguistic and the sociolinguistic situation admirably. Gardner-Chloros (1985, 1991) describes the interesting kinds of code-switching and other multilingualism that still occurs in Strasbourg, even in fancy shops and banks, not just by uneducated or rural people. Veltman and Denis (1988) give a pessimistic view of the future of Alsatian dialect, while Vassberg (1993) presents an eclectic overview of the history, attitudes, policies, conversational and code-switching behaviour, and results of a questionnaire-survey in upper Alsace (Haut-Rhin, centred around Mulhouse) and lower Alsace (Bas-Rhin, centred around Strasbourg).

5.2.3 The linguistic situation in Alsace in 1648

As we have noted, in the areas known as Alsace and Lorraine, German dialects, minimally distinguishable from other German dialects spoken on the German side of the border, had been spoken since pre-history. By the Peace of Westphalia, under the terms of which Alsace came under French jurisdiction, there emerged a policy on religion known as *cujus regio, ejus religio*, that is 'whatever the ruler, his religion', meaning that the rulers of each region determined what religion (Catholic or Protestant) would be tolerated. Believers whose religion was not tolerated in effect had to leave, and there was much emigration after 1648 to other like-minded areas. But there were also many anomalies, such as tiny residual enclaves that were under the jurisdiction of princes living far away, which may have been surrounded by a sea of the other religionists, but remained in the religious fold of that prince. Free cities, such as Strasbourg, could choose whatever faith was in the majority, or could even choose to tolerate all faiths.

Thus Lutherans and Catholics in Alsace ended up in a truce, with different parts of the province committed to one or the other religion. In order to enforce *cujus regio,* they tried a variant we might call *cujus regio, ejus lingua*, that is, they attempted to ban French, because it was associated with Calvinism. But it went underground and into hiding in smaller places, such as Molsheim. But *cujus regio* did not work in Alsace, because although it was part of the French Empire after 1648, it was not within the Kingdom of France, and *Villers-Cotterêts* technically did not apply. In exasperation on 21 October, 1737 the French administration ordered everybody to learn German.[5] In 1757 it was decreed that the Protestant Gymnasium drop Greek from its curriculum, increase the Latin, but also add French: yet the Gymnasium remained essentially a German language institution, and Strasbourg remained Protestant and Lutheran – none of its seven parishes were French. The French administration did not try to meddle with an organization of schools which benefited a religious sect that it tolerated against its will. (If anybody wanted French, they could go to Molsheim.) Some of this attitude was due to animosity against the Jesuits, who were the organizers of French *Catholic* schools in Alsace.

Strasbourg University continued to operate in Latin, which was the typical pattern in 'German' universities at this time, with some German and some French before 1789.[6] In 1788 the government aroused itself somewhat, noticed the German schools, and ordered the institution of some French Lower schools, because there was hardly any French taught except as an elective: even in the 'interior' of France, as we have seen, most schools operated in Latin. People who really wanted a French education went to France or hired governesses. For religious formation, all teaching was done in German, as if the motto was 'First save the souls, who cares what language they speak.'[7]

It seemed to be part of the attitude of the time that *les gens de la bonne société* tended to become bilingual: they looked out for both their German and their French. Thus even if the institutions were not supportive of French, or bilingualism, society was, and it was pushing *francisation*. Ordinary people of course knew no French, but 'higher' classes of people were reported by German travellers to speak it well. But Alsatian Catholics did not care for German, so a kind of polarization ensued: French became associated with Catholicism, and German associated with Protestantism.

Of course the French administration had extended the *ordonnance* of *Villers-Cotterêts* by an *arrêté* of the Council of state of 30 January, 1685, saying that all record-keeping should be in French, but because of the residual rights of the former rulers in Alsace, it had no effect. The Alsatians, especially the Strasbourgeois, were well known to be anti-French, and there was little that could be done about it. On 16 July, 1786, the *Conseil souverain d'Alsace* again demanded that all acts of procedure be in French: but again no action was taken, and records continued to be kept in German. Overall it is difficult to summarize any general 'policy' about language use in Alsace at the beginning of the French Revolution, except perhaps to say that people were ambivalent, they were 'hedging their bets', it was a hodge-podge, much like it always has been.

5.2.4 The penetration of French linguistic culture

As we can see from the foregoing, it is not easy, despite the excellent sources such as those just mentioned, to get an accurate picture of just what went on linguistically in Alsace throughout much of its history. Official sources on both sides of the Rhine have axes to grind, and are careful to emphasize only the linguistic features that they are interested in: it is especially important for them to convey the point of view that the other language was never very important. Thus a glance at German linguistic atlases of various sorts mention only the Germanic linguistic features, and ignore any Romance (i.e. French) data. The official French sources concentrate on French speakers and the re-establishment of French hegemony after the various periods of German 'occupation'.

Older models of linguistic analysis had no room for sociolinguistic variation either, so the idea that there was some kind of rule-governed diglossia or code-switching is also foreign to all but the most recent interpretations. The result has been much ignorance of the multilingual character of the region – the diglossia, the different domains of various languages, the code-switching, the important role of religion and in particular the Reformation in the propagation of one language or another – all combine to make for a fascinating but poorly studied subject. Officialdom on both sides has consistently failed to see that the multilingualism of the area is part of its linguistic culture and of its own linguistic identity, rather than something that has to be exponged.

One set of facts that is consistently misrepresented by the German viewpoint was the reality that French linguistic culture began to penetrate into Alsace long before the Treaty of Westphalia. It came early, it was fashionable, and it put roots down even in small towns (the *décapole*, a league of ten cities that did not include Strasbourg) long before 1648. Aside from being strategically placed on the eastern border of France and thus open to influences from the west, Alsace was seen as a place of refuge from all kinds of persecutions, and was sought out by Jewish refugees from the east as well as by Protestant refugees from France. At the time of the Reformation Alsace was at the apogee of its cultural importance (Philipps 1975: 25) and its dialect was a strong contender for status as a German *lingua franca*. Gutenberg was active in Strasbourg at the time, and the adaptation of movable type to printing Luther's translation of the Bible, as is well known, facilitated the spread both of Protestantism and of Luther's brand of German. Luther's ideas caught the attention of Alsatians early on: Mass was said in German in Strasbourg Cathedral from 1524, and the region figured prominently in the Reformation, becoming a haven for French Protestants fleeing the persecutions there. Strasbourg's conversion to Lutheranism did not last forever (it was later undercut by the principle of *cujus regio, ejus religio* after 1648 and 1681), but the result was that when French Calvinists sought refuge in Strasbourg, they were told to go to the towns of the *décapole*, which meant that French was able to penetrate into small towns of the region, not just the largest city, and establish deep roots for its domains.

As Philipps emphasizes (1975: 24), the choice of another dialect of German by Luther and its general acceptance as a standard German, even by Catholics, meant that Alsatian dialect was no longer a leader as a written form, resulting in the development of a diglossic situation that has lasted almost to the present day. It meant that dialect had to retreat into its own domains, and though attachment to dialect has waxed and waned depending on the vagaries of both German and French rule, the dialect began to suffer long before the French language began to penetrate:

> As for the Alsatian people, they used their Franconian dialect in the north and Allemanic in the rest of Alsace as their language of everyday communication. The better educated of their children had even managed to make of it a high-class literary vehicle. But the Reformation and the invention of moveable type printing favored the implantation and spread of a kind of common German, the use of which became more and more obligatory for educated people. Counted among these were Alsatians, completely at ease in dialect while also perfectly able to use the new form of German, and who also had a sufficient knowledge of French to keep themselves open to French cultural trends.[8]
>
> (Philipps 1975: 27)

5.2.5 The linguistic situation in the marginal territories

Let us now survey the sociolinguistic situation in various peripheral areas, regions which became part of France later rather than earlier.[9] There seems to have been a recognition by the monarchy that the *ordonnance* of *Villers-Cotterêts* would not just take effect in these areas automatically, so new territories had to have the edict imposed. Thus as each territory was added (by treaty, royal marriage, change of succession, etc.) the *ordonnance* of *Villers-Cotterêts* was pronounced to be in effect: but no action was actually taken to see that the edict was implemented.

1 *The Province of Béarn in the southwest* This province had joined France late (1620) and the medieval custom had been to write the Béarnais dialect. Basque was also spoken in this area, but Basque speakers knew neither French nor Béarnais, and their language was not taken account of. This was an area where Protestants had sought refuge after the revocation of the Edict of Nantes, because of the protection offered by the queen, herself a Protestant. With the accession of Béarn to France the *ordonnance* of *Villers-Cotterêts* was promulgated, but as with other areas, had no immediate effect. French did not actually begin to penetrate the area until the nineteenth century, with the development of schools, military service, railroads and tourism.

2 *Roussillon* This is Catalan-speaking country, around Perpignan. Joined to France in 1659, it had previously been attached to the court of Spain or of Barcelona, and *francisation* began in earnest, with schools and knowledge of French ordained, and sanctions for failure. The Church, seeing a need to win the souls of the children, pushed French (perhaps an idea influenced by the Reformation). After the revocation of the Edict of Nantes things got more zealous, but then there was a resurgence of Catalan. So in 1700 the administration reminded them of *Villers-Cotterêts* and how they needed to follow it. But there was still some attachment and nostalgia for Barcelona, and Latin was still a school language in this area.

3 *Brittany* Speakers of Breton, a Celtic language related to Welsh and Irish, came in waves from Britain before the eighth century and reached their widest territorial extension before the ninth century, but then the Normans invaded in the tenth century and pushed them back west. At this point they came under the orbit of the Normans, and there was intermarriage between Normans and Bretons: the grandmother of William the Conqueror was a Bretonne. Already by the time of the marriage of Anne de Bretagne with Charles VIII of France their monarchs spoke French. François I signed the solemn contract of union joining Brittany and France in 1532. Brunot sees Bretons as more stubborn than any other 'race', and feels that their language is destined to be conserved, even in difficult conditions. One thing that helped was that early French missionaries to Brittany became converts to and devotees of Breton, preaching in it and composing literature in it, which

retarded the pace of *francisation*. The two missionary priests Nobletz and Maurois were *bretonnant*, not perfect speakers, but their ardour and zeal was contagious. However the populations of the largest cities of Brittany, such as Rennes, Nantes and Vannes, were primarily French, and thus their aspirations for independence were confounded by their French-speaking municipal centres. (The same problem existed with Lorraine: Nancy and Metz were French areas.) The Church was one strong defender of Breton, but it made counter-productive moves by forbidding (actually by getting civil authorities to do it) the spread of amateur theatricals which vulgarized sacred stories, despite the fact of their being a strong expression of Breton culture. The plays were secularized versions of medieval religious and morality plays, and the Church did not like the competition.[10]

4 *Flandre Maritime* An examination of an historical atlas of France (e.g. *Petit Larousse* 1962: 1367) reveals that the northern border of France exhibits a ragged picture of zig-zag, piecemeal acquisition, giving and taking, ins and outs. In the south, southeast and west, however, the newer territories were acquired in larger chunks, and in most cases once acquired they remain part of France – they are not contested, fought over or repossessed like territories such as Alsace and Lorraine. Of the northern, Flemish-speaking territories, France once controlled a larger area, but this was pushed back to include only a sliver of Flanders, but with some Flemish speakers remaining. In the *cahiers de doléances*, the peasants in this territory composed their grievances in Flemish.

5 *Alsace* Alsace is definitely the most complex of all the marginal territories, and has been the most difficult 'problem'. We will deal with this in detail below.

6 *Lorraine 'allemande'*. The Duchy of Lorraine (German Lothringen), which of course derives its name from the brother (Lothaire) who was conspired against by Charles and Ludwig in 842 in Strasbourg, was by this time a territory with a mixed population. The dukes of Lorraine were French speakers but there were some small localities where German was spoken. The ordinary language (or dialect) was Lorrain, a *'langage fort grossier et corrompu'*.[11] There were still *baillages allemands*, meaning some tributary rights to German princes. The number of German-speaking villages had decreased in the seventeenth century because of the Thirty Years War, emigration, famine and massacre. They were resettled by French speakers, occupying places with German names (e.g. Metz). The Dukes of Lorraine could ignore the *ordonnance* of

Villers-Cotterêts because the territories acquired by the Treaty of Westphalia were part of the French Empire and not the Kingdom of France. The result was that Lorraine was perhaps the only really bilingual province at that time. Schooling, when not in Latin, was in French or German – sometimes in German even in French-speaking territory, into the eighteenth century.

In 1735, the province passed from the hereditary masters of Lorraine into the hands of King Stanislas of Poland, who ordained on 27 September, 1748, that all communications with the *baillages allemands* be carried out in French. But again this was not enforced: even then the Parlement of Nancy on 24 August, 1778 ordained that reports be made in German in the *justices seigneuriales*. In the *cahiers de doléances* of 1789 there were no protests at all about language except to demand the use of German in certain parishes. However one sees in Lorraine some indications of actual language shift (e.g. Thionville) over time, even in small villages, little by little, whereas in Alsace there is none by 1789, only pockets of French spoken by certain Frenchified Alsatians.

5.3 BRUNOT ON ALSACE

Brunot (1967) has devoted much space to the question of Alsace in his 13-volume work, since Alsace is in many ways the quintessential multilingual challenge to French monolingualism. No other region resisted linguistic assimilation so strongly, and of course no other region was taken away from France so many times by a powerful neighbouring state.

Brunot does of course admit that the Alsatians have some kind of point: he does distinguish between what he calls *langues héterogenes* or *idiomes* such as German, and dialects of French. Other writers use the term, as we have seen, to refer to either a substandard or regional speech form, but the term generally trivializes or marginalizes whatever it refers to, and is intended to. Brunot avoids using *patois* as part of his definition, but he does refer to *les patois* often. The French agenda, as it were, is to classify certain things as *langues héterogenes* in order to show that they are not really French, and therefore ought to be banned. As for the *patois*, they are casual, informal kinds of speech, also not worthy of any status. The idea that there might be indigenous forms of speech, neither French nor foreign, does not fit well into these schemes. One must either be able to subsume a speech form under the umbrella of French, or exclude it as a 'foreign' language.

5.3.1 Alsace during the Revolution

Early in the Revolution, on 14 January, 1790, a policy to translate new decrees and new laws was adopted: this was still during the period of the Constituent Assembly. Alsatians were among the most vociferous in wanting everything; translated in June, 1790 Alsace asked for a bilingual judiciary. When the idea of toppling the king gained favour, people began to question the doctrine of *cujus regio, ejus lingua*. That is, people in Alsace began to ask whether, if the purpose of a monarchy is to be of service to people – not for people to serve the monarchy – then by the same token was it reasonable to require the people to know the language of its judges when a judge is permitted to ignore the language of the people he is called to judge? One of those responding in letters to Grégoire said that it 'is impossible, sirs, to proscribe the German language from Alsace because of its topography, and most legitimate to require two languages' (quoted in Brunot, vol. 9: 81–2).

Brunot chastises the Alsatians for reacting too soon to claims of persecution. He indicates that there were already many examples of bilingual usage which had not been proscribed, so why were they getting hot and bothered? However, what ensued he himself characterizes as a *terreur linguistique*, so perhaps they had a premonition of what was in store for them.

5.3.1.1 Reports of représentants

As we have noted, the way in which the central legislative bodies of the Revolution (e.g. the *Convention*) actually implemented the new policies and carried out the decrees in the various distant marginal areas such as Alsace was by sending representatives (*représentants*), who had both the function of watchdogs (to report back to the *Convention* in Paris), and also were empowered to issue edicts in certain domains. The representatives for the department of Bas-Rhin were LeBas and St-Just. When they arrived in Alsace, they found the policy of translation of decrees in a state of disarray, and very little progress in *francisation*. They assessed the situation and discovered a disorganized army, intrigues, and threats of insurrection and secession. Becoming concerned about the continued attachment of Alsatians to the German language, they believed themselves in the right (by virtue of their unlimited power) to decree the creation of a French school in every commune of the *département* of Bas-Rhin. This was to be paid for by local resources, and budgeted at the amount of 600,000 livres, pending the establishment of a national policy. Needless to say, response to this decree was not enthusiastic: in fact, Alsatians began to see this as a kind of linguistic *terreur*, although the term was not yet in vogue.

As many have noted, including Brunot, there are good reasons why Alsace constitutes an especially problematic case within French language policy:

1 *German princes* Alsace was not just a province belonging to the king without restrictions and reservations. German princes remained *possessioné*, that is, they retained some rights and privileges. The people had constant contact with the right bank of the Rhine.
2 *The Alsation dialect* Dialectally, one should note that the linguistic isoglosses separating various German dialects of the area cut at *right angles* to the Rhine river, not parallel to it. The Alsatian dialect is part of the *Alemannisch* dialect complex, which extends from the Vosges across the Black Forest into Swabia and down into Switzerland. Northern Alsace (now the *département* of Bas-Rhin) has more in common dialectally with dialects just across the Rhine than it does even with the dialects of Southern Alsace (Haut-Rhin). Before industrialization brought air pollution, the cathedral of Strasbourg was visible to a large territory in Baden (Germany) and was a unifying symbol for people living on both sides of the Rhine.
3 *The Protestant Reformation* The people of Alsace and especially of Strasbourg were early and strong supporters of Martin Luther and did not want French Calvinist Huguenots settling there, especially at Strasbourg. Further, Louis XIV forbade the Reformed Church of Strasbourg from having its ministers use French in any way (for fear it would spread further?).
4 *The university in Strasbourg* The university had been founded when the dominant cultural language was German. Though at this point lectures were still given in Latin (German was not to become the general language of instruction in German universities until after the French Revolution), it was seen as a stronghold of *germanitude*. Germany's greatest poet, Johann Wolfgang Goethe, studied for a while at Strasbourg, and rhapsodically praised its cathedral in an essay entitled *Über deutsche Baukunst*, 'On German architecture'. German universities taught theology, and

this one maintained both a Protestant and a Catholic divinity school, which were both anathema to the Revolution.[12]

5.3.1.2 Failure of the translation policy

From the point of view of Paris and the *Convention*, the policy of translation now began to seem doomed to failure, and given the negative comments from representatives LeBas and St-Just, according to which the translation policy simply played into the hands of secessionists, the ensuing climate of terror unleashed by the representatives seemed justified. Brunot shows that in Alsace the translation policy actually made better progress than anywhere else, since German was a language capable of expressing most, if not all, of the ideas of the Revolution. Later a kind of essentialism developed, and it became fashionable to claim that only the French language was capable of expressing the ideas of liberty, equality, fraternity, etc., that French was the best language, and that French civilization was co-terminous with humanism and human civilization.

Brunot also wants to show that though the Alsatians were getting edgy about supposed controls to translation, they really had a free hand during this period. On 10 August, 1793 a correspondent from Colmar wrote that the *Convention* assured them complete independence. Even at a *culte de la raison* on *27 brumaire an II* German was used to inaugurate it. On the other hand it was difficult to find translators in every locality where they were needed, and since the French Revolution was coming up with new lexical items every day, as well as new meanings for old words,[13] it was very difficult to find an exact word that did not convey some meaning left over from the *ancien régime*. Thus it was very difficult to show that the translation policy was really working, and to satisfy the more radical revolutionaries. As we have noted, regional languages became tainted with the nuance of separatism, of counter-revolution, of resistance to the reforms, and they have retained this taint to the present day.

5.4 LINGUISTIC CULTURE IN ALSACE

Much as been written about the use and domains of French, German and Alsatian dialect in Alsace. What is not so clear from most descriptions is what kind of multilingualism we see exhibited in Alsace, and how this has changed over the centuries. Another way of putting it is to ask what kinds of sociolinguistic models we have to characterize what appears to some to be bilingualism, to others a curious kind of language mixing, and to others a horrible *salade* or *Kauderwelsch* or linguistic mish-mash.[14] Some writers even claim (e.g. Philipps 1975, quoting the poem of Weckmann) that Alsace is part of a larger linguistic culture, *la rhénanie* or what we might call the Upper Rhineland, a culture situated on both sides of the broad Rhine plain and distributed in three separate polities – that is France, Germany and Switzerland.

5.4.1 Sociolinguistic models

In terms of modern sociolinguistic approaches to the language situation in Alsace, there seems to be general agreement that what we have here is an example of diglossia in both the Fergusonian (1959a) sense, and in the Fishman (1967) sense, that is Alsatian is part of a 'genetic' diglossia with German, and it is part of an 'extended' diglossic relationship with French. Together they constitute a triglossia, to the extent that German even remains a viable part of the picture. There is also agreement that language *use* in Alsace exhibits characteristics of what is known as *code-switching,* since one often gets mixed samples of both Alsatian and French, in the same sentence, spoken by the same speaker. This differs from *lexical borrowing*, which would be to incorporate a French or German word in what is essentially a sentence of Alsatian, or vice versa. In code-switching, whole phrases are juxtaposed from both languages: we can also discern certain kinds of tendencies, such as beginning a conversation in one language and then switching to another; the use of politeness phrases from one language (i.e. one language is felt to be 'more polite' than another, or more emphatic, or more solidary, etc.). Seen by lay analysts, code-switching is often thought of as indiscriminate mixing and 'bad use', that is it is 'bad for people' or children or whatever to observe this or be observed. The idea that code-switching might be rule-governed does not occur to such casual observers.

Vassberg's study (1993) concentrates on conversations that perforce exhibit code-switching behaviour: one would have to conclude that almost no discourses exist in Alsace that are totally in Alsatian, except perhaps between elderly, rural people whose schooling did not involve much French – even then certain politeness formulae would probably be in French. The amount of switching then varies all the way to almost totally French conversations, with occasional Alsatian phrases, such as one I observed in a Strasbourg bank:

Alors, dix-neuf cent quatre-vingt cinq francs. *schtimts*?

'All right, nineteen hundred eighty-five francs. *Correct*?'

The following example from Vassberg is perhaps typical:

B: *Also, A ich will Di nit länger ufhalta* embrasse tous de ma part, et puis à samedi.

A: A samedi donc, et puis bon après-midi en dépit du temps.

B: Merci, *hoffentlich hammer schener watter.*

A: *Jo, jo,* c'est vrai, ce s'rait quand même mieux, hein, *wenn's nit ragna.*

B: Oui, oui.

A: Enfin ça fait rien *ma müess namma was kummt he.*[15]

(1993: 91)

Vassberg's analysis of this kind of activity shows how all kinds of different motivations are involved in the use of material from different languages. It is clear from the above that neither speaker has any problem in expressing themselves in either language, so switching from one to another is not done from a lack of facility in either language, or to gain advantage over the other speaker. Rather, choices are made to express solidarity and co-operation, to ratify previous decisions, to negotiate meanings, and in effect to express or construct meanings that are more obvious at the discourse level than at the lexical level. For Vassberg, following LePage and Tabouret-Keller (1985), these are 'acts of identity' that are specific to the Alsatian context. Saying the same thing in French or Alsatian only, would not be the same, and a mere translation into a third language also fails to express what code-switching 'means' here. We must keep in mind that each chunk of discourse takes its cues from the very specific characters involved: no two speakers, no matter how embedded in Alsatian identity, would make the same choices, but any discourse would make sense to others in the speech community, given the gender, age, residence (urban or rural), and educational level of the speakers. Each conversation is therefore both idiosyncratic and very typical at the same time. As with much linguistic activity, there may be an element of virtuosity involved, that is, it is something that only certain people can do well, and were this ability to be lost, something unique would also be lost.

So we see that Alsace is a diglossic speech area, meaning that different languages have different functions or roles, but we also see that in certain situations there seems to be overlap, and then we get code-switching, which seems to express something of its own, and is not to be thought of as a failure of some sort.

5.4.1.1 Other kinds of studies

Vassberg (1993) provides a very useful review of different kinds of studies that have been carried out recently in and on Alsatian:

- General descriptions: Verdoodt (1968); Olson (1974); Stephens (1976).

- Alsace in the context of other minority languages of France: Tabouret-Keller (1981).

- Regional advocates/activists: for example Philipps (1975, 1978, 1982).

- Educational and pedagogical issues: Vogler (1974); Hug (1975); Woehrling (1983).

- Statistical studies: based on data from INSEE (Institut National de la Statistique et des Etudes Economiques), a government body that does opinion research and census studies.

Many of these studies are descriptive or focus on explaining language shift, or decrying it. Many are arm-chair analyses, not based on empirical research or observation, while others limit their questions or focus on specific predetermined variables (age, sex, education, residence) but allow respondents to give answers without observing actual language use. Vassberg's preference is for the 'micro'-type of study, focusing on 'how speakers exploit their linguistic resources as a means of projecting their social identity' (Vassberg 1993: 29). Thus her emphasis is on individual variation, and eschews the broad-brush studies listed above, though exploiting them as revelatory of many of the social variables in question.

5.4.2 Diglossia and triglossia in Alsace

The history of Alsace is undeniably closely associated with various German states (Holy Roman Empire, Second Reich, Third Reich) interspersed with periods of French hegemony, and the various conflicts and facts of the situation are well known (Lévy 1929). Both France and Germany, as we have seen, have been eager to cleanse Alsace of the taint of the other culture and to show how deeply attached it was to their own polity and culture. The idea that Alsace exhibited its own linguistic culture, blending elements of the dominant others, has never been allowed to gain credibility. This is exactly what we ought to be focusing on in our discussion – what kind of linguistic culture now prevails (or prevailed until recently) in the Upper Rhine basin, on both sides of the river, between Strasbourg and Basel. An examination of the linguistic history of the area reveals that this area (known as *Rhénanie* in French) is part of a dialect area known as *Alemannisch*, specifically lower Alemannic (*Nieder-Alemannisch*), which encompasses most of Alsace, the state of Baden in Germany, and then proceeds on south into German Switzerland, all of which is classified as *Alemannisch*.

Whatever else happened or happens in the politics of the area, the people who speak this dialect see themselves as having a common history, troubled as it may be, and dialect speakers sometimes share more commonality with their brothers and sisters on the other side of the Rhine than they do with speakers 30 miles north or south of them: the isoglosses (dialect boundaries) within Alemannic run essentially east–west, rather than north–south. Germans from Baden can go to Strasbourg, speak dialect, and be understood. Swiss from Basel can cross easily into either France or Germany and not have to give up their linguistic identity for the day. Alsatians in increasing numbers cross both borders to work, and Strasbourg newspapers (such as *Dernieres Nouvelles d'Alsace*) carry advertisements for such employment *in German*.

But the existence of a common spoken dialect is not the whole picture, because in each of the three polities the relationship of dialect to standard language is different. Swiss-Germans are in a diglossic relationship between dialect and standard German, but their use of the latter is in exclusively written domains. Alsatians are in a diglossic linguistic culture involving French as H and dialect as L, and Germans are members of a diglossic linguistic culture in which diglossia is officially ignored, and is in the process of being *levelled*[16] so that the attitude toward the H-norm (*Hochdeutsch* in two of the cases, and French in the other) is different in the three linguistic cultures even though the linguistic habits and speech forms (of the L-form) may be almost the same. Germans from southwestern Baden who cross the border to do business in Basel find it curious and not unpleasant that the L-variety has more domains and is more highly valued on the southern side of the border: in their own linguistic territory they would be more likely to have to switch to *Hochdeutsch* or a regional variety of it, in an urban environment such as in Freiburg or Offenburg. Similarly, Swiss or Germans from the region who attempt to use their L-variety in Alsace (e.g. in Strasbourg) find it acceptable up to a point: but because code-switching with French also has certain rules and expectations, a conversation carried on in L can only go so far, and only with a certain percentage of the population.[17] There is also some residual hostility towards people of Baden who were resettled in Alsace after 1871 to serve as bureaucrats, officials, school-teachers, etc., since they could handle tasks requiring a knowledge of German, which Alsatian dialect speakers could not. These *Badois* cannot be identified by their speech or any other social characteristics, but if their ancestry is known, they tend to be shunned by 'true' Alsatians. Such persons are of course suspected of collabouration with the Germans in World War II, if not of other offences.

5.4.3 *La Loi deixonne* of 11 January, 1951

A discussion of the rights of regional languages would not be complete without mention of *la Loi deixonne*, a law passed in 1951 that seemed to relax somewhat France's monolingual educational policy. In fact the effects of this law are exaggerated: the law charged the *Conseil supérieur de l'Education nationale* to 'research the best methods to facilitate the study of local languages and dialects in regions where they are in use'.[18] Teachers are encouraged to use local languages in elementary schools and nursery schools, especially in teaching French. Teachers who request permission may spend an hour a week studying the language, which is *optional* for the students. Other articles concern the purchase of books and materials, the training of teachers, instruction at the secondary level, and provisions for higher education. Para. 10 states that the previous articles are applicable to Breton, Basque, Catalan and Occitan: the German language, or the Alsatian dialect, are not mentioned. But in a separate decree, dated 18 December, 1952, instruction in German is optional in schools in areas where the Alsatian dialect is in use: two hours per week in the last two years of elementary school is permitted for children whose parents have requested it. The following day this decree was followed by an *arrêté ministériel*, requiring *written* permission of legal guardians, and subtracting the time spent from physical education and other directed activities (Falch 1973: 218–19).

In reality, the Deixonne law has had little effect: none of the coursework was required, and was not tested at any level as a condition for graduation to higher levels of education. Other attempts to either expand the Deixonne law, or expand legal domains for languages other than French, have been proposed, but have not passed.[19]

5.4.4 Alsace: a failed triglossia – a failing diglossia?

In French Alsace the existence of two standard languages, *Hochdeutsch* and (standard) French has always been seen as a *competition* for dominance of the H-variety domains instead of as a dynamic structured interaction. That the spoken language of Alsace has until recently always been predominantly Alsatian dialect(s)[20] is also broadly noted. During the earliest period of French hegemony, and continuing into the German Empire period (1871–1918), a great deal of latitude for *Hochdeutsch* and/or French as competing H-varieties was allowed, and many Alsatians could report that they grew up bilingual in *Hochdeutsch* and French. Albert Schweitzer comments in his autobiography (Schweitzer 1931: 52) on the good fortune of having both German and French (and of course dialect) at his disposal. Although he was born after Alsace reverted to the German Empire, French was a language with its own domains even during that 48-year period.

What was usually not recognized by either regime, of course, was that Alsatian was *not* the same as *Hochdeutsch*, that is, neither regime recognized that there was a triglossic situation in effect, with two H-varieties in uneasy competition (and sometimes truce), but with an L-variety that occupied a very different position from *Hochdeutsch* in the hearts and minds of Alsatians than was thought to be the case by either sets of authorities. Only the Alsatians themselves recognize the difference. Philipps puts it as follows:

> Alsatian culture is the culture which *today's Alsatian* can and must be able to acquire by combining French, German and Alsatian elements which *together* give the culture *lived* in the Alsatian milieu its specifically Alsatian mark.[21]
>
> (1982: 151)

But a deaf ear has always been turned to their situation by both regimes. Some writers look wistfully to their Swiss neighbours, where German–French bilingualism in, for example the Swiss railways exists without great trauma to the employees who have to master a few phrases in each language. But in many ways the triglossia of Alsace has more parallels with that of Luxembourg reported by Verdoodt (1972), but without, of course, the institutional protection for the three varieties.

In 1956, for example, as part of the Census of that year, the French government carried out an extensive survey to determine to what extent the citizens of the *départements* of Haut-Rhin, Bas-Rhin and Moselle knew German, French and dialect. When they had determined that the only segment of the population that did not know French were over 65 years of age (people *scolarisé* before 1918 who had remained in rural areas or engaged in professions not requiring the knowledge of French) they considered the 'danger' of bilingualism to be past, and that their efforts to reintegrate these areas and their populations could be abandoned.[22]

What has never been permitted by the French in their periods of hegemony (1648–1870; 1918–40; 1945 to present) is any protection of any H-variety domains for *Hochdeutsch*. This is as much a reflection of French centrist monopolistic language policy as it is anything else. At least in the German Empire period French was never banned, and was even used as a language of elementary education in certain areas (Lévy 1929: 388) – albeit with the notion that this was a transitional phase. It is interesting, however, that the resistance to the *Verdeutschung* of Alsace-Lorraine in the Prussian period took the form of increased loyalty to *dialect*. Since French was not available as a language of resistance, loyalty to dialect and expansion of it into even H-domains (literary works, etc.) became the way to say 'no' to Germanization (Phillips 1975: 160): in fact it was a way of saying that Alsatians were neither French nor German, but *'un petit peuple qui n'acceptait pas qu'on portât atteinte à sa personnalité, sous quelque forme que ce fût'* (Phillips 1975: 161). From 1918 until 1940 centrist French policy became more obdurate, and this was followed by an even more hard-nosed policy during the Nazi period, when public use of French on the street was banned, and monolingual French speakers were deported into the occupied zone of northern France (Alsace having been incorporated into the Reich). This policy had the effect of outraging even Germanophile Alsatians, who still saw a role for French in H-domains in Alsace, so from 1945 onward the pendulum swung away from strong claims for bilingualism at the H-level even by erstwhile Germanophile Alsatians. The National-Socialists' language policy in occupied territories as well as in the Reich provoked exactly the opposite effect to what was intended – in both France (Alsace) and Alemannic Switzerland any residual sympathy for *Hochdeutsch* was obliterated and has resulted in an accelerated shift to French in almost all H-domains in Alsace, and the shift to L-variety Swiss dialects in many former H-domains in Alemannic Switzerland.

In Alsace, triglossia is now for all intents and purposes, dead: the question now is whether *diglossia* will survive, or whether there are any reserved domains for L (dialect) still viable. The latest studies indicate that while L can still be heard even in shops in urban Strasbourg (Gardner-Chloros 1985; Vassberg 1993) banks, etc., upwardly mobile adults, particularly women, do not seem to be speaking it as regularly with their children, even in rural areas (Tabouret-Keller and Luckel 1981: 59). There is still some nostalgia for former periods, and quite a cottage industry in books on the topic (both in French and in German), most of them bemoaning the insensitivity of both regimes for the special circumstances of Alsace.[23] Recently there seems to have been an upswing in the use of *Hochdeutsch*, albeit mostly passive, due to the flood of tourists from Germany, the response to which has been to train many young *dialectophones* in *Hochdeutsch* in order to cater to these money-laden foreigners. Another passive use is in the media, since German television (e.g. the *Südwest-Funk*) can be received easily in Alsace, and is generally thought to be more interesting than French programming.[24] A third passive use is that Alsatian dialectophones can sometimes get better-paying jobs in Germany and Alemannic Switzerland than they can in France: certain middle-level supervisory jobs (though not higher-level management jobs, because of their lack of literacy in *Hochdeutsch*) are available to Alsatians, whose services are preferred over guest workers (*Gastarbeiter*) from southern Europe because of their ability to converse with their superiors in a comprehensible form of German (i.e. Alemannic) and advertisements for such positions regularly appear (in *Hochdeutsch*) in newspapers such as *Les Dernières Nouvelles d'Alsace*.[25] Alsatians of this category can use their L-variety dialect as a spoken language in southern Germany and Alemannic Switzerland, and have the added advantage that they can also speak French, which is of some value in Germany for communication with Italians and Spaniards, and of course in Switzerland for communication with French-speaking Swiss. One can still find persons born in Alsace who cannot speak French, but they are now very aged.

5.4.5 Bilingualism in nursery schools: January, 1993

Given all this pessimism, it was with some astonishment that observers witnessed the signing, on 7 January, 1993, of an 'accord' between the state (*l'Etat*) and the *département* of Haut-Rhin, that is upper

Alsace, to begin bilingual classes in nursery schools – at the instiga-
tion of the *département*.[26] This accord was signed by Jack Lang, then
France's Minister of Education and Culture, Jean-Jacques Weber,
President of the General Council of Haut-Rhin, Alain Boyé, *Inspec-
teur d'Académie du Haut-Rhin* (an official of the departmental school
system), and Jean-Paul de Gaudemar, *Rector de l'Académie* of Strasbourg, each of whom committed themselves to public funds to reward
and recruit special teachers, pay for teacher training, etc. The accord
also foresaw expansion of the bilingual programmes into the lower
elementary grades, and perhaps the upper grades, with, for example
the possibility of examinations in history or geography in one of
France's regional languages. Similar agreements had already been
signed in the Basque region, and provisions for teacher certification
via CAPES (*Certificat d'Aptitude à l'Enseignement Secondaire*) have
been set up in the Occitan, Breton, Corsican, Catalan and Basque
regions, as was now done in Alsace.

The accord of 7 January, 1993, can be interpreted in two different
ways. One is that it is a momentous event, and promises to allow
France's regional languages to recapture domains now reserved for
French. We know that if a language has no young speakers, it stands
little chance of survival. On the other hand, as far as I can determine,
the accord received no attention outside Alsace. Parisian newspapers
such as *Le Monde* and *Figaro* ignored the event, though it took place
in Paris and not in Mulhouse. Perhaps a similar agreement will be
signed between the ministry of education and culture and the *départements* of Bas-Rhin and Moselle, but we are not holding our breath.
The socialist government of M. Bérégovoy is now out of power, and
M. Lang, who seems to have taken special interest in this bilingual
project, is no longer minister of education and culture. Whether these
initiatives will flourish or wither on the vine is anybody's guess. But
the accord at least seems to signal a reversal, if only temporarily, and
perhaps trivially, of France's monolingualism, which we have seen
displayed so prominently in these chapters. Perhaps it is only a blip:
perhaps it is the beginning of a sea change. Perhaps with European
Economic Integration the power of large states (*l'Europe des patries*)
will wane, and various minority groups will flower (*l'Europe des
ethnies*).

6 Indian linguistic culture and the genesis of language policy in the subcontinent

6.1 WHERE DO LANGUAGE POLICIES COME FROM?

We live in an age where increasing attention is paid to what is known as 'multiethnic diversity', and part of this attention is focused on issues of language. Nowadays it is not uncommon in discussions about language policy[1] for someone eventually to ask 'Why does there have to be a language policy? Why do we have to have a standard language? Why can't people just do what they like with language?' My reply is that whether or not there are explicit language policies, there will always be *implicit policies*, that is, there are cultural assumptions about language, about correctness, about the 'best' way to talk or write, and even if there is no explicit policy, these assumptions will constitute the implicit policy. That is, there is no such thing as *no language policy* – there is always a policy, whether or not it is explicit. Abolishing the explicit rules about language, or declaring 'standard' languages to be nothing but a 'myth' or an ideology does not make the cultural assumptions underlying these concepts automatically disappear.

An area of the world where we find very ancient cultural concerns about language is India and the South Asian subcontinent. If we wish to examine the origin of language policy in South Asia, we must first confront a whole set of cultural assumptions about where *languages* come from, and what purpose they serve in the scheme of things. That is, the conceptions of what is language, what is not language, what is language for, who may use it, and what powers it has over human behaviour, have deep roots in Indic culture, and have for a very long time perplexed those who have grappled with questions concerned with language policy. One cannot have a policy about language in India without being able to say that Sanskrit is a language and that the language of the *mleccha*s is not, or that Hindi is (or is not) a separate language from Urdu. The former question was the first one asked, and the latter question and others like it have been asked again and again, but have not in fact been satisfactorily answered.

Language-policy analysts would ideally like to have facts about language at their disposal when they analyse language policies, and they often turn to linguists to provide them with such facts. Under British rule, the Government of India asked George Grierson (1903–28) to come up with some answers, but his survey simply raised more questions than it answered. Disentangling a language from a dialect, finding clear dialect and language boundaries to correspond with political boundaries, etc. has been a problem in many polities: there is no time here to review all these controversies, except to say that hard facts are difficult to come by. I refer the reader to the review of this issue presented by Shapiro and Schiffman (1981: 16–107): but recall that even in the absence of hard facts, policy-makers have been known to make decisions that presuppose fact rather than fiction.[2] What they are doing when they do this, is what this book is about – trying to delineate where policies about language come from when they do not rest on hard data.

6.1.1 Language-policy study in the subcontinent

When one considers language policy and its operation in India today, it seems to be standard practice to look primarily at the outcome of the policy deliberations that led to the promulgation of the Constitution of 1950, and its 1965 revisions on language. Some daring souls even look back to the development of a policy by the Indian National Congress in the 1920s;[3] truly audacious researchers might hark back to the Macaulay Minute of 1835, but few turn their attention any further back.

In this chapter, as in this book in general, I am going to take the approach that a study of language policy in India (or anywhere, for that matter) cannot rely solely on overt, official, *de jure*, explicit, codified 'text' about language policy. I believe that an understanding of language policy in India (or anywhere else) requires also that we look at what I call covert (implicit, unofficial, unstated, unwritten, *de facto*) language policy. I will focus primarily on establishing some fundamental notions about South Asian *linguistic culture*, which is the sum totality of ideas, values, beliefs, attitudes, prejudices, myths, religious strictures, and all the other cultural 'baggage' that South Asians bring to their dealings with language from their culture. Since South Asian linguistic culture is deeply concerned with the transmission and codification of language(s) used in the area, we also need to examine what notions of the value of literacy and the sanctity of texts are current in the area.

The perspicacious reader will note that there is a great deal of difference between covert policy in a linguistic culture like that of the United States, and covert policy in a polity like Tsarist Russia. In the first, covert policy is in fact *the* policy, since there is at the federal level in the USA *no* overt explicit policy. In the case of Tsarist Russia, the covert policy (as exemplified by Poland pre-1918) was in deep conflict with the overt policy. It was underground and in fact *subversive*, and was successful in circumventing official policy, while still paying lip-service to it.[4]

In Nagaland, in northeast India (Sreedhar 1974), the policy of overt use of English and covert use of Nagamese is a compromise, since Nagamese, though it is the only language that all Nagaland children understand, lacks the prestige to be fitting as an official language of education or the state. Assamese, though known by many, is not acceptable for political reasons, so English, prestigious and neutral, makes a nice face-saving solution. In Nagaland, just as in the USA, rather than being subversive, the covert policy is supported at all levels by majority culture members, and is only in conflict with it when squabbles arise over the use of other languages (e.g. in education).

Though I have identified only two kinds of covert policies ('promotive/supportive' and 'subversive') one could conceive of other possibilities that might be applicable in other linguistic cultures. I want only to show that what India had at at least one point in its history was a covert policy that was in tune with the overt policy, but that the advent of colonialism and the Independence Movement brought in ideas about policy ('monism') that were no longer in tune with its long-standing linguistic culture, and finally resulted in an overt policy that was dramatically out of line. In fact, I will argue, the 1950 policy was without any doubt a clone of the Soviet model developed and implemented by Lenin in the USSR in the 1920s (and by Stalin in the 1930s), with the role occupied by Russian in that policy tailored for Hindi in India's policy. More or less slavish imitation of this policy, I claim, has led to incongruities that have plagued the policy from its inception to this day, and are now quiescent only because of the stalemate arrived at in Shastri's 'Three-Language Formula' of 1964–5.

6.2 LINGUISTIC CULTURE AND LANGUAGE POLICY IN SOUTH ASIA

It is no secret that South Asian culture is one of extreme linguistic diversity,[5] the parameters of which are on a scale and of a nature that are difficult to imagine for someone who is accustomed to conditions in a monolingual egalitarian society. But not only is there this great diversity and complexity, the culture is also one that is highly concerned with language: it is one that has been concerned with language, with the transmission of its culture through language, and with the codification and regulation of language from its earliest records.[6] The very existence of the earliest texts as we know them today is dependent on this concern for language and its control. That is, the existence of these concerns, myths, attitudes and elaborate cultural 'baggage' about language are evidence for what I am calling not only linguistic culture, but a highly developed, deeply seated, long-standing tradition of linguistic culture.

In India,[7] language is tied up with religion, it is affiliated with caste and social structure, it differs from region to region, group to group, and cannot be understood without reference to the long-recorded history of the region.

6.3 LANGUAGE IN ANCIENT INDIA

Scholars who study language policy in Europe and correlate it with the Renaissance and the rise of nation states, expect South Asian language policy to have its roots in the same phenomena. Superficially, of course, this kind of development can be discerned. Yet the existence of classical languages such as Sanskrit and Tamil cannot be ignored, allegiance to which is strong in modern India, and which cannot be overlooked in the development of a language policy. The fact that Sanskrit was codified in Pāṇini's grammar in non-metrical *sútra*s in perhaps 500 BCE, and that Tolkāppiyanār's grammar of Tamil dates from around the beginning of the CE, the fact that students still can learn Sanskrit and Tamil at the feet of pandits by the time-honoured rote methods worked out millennia ago, attest to an unbroken linguistic and cultural tradition that still influences thoughts and feelings about language in South Asia today. Though modern linguistics as developed and practised in the West since the early nineteenth century is inextricably linked both to the 'discovery' of Sanskrit by Europeans in the late eighteenth century[8] and to the discovery along with it of the Indian grammatical tradition that itself enabled the transmission of this culture, modern linguists in the subcontinent have to fight a thousand battles to get modern Indian students of language to disengage themselves from Pāṇini and Tolkāppiyaṉār and look at the modern languages as independent from their classical precursors.

Perhaps the most salient feature of ancient Indian linguistic culture was the concern for the preservation of sacred texts and the purity of the language in which they were composed. This concern arose out of the willingness of the society not only to commit the resources (time, human resources, energy, material resources) for this transmission, but also to the development of a technique that would guarantee the purity and constancy of the texts. The decision or strategy devised was to commit the sacred texts to memory and to transmit the sacred texts orally, but in a highly controlled way that was rightly felt to be the only way to avoid the introduction of error into the texts. As anyone who has witnessed a demonstration of this technique can attest, the outcome seems to be fairly foolproof,[9] better anyway than via literacy and handwritten transmission, where scribal error and individual additions and emendations can often be introduced.

The reliance on orality is motivated in part by the power of spoken words to invoke the intervention of the gods. In the Indic tradition, if the text has been learned in the proper way, and by the proper person[10] then the power of the word, when spoken, is irrevocable – the gods *must* act, and will act. Writing the word on paper (stone, copper, whatever) is not a substitute for pronouncing it. The utterance of an invocation is thus automatically what modern speech-act theorists would call a *performative* speech act. In the saying of the word, something is also *done*, and cannot be undone. Indian literature is full of tales in which a word was misused, uttered capriciously or wrongly, with mischievous or even disastrous consequences. The term 'magic' comes to mind here, and in some ways the power of words can be seen as magic: but this is not mere magic.

This oral tradition is in some sense the epitome of orality, and not just a poor substitute for literacy. It differs from puristic traditions of other sorts (religions of 'the book') where language is kept pure because it is holy, the word of God, the truth immutable.[11] In traditions such as Islam, the Qur'an is the word of God, and cannot be changed. But the word of God is kept in a book (the Qur'an) so that mortals can consult it to see what God has said. The purpose of the Indic oral tradition is to enable mortals to speak to (the) God(s), not to know what God has spoken to mortals. And if one is going to speak to God effectively, one must do it in a way that has been pre-ordained.

We are dealing here with two cultural ideas, one a concern for the purity of language, another for the mode of transmission or preservation for future generations. The mode of transmission, orality, involved memorization from a young age, and the willingness to devote great amounts of the society's labour and resources to achieve the goal of maintenance and transmission of this textual tradition. Having set this in motion, it also became a cultural value to preserve the infrastructure needed to propel the system – a system of gurus, pandits, disciples, and in some cases monasticism – and of course the caste system with a special niche and privileges for the (hereditary) priesthood.

Cultural literacy in ancient India, though at first totally oral and focused on the magical power of language, became wrapped up in the issue of transmission and survival of the culture. This has been summarized quite succinctly by Madhav Deshpande:

> The Aryans generally looked at the mass of non-Aryans from a singular perspective. . . . Thus, all the non-Aryans seem to have been normally lumped together in the category of Dāsas. . . . The non-Aryan language could not have pleased the Aryan gods, and hence was held to be ritually inferior to the Aryan language . . . [and] . . . nondivine language at the very least.
>
> (1979: 2–3)

As the Vedic Aryans gradually moved into the interior of India, they began adjusting themselves to the local scene. . . . At the same time, the Aryan language of the early Vedic texts was fast becoming archaic, and new forms of Aryan language had begun to develop. This forced the Aryans to look at their own language more carefully, and herein lies *the beginning of linguistic speculation in India*. This stage is reflected in the later Saṃhitās and in the *Brāhmaṇa* literature, and Pāṇini (about 500 BC) probably marks the end of this stage.

This concern led to the development of many technical sciences, of which phonetics, etymology and grammar are particularly significant in this respect. Here we find an attempt to capture and define various aspects of the Aryan language as it had been orally preserved in the ancient texts, and also an attempt to describe the Aryan upper-class language as it was currently spoken.

However, we must not forget that this most normal title *bhāṣā*, 'language', in fact refers to the spoken dialect of the upper classes. . . . We may safely assume that other forms of Indo-Aryan, and the non-Aryan languages, were viewed as 'substandard' languages, as those peoples themselves were placed in the lower slots of the social hierarchy. . . . Thus, during this period, there seems to be a general idea emerging among the upper-class Aryans that the lower forms of Indo-Aryan as well as the non-Aryan languages were somehow substandard and inferior.

(Deshpande 1979: 3–4, emphasis added).

The origin of the Mīmāṁsā conception that language is eternal lies in the Brahmanical concern for preservation of the Vedas which the Mīmāṁsākas shared with the Sanskrit grammarians. However, this conception of eternality of language is not a universal principle, but it applies only to Sanskrit. To be more specific, only the Sanskrit language is the eternal language, while all the *apabhraṁśa* 'fallen, substandard' languages are noneternal.

(1979: 18)

One could give many more examples of this, but it is clear that the groundwork was laid at an early stage for all kinds of infrastructure to preserve the language, and that attitudes about high and low language were extant from the earliest recorded history. What we must also assume is that although the Aryans saw themselves at the top with all other peoples and languages in an undifferentiated mass below them, those below them did not accept the lack of differentiation, but in fact applied the same dichotomy to themselves and people/languages they felt were below *them*. That is, even *mleccha*s like Tamils also imbibed these attitudes and hierarchized themselves in the same manner. Thus there were high Tamils, and there was good Tamil (*centamiṟ*), and there were lower Tamils and 'broken' Tamil (*koḍuntamiṟ*), and we can see that this kind of attitude was prevalent all the way down: even the tribal peoples of the Nilgiri Hills of South India hierarchize themselves, as Emeneau describes.

In the local caste system of the Nilgiris, the Todas rank highest. Small as the community is, numbering approximately 600 people, it has a most complex social structure.

(1964: 332)

They are peculiar, even a self-consciously peculiar, people, as befits a segment at the top of a local caste system of the Hindu type.

(1964: 340)

My point here is not so much to document these aspects of Indic linguistic culture (which in any event are well known to classical

Indologists, at least) but to show that this linguistic culture, often thought of as only a thin veneer, or a characteristic of only a tiny minority in the society, is deeply suffused through Indian culture, so intrinsically rooted that even illiterates of the lowest castes share the same value-system about language, its preservation, perpetuation, and its pivotal role in the transmission of the culture. Thus for the pre-literate (or only orally literate) Toḍas, we can discern three distinct varieties of speech: spoken Toḍa, sung Toḍa (not automatically comprehensible to someone knowing spoken Toḍa) and trance-language Toḍa (probably a pidginized kind of Malayalam, but as yet unresearched). The central position of Toḍa songs in Toḍa culture has been documented thoroughly by Emeneau (1964, 1974).

So whereas in some cultures the attitudes toward language held by educated élites may be scorned, despised, or simply ignored by less privileged members of the society, such that it would be easy to conceive of removing these élites and substituting some other policy or set of attitudes, in Indian culture such a notion is inconceivable. (This has deep repercussions for what came later, as I will show[12]).

To make a long story short, the evidence for the claim that Indian culture has devoted an inordinate amount of resources to linguistic culture, its preservation and transmission lies in the following:

1 The existence of a hereditary priesthood: guru/pandit/disciple system, dedicated to the preservation of texts.
2 Purity of text (language of the gods, word of god): desire to preserve purity of language – death to non-Brahmans who hear or learn the pure language.
3 Notion that language is eternal: there are no time limits on it – pure language does not change.
4 Existence of diglossia as a way to keep language pure and separate: freedom to use spoken language informally. Opens door for toler-ance of multilingualism, since only H-languages are pure – spoken language is outside the pale.
5 Extreme hierarchization of language: connection between language and religion.

The above are observations that can be made about linguistic culture in India, but they are not the whole story. They have implica-tions that fundamentally affect the symbolism, the instrumentality, and the perpetuation of anything having to do with language.

6.3.1 Diglossia

In this section I will focus on one factor, that of diglossia, to illustrate how by deliberately turning their back on their own indigenous values about language, India's policy-planners caused chaos in post-independence language policy. Diglossia as a concept and as a feature of language has been well known since at least the appearance of Ferguson's seminal article (1959a), and an extensive literature on the subject attests to its widespread manifestation in the languages of the world, not the least of which are those of India, classical and modern. To me it is clear that diglossia is so deeply rooted in Indian culture that it is not only probable that we will find it no matter which language we look at, it is almost an *inevitable* feature of the Indian linguistic scene. I have claimed before (Schiffman 1978) that diglossia is rooted in a concern for purity that is parallel to, if not related to, the purity/pollution complex. I would now expand this to say that it is rooted in Indian linguistic culture *per se* (witness Deshpande above). It is not just a concern for purity, but for purity of language(s) as a way of maintaining the purity of the channels for the transmission of culture. But the underside of diglossia is that all sorts of things are allowed *outside* the arena of purity, so long as they are not dignified by any attention being paid to them.

6.3.2 Diglossias of various types

Diglossia of the Ferguson (1959a) type also implies non-genetic diglossia of the Fishman (1967) type, which then licenses linguistic diversity at the grass-roots level. Since diglossias typically reserve their concern[13] for purity and uniformity at the H-level, but ignore the linguistic habits at the L-level, an illusion of uniformity and purity is maintained, while L-variety diversity can be tolerant of all kinds of things. This system thus unites the well-known diversity-within-unity paradox that India is famous for: unity at the top (H), overt level, diversity at the unofficial L-variety level.

Note that the regulation of language here is a kind of language *policy*. It falls within the realm of what is called 'corpus planning' – structural control of the H-variety in order to control its accuracy. It is also an example of 'status planning', in that it regulates the status of the H-variety, and not that of the L-variety. L-variety language remains unregulated in terms of its status and its corpus.

In my understanding of language policy, the regulation of the status and corpus of the H-variety is a prime example of *overt* policy, while the non-regulation of L-variety languages is an example of covert policy. It is not the case that there is *no* policy toward the L-varieties, but that *de facto* their status is purposefully unregulated. Both of these facts, the overt and the covert, are deeply rooted in Indian linguistic culture, I would hold. Both are part of the situation that persisted for centuries, perhaps millennia, as is clear from all the evidence we have from writing about language in the subcontinent.

Occasionally, however, the stability of this H/L dichotomy would be shaken by forces from within or from outside the society. An example of an 'inside' force was that of Buddhism, which profited from the wide gap between the ritual forms of Sanskrit and the spoken vernacular by leaping into the breach and using the L-varieties as vehicles for the dissemination of Buddhism. This disturbed the system profoundly, led to a shake-down and abandonment of the exclusive dominance of Sanskrit, but still allowed diversity to flourish – Buddhist Hybrid Sanskrit, Pali and other linguistic traditions arose: Tamil was already on the ascendant in the south – but without displacing Sanskrit from its niche. Diversity was preserved.

An outside challenge to India's linguistic culture came with the arrival of Islam and the introduction of Persian as the 'official' language of the Mogul Empire. Needless to say, Persian may have claimed a domain in government, law and commerce in Mogul India, but it never displaced any other variety from its domains. It did have an effect on spoken Hindustani resulting in the development of a literary language written in Perso-Arabic script (Urdu), but again no exclusive domain was claimed by Urdu except perhaps eventually to replace *Persian* in the scheme of things.

Even the arrival of European languages (chiefly Portuguese and then English) did not deeply disturb the equilibrium of Indian linguistic culture at first (English replaced Persian), and even after Macaulay's famous Minute and the development of English-style education, English was not thought of as displacing others, but as a variety that would allow the British better to govern India and bring it into the modern world. Most of the population of India was totally unaffected by English education, since they received no education at all, in any language.[14]

Before Independence a kind of administrative and linguistic chaos, similar to the diversity of the Austro-Hungarian Empire, reigned all over India. Moslem rulers ruled over Hindus and Muslims; Hindu rajas ruled over Hindus and Muslims, and what languages they spoke was largely irrelevant (at this point there was neither *cujus regio, ejus religio* nor *cujus regio, ejus lingua*). It was not until the twentieth century that a large-scale linguistic census of India was undertaken (Grierson 1903–28) and then only in the northern parts of British India.[15]

Perhaps the greatest challenge to Indian linguistic culture originating from the impulse of English was that English education, English rule and English-imposed modernization created *expectations* that had not existed before, and created domains (e.g. Western professions, the postal and railroad system, the civil service) that were new, and with these domains, economic expectations that had hitherto not existed. As time went on it became clear that whoever controlled these domains would be crucially linked to whoever controlled the language dominating them.

6.4 LANGUAGE AND COLONIALISM

Language policy in the British period evolved along with the development of various forms of centralized rule, and can be roughly divided into at least two stages, one pre-Mutiny and the other post-Mutiny. When Europeans first came to India in the early sixteenth century, they communicated in whatever languages were already in use, which would have been Persian and Urdu at the official levels, and local languages, including Portuguese or some form of it, at the grass-roots level. We have evidence of the development and use of a specific Indo-Portuguese pidgin (later Creole) in the coastal ports from this early time, and even after the Portuguese star had waned, Dutch, Danish, British, French and other colonial powers often used Portuguese pidgin in their dealings with Indians. A number of events changed this.

6.4.1 Oriental Jones and the 'discovery' of Sanskrit

The discovery by Sir William Jones and other Orientalists that Sanskrit was probably related to European languages, but in a genetic relationship that involved descent from a common source that 'perhaps no longer exist[ed]' certainly changed the 'Orientalist' equation, no matter what critics of Orientalism might say. Sanskrit became a language that was no longer inherently exotic or 'oriental', but a language with deep affinities with European classical and modern languages. It became a *sister* language, rather than a subaltern language, and its 'discovery' had direct impetus for the development of historical and comparative linguistics, and modern linguistics in general. It spurred inquiry into the genetic relationships of the daughter (and 'grand-daughter') languages of Sanskrit by scholars and missionary-grammarians of all sorts, which perhaps raised as many questions as it solved. It encouraged efforts to standardize and modernize Indian vernaculars for use in the administration of the East India Company (and post-Mutiny, of British India), and it legitimized the status and aspirations of certain languages and discouraged the hopes of others, as linguists were forced to make decisions of various sorts about what were 'real' languages and what were 'mere dialects'.

One must not assume, however, that the 'Orientalists' (now much reviled by critics from post-modern and subaltern studies) were to carry the day on language policy in India. Though Jones and others praised Sanskrit for its 'wonderful structure, more perfect than the *Greek*, more copious than the *Latin*, and more exquisitely refined than either' (de Bary 1958: 38) these sentiments were not shared by the Anglicists who came later.

6.4.2 Missionary activity on behalf of other Indian languages

Missionary activity was, as is well known, discouraged in India until the Act of 1813, which allowed, in its thirteenth resolution, 'such measures . . . as may tend to the introduction amongst them of useful knowledge, and of religious and moral improvement' (Spear 1958: 526). Almost immediately, we begin to see missionary activity focusing on language, since it is impossible to save souls and otherwise evangelize a population if their language is not known (especially in the Protestant approach). Thus began the tradition of the missionary-grammarian, the English-educated divine[16] whose classical education (in Greek, Latin and often Hebrew) had prepared them to look at language within a particular paradigm. The list is too long even to begin to mention, but for each literary language, and for many non-literary ones as well, the nineteenth-century production of grammars, dictionaries, guidebooks, textual editions, etc., is impressive.[17]

6.4.3 The Macaulay Minute and the imposition of English

Simultaneous with this activity we have the development of another point of view, which eventually led to the momentous decision to place English education above education in Sanskrit, Arabic or Persian: the famous (or infamous) 'Minute on education' of 1835, formulated by Thomas Babington Macaulay, according to which government funds would be used to support education in English in

India, and the curriculum would be based on that prevalent in schools in England. As de Bary put it:

> The Committee on Public Instruction . . . was hopelessly divided between the 'Anglicists' and the 'Orientalists'. The former saw the need to train a host of loyal government servants able to conduct the routine clerical work of the Company. The latter feared that a Westernizing policy would offend the sensibilities of the Indian upper classes and possibly lead to their general rebellion. Seeing that a decision was needed, Macaulay ended the stalemate by supporting the Anglicists with all the weight of his influence and all the power of his pen.
>
> (1958: 36)

And Macaulay did not mince words:

> All parties seem to be agreed on one point, that the dialects commonly spoken among the natives of this part of India contain neither literary nor scientific information, and are, moreover, so poor and rude that, until they are enriched from some other quarter, it will not be easy to translate any valuable work into them. It seems to be admitted on all sides that the intellectual improvement of those classes of the people who have the means of pursuing higher studies can at present be effected only by means of some language not vernacular among them.
>
> (Macaulay, *Prose and Poetry*, quoted in de Bary 1958: 44).

Macaulay and the Anglicists were, of course, strengthened in their resolve by the great interest already evidenced among many educated Indians for an English education. Rāmmohun Roy was one of those Bengalis who had founded his own English school, and wrote to the governor-general, Lord Amherst, to protest the use of government funds to found and support (in 1823) a college for Sanskrit studies:

> We find that the government are establishing a Sanscrit [*sic*] school under Hindu pandits to impart such knowledge as is already current in India. This seminary . . . can only be expected to load the minds of youth with grammatical niceties and metaphysical distinctions of little or no practical use to the possessors or to society. The pupils will there acquire what was known two thousand years ago with the addition of vain and empty subtleties since then produced by speculative men such as is already commonly taught in all parts of India.
>
> (quoted in de Borg 1958: 41)

6.4.4 The (re)discovery of Tamil and other roots of tradition

The debate between the Anglicists and the Orientalists was not ended by the Minute of 1835, because their goals and their constituencies were different. The study of indigenous languages was not suspended with the advent of English education: it continued under the care of traditional pandits and missionary-grammarians alike, and led in fact to a polarization of language policy that had then to be resolved in post-Independence India.

In the case of Tamil, it was the missionary-grammarians such as Caldwell who helped establish the notion that Tamil and the Dravidian languages were separate genetically from Sanskrit, but it was Tamil 'Orientalists' such as U. Ve. Cuvāminātaiyar who 'rediscovered' ancient Tamil literature and made it available to a wide audience. Before 1881, when Cuvāminātaiyar first laid eyes on manuscripts written in a kind of Tamil he had never seen before, few in the Tamil tradition knew of any pre-Aryan Tamil culture.[18] The subsequent development of the Pure Tamil Movement (*tanit tamir iyakkam*), the renaissance of Tamil literature, and the development of a Dravidian political movement (Justice Party, DK, DMK) must be seen both as stimulated by and as a reaction against the rise of English education and the work of 'Orientalist' missionary-grammarians. We deal with this in more detail in the next chapter, that devoted to Tamilnāḍu.

6.5 LANGUAGE POLICY IN INDEPENDENT INDIA

Even before India gained its independence in 1947, there were attempts to evolve a policy that would be more suitable to the needs of a self-governing India than that which was in effect in the British Raj, that is a policy that favoured English. Some of the developments that had to be considered were such factors as the following:

- Gandhi's recommendation to replace English with Hindustani (not Hindi, not Urdu).

- Congress Party's language policy favouring Hindi (not Hindustani) and the first protests about this in the 1930s.

- The fragmentary hegemony of British India and the incomplete control of the territory, especially the 'Princely states'.[19]

- The feeling in some non-Hindi areas that Delhi was 'not our country' and Hindi 'not our language'.

- The pressure to reorganize the patchwork of states and principalities into linguistically-based states, beginning with the movement for a Telugu-speaking state (Andhra Pradesh) in 1953, leading to the appointment of the states Reorganization Commission, which delivered its recommendations in 1955.

6.5.1 The fatal error: the importation of the Soviet language policy model

When independence came to India, most people seemed to be in agreement that the colonial language, English, was inappropriate for Independent India. What it should be replaced with, and how, was not so clear. Since India had been rushed to independence by Mountbatten in 1947, agreement on a constitution and what it should contain had been lacking. As far as language was concerned, it was decided to appoint a Language Commission to study the matter and make some recommendations. The commissioners heard many reports, read many sources, and even made trips abroad to study other multilingual polities. Though it is not usually explicitly characterized as such, the recommendation they arrived at was essentially to adopt a modified 'Soviet' model of language policy. The most telling document in this regard is the report of the secretary of the commission, S. G. Barve, who travelled to the Soviet Union to observe conditions there and see whether the Soviet experience could serve as a model for India. His report 'note' is a very insightful analysis of the Soviet model, and he contrasts conditions in the USSR with those in India, pointing out similarities and differences as they appear to him. At several places in the report he explicitly warns against *borrowing any model without adapting it* to local conditions:

> Obviously no two cases in a field like this are exactly or even broadly similar; therefore any lessons to be had from the experience of like circumstances in other countries must be drawn with great care. Ultimately the language problem of our country can be solved only in terms of solutions we can devise ourselves for our specific requirements; it would be manifestly wrong to expect to find anywhere else a ready-made policy of prescriptions immediately applicable to our particular problems.
>
> Nevertheless, broadly-speaking the experience of the U.S.S.R. which is the only experience yet extant as to the successful tackling of multi-lingual problems would appear to lend support to the following broad propositions.

(Barve 1957 [1956]: 494)

He then lists a number of ideas, principles, and recommendations which the commissioners ought to take into account in deriving lessons from the Soviet experience. Most of them are quite laudable – the need for pragmatism and objectivity, the problems associated with a multiplicity of scripts, the desirability of promoting all languages, no matter how small, but noting the limitations of small languages for such purposes as higher education, etc. He also notes the need to teach whatever common language is chosen as a common linguistic medium as widely as possible and as systematically as possible.

But his final warning was apparently ignored by the commissioners:

> In a sense, the Indian problem is not similar to but sharply contrasted to the Russian [i.e. Soviet model]. In Russia they had a historical tradition as well as the elements of a situation in which a strong pan-Russian medium of expression was readily available; their undertaking was the comparatively easier, congenial and 'flattering' task of developing and 'enfranchising' local languages that had been suppressed under the weight of too great an insistence on the common linguistic medium. In Indian conditions the problem is that we have strong regional languages and we have to evolve anew a linguistic medium for pan-Indian purposes out of the regional language spoken by the most numerous linguistic group in the country. While the Indian problem is obviously far more difficult than the Russian problem ever was (as was readily conceded in all the numerous discussions I held with Russian scientists and scholars) the broad principles of the Russian experience are not without an element of benefit for our purposes.
>
> (Barve 1957 [1956]: 494–5)

Despite these caveats and warnings, however, it seems clear that the commissioners modelled their recommendations on the Soviet policy. Barve, and the commissioners after him, accepted at face value the pronouncements of Soviet planners on the successes and advantages of their plan, and despite Barve's careful exposition of the differences between Russian and Hindi ('the most numerous linguistic group in the country'), India's planners ploughed ahead.

That is, they saw the model that had been developed for the Soviet Union under Lenin, with Russian as *primus inter pares*, and territorial rights for other 'minority' languages, as an appropriate one for Independent India.[20] But they turned a blind eye to the differences, and with disastrous consequences.

6.5.2 The Soviet model

The circumstances underlying the development of Soviet language policy (which has now become a type or model that has been implemented in Eastern Europe, China and elsewhere) were of course rooted in the historical circumstances emerging from monolingual Tsarist Russia, and the desire to remedy the linguistic oppression inherent in that model.[21]

6.5.3 Discongruities between the Soviet model and Indian circumstances

The peculiarities of pre-Soviet and Soviet language policy can be summarized as follows:

1 Russian had been the *dominant* language in Tsarist Russia, and in the late nineteenth century had been in fact the *only* language permitted during the period of the most intense Russification (with a few exceptions, e.g. in the Grand Duchy of Finland).

2 In 1919, Russian was also the *majority* language, that is, had more speakers than all minority languages combined, and despite the dissolution of the Soviet Union, still is the majority language in the Commonwealth of Independent States (although its numerical superiority is of course being encroached upon because of the tremendous birth-rate among Turkic speakers in Central Asia) and continues to be the language used for interregional communication even among the newly independent former republics.

3 The territory associated with the Russian language was the largest territory, and Russian had been the vehicle of expansion into the Far East, as the Russian Empire expanded to the Pacific. Russian thus had a history as a *lingua franca* in every territory and region of the Soviet Union, even if feelings about it were not always positive.

4 Soviet policy was (at least at first) designed to *reduce* the hegemony of Russian, and to allow other languages to be used in many domains from which they had previously been barred. Depending upon the size of the linguistic group, some language groups that had previously not been allowed the use of their languages except for private or religious purposes found their domains expanded under Soviet policy. Even smaller groups gained domains, with their language being used for primary literacy, for example.

5 Soviet policy (covertly, of course) saw the non-Russian languages as a possible vehicle for *Sovietization* (collectivization etc.) of territories that could not be Sovietized through Russian, so the policy of new domains for previously non-literate languages was a hidden agenda of the new policy.[22]

6 Later, under Stalin, there was a tendency to emphasize the importance of Russian as a linking language, as a source for new vocabulary, and as a kind of Big Brother, a *primus inter pares* that would lead the other nationalities. Groups that had at first been allowed to use roman or Arabic script for their orthographies later (in the 1930s) found this right removed, and a Cyrillic version imposed.[23]

7 Rights of Russian speakers to schools and broad use of their language were never restricted: the right to Russian was a 'personal' one, whereas rights to other languages were strictly territorial. Russians could go anywhere in the Soviet Union and always find Russian schools available: other language groups could not.

8 A covert aim of Soviet policy was to encourage individuals and groups to assimilate to Russian, since incentives to do this were built in. The greatest incentive was that non-Russian minorities living in another non-Russian republic generally had no guarantees for their language: if Armenians living in Georgia did not wish to attend Georgian schools their only option was to attend Russian schools. No incentives to assimilate in other directions existed, and very little assimilation to other languages ever took place (Breton 1991). Similarly in India, linguistic minorities in a given other-language-dominant state are provided with few opportunities to learn their mother tongue: Indian government servants thus are provided with Hindi-medium schools, but others have to fend for themselves.

The biggest mistake of post-independence language policy in India was not that planners sought a policy that would remove English and better suit Indian circumstances, but that they chose another foreign model for their language policy, one that on the surface seemed egalitarian and multilingual but was otherwise ill-equipped for Indian circumstances.[24] In addition, they ignored the tremendous power of Indian linguistic culture and its built-in attitudes and assumptions about language, in particular the deep-rooted propensity toward *diglossia*.[25]

Error number one was to assume that in the place occupied by Russian in Soviet policy, Hindi could fit the bill for India. This was problematical for the following reasons:

1 Hindi had not been the majority language of pre-Independence India, though it was numerically superior to any other.
2 Hindi had not been the *lingua franca* in all of pre-Independence India (though it was widely used in *North* India).[26]
3 Hindi was not a prestige language in the same way that Russian was: other languages such as Urdu, Bengali and Tamil had longer literary histories and were seen by their speakers as vastly superior in prestige. (Few languages in Tsarist Russia could make this claim.)[27]
4 Planners mistook the numerical predominance of Hindi-speakers in the Congress party and its consensus about Hindi (or in fact Hindustani) as the link-language of post-Independence India, for a *national* consensus.
5 Planners failed to reckon with the *inevitability of diglossia* and the tendency of Indian linguistic culture to deliberately diglossify languages that were not diglossic to begin with. Thus the decision to make Hindustani the 'national language' played into the hands of Hindi chauvinists and pandits, who inexorably Sanskritized Hindustani,[28] making it impossible for non-Hindi speakers[29] to master. For their part, the pandits were simply acting like predictable members of the Indian linguistic culture – to them Hindustani was an inappropriate vehicle[30] for a national language, and it had to be gussied up to occupy the formal role. As Das Gupta points out (1969: 588), a century of rivalry between Hindi and Urdu had resulted in both varieties purging themselves of the vocabulary of the other classical source, while moving toward classicization from its own source. Classicization was thus confused with standardization, and divergence from the language of common speech proceeded apace. Sanskritization of Hindi was, of course, inevitable (just as Persianization of Urdu was inevitable), given the value system of Indian linguistic culture, yet it undermined any possibility that Hindi would be accepted as the national language by many non-Hindi speakers, especially the vociferous Tamil community.

Das Gupta reviews the way the task of 'developing' Hindi as a vehicle for ordinary literacy eventually passed from the Gandhian associations into the hands of the orthodox Hindi associations.[31]

By the time Hindi was declared the official language, they [the orthodox Hindi associations] alone had the manpower, skill, and tradition to contribute to and control this level of work [language planning] for Hindi. At the same time, this control enabled them to impress their favored classicalization as the dominant style of Hindi. *True to the tradition of the traditional Indian literati,* they are developing Hindi in a direction that tends to make the new Hindi a compartmentalized preserve of the Hindi literary elite. Their logic of language development seems to go contrary to the logic of mass literacy, effective access of new groups to the educated communication arena, and to social mobilization of maximum human resources in general.

(1969: 590, emphasis added)

6.6 'THREE-LANGUAGE FORMULA'

What then, is India's language policy today and what is it an expression of? As Das Gupta points out, the issue of official language eventually became more than just a language issue, it became a regional issue, since the non-Hindi states were the strongest opponents of it. They attacked the policy promulgated by the national parliament (*lok sabha*) and organized regional opposition to it. As a counter-weight to proposals made in the *lok sabha*, a conference of chief ministers of states developed a compromise formula known as the 'Three-Language Formula'. According to this proposal, three languages would be taught at the secondary-school level: English, the local language and Hindi. In Hindi areas, another Indian or European language would be taught.

In practice, of course, this proposal has been honoured in the breach more than in observance, but it took widespread rioting and loss of life to force a compromise. Meanwhile, support for Hindi that had previously been accorded to the Congress Party was transferred to other, often rabidly fundamentalist Hindu parties, thus draining Congress of its traditional support. In reality then, in Hindi areas there is little attention paid to English and even less to a third language. In non-Hindi areas, such as Tamilnāḍu, Hindi is only taught *sub rosa* if at all, while great support can be found for English (as well as Tamil, of course). In other areas, such as Kerala, a more open outlook allows the teaching of as many languages as are deemed useful.

I would argue that the 'Three-Language Formula' is in fact consonant with the traditional multilingualism and linguistic diversity of the subcontinent. It fits the linguistic culture of the area, and it rejects the monism of policy-planners who have tried to impose imported policies of the Soviet or other types. It does not make the Hindi areas happy, and it may result in the end in the disintegration of India as we know it, but as we have seen in the recent disintegration of the Soviet Union, their language policy did not succeed in making various linguistic groups happy, either. We should not expect it to succeed in India, where it was perhaps doomed from the outset, but a policy that recognizes historical multilingualism, linguistic diversity, and reverence for ancient classical languages is more likely to succeed than an imported model of any sort.[32]

What is lacking from the current policy is the unity at the top levels that I mentioned earlier: the 'Three-Language Formula' does not make it clear what is at the top, and this is perhaps its fatal flaw. Perhaps the best that could be achieved would be to enshrine Sanskrit as India's national language, and then go ahead and use any other language at the instrumental level, with no claims to sanctity, purity, antiquity, or whatever that seem to be inherent in the current quest for a language that fits the bill. What seems to have been lost is the *symbolic* function that special languages often have in various polities: India lacks a candidate for the symbolic function, though Sanskrit used to suffice. Now individual languages such as Hindi and Tamil have taken on symbolic functions, and the instrumental value of either language is diminished;[33] the tendency then is for English to take over as the instrumental language, to the detriment of all others.

6.7 GUARANTEES AT THE STATE AND REGIONAL LEVEL

One other factor that ought to be mentioned in any discussion of overall policy is what happens to small linguistic groups that are *not* given control of a territory or linguistic state, but still expect the same rights as larger groups. India has many minorities with population sizes on a par with such European nations as Denmark or the now independent Baltic states, such as Tuḷu, a Dravidian language spoken around Mangalore in Karnataka state. Tuḷu possesses a grammar, a dictionary, and a folk literature of some amplitude, but it controls no territory and has no independent script, so Kannaḍa script is used for whatever is written in Tuḷu, and Kannaḍa is the language of literacy in the area. Similarly, further north, Konkani struggles for recognition as a language separate from Marathi, though with less success: Maithili in the Hindi area is another candidate for language status, but has not been recognized.

When the Indian language-planners borrowed the Soviet model, they seem to have ignored the fine print. Though minorities as small as the Abkhazians (with a population less than 100,000 speakers (Lewis 1972: 58)) were entitled to use their language for at least elementary education in the USSR, the only guarantees that linguistic minorities (those not mentioned in the Eighth Schedule) possess at the substate level are vague references to rights to maintain the language. Language groups mentioned in the Eighth Schedule, who have a right to some schooling at state expense in areas where they are strong enough, nevertheless have little to fall back on in terms of meaningful guarantees when they feel that violations of these provisions have occurred.[34]

In order to ferret out just what rights linguistic minorities have who live in states where other languages are dominant or official, one must consult such sources as the Andhra Pradesh Government's *Brochure* (Andhra Pradesh 1989), the Karnataka Government's statement on provisions for linguistic minorities in Karnataka (Banakar 1982), or the periodic reports of the Commissioner for Linguistic Minorities in India (e.g. *Government of Republic of India 1971*). The latter outline various 'scheme[s] of safeguards for linguistic minorities', but despite avowals of freedom to language, culture, speech etc., contained in the Constitution of India (e.g. Article 29(1) which empowers people having a distinct language, script or culture to conserve the same), linguistic groups having a grievance must petition the president of India, who may direct the state to officially recognize such language. These articles were incorporated into the Constitution in the revisions of 1956. Article 350A states that:

> It shall be the endeavour of every State and of every local authority within the State to provide adequate facilities for instruction in the mother-tongue at the primary stage of education to children belonging to linguistic minority groups and the President may issue such directions to any State as he considers necessary or proper for securing the provision of such facilities.

Further, Article 350B(1) specifies that the president may appoint a special officer to investigate all matters relating to the safeguards provided for linguistic minorities. In fact the central government provisions are so weak that states have had to resort to regional solutions to these problems. Even before the Indian Constitution of 1952 was ratified, provincial (now state) education ministers met in 1949 to decide what provision of facilities for instruction through the mother tongue should be made. Then in 1956, a joint Government of

India and chief ministers of the States memorandum was issued. In 1960 the Southern Zonal Council, representing the four southernmost (Dravidian language) states, made decisions regarding safeguards of linguistic minorities, that is what rights should be guaranteed to Telugu minorities in Karnataka, Tamil minorities in Andhra, etc. But though these regulations are quite specific and useful, they are essentially *ad hoc* solutions, and depend on the good will of the states involved, rather than providing legal and statutory teeth. Some states are more proud than others of their record in this area: Indian states vary, of course, in the percentages of mother-tongue speakers. Interestingly, the state with the highest percentage of mother-tongue speakers, Kerala, with 96 per cent in 1971 (Panikkar 1985) also has the highest literacy rates. One wonders whether there is any correlation between the two.

6.8 SUMMARY: ANTIQUITY, UBIQUITY, ORALITY, DIVERSITY

Students of language policy in India may be well motivated to ask what, if anything, is distinctive about its linguistic culture, and how it is different to what is found in other puristic traditions. It seems to me that the four unique features of Indian linguistic culture are its antiquity, its ubiquity (the pervasiveness of values about language distributed widely throughout the culture, even unto the 'lowliest' tribal cultures, as we have seen with the Toḍas), the primacy of the oral tradition, and its linguistic diversity.

- *Antiquity* There are many puristic linguistic traditions in the world, and many linguistic cultures have gone through periods of purism as a result of a perceived threat from some other language. Purism is also often related to a concern for the preservation of holy or magical texts, and can be allied with religious fundamentalism of various sorts. What seems different to me about such other traditions is that the puristic phase is usually not the most ancient stage of the language. Arabic purism is closely allied to Islam and the Qur'an, but there exists a pre-Islamic Arabic literary tradition, and furthermore Islam seems to have arisen from a need to purify corruption in Arab society at the time, including a need to 'rebut', as it were, Christianity and Judaism. What seems distinctive to me about the Indic tradition is that it is so old: it is the bedrock of the culture, and has not arisen as a response to something else, except when purism is resorted to as a way to return to a former and original purity. Thus the Sanskritization of Hindi and the Pure Tamil Movement both wish to return to a former state, a linguistic Ur-paradise, when there was no mixture of language and no strife between people. The discovery of Tamil Sangam litera-ture allowed the Pure Tamil Movement, on its part, to give the Tamils back their antiquity, their ancient 'pure' state. This must be seen as a kind of empowerment that cannot be minimized.

* *Ubiquity* By this I mean the pervasiveness of Indian linguistic cultural norms – the fact that not only the Sanskrit tradition has a hierarchical view of language, with different versions of the language specialized for different domains, with diglossia deeply seated and deeply rooted in all its linguistic subcultures, even the Nilgiris tribal microcosm. Values about language and its preser-vation and tradition are shared throughout the Indic area, and multilingualism is pervasive. The tremendous linguistic diversity of the area is not accidental or exceptional, therefore: it is a *product* of the culture.

* *Orality* Another cornerstone of Indian linguistic culture is surely the reliance on orality and the elaboration of complicated methods of oral transmission of language. This continues to be one of the hardest facts about Indian linguistic culture for outsiders to the tradition (e.g. Goody 1986) to accept, because it contradicts their theoretical notions of what is possible and what is not possible. Were their theories grounded in empirical observation of Indian linguistic culture, they might be less sceptical, but to most obser-vers who have studied the culture profoundly, and to most native speakers of the tradition as well, orality and all it implies in Indian linguistic culture are fundamental and revelatory. Staal's evalua-tion of the Goody–Watt hypothesis (according to which literacy is more reliable than orality) is worth quoting:

> We thus find in India at least two traditions of transmission that are formal and more or less reliable in their preserving function. One is written and of relatively recent date; it exhibits structures that are also found in other similar traditions. The other is oral and very ancient; it is closely related to typically Indian forms of science. This latter tradition is by far the more remarkable, not merely because it is characteristically Indian and unlike any-thing we find elsewhere, but also because it has led to scientific discoveries that are of enduring interest and from which the contemporary West still has much to learn. The existence of

this latter tradition demonstrates in passing that the Goody–Watt thesis is not without important exceptions and therefore not generally tenable.

(Staal 1986: 27)

This ability to memorize things seems to be highly valued in the culture in many ways, and can be observed in many other contexts, for example, the recent press reports of a young Indian man, Mr Rajan Mahadevan, who, having already memorized the value of π to 31,811 places, has now declared his intention to memorize it (the value of π) to the millionth place. It is hard to imagine another culture on earth where anyone would even want to do this: in Indic culture it seems not at all extraordinary.[35]

- *Diversity* We have presented the view that India's great linguistic diversity has been seen as a source of conflict in the post-independence era, as India has attempted to throw off vestiges of colonialism and find a language policy that suits its own conditions. But India's linguistic diversity can be viewed not just as a problem, not just an impediment to modernization or industrialization or whatever, it can also be seen as a resource. India's linguistic diversity, I contend, is deeply rooted in its linguistic culture, and is in fact a *product* of the culture, an outcome of its cultural policy, rather than a vexatious hindrance. The 'Three-Language Formula', rather than being a stalemate, a failure of policy, is a negotiated outcome, a middle way between unfettered diversity and monolingualism. It recognizes the value of local linguistic resources and the need for a language of wider communication, indeed of international communication. It allows different interpretations of the policy, depending on local sentiments and needs. In fact, if left to their own devices, many Indians will learn more than three languages, and expect the same of their children, and of their children's children.

7 Language policy and linguistic culture in Tamilnāḍu

As we have seen in the foregoing chapter, South Asia is an area of tremendous linguistic diversity, and one that is plagued with perplexing language-policy issues. One example of a regional linguistic subculture within South Asia that is perhaps quintessentially problematical, in whatever polity it is spoken, is that of the Tamils of the Dravidian south and Sri Lanka.[1] It is one that sees itself as separate and different from Indo-Aryan culture, and it has asserted that sense of difference in many ways that have challenged the hegemony of the dominant culture in both India and Sri Lanka. In what follows, I would like to show what Tamil linguistic culture consists of, what cultural notions underlie and inform it, and how different it in fact is from the dominant cultures it is in contact with.

7.1 ANCIENT TAMIL LINGUISTIC CULTURE

It is a challenge to describe the historical development of Tamil culture and its linguistic culture without immediately plunging into a morass of imprecision, historical inexactitude, and outright mythology. This is perhaps par for the course, since Tamil linguistic culture in fact thrives on myth, as does Indian linguistic culture[2] in general. It would be convenient if we could filter out the myth for later and separate treatment, but in what follows this will not be consistently possible. As we will see, Tamils do not only rely on ancient myths in their linguistic belief system, they actively construct and continually embellish new versions of old myths as it suits their purposes. Thus attempts to separate out myth as if it were some kind of *a priori* element are necessarily fruitless.

As we have seen in the previous chapter, it seems to be agreed that the earliest record of Tamil is a grammar, the *Tolkāppiyam*, composed around the beginning of the Common Era, give or take a few centuries.[3] Marr (1985: 2) has attempted to deal with the difficult historiography of the period, confronting such vexatious questions as chronology, absolute dating, authorship, order of original works, editorship of anthologies, all embedded in traditional accounts (some of it mythologized), and, as if this is not enough, there is also the question of the 'divine' origin of the poems themselves. As an example of the difficulties facing such analysis, Marr gives the following:

> Strong tradition in the Tamil country says that the poets who 'contributed' to the eight anthologies, and the authors of *Pattupāṭṭu and Tolkāppiyam* lived in an age of one or more literary academies, centred latterly on Maturai, the capital of the Pāṇṭiya kingdom. The main sources for the tradition of the *caṅkam* are the *Tiruviḷaiyāṭarpurāṇam* of Parancōtimuṉivar and the commentary on *Iṟaiyaṉār Akapporuḷ*. It may be convenient to consider the latter first. . . . The author of *Akapporuḷ*, Iṟaiyaṉār, is traditionally the god Śiva. . . . The tradition regarding the authorship seems to rest on little but the name of the author, Iṟaiyaṉār. . . . It may be suggested that a poet of the name Iṟaiyaṉār did exist and write the verse in *Kuṟuntokai* and perhaps the *Iṟaiyaṉārakapporuḷ* also, and that in medieval times the legend of the divine authorship of both developed.
>
> (1985: 2–4)

Tolkāppiyam is a grammar of a language for which we have no texts except the grammar itself. The name of its author, *Tolkāppiyaṉār*, means no more than 'the author of *Tolkāppiyam*'. The theory of grammar underlying it shows unmistakable and irrefutable influences of the 'northern' grammatical tradition, that is, of the tradition of analysing Sanskrit.[4]

A perhaps later body of literature, now referred to as Sangam Tamil (*caṅkat tamiṟ*), consisting of a large amount of poetry in two genres, love and war poetry, and showing an original style with little influence from Sanskrit, was 'lost' for many centuries, only to be 'rediscovered' in the second-last decade of the nineteenth century in a manner that itself had interesting repercussions for Tamil culture. But before even this amateur archaeologist's dream could come true, a number of other factors must be taken into account.

7.1.1 Origin myths

One of the most fundamental myths pervasive in the Tamil area is one concerning the origins of the language. As Shulman describes it:

[t]he Tamil myths themselves often emphasize the importance of the Tamil language, and in this connection they mention the Vedic sage Agastya, who is believed to have come from the north to reside on the Potiyil Mountain near the southern tip of the subcontinent. The Agastya legend is in essence an origin myth explaining the beginnings of Tamil culture: according to a widespread tradition first found in the commentary ascribed to Nakkīrar on an early work of rhetoric, the *Iṟaiyaṉār akapporuḷ*, Agastya was the author of the first Tamil grammar.

(1980: 6–7)

Shulman then goes on to quote another later myth that explores Agastya's involvement with both Tamil and Sanskrit. In the myth, the sages are faced with the dilemma of knowing which of two *avatars* were greater, Agastya, a form of Shiva, or Vyāsa, a form of Viṣṇu. Agastya leaves the assembled sages to worship Shiva, who appears and teaches him a *mantra*, saying:

This is sweet Tamil. Murukaṉ [the son of Shiva] will teach it all to you without leaving anything out. . . . Murukaṉ instructed him in the Tamil syllabary and the other parts of grammar, then disappeared in his shrine.

When Agastya returned to the sages, he was welcomed by Vyāsa and the rest: 'You have brought mountains here so that the south will flourish, and you have enabled all to taste the divine drink of Tamil'. Agastya put Tamil grammar in the form of aphorisms for the benefit of the land between Vaṭaveṅkaṭam and Teṉkumari, and he expounded his book to his twelve disciples.

(ibid.: 7)

In this myth, it is clear that Tamil is placed on an equal plane with Sanskrit; to my knowledge, no other language in India has such a myth, nor does any other language claim this kind of equal status with Sanskrit. In it, the lineage of Tamil is associated with one of the two most powerful gods of the Hindu pantheon, Shiva, who showed the sage Agastya the beauty and sweetness of Tamil, and then had his son Murukaṉ instruct him in it. Tamil is shown to have a divine origin, as lofty as that of Sanskrit, and certainly (therefore) more divine than any other contemporary language. Why then should Tamil take second place to any other language in India, one might ask.

In an article published more than 20 years ago (Schiffman 1974) I characterized the situation in the following way, which seems to me in little need of change still today:[5]

The study of the language issue in Tamilnāḍu should begin in approximately 1000 BC, or even earlier, for one of the cornerstones of this problem is the argument of the antiquity of Tamil culture. Tamilians know, and they are constantly being supplied with new evidence to support it, that the Dravidians antedated the Indo-Aryans on the Indian subcontinent. The Dravidian languages have not been proven to be related to any other family, and they are spread across India in a configuration that suggests that speakers of Dravidian once occupied a much larger area. The isolation of the Brahui in the northwest, the coterritoriality of many of the central Dravidian languages with non-Dravidian and with Munda languages, with the contiguous languages in the south of India having the largest numbers and the oldest literary traditions, all suggest that Dravidians once occupied the whole of the subcontinent, but that their culture was 'destroyed' in the north by the coming of the Aryans. The Aryans then intermarried with Dravidians or somehow imposed their language on them, not without, however, the infiltration of the Dravidian substratum into Sanskrit through the conditioning of retroflex consonants, Dravidian patterns of syntax, and so on.

Not only do Tamilians know that their language has the oldest literary tradition among the Dravidian languages (dating from the early centuries of the Christian era by the most conservative estimates), but Tamilians know that the oldest of the Tamil literature of the 'Sangam' period is also the most prestigious of all Tamil literature. I think things might be different if not the oldest of the Tamil literature, but, say, the literature of the tenth century AD happened to be the 'best' of Tamil literature. That the oldest literature is the most original suggests to Tamilians that there was an even older literature, documents from which are no longer available; upon the fact of an ancient culture, Tamilians are wont to build an elaborate myth, some of whose aspects might someday be provable, but others of which are nothing but flights of the imagination. One of the first jumps that is always made is that the Indus Valley civilization, known through the excavations at Mohenjo-Daro and Harappa, was a *Tamil* civilization. It is highly probable that the Indus Valley civilization was Dravidian, but certain advocates have assumed the probability to be fact, and have already 'translated' some of the seals into Old Tamil. From there they extend Tamil influence to Mesopotamia, specifically to the Sumerians. Next the Tamils are found to be trading with the Egyptians, and so on.[6] Other well-meaning philologists, on the basis of skimpy linguistic evidence (one or two lexical items) have tried to set up phonological correspondences between Sumerian and Dravidian (Sadasivam 1968). What is important here is not *whether* such an early Dravidian civilization might have existed. Rather, that it *might* have is taken as tantamount to an assumption that it *did* and vague hypotheses are interpreted as if proven.

Thus we have the assumptions that Dravidian culture once extended beyond the subcontinent and was represented in its highest development by ancient Tamil culture, but was attacked and destroyed by invading Indo-Aryans, so that Dravidians are now second-class citizens in their own homeland, at least compared to the descendents of the Indo-Aryans, the Hindi speakers. Since Tamil is assumed to be more ancient than Sanskrit, and Sanskrit far more ancient than Hindi, why should Hindi be honored by being enshrined as the official language? Since almost any other language – Bengali, Telugu, or Urdu, for example – has older literary traditions than Hindi, why choose Hindi?

An evaluation of the claims of the Tamils to a separate, independent, more ancient culture must include the implications of the [rather] late political incorporation into India of the ancient kingdoms of Tamilnāḍu, the Chola (Cōṛa), Ceera (Cēra), and Pāṇdya dynasties. The Tamil kingdoms were independent of any political control from North India until the Vijayanagar period . . . [P]olitically, the present Tamil and Malayalam speaking areas were not united with the north until the British period.[7]

Thus both an ancient culture and former political independence give Tamilians great pride in their language and traditions. There is a third factor, which has only recently gained some attention, but is of particular interest to linguists. It is the idea that 'Tamil' has never changed.

(1974: 127–9)

Thus we see how fact and myth are interwoven: Tamil *is* an ancient linguistic culture, the Dravidian family *is* separate from Indo-Aryan, but these facts are then exaggerated and mixed with fiction until it is hard to disentangle them.

7.1.2 The myth of immutability

The idea that 'Tamil has never changed' is an example of a fairly recent myth about Tamil, since it would not have been possible before the rediscovery of Old Tamil and the archaic linguistic forms it displays. In this myth, as with all others, there is a kernel of truth. Modern literary Tamil is open to borrowing from its earlier stages, and writers who use Old Tamil material in their writing are admired for their erudition. But it is only because of the severely diglossic nature of the language that this is possible. The literary dialect of Tamil (the H-variety) exhibits few if any changes that have occurred since about the time of its thirteenth-century codification by the grammarian Pavanandi.[8] Furthermore, 'borrowings' from older Tamil sources are permissible in literary Tamil (especially the variety known by some as 'Pandit' Tamil), so that no words are excluded from the lexicon on the grounds of archaicity. Thus the definition of what constitutes Tamil is open-ended in one direction only: into the past. It is not open to modern colloquial forms, which would of course show changes. Since in diglossic linguistic cultures the L-variety (spoken Tamil, which has changed radically since the thirteenth century) is usually treated as if it did not exist, the lack of change in the H-variety is taken as proof that Tamil has never changed. This is because L-variety Tamil is dismissed by such people as not real Tamil,[9] so they are able to add another argument to their arsenal, that of the *immutability* of Tamil. In diglossic linguistic cultures, the fact that an illiterate person who knows only the L-variety *might not understand* the H-variety, is not a fault of the H-variety, but of the ignorance of the speaker. That is, one cannot advance arguments that archaicized Tamil is not real Tamil, because the culture-bearers would argue the contrary. In their view, the pure Tamil of the past has *only* changed by the addition to it of foreign elements; remove those foreign elements, and the language remains unchanged.[10]

Such arguments are of course difficult to refute, since they permit no recourse to factual argumentation, and much is based on myth or mythologizing. Arguments from the methodology of historical and comparative linguistics are given only as much weight as is useful, and any counter-evidence is dismissed as not relevant.[11] And as anyone who has tried to deal with the history of the subcontinent has discovered, the culture has little use for what Westerners think of as historical methodology, since the Indian view is rooted in the cyclicity of time and events, not in its linear progression.

7.1.3 Portuguese and early Europeans 'discover' Tamil

Early European explorers seem to have followed the maritime trade routes that were already established by Arab and other traders of the area, and because of the monsoon winds, the spice trade and other conditions, they came into contact with the Dravidian southern coastal areas earlier than with much of the Indo-Aryan north. Thus the Tamil area in particular was an early theatre for European contact. Tamil seems to be the first Indian language to have had type fonts cast for it and works printed in it; and the Malabar and Coromandel coasts were sites of early trade and missionizing by Portuguese and later missionaries, some of them using tracts and missals, etc. printed by the Portuguese presses. A number of missionaries, especially the Italian Jesuits Robert de Nobili and Constantine J. Beschi, learned Tamil and distinguished themselves by their knowledge, erudition and oratorical skills.[12] These missionary-scholars, followed by others, began to propagandize for Tamil better than the Tamils could have ever done for themselves, extolling the virtues, the beauty and the antiquity of the language. Eventually the British missionary-scholar Robert Caldwell published his *Comparative Grammar of the Dravidian or South-Indian Family of Languages* in 1856 (reprinted in 1961), establishing that the Dravidians were a family of languages and linguistic culture separate from the Indo-Aryans. This was done at a time when comparative linguistics was still in its formative state, and comparable work for many other language families had still not been attempted. Nevertheless, the notion that Dravidian culture – exemplified by its most pristine and un-Sanskritized member, Tamil – was separate and independent from Sanskrit and Indo-Aryan was legitimized by having been propounded by a member of the English conquering race, and the stage was now set for the dramatic rediscovery of the most ancient sources, which would occur on 21 October, 1880.

7.2 PURISM AND TAMIL

It is perhaps not surprising that the rediscovery of an ancient past coupled with the flattery of Europeans should stimulate the Tamils to embark upon a linguistic renaissance. This revival reached the point of ebullience in the last decades of the nineteenth century – when the glories of the Sangam literature began to be apparent, and when the challenge of English education had backed some Tamils against the linguistic wall, but had led others to vow to fight tooth and nail against all 'foreign' languages (which, depending on different reformers, could mean English, Sanskrit, Hindi, or all three).

Such challenges have led many linguistic cultures to opt for purism or linguistic 'purification', that is, movements to cleanse themselves of elements that sap their strength and weaken their linguistic moral fibre. What often begins as a language-*maintenance* tactic then often becomes a corpus-*planning* strategy, i.e. an endeavour to control the vocabulary and structure of the language.

Linguistic purism has been defined (Annamalai 1979b) as the closure of the language to modern sources, and the opening of it to more ancient (classical, indigenous) sources. That is, as far as sources for new vocabulary in the language are concerned, the linguistic culture opts for indigenous roots and word-formation processes, and develops a policy of not borrowing terminology of any sort from 'non-indigenous' sources. Of course it is not always easy for a linguistic culture to decide what is or are its own sources, and the literature on purism is rife with descriptions of inaccurate and often downright silly interpretations of what is indigenous and what is foreign. But the point is that it doesn't really matter so much what the details are, as long as there is a *perception* in the culture that linguistic purism is a necessity for the survival of the language, the culture, or whatever, and that speakers are mobilized to participate in a movement to reconnect the language with its roots. Given the myth of divine origin of the Tamil, however, it is clear what the motivating factor ought to be – ridding Tamil of admixtures from other languages, whether Sanskrit or others, to return to the sweetness of Tamil as it was first taught by Murukaṇ.

7.2.1 Purism: a world-view

The movement for linguistic purism[13] began, then, when a number of factors coalesced to spark new thinking about language in the subcontinent. One of these was the attention paid to Tamil by the aforementioned Caldwell, who was the first to use the term 'Dravidian' for the languages of South India, and who declared them to be unrelated to Sanskrit (i.e. not genetically descended from it), with Tamil as its most ancient manifestation. A few decades later, there was the 'discovery' by U. Ve. Cāminātaiyar of some ancient Tamil texts, and with their publication the antiquity of Tamil was pushed many centuries further back in time. At the same time, the influence of English education and the confrontation between English and Indian languages in many cases stimulated indigenous linguistic cultures to stand up and assert themselves. As many researchers have noted, the spread of a language of prestige and power often engenders a counter-reaction in the areas it affects, and this seems to have been the effect of the introduction of English into India. But even before the famous Macaulay Minute became policy (establishing English as the language of education in British India, in 1835), English was in demand in the areas the British had established early beachheads in, and Madras in the Tamil area was one of these.

7.2.1.1 Rediscovery of ancient Tamil and linguistic purism

The movement for purism in Tamil has been described in its general outlines by Annamalai (1979a); I will summarize the details as follows:

1 The discovery of uniqueness by European missionaries; coinage of the term 'Dravidian' (from Sanskrit *ḍirāviḍa* 'south Indian, Tamilian').
2 Rediscovery of ancient Tamil by U. Ve. Cāminātaiyar and publication of texts by printing press.
3 Maraimalai Aḍigaḷ takes a vow to speak only pure Tamil (1915–16).
4 Non-Brahman political movement: E. V. Ramasami Naickar, the Justice Party, the DK and the DMK.

Dating the clear beginning-point of the movement for linguistic purism, sometimes referred to as *taṇit tamiṟ iyakkam*, is problematical. Caldwell's *Comparative Grammar* was published in 1856, and this marked the beginning of a new look at the Dravidian languages; the date 21 October, 1880 is also one that can stand as a clear milestone, since it was on that day (as he recorded in his journal) that Cāminātaiyar first saw the ancient texts.

But first let us review the state that Tamil was in – the lowest ebb, as it were – when it began its renaissance. As Annamalai has pointed out, Tamil had become highly Sanskritized with the establishment of the Vijayanagar Empire in South India.[14] From the twelfth century onward the flood-gates opened and Sanskrit and Indo-Aryan loan words poured into the language.[15] By the time of the arrival of European colonial powers and missionaries, Tamil and the other Dravidian languages were so replete with Indo-Aryan vocabulary that they seemed to be no different from other North Indian languages. But as we have seen, as the European missionaries (Beschi, de Nobili, Fabricius, Caldwell, etc.) began to study Tamil and the other Dravidian languages, some of them began to realize that here was something different. With the development of the new discipline of historical linguistics in the nineteenth century (itself stimulated by the European 'discovery' of Sanskrit), a picture of Dravidian separateness began to take shape, formed as we have seen by missionary-grammarians such as Caldwell.[16]

However, the dominance of Brahman castes, through their monopoly over education, their heritary status as priests, and their control of language in general meant that the attitude toward language was Sanskritophilic. Sanskrit represented the highest ideal, and the notion that Tamil was perhaps on an equal footing with it (as we have seen present in the myths and elsewhere in the culture) was hardly part of what Brahmans were taught – nor did they impart these ideas to their students. So it was something of a surprise to U. Ve. Cāminātaiyar, a Brahman scholar,[17] when his attention was called to the existence of manuscripts that he knew nothing of, and written in a kind of Tamil that he could not readily decipher:

> He was entirely unaware even of the existence of the twin epics and the breathtaking poetic anthologies of Tamil literature, till he met a liberal-minded *munsif* named Rāmacuvāmi Mutaliyār. . . . The munsif had just been transferred to Kumpakōṇam. Cāminātaiyar says that his own merit and the good fortune of his past lives took him there, and opened up a new life for him. Mutaliyār asked Cāminātaiyar under whom he studied and what. When Aiyar gave him a list of all the purāṇas and religious poems and grammars he had slogged at – Mutaliyār said 'That's all? What use is all that? Have you studied any of the old texts? Cīvaka Cintāmaṇi, Cilappatikāram, have you read them?' Aiyar . . . was aghast that he had not even heard of them. Mutaliyār gave him a hand-written manuscript to take home and read. Cāminātaiyar devoted the rest of his life to unearthing, editing and printing the greatest of Tamil literary texts, the Cankam works.
>
> (Ramanujan 1970: 68)

Ramanujan reminds us that because of the religious taboos and sectarian isolationism, Vaishnavites knew nothing of Jain texts, Jains knew nothing of Saivaite texts, and none of them knew anything about Buddhist texts, since with the triumph of Saivism and Vaishnavism over Buddhism there was no need to know the works written by Buddhists. (The best that could be expected of pandits of one sectarian tradition was that they had memorized the *refutations* of doctrinal texts of the other traditions, but not the texts themselves.)

The extent to which the palm leaf manuscripts were intimately tied up with the caste-system is not always realized. Teachers were specialists in certain texts, and a scholar roamed from teacher to teacher. Some teachers did not take students of religious persuasions other than their own, though there were startling exceptions. . . . Or if they were liberal enough to do so, the young scholar had often to change his name at least. . . . Thus the channel or the medium of the palm leaf carried with it a whole oligo-literate caste-enforcing class.

(ibid.: 69)

Though Tamil in its modern written form is remarkably (and blessedly) free of caste connotations, and modern Tamil speakers of any sectarian (Saivite, Vaishnavite) or religious (Hindu, Muslim, Christian) background can unite around their love of Tamil, this was not true at the beginning of the Tamil renaissance, as Ramanujan has pointed out. And unfortunately for the Tamil movement, caste-oligarchical attitudes persisted for decades, hobbling the movement and sapping its strength with caste-hatred. This kind of squabbling was nothing new, however. Appadurai (1981) has chronicled the conflict that arose even between Brahman subcastes, a conflict over whether Sri Vaishnavism should be expounded in Sanskrit (the Sanskrit school, or *vaḍagaḷai's* 'northerners') or in Tamil (the Prabandic school, or *teṅgaḷai's* 'southerners'). In fact what began as a doctrinal dispute bore with it the seeds of a language-policy dispute:

The overall issue . . . was the question of whether the Sanskrit tradition, represented at its peak in Rāmānujā's *Śrī Bhāsya*, or the Tamil Prabandam devotional poetry of the āḷvār poet-saints was to be the focus of religious study, exposition, and sectarian mission-ary activity. This issue, in part, had tremendous significance as a linguistic question, because the choice of Tamil over Sanskrit as a religious language automatically ensured a wider audience in South India, greater popularity for its proponent ācāriyas, and most important, the accessibility of the greatest religious truths to all four varnas [castes] of society. Emphasis on Sanskrit, on the contrary, implied a socially and historically conservative position, retaining a relatively Brahmin-exclusive mode of religious dis-course, which was certainly closed to Sūdra participation and closely linked to the varna scheme as a system of mutually exclusive roles and duties. The question of which language (and therefore which set of texts) was to be the preferred center of dogmatic attention, Sanskrit or Tamil, was, in fact, the linguistic expression of a considerably wider set of issues that divided the followers of Rāmānujā.

(Appadurai 1981: 78)

Ironically, though this was a conflict over the use of Tamil instead of Sanskrit in South Indian temples, and even though the *teṅgaḷais* (Tamil faction) won in many cases, this earned them no merit in the eyes of non-Brahmans when the language battle became secularized.[18] The temple-language battles simply carried over into Brahman versus non-Brahman, northerner versus southerner, Hindi versus Tamil, and today have nothing to do with the language of ritual. But we see here another cornerstone for future debates over the legitimacy of Sanskrit and Tamil as liturgical languages: if Tamil is 'as good as' Sanskrit even in Vaishnava temples, Tamil needs to bow down to no other language. This is an assertion of the purity and appropriateness of Tamil even in the most sacred places, and contributes to later assertions that Tamil should cede nothing to any other language. I know of no other regional language in India that makes this claim, although Panjabi as the sacred language of Sikhism may be a distant second.

7.3 CONFLICTING PROJECTS

It would be an oversimplification, however, to treat the Tamil revival as a project with one goal, with actors who were totally in agreement with each other, at all times and under all circumstances. In fact the revivalist *iyakkam* 'movement' had many strands, and often differing goals. Sometimes the main actors worked in concert, giving credit to others where credit was due, and at other times they worked at cross-purposes, and condemned each other's efforts. In a recent dissertation, Sumathi Ramaswamy has teased out and disentangled these different strands, and identified their main actors:

> The periodic shifting of registers or styles of speaking and writing, in response to shifting demands and imperatives, is one other reason that I propose that Tamil revivalism is a melange of shifting consensual and contestatory positions that change through time. It is important to emphasize both. . . . On the one hand, revivalist texts were generated within a shared interpretive community that was itself embedded within the changing social and institutional matrices of late colonial and post-colonial Tamilnāḍu. . . . Certain shared notions about Tamil and its place in the community do emerge and abide within each idiom, and even across the various idioms. . . . On the other hand, the obverse side to the consensual aspects of revivalist activity is the highly contestatory nature of revivalist pronouncements. . . . I have iden-

tified a 'revivalist' text as one which proposes that language held the key to the Tamil past, present and future.

(Ramaswamy 1993: 36–7)

Ramaswamy identifies the following 'idioms' (her term for the various revivalist submovements or projects) as follows:

- *The Religious Idiom* Religious reform; Neo-Shaivism; countering the disparagement of Dravidian religion in colonial texts, and the recasting of Hinduism as Aryan, Sanskritic, Brahmanical religion. Oppositional identity of non-Brahmans.

- *Counter-Orientalist Classicism* Two groups, Compensatory versus Contestatory, with different goals and agendas:

  Compensatory classicists were distressed at the way 'metropolitan' Orientalism (essentially a North Indian, Sanskritophile enterprise) vilified the Dravidians in general and the Tamils in particular. They attempted to elevate Tamil civilization, literature and culture to be on a par with the Sanskritic.

  The Contestatory classicists, on the other hand, were convinced that Tamil was not only equal with Sanskrit, it was purer, richer, more ancient and more beautiful. Sanskrit had debauched the pure Tamil, and must be driven out. Pure Tamil must be revived. Tamil was also alive and modern, the only Indian language to have both a classical and modern form. But modern Tamil must be rooted in classical form and draw strength from it.

- *The Nationalist Idiom* The British and the English language as the main protagonists, willing to participate in nationalist (pan-Indian) renewal, participatory and consensual with regard to 'India'. Anti-Neo-Shaivite; anti-contestatory classicist; anti-ethnic revivalist. Opposed to use of term 'Dravidian': paradoxical, because under attack from these formerly, and because some of best eulogies of Tamil were by nationalist Tamil poets. Tended to defend Brahmans; were opposed to archaizing and classicizing/panditizing Tamil; anti-pure Tamil, but wanted a *taṇit tamiṟ* free of foreign words, both Sanskrit and English. Populist approach: give the language back to the people.

- *The Ethnic Idiom* Ethnic resistance and political religion. Anti-Shaivite, anti-religious for most of its history; anti-nationalist and anti-Hindi. More populist and 'lower' caste than any other group. Political mobilization through Justice Party, DK and DMK – takes power from Congress in 1967.

Table 7.1 Summary of tenets and goals of Tamil revivalist subgroups

	Taxonomy of Tamil revivalist tenets			
	Neo-Shaivite	*Classicists*	*Nationalists*	*Ethnicists*
Is Tamiḻtāy salvific?	Absolutely	Yes	Okay	Yes!
Chief means to revival?	Revive the community **religiously**	Insist on high **classicality**	Make Tamil the language of politics, government, admin., education, etc.	Establish a *tirāviḍa nāḍu*
Chief enemy?	Brahmans	Brahmans (CnC)	British	Brahmans
Enemy language?	Sanskrit	Sanskrit	English	Hindi
What kind of Tamil is required?	Pure (which means panditized)	Pure, but historically correct	Simple, pragmatic, modern, populist	People's Tamil
Is Tamil divine?	No	Contestatory: yes! Compensatory: okay	Divine, but room for improvement	No!
Which religion is needed?	Neo-Shaivite (what else?)	Any; Tamiḻtāy is mother to us all	Neo-Hinduism, purified of its faults	None!
Emphasis on Classicism?	Absolutely	What could be more important?	Yeah, fine (but don't get carried away)	Popularize it

Sangam period?	Milk & Honey	Garden of Eden	Free of strife	Popularize it
What is linguistic pride?	*taṉit tamiḻ*	Sangam Tamil	Sanskrit and Tamil	*taṉit tamiḻ*
Source for new scientific terminology?	*taṉit tamiḻ*	Mixed reactions	Eclectic: translate, but write in modern Tamil	*taṉit tamiḻ*
Prose style?	*taṉit tamiḻnaṭai*	CnC: *taṉit tamiḻnaṭai* CmC: *centamiḻnaṭai*	*marumalarccinaṭai* 'renaissance prose'	*centamiḻnaṭai*
Class background?		Upper-caste, middle-class, urban, educated, professional		Middle/lower castes
Arena of activity?		Religious writing, learned academies, scholastic journals		Public spaces, street confrontations

Note: *taṉit tamiḻ* can mean a number of things: *tani* means 'alone, unique, sole, one's own', so *taṉit tamiḻ* can mean: (a) 'Tamil only' (with no other language added to it, hence 'purified' Tamil); (b) 'unique Tamil' i.e. something unlike other languages; Tamil 'on its own', i.e. getting no help from any other languages; (c) 'one's own Tamil' the Tamil that belongs to oneself, and is inalienable. These meanings are fluid and sometimes blend; at other times different aspects can be emphasized or perceived. *Centamiḻ* is the name for the earliest 'pure' Tamil (distinguished by early grammarians from *koṭuntamiḻ* 'broken' Tamil), either as it was in the Augustan Sangam age, before it was adulterated, and/or now cleansed and pristinized.

I have attempted to summarize the tenets and goals of each idiom in the Table 7.1.

Let us examine each of these paradigms (idioms, discourses, projects, enterprises, etc.) one by one, since it is instructive to see in what ways they acted in concert to achieve some of the goals of the Tamil revivalist project, and, on the other hand, worked to counter each other and sometimes bring about stalement and stagnation. We need to see why there was failure to achieve the goals, because from the viewpoint of the last decade of the twentieth century, the attempt to reclaim a unique cultural space for Tamil seems to have been less than successful.

7.3.1 The Religious Idiom

The main goal of the Religious Idiom is religious reform, under the umbrella of Neo-Shaivism, and the countering of the disparagement of Dravidian religion in colonial texts, which recast Hinduism as an Aryan, Sanskritic, Brahmanical religion. It tried to establish the oppositional identity of non-Brahmans, part of the radical polarization between Tamil and Sanskrit as approprite ritual languages for two formations: non-Brahman, Dravidian/Shaiva versus Brahman/Aryan/Hindu. They saw Tamil as the sole appropriate divine language for all true Tamilians. Attempts to institutionalize this took place in the early 1920s. Its proponents call for a return to imagined pristine religious fundamentals as a means for rejuvenating society. Language is the medium of expression and also the means through which religious revitalization was enabled in colonial Tamilnāḍu. Attempts to put Tamil in 'the same space in the life-world of devoted Tamilians that has been inhabited by their traditional deities, and until recently, by their sovereigns' (Ramaswamy 1993: 53). As Ramaswamy reminds us, there is a long tradition of praise poetry dating back to the oldest period of Tamil literature, the Sangam period. Most praised kings, deities and spiritual masters, but in the seventeenth century we see Tamil cast as a 'divine messenger'; this emphasis increases in the early twentieth century, and attempts to convey to devotees the 'salvific powers of the divinized language' (Ramaswamy 1993: 53).[19]

With this idiom there is a need to archaize Tamil; it uses pre-modern genres and linguistic styles (archaic grammar, vocabulary, etc.) and venerates the primordiality, *muṇmai*, and antiquity, *toṇmai*, of Tamiḻtāy.[20] Its advocates tried both to archaize the modern, and simultaneously to scientize the legend by pseudo-philologizing, making Tamil the oldest of languages, the mother of all Dravidian languages, of all Indian languages, etc.). There are parallels with the pan-Hindu Saraswati (goddess of knowledge and learning) but also with goddesses of polities, which we see emergent in nineteenth-century language nationalism – such as Mariane in France, Britannia in Britain, etc. According to this group, Tamil is empowered by mobilizing the *sakti* 'divine power', that is associated with deities.[21]

The colonial authorities, for better or for worse, recognized some of these pre-Aryan elements, and praised the egalitarian nature of non-Brahman Dravidian society. Here British orientalism joined forces with Neo-Shaivism: George Pope, a missionary-grammarian who died in 1907, translated and commented on a medieval Shaiva text, the *Tiruvācakam*, saying that:

> The Çaiva Siddhānta system is the most elaborate, influential, and undoubtedly the most intrinsically valuable of all religions of India. . . . Çaivism is the old pre-historic religion of South India. . . . (Classical Tamil is very little studied, yet this key alone can unlock the hearts of probably ten millions of the most intelligent and progressive of the Hindu races.)
>
> (Pope 1900: lxxiv)

With such august praise and the support of foreign scholars, the contemporary Neo-Shaiva assertions were buttressed and 'reauthorized'. When the Indus valley civilization was discovered, it was declared to be pre-Aryan, and the Dravidian revivalists claimed it for Shaivism; Saiva Siddhantism was given highest seat.

7.3.2 Counter-Orientalist Classicism

Another nucleus of cultural revitalizers was the group that we may refer to as the Classicists. Sumathi Ramaswamy divides them into two groups, because of their different goals and agendas, though individuals often 'crossed the line' and preached from other pulpits, such as the Neo-Shaivite. She refers to the two subgroups of Classicists as 'Compensatory' and 'Contestatory'.[22] In her analysis, this group shares much with the religious revivalists (Neo-Shaivites) but they have different emphases.

The Compensatory Classicists (CmC) were distressed at the way 'metropolitan' Orientalism (essentially a North Indian, Sanskritophile operation) treated the Dravidians in general and the Tamils in particular. This 'metropolitan' Orientalism had the colonial regime as its sponsor, and could rest on the plaudits of Sir William ('Oriental')

Jones, Monier-Williams, and others who were intent on showing the purity and elevation of Sanskritic and Indo-Aryan culture, and distancing it from the low, corrupt, debased Dravidian elements of modern Indian reality. Relying on their own Orientalists, such as Caldwell and Pope, the CmCs attempted to elevate Tamil civilization, literature and culture to a par with the Sanskritic. This branch drew support from various communal backgrounds, whether Brahmans, non-Brahmans, or even Christian Tamils, and sought to harmonize the various elements of Indian civilization as part of a project to revitalize India and expel the British. (Their efforts fed naturally into the goals of the Nationalists, whose 'idiom' is slightly different.) CmCs are still to be found within academic circles in South Indian universities, though they are often eclipsed by CnCs and Ethnicists in present-day parlance.

The Contestatory Classicists (CnC), on the other hand, were convinced that Tamil was not only equal to Sanskrit, but that it was purer, richer, more ancient and more beautiful. Sanskrit had debauched the pure Tamil, which had existed in a state of perfect harmony before the arrival of the Aryans. Life then had been beautiful, a linguistic Garden of Eden, corrupted only by the arrival of the perfidious Sanskrit. Sanskrit must be expunged from all domains in the Tamil lands, according to this line of thinking. The CnCs blamed Brahmans for bringing Sanskrit to the south and would have no commerce with Brahman Tamils, even those responsible for reviving the Sangam classics such as U. Ve. Cāminātaiyar. Given the hostility of the CnCs, the Brahmans naturally gravitated to the compensatory camp. Among the CnCs, therefore, there are often gaps in the historiography – they cannot bring themselves to give credit to Brahmans who helped revive the classics, and the tendency to mythologize wildly about the Tamil past is therefore most highly developed among this sector. In their view, Tamil civilization was once dominant in all of India, and was only displaced by the invading Aryans. Tamils had once traded with all of the known world, theirs was the civilization of Mohenjo-Daro and Harappa, and of an ancient continent known as Limuria, now sunk beneath the Indian ocean. In linguistics and some other disciplines, this kind of theory would be known as a 'strong theory', because it is totally unconstrained. The methodology available to compensatory classicism – such as the comparative method of historical linguistics, which would mute unverifiable claims – seems not to have been found useful for the goals of the Contestatory Classicist paradigm, and no wonder. Still today, this paradigm is uncomfortable with challenges to its epistemology.

Both however, worked alongside the religious revivalists, to unseat Sanskrit from university study as a 'classical' language, and among this group there was much adulatory poetry and prose about the wonders of classical Tamil.

7.3.3 The Nationalist Idiom

The Nationalist Idiom was one that was in tune with the goals of the Indian nationalist movement, Gandhism and the Congress Party. It sought to enshrine, not the goddess *tamiṛtāy*, but a pan-Indian Mother India figure, Bharata Mata. The pan-Indian strategy on language was to dethrone English and introduce Indian languages, and Tamil would take its place along other Indian languages, flowing together as waters of tributary rivers flow into the Ganges. Its poets, such as Subramania Bharati, are recognized as epitomizing praise and devotion to Tamil, but they often found themselves between a rock and a hard place. As Sumathi Ramaswamy points out:

> [t]he widely-acknowledged poet-laurate of the Dravidian movement, Bharatidasan, proclaimed himself (as his pen-name indicates) a 'devotee' of Subramania Bharati, the paradigmatic nationalist Tamil. . . . In other words, the Nationalist Tamil Self is paradigmatically a divided Self, or to borrow a contemporary metaphor, it is a Self which is caught between devotion to Bhārata Mātā and Tamiḻttāy.
>
> (1993: 200)

They opposed the Neo-Shaivites, the Contestatory Classicists and the Ethnic Revivalists, and were reviled by these in return. They wanted a *taṇit tamiṛ* free of Sanskrit, archaic Tamil, and English, and would have worked to modernize the language for use in technology and science. After Independence they steadily lost ground and any sentiments still extant in favour of this idiom are rare: their proponents dare not publicly expound their views. They tended to defend Brahmans and to appear not to defend Tamil enough. Rampant Hindi nationalism and modern Indian language policy have made this position almost untenable in the present situation, as its critics warned early on.

7.3.4 The Ethnic Idiom

7.3.4.1 Ethnic resistance and political religion.

This strand of revivalism is the most difficult to describe because it has changed the most from the time of its founding to the present day. Originally allied most closely to Contestatory Classicism, it took as its chief enemy the Nationalists, and also chose political means toward enshrinement of Tamiḷtāy. Early leaders were Maraimalai Adigal and the poet Bharatidasan, but it became political with the founding of the Justice Party by E. V. Ramaswamy Naikker (known in Tamil as EVR).[23] EVR believed the salvation of Tamiḷtāy to be in secularism, and denounced the religiosity of the Neo-Shaivites, just as he criticized the positions of antiquity and motherhood in favour of his own 'Self-Respect Movement'. In fact EVR's vision was originally pan-Dravidian, but this did not catch fire with other Dravidians. Eventually the Justice Party was replaced by the DK, or *ḍirāviḍa karakam*[24] which emphasized the Tamil version of *Blut und Boden* rather than language, though opposition to Hindi was pervasive. After Independence the DK was gradually replaced by the *ḍirāviḍa munnēṟṟa karakam* or DMK,[25] which toned down the anti-Nationalist, anti-Brahman, and even anti-religious rhetoric of the DK, so that eventually (in 1967) the DMK could wrest power from Madras State Congress Party. In many ways this idiom united all variegated strands of Tamil revivalism, even when some of them were in direct contradiction. As Ramaswamy puts it:

> [A]ny analysis of the ethnic idiom has to be carried out with the awareness of all these internal contestations and differences, ranging from EVR's iconoclastic critique to the passionate declarations of ardent Tamil devotees who claimed a readiness to give up their lives and souls for the sake of their language.
>
> (1993: 295)

Thus the Ethnicists were able to radicalize, if only temporarily, those who belonged primarily to other subgenres of revivalism, especially in times of political crisis, such as the anti-Hindi protests.

7.3.5 Non-Brahman puristic movements and the development of the *taṇit tamiṟiyakkam*

The picture of language nationalism in the Tamil area that we can now see the outlines of is thus a confused one, one in which different figures and forces sometimes work at cross-purposes with one another. Until recently there was no comprehensive view of this movement that could be gleaned from any one source (either in English or in Tamil), despite the widely-known oral folklore about its development, because different communities in the Tamil area emphasize only those aspects and personalities that they revere, giving no credit to those whose influence may have been important in the Tamil renaissance, but who are on the wrong side of the communal fence.[26]

What began as a renaissance of a language struggling to recapture the glories of its past, revealed both through the efforts of European missionaries and of scholars like U. Ve. Cāminātaiyar and C. W. Damodaram Pillai, now turned into a political movement, with various agendas. Though the Tamil revival movement appears to outsiders to speak with one voice[27] its origins are not, as we have seen, uniform, and the directions it moved in were certainly never attuned to the same compass. Unfortunately for this movement, it failed to develop a supra-caste ethos, but continued the communal parochialism current in the late-medieval period, perpetually hobbled by issues of communal origin, specifically that of caste.[28]

In some ways Tamilnāḍu resembles a polity like Norway, where two distinct directions of language reform developed almost simultaneously. In the Norwegian case, a primarily urban community centring around Oslo and speaking a Norwegianized form of Danish pushed its dialect as standard, while in the western and more rural parts of Norway a norm that more closely resembled folk-varieties of that region competed for ascendancy. In the Tamil area, the conflict was between Brahmans, the hereditary priestly caste in the Hindu hierarchical order, and those who saw themselves as more authentically Dravidian (non-Brahman), as well as victimized and oppressed by the Brahmans, who they saw as interlopers from North India. The Brahmans were of course the bearers of Aryan and Sanskrit culture, and spoke and wrote a more Sanskritized variety of Tamil than did non-Brahmans. As the non-Brahman movement gathered momentum, the contributions of language reformers like Cāminātaiyar and Bharadiyaar were shoved aside, and anti-Brahmanical crusaders began advocating a cleansing of Tamil of all foreign elements, in particular Sanskrit, Hindi, and English loan words.

The movement that came to be known as *taṇit tamir̲ iyakkam* eventually succeeded in motivating a puristic movement in Tamil, and its energy can be felt to this day. Three political parties arose out of this same energy: first the Justice Party, then the Dravidian Party (*ḍirāviḍa kaṛakam*) and finally the DMK (*ḍirāviḍa muṉṉēṛṛa kaṛakam* or Dravidian Progressive Party) which eventually won political power in the elections of 1967, changing the name of Madras State to Tamilnāḍu.[29] There is also a tendency in some sources to refer to the Tamil Renaissance/Revival as the *taṉit tamiṛ iyakkam* – the picture one gets in current (non-Brahman) accounts. As mentioned above, if Tamil sources are consulted in this area, one only hears of the contributions of Maraimalai Adigal; no credit is given U. Ve. Cāminātaiyar or Brahmans of any sort, despite the monumental importance for this movement of the rediscovery of the Tamil classics in 1881. The received non-Brahman orthodoxy today gives credit to the Pure Tamil movement, since this suits the purposes of the currently dominant revivalist paradigm, that of the Ethnicists.

One Tamil history of the Pure Tamil Movement describes it as follows:

> 'Pure Tamil Movement' is a literary Tamil movement founded and propagated by Maraimalai Adigal in order to avoid the use of foreign words especially words from Sanskrit, and to write only indigenous words. Maraimalai Adigal argues that even if foreign words are found in proper names they should be eliminated and should be substituted with pure Tamil words. For this very reason he translated his own name from Suvāmi Vēdāccalam to 'Maraimalai Adigal'.
>
> (Sivattambi 1979: 1)

It would be difficult to imagine the development of Tamil pride and self-consciousness as it later grew in the *taṉit tamiṛ iyakkam* without the knowledge of the existence of Sangam literature; indeed it is hard to imagine a linguistic culture *not* being affected by the sudden discovery of an ancient literature that rolled its origins and history another millenium into the past. It would be hard to imagine that the kind of mythologizing about language that Tamils do could ever have been possible without awareness of this early new material, and the Tamils were indeed quick to use this to feed the myth. I am tempted to say that it is *precisely* this discovery that makes the Tamils so avid in their filiopietism, and so avidly anti-Sanskrit and anti-Hindi. It is thus almost impossible to imagine that Maraimalai Adigal could have carried off his vow to write only pure Tamil had not the treasure-trove of ancient Tamil words been made available.[30] But when one consults the writings of Maraimalai Adigal and Bharati, one sees no mention of how it these works came to light.

This recognition gap is not a trivial point, I think, for much of the Tamil energy on this issue went into internecine attacks on Brahmans and their supposed degradation of the Tamil language (by the importation of Sanskrit vocabulary, etc.), instead of cooperating with those Brahmans whose erudition could have been of service in the development of Tamil language and literature. But as we have seen, Neo-Shaivite, Contestatory Classicist, and Ethnicist strategies required a visible enemy, a villain at whose feet all blame can be laid, and the Tamil Brahmans became the early scapegoat. The tendency to litigate over temple control was already well established, as we have seen. Later, of course, Hindi speakers and North Indians (all cut from the same cloth, the non-Brahmans would claim) got the blame as the Ethnicist discourse attracted the most attention.

Two names come to mind as the best-known 'fathers' of the revivalist movement: Subramania Bharatiyar and Maraimalai Adigal (who changed his original 'Aryan' name from Suvāmi Vēdāccalam to Maraimalai Adigal (Adigal 'sage, seer')).

Maraimalai Adigal's daughter Nīlāmbikai, who actively participated in the movement with her father, writes about their common vow to write only in Pure Tamil:

> The first time I realized how Tamil loses its sweetness [*iṉimai*] and purity [*tūymai*] because of the influence of Sanskrit [*vada moṟi kalappu*] *mixture of northern language* was when I was thirteen years old. One day I was enjoying being with my father in our garden. My father sang a song of Ramalinga Adikaḷār [*peṟṟa tāytanai maka marantālum*] '*even if a child forgets his own mother . . .*'. When he sang the second line of the song [*uṟṟa tēkattai uyir turantālum*] '*even if life leaves its dwelling place, i.e. body*', he said

> > 'My dear! Look how beautifully Ramalinga Adikalār has made this song. But it would have been far better if he had substituted the Sanskrit word *tēkam* 'body' with the pure Tamil word *yākkai*. Use of Sanskrit words in Tamil causes the loss of sweetness [*iṉimai*] in it and many Tamil words become obsolete.'

> From this moment on my father and I took a vow to use pure Tamil in our speech and in writing.
>
> (Nīlāmbikai, Nakai 1925, quoted in Sivattambi 1979: 51–5)

7.3.6 Purism and mythology

As we have seen in an earlier section on origin myths, the Tamil puristic movement relies heavily on mythological elements to buttress and strengthen the notion of an original linguistic Garden of Eden, which has been sullied and corrupted, as it were, by a serpent named Sanskrit. There are a number of myths that have coalesced around the language, and both feed on and in turn nurture a mixture of fact and fiction.

7.3.6.1 The myth of distinctness

One of the myths that appeals to Tamil linguistic culture – one that has been pushed most strongly by the Contestatory Classicists and the Ethnicists – is that Tamil is a distinct (*taṇi*) language, unlike any other.[31] Because of Tamil's distinctness, they believe, no foreigner can ever succeed in mastering it. To some extent this is a correct observation, but not, I would hold, for the reasons Tamils believe. As one foreigner who has spent some 30 years trying to master the language, I would say that the main barriers to learning Tamil are sociolinguistic, not structural (i.e. internal linguistic) reasons.

The aspiring student of Tamil who attempts to speak Tamil in the areas where it is spoken often experiences a rude shock the first time she or he attempts to speak the language she or he has spent so many arduous hours studying. Tamil speakers, after an initial moment of surprise, usually respond in some language other than Tamil. Even monolingual Tamils will often respond in some variety other than the spoken language, attempting literary Tamil, Hindi, anything, it seems, but the common speech of 60 million Tamils. This tendency is exceedingly distressing to the Tamil learner, given her or his notion that the best way to really learn to speak a language is to try to speak it with mother-tongue speakers on a day-to-day basis. The only Tamils who demonstrate proficiency in no other variety than their mother tongue are monolingual illiterates (or semi-literates), who genuinely seem to appreciate that foreigners[32] have taken the trouble to learn their language. The problem with this is that their variety of Tamil bears with it connotations of rusticity and lack of education, and if learned by a foreigner, results in other kinds of negative reactions from educated speakers, i.e. one's peers. The foreign learner is thus confronted with a dilemma – the people she or he most wishes to speak to and with will not speak Tamil with her or him, but those Tamils who will speak to her or him speak a variety that will eventually prove to be a kind of sociolinguistic liability.

Refusal to speak when spoken to in one's mother tongue is a kind of linguistic behaviour that has ramifications for a number of disciplines concerned with language use. One might view this as a variety of cross-cultural communicative disorder, or catalogue it as yet another impediment to language learning, but these kinds of negative evaluations do little to explain why this behaviour exists, or what one might do to rectify it. In this section I will discuss it only briefly in terms of 'language-learning difficulties'; it is actually a much more important facet of language behaviour, having its roots in Indian linguistic culture, but has been buttressed by colonialism and persistent attitudes about language appropriateness that are then further reinforced by the diglossic condition of the language.

7.4 TAMIL DIGLOSSIA, WITHOUT WHICH THERE CAN BE NO MYTH

It is my strong contention that one or more aspects of Tamil myth-making rests on the existence of severe diglossia in Tamil. But before we can discuss the interaction of Tamil diglossia and mythologizing about Tamil, we must define some terms.[33] Fishman (1980) has provided a taxonomy of diglossia that classifies Tamil diglossia as a type (a):

(a) *H as classical, L as vernacular, the two being genetically related,* e.g. classical and vernacular Arabic, classical or classicized Greek (Katarevusa) and demotiki, Latin and French among francophone scholars and clergy in earlier centuries, classical and vernacular Tamil, classical and vernacular Sinhalese, Sanscrit and Hindi, classical Mandarin and modern Pekinese, etc.

(b) *H as classical, L as vernacular, the two **not** being genetically related,* e.g. Loshn koydesh (textual Hebrew/Amaraic) and Yiddish (Fishman, 1976) (or any one of the several dozen other non-semitic Jewish L's, as long as the latter operate in vernacular functions rather than in traditional literacy related ones (Weinreich, 1980).

(c) *H as written/formal-spoken and L as vernacular, the two being genetically unrelated to each other;* e.g. Spanish and Guaraníin Paraguay (Rubin, 1972 [1968]), English (or French) and various vernaculars in post-colonial areas throughout the world (Fishman *et al.*, 1977).

(d) *H as written/formal-spoken and L as vernacular, the two being genetically related to each other.* Here only significantly discrepant written/formal-spoken and informal-spoken varieties will be admitted, such that without schooling the written/formal-spoken cannot even be understood (otherwise every dialect-standard situation in the world would qualify within this rubric), e.g. High German and Swiss German, standard spoken Pekinese (Putonghua) and Cantonese, Standard English and Caribbean Creole.

(Fishman 1980: 4)

In actuality, type (d) fits Tamil as well as type (a), since as some researchers have pointed out, there is a range of styles of Tamil that is in use in various domains, from the classical through modern literary to educated spoken, regional spoken dialects, and non-standard colloquial dialects. Further, English does occupy a space in the domains of language use in Tamil-speaking territory, even though it is not controlled by a large segment of the population. For that matter, though, neither is literary Tamil, yet it also has reserved domains that spoken Tamil cannot be used in. In some sense it could be argued that Tamil linguistic culture is a multiglossic linguistic culture, rather than 'merely' a diglossic one, and that the range of styles mentioned above also makes place for English, i.e. some domains are reserved for English and no other language would ever be used to discuss them.[34]

7.4.1 Diglossia and linguistic culture

In an earlier chapter I defined what I mean by 'linguistic culture'. Diglossia is one aspect of Tamil linguistic culture that is deeply rooted in the culture, and that has ramifications for other aspects of the linguistic culture and for language policy (writ large) in Tamilnāḍu. That is to say, the fact that a Tamil is diglossic is actually a feature of the linguistic culture of Tamilnāḍu, rather than of Tamil *per se*.[35] *Speakers* of a particular language cannot be characterized as diglossic; only their behaviour – or the behaviour of the speech community – can be considered diglossic. And, I think it can be shown, beliefs and attitudes about the language condition the maintenance of diglossia as a fact of linguistic culture. In the case of the Tamils, for example, it is the set of beliefs about the antiquity and purity of Tamil that unites all members of the linguistic culture in its resistance to any change in the corpus or status of Tamil, by which of course is meant H-variety Tamil (Schiffman 1974: 127). And it is the fact of diglossia that allows this purity to be observed – the corruption is all in the spoken language, while the purity is all in the written form. Diglossia is therefore necessary for these myths to exist.

7.4.1.1 Diglossia and literacy

In a society where literacy is not only not universal, but actually quite minimal, not all speakers control the use of multiple norms.[36] The norm that illiterates lack control of is the H-variety. This does not mean that they have the option of using the L-variety in H-variety domains; rather, the expectation is that they will remain silent[37] rather than exhibit inappropriate linguistic norms. Their linguistic behaviour is in fact restricted to the L-domains, and use of H-domains is *de facto* the monopoly of the educated few. The same is true of domains restricted to English, but with some shifting in this area. That is, in the spirit of modern democratic India, it is recognized among élites that having domains restricted to English effectively disenfranchises some speakers, and whenever challenged, concessions to Tamil will usually be made. But challenges to reserved domains for English remain *ad hoc*, and in the absence of them, speakers revert to English when discussing linguistics or computer science or medicine.

7.4.1.2 Shifting domains and diglossia

While diglossia may be a stable feature of linguistic culture, the distribution of domains reserved for one variety or another can vary: the dominance of a particular domain by a particular variety can shift, with one variety encroaching on domains previously restricted to another. In Tamil, the political speech was once restricted to the domain of the H-variety, but nowadays political speeches only begin and end in H; in between, L-variety predominates (probably as a mark of solidarity). In journalism, especially in political cartoons, movie magazines, etc. one also sees a shift from H to L in many linguistic cultures. In Alemannic Switzerland, the development of television has opened up a domain that has become almost exclusively that of the L-variety, especially in 'live' interviews, talk shows, game shows, etc. where use of *Hochdeutsch* would seem stilted and unnatural. In Tamilnāḍu, one of the domains that has become almost exclusive for spoken Tamil is that of the film, especially the so-called 'social' film.[38] But this does not mean that diglossia in Alemannic Switzerland or Tamilnāḍu are doomed; many Swiss and many Tamils, while welcoming the expansion of L-variety domains,[39] see a need to retain domains for their H-variety languages for a number of reasons.

On the other hand, social forces within a particular linguistic culture can act to eliminate diglossia – as was the case when medieval Latin was displaced during the Renaissance by various European vernacular languages; diglossia seems to be giving way (to a certain extent) in present-day Greece, where it had held sway until a recent (1975) government decree ordained the shift from H (*katharevousa*) to L (*demotiki*) in many domains. This shift was not a slow and 'natural' one but was ordered by the government in response to pressures from 'democratic' sectors of the society; some elements of society continue to resist, many feeling they are being forced to choose between *katharevousa* and *demotiki*, whereas in fact what is evolving (or has already evolved) is a modern Greek *koiné* (Babiniotis 1979). Diglossia was more extreme in pre-modern Bengali and Telugu than it is today, although there still are some reserves held by the older norms. Latin held on in German linguistic culture until the early eighteenth century in a number of restricted domains (scholarly writing, university lectures). When and if diglossia is more or less eliminated[40] we would by rights, have to, speak of a kind of language shift. To ignore shift when it takes place within a diglossic continuum would be to perpetuate the notion that the L-variety is not the real language, and/or that diglossia is in effect irrelevant.

7.4.1.3 Diglossia and linguistic areas

If diglossia is an aspect of linguistic culture, it may result from and be maintained by the same forces that lead to the existence and maintenance of linguistic areas (Emeneau 1956); that is, diglossia may be an areal feature as well as a feature of a particular linguistic culture within the area. In South Asia, as we have seen in the foregoing, diglossia seems to be almost an inherent characteristic of the pan-Indian linguistic culture, since there is a tendency to develop diglossia even in languages that originally may not have exhibited a great degree of it. When Hindustani was chosen as the national language of Independent India, supposedly because of its wide use as a *lingua franca* in the area, other forces became operative that resulted in the development of a more appropriate H-variety – highly Sanskritized in vocabulary, since the vernaculars of Hindi then in existence seemed to be too 'low' for many citizens of the country. This was exacerbated, of course, by the desire of Hindi proponents to make a claim to complete separateness from Urdu, and led to a polarization of the two. The perception that Sanskritized Hindi was then the rightful heir to Sanskrit led Hindi proponents to make claims for it as a national language that could not be accepted by speakers of other languages. Of course diglossicization as a value may vary from subculture to subculture in the region, but it cannot be denied that the overall view in South Asia is pro-diglossic. That its existence is also *a priori* antithetical to rational decision-making about language is usually ignored.

7.4.2 Diglossia and solidarity

One of the reasons that Tamilians give for their shift to English when confronted with a foreign-looking person, even one speaking Tamil, is that the notion of speaking Tamil with such persons makes them ill-at-ease, nonplussed, embarrassed; they experience a kind of cognitive dissonance, or contradictory emotional reactions – they cannot believe their eyes and their ears at the same time. Many report that they have *never* met a foreigner who spoke Tamil; many express their joy and delight (*makircci*) at hearing Tamil from the mouth of a foreigner. But more often than not they do this in English, rather than in Tamil.

Tamil culture is not alone in constructing barriers around its spoken language as a reserve for in-group members. Miller (1982) reports that the Japanese have a notion that Japanese as a language is not easily learned, or indeed, ought not properly to be learned by *gaijin* (foreigners). When a foreigner begins to learn Japanese, he will be praised lavishly for his efforts, often with comments about how he 'speaks Japanese better than we do ourselves'. But as he progresses, the learner encounters more and more resistance – the Japanese become increasingly disconcerted, even resorting to other languages or feigning incomprehension. Miller refers to this as the 'Law of Inverse Returns':

> In most cultures, a foreigner who makes the attempt to learn the language of the society in question is thought, by the members of that society and by the native speakers of that language, to be providing a significant indication of the high esteem in which he or she holds both the society and the language. The gesture of learning a foreign language is consequently usually interpreted elsewhere in the world as one respecting, if not actually honouring, both the

society and the language in question. Put more simply, the members of most societies are pleased when a foreigner tries to learn and use their language, and they reward such a foreigner with approval in direct proportion to the degree of success achieved with the same.

Thus, it always comes as a particularly rude awakening when the foreigner who is resident in Japan for any length of time finally realizes that Japanese society behaves in a fashion that is directly contrary to this general rule. Japanese society usually distrusts and dislikes any attempt by a foreigner to learn and use the Japanese language. The distrust and dislike grow stronger and show themselves more and more stridently, the more the foreigner gains fluency in understanding and using the language.

(Miller 1982: 154)

Miller's analysis is that the Japanese language is the last vestige of the myth that the Japanese as a people (one might even say 'race') are somehow special, so that when foreigners learn it, the Japanese feel in some way threatened. They feel 'funny' – invaded, stripped of identity. In effect, a foreigner who speaks Japanese (or Tamil) is performing an unnatural act, and one of the ways Japanese have to deal with this (other than ostracism or the above-mentioned confusion, distrust and dislike) is to ridicule such behaviour on television game shows, situation comedies and variety shows: there is even a term for such foreigners – *hen na gaijin*, or 'crack-brained' foreigner.

Another culture that was once more open to its language being learned by non-native speakers is that of the Aymará of Andean Bolivia. Heath and Laprade report that:

[T]here is extensive bilingualism among native Aymara speakers in La Paz. Aymara can be heard among market women, masons, maids and security guards, but it is not uncommon that as soon as a native Spanish speaker comes on the scene, they switch to Spanish, often spoken imperfectly and with an accent, but Spanish nonetheless. . . . Using Spanish with outsiders has become the norm with many Indians. . . . Some upper- and middle-class 'Hispanic' women, who years back had the advantage of being bilingual – at least for practical purposes of bargaining in the marketplace – today lament the fact that they have little opportunity to use their Aymara.

(1982: 134)

One of the most useful things Miller says about this phenomenon is that 'any individual act, behavior pattern, or cultural trait actually has meaning or significance only when it is understood in terms of the part that it plays in the overall structure, in other words, in the larger cultural complex of which it is a part' (Miller 1982: 161). I would concur with this in the evaluation of this phenomenon in Tamil – it is part of a larger picture, the purism picture, the antiquity myth and the myth of separateness, and these myths cannot live if contradicted by a living, breathing foreigner, who speaks Tamil.

7.4.2.1 Languages of power and solidarity

It is perhaps instructive at this point to look at work done by Brown and Gilman (1972 [1968]), who introduced the notion that the use of certain pronouns (epitomized as T and V) can be an expression of power and/or solidarity. Rubin (1972) [1968] extended the analogy of T and V pronouns to the use of L and H varieties in Paraguay, a (predominantly) bilingual linguistic culture in which the two languages, Spanish and Guaranì, are in an extended diglossic relationship.

In some of the linguistic cultures under consideration in this study, the use (or misuse) of L and H varieties can also perhaps be interpreted in terms of these same polarities. Certainly the use of L where H is expected (or *vice versa*), constitutes a violation of communicative competence rules. If an outsider speaks Spanish to a representative of the Immigration and Naturalization Service in Seattle, *Hochdeutsch* in Alemannic Switzerland, Hindi to a hotel clerk in Madras, or begins a conversation in *Hochdeutsch* (or even in dialect) in French Alsace, these are mistakes that stem from an inadequate understanding of the linguistic culture, and are threats to the linguistic balance of power in ways that may be very unclear to the outsider.

Brown and Gilman established the notion that use of T pronouns (the familiar, non-respect form) can have several social meanings. Reciprocal use of T by equals expresses solidarity, but between non-equals the giver of T is putting himself in a position of power, and the receiver is expected to respond with V. Similarly, reciprocal V usage implies mutual respect and social distance; any non-reciprocal use of these pronouns is an expression of a differential of power.

As Rubin demonstrated, in diglossic situations the use of H or L varieties in a given social exchange (as distinguished from societal patterned usage as a whole) may be seen as the same kind of T/V situation. The use of L may be an expression of solidarity and may not be offered to speakers whose social position is superior or at least distant. Similarly H may be the only variety appropriate in a given situation because the use of L would imply a solidarity that is only reserved for members of a particular in-group. The use of Black English by White speakers of American English in conversations with Blacks would probably be considered insulting – unless individual allowances had already been worked out. The use of L-variety Tamil by non-Indians is considered inappropriate by many educated Tamilians; they may respond in H-variety Tamil or in English unless the use of L-variety has already been negotiated (with explanations about the goals of the speaker and disclaimers about intended slurs and put-downs). The use of H-variety German in Alemannic Switzerland conversely may be seen as a power-trip designed to put the Swiss speaker at a disadvantage. The fact that the *Hochdeutsch* speaker may have no alternative linguistic vehicle may be irrelevant; it certainly explains the desire to switch to 'neutral' English or French. In Luxembourg, L-variety and its use are expressions of *Lëtzebuergesch* nationality and ethnic solidarity, so while Luxembourg nationals expect L from all Luxembourgers, they switch readily to French or *Hochdeutsch* or English with foreigners, with no expectation that they will or should be able to speak L.[41]

The dynamics of H and L exchange, like the exchange of T and V, are specific to particular linguistic cultures, and cannot of course be predicted without recourse to a knowledge of other aspects of the linguistic culture.

There are some ways to get around what foreigners in Tamilnāḍu perceive as a linguistic roadblock, and that entails what I call 'negotiated language choice', a concept I do not claim to have invented, but one that is particularly apt in the Tamil context.[42]

7.5 LANGUAGE POLICY IN TAMILNĀḌU AT THE END OF THE TWENTIETH CENTURY

As we approach the end of the twentieth century, there are a number of milestones to observe in any attempt to ascertain what kind of overt and covert policies are in effect in Tamilnāḍu. India became independent in 1947 of course, and the Madras Presidency became part of the Indian Union, later the Republic of India, as Madras State. In the 1950s there was agitation for a Telugu-speaking state, and after much pressure and a fast until death by one Sriramulu, an act known as the [Linguistic] States Reorganization Act was passed, by which the boundaries between states were to be redrawn along linguistic lines. Parts of Madras Presidency were then carved off and areas with a majority of Telugu, Malayalam or Kannaḍa speakers went to Andhra Pradesh, Kerala and Mysore (later Karnataka) states, respectively. With the loss of these areas, Madras State (later Tamilnāḍu) then became a state with a majority of Tamil speakers – 89 per cent according to the 1971 census.

1 In 1956 it became feasible to declare Tamil the official language of the state, though not much was done to implement this change.[43]
2 In 1967, the DMK party gained a majority in Tamilnāḍu for the first time, displacing Congress Party, and the name of the state was changed to Tamilnāḍu.[44]
3 In 1970–1 there was an abortive attempt to make Tamil the liturgical language of Hindu temples; we have discussed unofficial attempts before this above.

In the ensuing years, however, the era of milk and honey promised by the DMK has not materialized. Tamil has become the medium of instruction at most levels of state-funded elementary and secondary schooling in the state, though not at the level of higher-education except in subjects like Tamil literature. Large amounts of state funds are expended on splashy filiopietistic projects like the construction of statues and monuments to Tiruvalluvar, or the founding of a Tamil University in Tancāvūr (Tanjore), and international conferences on Tamil studies. The political victory of the DMK has degenerated into in-fighting between factions such as M. G. Ramachandran's DMK versus Karunanidhi's AIDMK (All-India DMK). Following the death in 1988 of Chief Minister M. G. Ramachandran, a former movie-star, his long-time companion Jayalalitha, also a former film star, took over as Chief Minister and she continues to hold this office up to the present, though constantly carped at from the sidelines by Karunanidhi, whose extraordinary oratorical prowess in Tamil is unmatched.

Tamil creative writers also have expressed themselves with increasing exasperation at the stagnation of life in Tamilnāḍu, and the continued emphasis on puristic Tamil instead of the flexibility and creativity of the colloquial language. Though many writers now compromise by using spoken Tamil in the dialogues of their novels and short-stories, the narrative portion is still in literary Tamil, and writers who deviate from perceptions of pure language are still condemned. The difficulties of attaining literacy in a form of the language largely divorced from the modern spoken norm are ignored by the educational authorities. The poet C. Mani expresses his frustration in a poem entitled *narakam*, 'Hell':

. . .
Tamilnāḍu is
neither in the east
nor in the west.
After placing the pan
on the stove
she refuses to cook.
Hunger and loss
are the result.
She moves
neither forwards
nor backwards.
The present is
hanging in the middle.
The hardened tradition
and the door locked from inside
refuse to offer a hand
to cut the knot.
What is there to do?
. . .

(Annamalai 1968: 26–7)

Another modern writer, Jeyakanthan expressed his hostility about the purist movement in the introduction to one of his articles, entitled *munnoottam.*

tamiṟum taṉittamiṟum!

tamiṟ oru moṟi. taṉit tamiṟ oru muyaṟci. taṉit tamiṟeː tamiṟ moṟiyalla. intat telivu eṉakkiruppataːl taṉittamiṟ miːtu eṉakku veṟuppillai. intat telivu illaːtatiṉaːl taṉittamiṟp piriyaːrkaḷ tammai ariyaːmaleːye tamiṟai veṟuttu varukiṟaːrkaḷ.

Tamil and the Pure Tamil Movement

Tamil is a language. The Pure Tamil Movement is an endeavour. The *taṉit tamiṟ* Movement all by itself is not the Tamil language. Just because I have this understanding does not mean that I hate the Pure Tamil Movement. Lacking this insight, the *taṉit tamiṟ* separatists are themselves bringing Tamil into disrepute.

(Jeyakanthan 1972: 189)

7.5.1 Linguistic minorities in Tamilnāḍu

One issue that cannot be ignored in any discussion of language policy in India or Tamilnāḍu is the fate of linguistic minorities in states dominated by Eighth-schedule languages. That is, much has been made of the attempts to officialize languages other than Hindi at the state level, but little exists in the way of constitutional guarantees for speakers of languages other than the majority language in any given state. Thus, if one is a speaker of Telugu, Kannaḍa, Marathi, Hindi or Malayalam (these being the main minorities in Tamilnāḍu), what kind of rights does one enjoy? As we have seen in the previous chapter, safeguards for minorities in various states are not dealt with in a very explicit way.

7.6 SUMMATION: TAMIL LINGUISTIC CULTURE AND POLICY

It should be clear that Tamil linguistic culture is one that, even within the context of Indian linguistic culture, is acutely concerned with language as the defining quality of Tamilness (Tamil *taṇmai*). The rediscovery of Tamil antiquity and its intense connection with the Tamil language is a replay of the rediscovery of the roots of Indian culture and its close alliance with linguistic issues that began with the arrival of the British and the development of colonial Orientalism. To mix metaphors somewhat, a sleeping demon was awakened and aroused, and then a sleeping goddess awoke, too, and slew the demon.[45] Some would say the battle is not over; others would say that a stalemate has been reached (the demon didn't actually die), and with many regional Davids (Panjab, Bengal, Kashmir, Tamilnāḍu) attacking him, the giant is now weak and distracted. The Indian metaphor, of course, is a battle between a virtuous goddess (like Parvathi) and an evil demon (Rāvana) – where devotion to the goddess is salvific, both for the language and for the devotee.

In India in general a number of questions arise about Tamils and the language issue. One is why those Tamilians are so fanatical about their language. Another is whether they are perhaps exaggerating the whole language business out of proportion, for some other reason. Given the perception that the language issue is a no-win issue for India, counter-arguments are usually raised about the efficacy, the rationality, indeed the very sanity of Tamilians and their linguistic goals.

I think I have shown that when all is said and done regarding Tamil and language issues in India, and when all the irrationality and mythology are disregarded, most Tamils feel that their language and their linguistic culture really are different from most others in India, and that the language policy of the Centre is seriously mis-guided. For them, Hindi did not inherit the mantle of Sanskrit, and in any event, devotion to neither of these two languages is salvific. As we have seen in the previous chapter, there is strong evidence that the choice of a Soviet-model policy was flawed, and was in violation of India's own history and linguistic-cultural values. It failed, and it deserved to fail. What type of policy would have pleased a majority of Indians is not clear to me – there may have been nothing that would satisfy proponents of Hindi, besotted as they were and are with the raging desire to squelch Urdu, and find a modern language that could lay a strong claim for the domains dominated by English. Some sort of face-saving device, to pay obeisance to some language like Sanskrit, while pragmatically retaining domains for English and regional languages, might have been beneficial for all. One is reminded of the *de facto* language policy in tiny Nagaland in north-east India. English was chosen as the 'official' language, and it is the language that appears on paper. In the schools of the state, however, teaching is done unofficially in Nagamese, a pidgin containing ele-ments of Naga languages and Assamese. Some variant of this policy is actually in effect in many offices and businesses in all parts of India. Would that it could be accepted as the *status quo* – since it is the *status quo*.

Within the Hindi-speaking areas of North India, it must be noted, the attempt to claim domains for standard Khari Boli and eradicate Urdu, Maithili, Rajasthani, Panjabi, etc. has been successful. The *śuddh* Hindi campaign has been a success, for Hindi in the Hindi areas. Its very methods and emphases there, however, have doomed it to failure elsewhere. With the disintegration and failure of Soviet minority policy and the resurgence of regional ethnicism throughout the former Soviet Union and other areas where Soviet language policy was adopted (Yugoslavia, Czechoslovakia, etc.), one cannot promise much for current language policies in India, which we have seen are clearly based on the Soviet model. And in Sri Lanka, Tamils have been resisting Sinhala-only policies for decades; it is difficult to know whether the Sri Lankan state still exists as it is imagined in Colombo, or whether it has in effect lost out to Tamil separatism.

Perhaps the scene of conflict has shifted from the linguistic stage to the more overtly religious stage, as Hindi/Sikh conflicts erupt in Panjab, and as Hindu/Muslim tensions explode in Bombay, Ayodhya, and elsewhere. The South was relatively quiet during the most recent disturbances, except of course for the assassination of Rajiv Gandhi by a Sri Lankan Tamil suicidal terrorist, who probably believed that she would achieve *moksha* in the process of delivering retribution to the enemies of Tamil. Tamiḷtāy seems to retain its salvific power.

8 Language policy in the United States

CAJUN WOMAN: I don't know how it could happen.
MASKED MAN: It was too easy; they preyed upon a basic fear of human nature.
WOMAN: What is that?
MASKED MAN: The fear of people who speak a foreign language. (*Exits, with Tonto.*)
WOMAN (*to her son*): And I don't even know his name!
SON: *C'est le chasseur solitaire!*
WOMAN: The Lone Ranger![1]

8.1 WHAT IS THAT MASKED POLICY, ANYWAY?

There is a significant literature on the history of language policy in the United States (at least *overt* language policy) and we shall begin this section by reviewing some of the more important studies.[2] Our thrust however, will be, to examine how both overt and covert policy in the USA have evolved since the the earliest contact between Europeans and Native Americans, and how early strategies influenced the development of somewhat more explicit, but still not official policies after the independence of the republic. Then we will focus on the way a consensus about covert policy seems to have come together in the late nineteenth and early twentieth centuries, and crystallized as it were in the period of 1917–23.[3] As covert policy became more overt, some aspects of it have actually become officialized, that is overt policy has reflected more and more the reality of the covert polity, for example in court decisions regarding naturalization of foreign-born citizens lacking adequate English skills (Mertz 1982).

8.1.1 The task at hand

Nothing can be more challenging to the language-policy analyst, I think, than to try to make sense of US language policy, given the almost total lack of a coherent explicit policy at the *federal* level. Again and again in the literature we see attempts to explain this phenomenon or that issue by grasping at one weak reed of 'official' policy pronouncement or another, such as Supreme Court decisions like *Meyer* v. *Nebraska* or *Lau* v. *Nichols*.[4] Many analysts consistently fail to notice that the strength of American language policy is not in what is legally and officially stated, but in the subtler workings of what I have called the covert and implicit language policy. Or, they conclude that because the USA has no overt stated policy regarding the English language, the statement that the USA 'has no official policy' is equivalent to 'has no policy' or is 'neutral' with regard to English or any other language. This totally ignores the very strong *implicit* policy with regard to the *English* language (and other languages) that is obvious to any casual observer.

8.1.1.1 The main issue

The main issue in the study of language policy in the USA, it seems to me, is what is *causal* in American language policy; that is, are various features of the linguistic situation in fact *results* of the policy (however we define it), are they the result of some *contradiction* or *weakness* in the policy, or have they come about *despite* the policy? Kloss (1977a) gives an answer to this question in a way that I think puts it in the right focus:

> As our study shows . . . the non-English ethnic groups in the United States were Anglicized not *because of* nationality laws relatively *favourable* to them. Not by legal provisions and measures of the authorities, not by governmental coercion did the nationalities become assimilated, but rather by the absorbing power of the highly developed American society. The nationalities might be given innumerable possibilities for systematic language maintenance; the manifold opportunities for personal advancement and individual achievements which this society offered were so attractive that the descendants of the 'aliens' sooner or later voluntarily integrated themselves into this society.
> (Kloss 1977a: 284)

The focus of this chapter, as is the focus of this book, will be on what Kloss calls 'the absorbing power of the highly developed American society', which I would prefer to interpret rather as the absorbing power of the highly developed American *linguistic culture.* As Kloss goes on to say, 'not only achievements of American society are responsible for the shrinkage of communities of non-English speech, but also societal attitudes displayed toward (and sometimes against) members of linguistic minorities' (ibid.).

8.1.2 English: a 'dominant' language?

It does not take sharp powers of observation to be able to perceive that English is the pre-eminent language in the life of the citizens of the USA (or indeed in North America as a whole, as our French-Canadian neighbours readily note). It is the primary (in some cases the exclusive) language used in schools, colleges, business; in state, federal, and local administration; in health-care delivery, in the media, in sports, in entertainment, and is the primary language used by religious bodies in America (including some that once used other languages). Outsiders to US anglophone culture (e.g. francophone Canadians) see English as an irresistible force, a vibrant, powerful linguistic culture that overpowers all other languages.[5] The fact that English is not legally protected, guaranteed, promoted, etc. does not mean automatically that some other language might be able to mount a strong challenge to it, that is, one cannot assume that there therefore is a level playing field when it comes to competing for any of the domains now dominated by English.

One way to look at the notion of dominance of English and the subsidiary role of other languages it to consider the question of whether US language policy ever had a potential for being a multi-lingual one, that is, something along Swiss or Soviet lines, or even that of Singapore, also an immigrant society. Most studies of US language policy never ask this question; others claim that US policy is actually extremely tolerant and in principle would tolerate multilingualism of the Swiss or Soviet types. My claim is that the seeds of monolingu-alism are inherent in US linguistic culture as inherited from English linguistic culture, and that the goal of a bi- or multilingual commu-nity, though explicit among some immigrant groups such as the Germans, has never been a real possibility, either now or in the past.[6]

To take a hypothetical example, let a politician address his or her constituents (or any legislative body, for that matter) in some lan-guage other than English, or let some parents demand the *right* to public schooling in a language other than English, for the furore to erupt. One could list many more examples of what might happen if American citizens were to attempt to carry on various kinds of public business – applying for a job, registering for unemployment, enrolling in school, applying for a driver's licence – and were to insist on the 'right'[7] to do it in some language other than English. Then we would hear something about the (covert) policy of the United States; we would hear that 'everybody knows' that the default language is English, and attempts to use another language are illegitimate in some way.

In other words, the *covert* language policy of the United States is not neutral, it *favours* the English language. No statute or constitutional amendment or regulatory law is necessary to maintain this covert policy[8] – its strength lies in the basic assumptions that American society has about language. These basic assumptions range from simple communicative competence in English to deeply held prejudices, attitudes, biases (often supported by religious belief), and other 'understandings' that constitute what I call American linguistic culture, which is the locus of covert policy in this (or any) polity.

As for the question of whether American linguistic culture ever had the possibility of tolerating multilingualism, we will find instructive the case of the German-Americans, the largest non-English speaking immigrant speech community that nineteenth-century America had to try to absorb. Here the 'cleavage' between overt and covert policy in the American context emerges quite clearly.[9] An examination of the literature on this subject of language shift among German-Americans reveals that most previous researchers have looked only at the official documents, statistics and policies of German-American religious bodies. They ignored grass-roots developments of various sorts[10] that in fact laid the groundwork for the later 'abrupt' shift (or what was perceived to be an abrupt policy shift, but what was actually a *de jure* recognition of the *de facto* shift that had occurred much earlier).

This ignorance was made possible by the diglossic nature (Ferguson 1959a) of German at the time of emigration, as well as by the extended diglossic relationship (Fishman 1967) between German and English in the Church bodies. As we shall see, diglossic linguistic situations often mask the true nature of linguistic repertoires (and therefore of language policies) by presenting a view of language that is skewed in favour of the 'high' language, ignoring the actual domains of the 'low' language. In the German case, this had disastrous results for the German language in America, since policy-makers in the German-American churches turned a blind eye to the reality of actual (multilingual) linguistic use within the local congregations.

8.1.2.1 Dominant or hegemonistic?

A number of studies on the market today (Grillo 1989; Phillipson 1992) reflect an analytic mode that aims to show that languages like English are hegemonistic; they represent a kind of imperialism that rolls over other languages and subjugates them; languages do not (to paraphrase this approach) 'reflect social structure, they *are* social structure; they do not reflect power, they *are*   power'. I do not subscribe to this theory, because it is overly simplistic in its analysis of what is causal and what is resultative when it comes to language issues. As we saw in the chapter on religion and myth (Chapter 3), this idea is perforce based on a conception of language that confuses the code with the context it is embedded in, and confuses language with *use* of language. It attributes power to 'language' as an undifferentiated 'black box' of code, context and culture, all shot through with 'ideology'. This kind of vague over-generalization can only confuse and waylay us in our attempts to understand language policy.[11]

8.2 THE COLONIAL PERIOD AND NATIVE-AMERICAN LANGUAGES

The study of pre-independence language policy, especially covert policy, in the US colonial period of course must begin with a look back at the roots of the policy in England. This is because, as we have noted before, covert policy is rooted in linguistic culture, and the predominant linguistic culture in colonial America was an English-speaking one.[12]

There are a number of aspects to this situation. As power in Britain was consolidated under the English kings, there were linguistic minorities in Wales, Scotland and Ireland that fared poorly under English hegemony. We may note that in the switchover from French as a court language to English in 1536, other tongues in use in Britain were also disenfranchised. We may recall that English was the language of education and established religion, and in the anti-Catholic measures directed at subduing Ireland, the Irish language was an early victim. We must also recognize that though the English were late in undertaking exploration of the New World, they did send Cabot and Hudson (neither of them Englishmen) to explore and claim parts of North America that the Spanish and Portuguese had overlooked. We should remember that Spain was England's arch-enemy in both Europe and the New World; that the British defeated the French in 1663 on the Plains of Abraham; that they conducted a number of pre-revolutionary wars against the French and Indians, and that the only languages other than English tolerated in the English colonies were Dutch in the former New Netherlands colonies of New York and New Jersey, and German (in a minor way) in the Quaker colony of Pennsylvania.

8.2.1 Policy toward Native-American languages

We will deal with this issue in somewhat more detail in the next chapter – that devoted to California. But overall, we note a great gulf between policy toward Native-American languages and policy toward other European languages, though the latter did not exactly receive warm tolerance.

Policy toward Native-American languages has to be viewed as neither planned nor coherent in its overall effect, or we will fail to make sense of it. We must remember that colonists came to America with different motivations; some had suffered religious intolerance in England and vowed to be peaceful in their relations with the inhabitants of the New World. Others saw themselves as a chosen few destined to prevail in an otherwise sinful world, and Native Americans were heathens, and therefore sinners. Others saw a need to bring the word of God to the Native Americans: a translation of the Bible into Massachusett, a language of the Algonkin group, was one of the earliest books printed in America.[13]

But the Native-American languages were many and diverse; effort spent learning any one of them did not provide a key to knowing any others, especially when the multiplicity of languages and the complexity of the task became known. As we will see in the next chapter, differing concepts of land ownership and rights to the land got in the way of any understanding of what belonged to whom. There was also the long-term problem of the French and their behind-the-scene manoeuvrings, 'stirring up' the Indians and waging guerilla warfare against English settlers everywhere north and west of the English colonies. This put the Native Americans in the category of 'enemy', since they were allied with the French in the long and fitful 'French and Indian Wars'.

Even where there were treaty relations with Native Americans, the conception of what actually constituted the treaty was problematical: that is, was it just the final summary document recording a particular agreement, or did the treaty consist of all speech events involved in the negotiation of it? Apparently the French recorded all of the negotiation as part of the treaty; the English recorded only the final agreement as the treaty (Deloria 1992). Since the Native Americans were not (except for the Cherokee and some other exceptional tribes) literate, their memory of what happened was the only record they had, and it was often not congruent with the British record. No wonder then than bitterness and a feeling of having been consistently cheated has become the predominant view of the Native American when treaty relations are discussed. Add to that the blatant disregard of the treaty when to do so was in the self-interest of the British (and the Americans after them), and a bleak picture emerges.

8.2.2 Linguistic rights

As we shall see again and again in this study, language *rights* are nowhere guaranteed in Anglo-American tradition. Unlike France or other polities,[14] where explicit texts and provisions have been proposed as a way to guarantee the rights of particular languages, or their speakers, our tradition glosses over and/or ignores any notion of specific language rights.[15] And though English colonists came to America because of religious or other persecutions, nobody came because of *linguistic* persecution, and the idea that linguistic rights needed protection, or should be explicitly stated, was not and never has been part of our linguistic culture. On the other hand, framers of early laws were aware of the notion that language rights might be connected with religious rights, which are guaranteed in the Constitution, but preferred to treat this as a local and regional issue (Heath 1977: 270). Since rights not conferred to the federal government are reserved to the states, and the citizens thereof, the very lack of mention of language in the US Constitution can be taken as an instance of rights reserved, and therefore of the *incompetence* of the federal government to legislate in this area. But as we know from other issues such as slavery – that were thought to be primarily issues of 'states' rights', the federal government does not stand idly by when state laws run roughshod over the civil rights of the general citizenry. But a 'rights' issue that begins as a local and/or state right and eventually becomes federalized goes through stages where local and federal views of the issue are in conflict. Language 'rights' are one of these issues: as Cloonan and Strine show (1991), surveys of 17 states about the use of minority languages in welfare and driver licencing bureaux reveal that language-policy development in the

USA is *decentralized* and may develop at the grass-roots level in response to a client-based need, rather than at the state level or through initiatives or referenda. In some situations (see California, next chapter) we see these two forces working at odds with each other – the one to expand access to services, the other to restrict access, in the same jurisdiction.

The idea (that language rights may develop at the grass-roots level in response to needs of citizens) has not always been foremost in the public understanding of linguistic issues, and now that some voices are calling for overt statutory protection of linguistic rights, many Americans are at a loss to see how this is to be reconciled by the US legal tradition. That is, some people would understand the lack of explicit rights for any one language as a defence of all languages, while others see it as a common law recognition of the status of English.

In sum, linguistic rights are not overtly protected in English or American law, and the English colonists, if they had any thoughts about the matter at all, dismissed them in their dealings with both Native Americans and with speakers of other languages. With the latter, tolerance was grudging, for limited purposes and behind closed doors. (In Canada, where Anglocentric notions of language rights clashed with French ideas about language, an ongoing struggle to reconcile the differences continues.)

8.2.2.1 *English linguistic culture*

In some ways, Anglo-American linguistic culture is subtle: it is not heavy-handed; it does not go in for fancy linguistic academies and draconian repressive measures like the ones we have seen in Chapter 4 on France. The intolerance for religious diversity that led to repressive measures against Catholics, Quakers and other non-conformists may have had linguistic side-effects in Ireland and Wales, but there was also enough tolerance to allow religious minorities to emigrate to English colonies in the New World, where non-conformists were allowed to settle and practise their religion with no interference from the British.[16] But with the ascendancy of English power in the UK (and the waning of Welsh, Scottish and Irish power), the English language flourished and other languages were expected to take a back seat. English colonists to America brought with them English bibles, English catechisms – or if they were non-conformists, other literature written in English. There was not to be much tolerance for other languages in the colonies. Penn's colony may have been an exception because of the suffering Quakers had undergone in

English prisons; William Penn recruited German non-conformists (Mennonites, etc.), and never questioned whether they would maintain their language; it is not a coincidence that language maintenance among the Amish, Old-Order Mennonites and others persists to this day.

Benjamin Franklin, celebrated as a founder of the republic, and founder-publisher (in 1732) of the first non-English newspaper in America, the German-language *Philadelphische Zeitung*, was nevertheless capable of intemperate denunciations of the Germans in Pennsylvania:

> Those who come hither are generally the most stupid of their own nation, . . . and as few of the English would understand the German language and so cannot address them either from the press or pulpit, it is almost impossible to remove any prejudices they may entertain. Their clergy have very little influence on the people, who seem to take pleasure in abusing and discharging the minister on every trivial occasion. Not being used to liberty, they know not how to make a modest use of it.
>
> (quoted in Ferguson and Heath 1981: 10)

8.2.3 Language policy toward African languages

No discussion of policy and language in colonial America would be complete without some attention to the question of language and slavery, and the language of the descendants of enslaved peoples. Slavery was part of the economic system of the first English colony in America (Virginia), as it was also a part of the colonial system everywhere – the French, the Spanish, the Portuguese, the Dutch, all took and used slaves – and there seems to have been a policy from the beginnings of slavery as it was practised in New World colonialism, to separate the speakers of various language groups so that they would not be able to communicate with each other.[17] This led to the development and use of pidgin languages, and eventually of creolized versions of European languages as the slaves and their descendents intermarried and their children grew up knowing nothing of their parents' African linguistic heritage. This practice seems to have been prevalent even before the colonial era, so that we find that pidgin and creole English (Portuguese etc.) arrived with the first slave ships, rather than developing on the soil of the New World (Cassidy 1971: 203).

Today the issue is one of African-American Vernacular English (previously referred to in the literature as Black English and/or Black English Vernacular) and its place in a public school system that prefers 'standard' American English and highly stigmatizes anything else. We will discuss the repercussions of this issue below, in the review of the so-called *Ann Arbor* decision.

8.3 THE FEDERAL PERIOD

Heath (1977) has dealt with the issue of there being some support, in the federal period, for a language academy, but aside from a few strong advocates such as John Adams and William Thornton, there was little enthusiasm for academies or for regulation; detractors from such proposals looked down on them as un-American (or un-English); they were viewed as monarchistic or as reminiscent of the French Revolution.

8.3.1 The Muhlenberg legend

One of the myths that has arisen during the early federal period is the so-called 'Muhlenberg legend', according to which the German language failed by *one vote* to be accepted as *the* official language of the United States (Kloss 1977a: 28). The actual situation seems to have been that German-speaking citizens of Virginia petitioned the Third Congress in 1794 to print some copies of federal laws in German. The matter was debated several times and came to a vote in January, 1795. The speaker of the house was one F. A. Muhlenberg of Pennsylvania, who had been one of the original sponsors of the proposal. But he ceded the gavel to someone else in order not to prejudice the vote, and the result was that the measure lost, by one vote. Had he remained in his Chair, he could have tipped the balance of a tie vote. This minor incident has been inflated to the supposedly hair-breadth decision whereby German 'failed by one vote' to become *the* official language of the United States. There were other attempts like this in the early days of the republic, and these attempts continued up until the Civil War: each proposal to print laws, or agricultural reports, in German (or French) was defeated on the grounds that English was already the official language of the republic. Support for German was of course very strong in the Midwest, where German speakers were concentrated; except for the Mid-Atlantic region, eastern seaboard states had no interest in giving German speakers any special recognition.

8.4 THE NINETEENTH CENTURY: IMMIGRATION AND CONSOLIDATION

After the American Revolution there was a kind of lull, if one can use this word, in the development of language policy. The proportion of English speakers in the new nation was fairly high: Kloss (1977a) gives estimates, based on the 1790 census, of a population of over 90 per cent English descent. The 1790 census, it must be noted, did not ask questions about language, so language status must be inferred from other data, including family names. Those that were not English speakers were either German (perhaps 7 per cent), French (in the territories west of the Appalachians but east of the Mississippi) and Dutch.[18]

As Kloss points out (1977a), there exists in American language policy a principle (nowhere stated overtly) that languages spoken by what he calls 'pioneers', that is the first settlers in any territory, are granted a sort of tolerance not granted to languages of later settlers. When the territory in question was not originally American, or was not settled by Anglo-Americans during the colonial or pre-US period, European-language settlers are considered to be pioneers, and they are usually granted some tolerance of their language, if only for a limited period. Thus Germans settled in Pennsylvania between 1683 and 1776; Dutch speakers in New York and New Jersey when it was still New Netherlands; French in the Louisiana Purchase territories; Spanish speakers in New Mexico, California, etc. Russian speakers in Alaska, Hawaiian speakers in Hawaii all enjoy (or enjoyed for limited periods) some tolerance of their languages. In some cases these languages are given privileges enshrined in state constitutions; but sometimes these tolerances seem to shrivel up and die, and they do not seem to be transferrable 'upwards' that is to the federal level. This tolerance is *not*, however, accorded to Native-American languages, and it is during the second quarter of the nineteenth century that we witness the rise of xenophobic 'nativist' elements, later known as 'Know-Nothings' from the name of a political party founded to defend the rights of 'native' (i.e. English-speaking) elements.[19]

Thus after the American Revolution, and for a period of about 25 years, the linguistic situation concerning languages other than English was fairly stable. Immigration slowed after the Revolution, and during the French Revolution and Napoleonic period was at a standstill. Not until after 1815 was there a renewed trickle of immigration from Europe, bringing the dispossessed and uprooted from the disruptions of the Napoleonic wars. The American tolerance policy toward 'pioneers' like Germans and Dutch was not tested during this early period. The USA passed an immigration law in 1819, after which some statistics about national origin are available. In the period between 1820 and 1850 immigration consists primarily of northern Europeans: Irish, Germans and Norwegians. The Irish were never perceived as a linguistic problem in the USA, though it is certain many were not mother-tongue speakers of English when they arrived. Norwegians left Norway in large numbers proportionate to the population of Norway, but in proportion to US population, they were not a threat.

But Germans began to leave Germany in many waves after 1820; failed revolutions after 1830 and 1848 brought many more, and by the late 1870s, German immigration was in the neighbourhood of 250,000 per year. The territory that was open for settlement at this time was the Midwest, and Germans flooded into the Ohio valley and the Mississippi and Missouri basins, and had a significant impact on cities like Cincinnati, Milwaukee, Minneapolis, St Louis and Chicago. This did not go unnoticed among Anglo-Americans, and the tolerance accorded 'pioneers' began to dry up; some researchers have proposed that linguistic tolerance was associated with religious tolerance. Since the nineteenth-century settlers' motivation for leaving Germany was less religious and more political or economic (there were exceptions), linguistic tolerance also declined.

8.4.1 Origins of schools

But where religion had been the motivating factor in emigration, there tended to be schools founded as well. As we have noted, Protestants were constrained to become literate as a path to salvation; in areas where they settled in large numbers, schools devoted to literacy in German were founded; in other areas, Germans found American schools inadequate and antiquated. Their own pedagogical methodology was better, and midwestern cities found German schools highly competitive, and offering services and curriculum not available in the American public school.

Recall that the movement to found and fund public schools with public monies did not get rolling in this country until the third decade of the nineteenth century, in Massachusetts. The new raw territories in the Midwest, lacking roads and other amenities, did not have anything resembling decent public schools until after the Civil War. German-founded parochial schools were often superior to anything else that existed; in fact public money was often used to teach in German in certain areas (e.g. rural Missouri) where Germans were in the majority; though this was technically illegal, it happened, and Anglo-Americans definitely did not like it.[20]

Another way that German became part of the curriculum of public 'American' schools was that pre-existing sectarian/parochial schools, many of which had been founded by Germans, were secularized, that is began to receive state (i.e. local) funds from taxes. This may have been in the form of a subsidy, or by paying the salaries of teachers, or by purchasing the building. In areas where there had been no pre-existing public schools, this was quite frequent. Though the 'Public School Movement' had its origins in the early part of the nineteenth century, there was much controversy over separation of church and state until a resolution of this issue in 1842 in New York State, which became a watershed for developments elsewhere – the gradual establishment of the principle of non-parochial public schools.[21]

The result was a patchwork, and the language issue was often beclouded by the religious issue:

1 New Mexico (a territory until 1912) financed parochial schools until 1891.
2 Georgia and other southern states were essentially 'state Protestant' schools until 1890.
3 In Utah, state schools were really Mormon schools until 1890.
4 New York: battle over school fund – should school taxes go to support parochial schools? Landmark law of 9 April, 1842: established non-parochial state schools, rejecting Catholics' attempts to get funding for parochial schools.[22]

8.4.2 1842 and after

• The New York decision of 1842 became the prevailing policy: secular state public elementary schools. Bible reading continued until 1948; prayer in schools was outlawed in 1962, though the issue continues to be a controversial issue into the 1990s.

• In most places Protestants accepted secular state schools and have not asked for state help with their parochial schools, but Catholics have persisted in asking for funds, claiming their members are poorer, requesting help with books, busing, secular subjects, buildings. In the 'Poughkeepsie compromise' the Catholics built the building and supplied the teacher, but the state subsidized 'secular' portions of curriculum, paying teacher's salary for that portion.

- In the 1840s there was a rise of xenophobia, 'nativism'; the Native-American Party and the Know-Nothing Party (1855) were against (among other things) parochial schools.

- The Catholic hierarchy was dominated by an Irish (i.e. English-speaking) priesthood, who wanted American Catholicism to be untainted by 'foreign' languages. They attempted to outlaw 'private' parochial schools and make Catholic schools state-supported (and English-speaking). Their goal was to eliminate German, Polish, Italian and French diocesan schools within the Roman Catholic Church – to change the image of Roman Catholic Church from 'foreign' to American. Thus the Irish hierarchy colluded with nativistic elements. They wanted 'compromise' schools – state-funded, but Catholic/Protestant (a solution adopted in the Netherlands). This compromise formula was a threat, for example to conservative German Catholics as well as to German *Freidenker* (atheist) parochial/private non-English schools.[23]

In any event, the principle was established, and defended in different states in different ways, that languages other than English could be taught as subjects and even as the medium of instruction, with public monies. As the institution of public schools became established, state School Laws were drafted to govern them, and different states handled this in essentially three different ways:

1 Laws stated nothing about language, even English, allowing whatever local conditions required.
2 Laws specifically forbade certain languages (but not always German!).
3 Laws specifically permitted certain languages and specifically banned others.

It must be noted that tolerance for languages like German may have varied in different segments of society; many well-educated Americans recognized that German was an important language of culture, that the German educational system, especially its university system, was the best in the world, and that German was an important language for science and medicine. American universities borrowed the concept of the 'graduate school' and the doctorate from German universities in the nineteenth century, since this had not been something inherited from English ideas about the university. But at the grass-roots level of society, Know-Nothingism and nativism would have represented the prevailing view of 'foreign' language, and still does.[24]

8.4.3 Attacks on 'language schools'

Attacks on 'language schools' began towards the end of the century – essentially at the point when immigration ceased to be strongly German and began to originate in eastern and southern Europe. The tide of German immigration peaked in 1882 at 250,000, but after that, immigration by Italians, Greeks, Jews and Slavs increased dramatically. Immigration from Asia, though never strong, had increased during the last half of the nineteenth century, and had led to riots and bans on Asian immigration, especially on the west coast. However, the rise of nativism took an anti-German turn (despite the decline of German immigration), and attempts to legislate against German increased:[25]

- In 1889–90 attempts were made in various states to legislate against German or in favour of English. At this time only three states, all in New England, required English: Connecticut (1873), Massachusetts (1873), Rhode Island (1883–7). New York required English grammar to be taught in non-English medium schools.

- 1889–90: attempts to control language in New York, Ohio, Illinois, Wisconsin, Nebraska, Kansas, South Dakota and North Dakota. New York law was vetoed by Governor.

- 1889–91. General attacks everywhere: German discontinued in big city schools: St Louis, Louisville, San Francisco, St Paul. Under attack in Cincinnati (Kloss 1977a: 157) and Milwaukee. Question: were attacks co-ordinated by the 'American Patriotic Association?' Was there collusion by the (Irish) Catholic Church? Claims were made that German had been 'illegally used' in St Louis. Two-pronged attack: against the languages, and against the churches.

- 1889: Bennett Act in Wisconsin (Edwards Act in Illinois): children aged 8 to 14 in public or private schools had to be instructed in English in the '3 R's, American History, and (in Illinois), Geography.[26]

- 1890: the Bennett and Edwards Acts were repealed, but had taken their toll; Kloss refers to this as an *axiom* of American language policy:

  AXIOM: A foothold gained by English is never lost
  COROLLARY: A loss to English is never regained

By this point German was taught as a subject only, except for religion. An interesting document from a German-American teacher's journal of the time (*Pädagogische Zeitschrift* 1893) showing a proposed *Stundenplan* reveals that secular subjects may indeed have been taught in English, with German reserved for religious subjects and German itself. Nevertheless, the *Stundenplan* does indicate that the balance between English and German 'hours' is about equal.[27]

8.4.4 Who were those masked Germans, anyway?

The purpose of this section[28] is to take a close internal look at the case of the one linguistic minority that posed the biggest threat to the development of monolingualism in the USA in the nineteenth century, that of German-Americans. It is important to do this because the German-American Church was attempting to preserve the German language for its members at a time when US language policy was beginning to change from a very *laissez-faire* tolerance policy to a less tolerant one, and the elaboration (some might say 'construction') of the general less-than-tolerant American policy was largely *in response to* the German 'threat', as we have seen from the evidence presented in the last section.

An analysis of this policy and the resultant assimilation to English demonstrates how a minority such as the German-Americans, who operated a large and sophisticated private German-language school system (how German it actually was we will see below), nevertheless found that this effort did not succeed in preserving the German language for their children, especially after 1918. My purpose here is not so much to examine what US language policy might have been like had the *laissez-faire* policy been truly tolerant of multilingualism, but to see what subtle obstacles to fulfilment of the policymakers' goals lay in American linguistic culture as it came to fruition in the late nineteenth century.[29]

Some of these questions have not been raised until quite recently, while others have never been explicitly dealt with in the literature on bilingualism or bilingual education. I will draw my conclusions about the development of American policy from the case study of the chief protagonist (as it were) – the schools of the German-American churches: other ethnically affiliated religious-supported language-maintenance schools in North America furnish comparable data.

8.4.4.1 Previous studies

Linguistic assimilation in the German-American Church has been studied by Hofman (1966, 1972 [1968]) and tangentially by Schneider

(1939); Beck (1939); Dietz (1949); Stellhorn (1963); Graebner (1965) and Kloss (1966b). Except for Hofman and Kloss, most of these studies have accepted the notion that linguistic assimilation was a foregone conclusion, and that the process only needed to be documented. Most have also studied the 'official' change in language policy (from German to English) in the German-American churches by examining the statistics on number of churches offering English-language services, confirmation classes in English, and number of church publications sold in English as against German. Hofman for instance, concludes that:

> the most crucial variable in the relatively greater persistence of German [as opposed to Scandinavian or other ethnic languages] may well be the greater numerical concentration of Germans. . . . Conservatism is an unnecessary assumption in order to account for the somewhat greater retentiveness of German.
>
> (1972 [1968]: 623)

Kloss (1966b) goes beyond this to offer a useful taxonomy of factors affecting language maintenance, but admits the contradictory effect of some of them (in some cases a given factor will aid maintenance, while in others the same factor will hasten assimilation). He also allows for a general-purpose fudge-factor, the 'special ethnic and cultural characteristics of the group as a whole', which may influence cases in otherwise unpredictable ways. I interpret this fudge-factor to be the same as what I call the linguistic culture of the retentive group.

While these studies are important for our understanding of the linguistic assimilation of the largest body of non-English-speaking immigrants the USA has ever had to deal with, none of them discusses any differential rates of assimilation within the rubric of the so-called 'German-American Church'. None address the reasons for the failure of the large school system(s) operated by many of these denominations (including the Missouri Lutherans, the Evangelical (and Reformed), the Roman Catholics, and other bodies – to say nothing of schools operated by 'non-church' Germans such as *Freidenker* and others), to produce bilingual individuals. Balanced bilingualism has not been the natural outcome of these schools, therefore stable and balanced bilingualism never became an accepted part of German-Americans' linguistic make-up, and thus a natural and accepted part of the American linguistic personality. That some bilingual individuals resulted from some of these schools is an accepted fact, but that the next generation were monolinguals or

English-dominant bilinguals also seems to be accepted as natural. No one has asked why the 'bilingual' schools operated by German-American and other denominations during the nineteenth century did not produce stable community bilingualism among these groups. The literature seems to assume that the official-language policy of these German-American churches is representative of the *de facto* language preference of their members, and then attributes the quick change-over to English after World War I to the harsh regulations of that era. Alternatively, these groups are acknowledged to be already English-preferential, but their English dominance is attributed to the 'enormous assimilative power of American civilization' (Glazer 1966: 360). The overwhelming evidence from internal documents of these churches, and particularly their schools, however, indicates that the German-American school was a bilingual one much earlier than 1917 (perhaps a whole generation or more), and that the majority of the pupils may have been English-dominant bilinguals from the early 1880s on; the *Stundenplan* in Figure 8.1 indicates this as a strong possibility.

Since at least some immigrant societies in the world are not monolingual, and linguistic minorities in some of them have remained distinct (for example in Canada, Singapore and South Africa) it seems incumbent on us to ask, not why immigration in some societies results in bilingualism, but why immigration in American society did *not* result in widespread bilingualism. Why did bilingual schools – whose goal was to maintain German and other languages (with concessions to English for 'practical' subjects such as arithmetic and geography) – produce in effect assimilationist English-dominant bilinguals who melted into the American mainstream?

In my earlier study (Schiffman 1987) I emphasized the internal contradictions of German-American Church policy, contradictions that led to a covertly and unwittingly assimilationist policy. Here I would like to focus on those aspects of American linguistic culture (Glazer's 'enormous assimilative power of American civilization') that in the end may have been an irresistible force, that combined with factors such as those enumerated by Kloss (1966b: 206–12), simply overwhelmed all the language-maintenance efforts of the German-Americans. I think we will see that a balance of social factors, combined with the internal contradictions eventually destroyed the schools of the German American Church, and with them, the German language in America. Had there been no German schools, assimilation would have been more rapid, but even with the

Stunden = Plan

Stunden.	Montag.	Dienstag.	Mittwoch.	Donnerstag.	Freitag.
Von 9 Uhr bis ¼10 Uhr	{ Biblische Geschichte.	{ Katechismus.	{ Kirchenlied.	{ Biblische Geschichte.	{ Katechismus.
Von ¼10 Uhr bis ¼11 Uhr	I Schönschreiben. II } Lesen. III	I Lesen. II Schönschreiben. III Lesen.	I Bibellesen. II Bibl. Gesch. Lesen. III Schreiben.	I Schönschreiben. II } Leseu. III	I Lesen. II Schönschreiben. III Lesen.
Von 11 Uhr bis 12 Uhr	I II } Arithmetic. Schreiben. III	I II } Arithmetic. Schreiben. III	I II } Buchstabieren. Lesen. III	I II } Arithmetic. Schreiben. III	I II } Arithmetic. Schreiben. III
Von 1 Uhr bis 2 Uhr	I Reading. II Writing. III Reading.	I II } Sprach-Unterricht. III Writing.	I English II } Grammar. III Writing.	I Reading. II Writing. III Reading.	I II } Sprach-Unterricht. III Writing.
Von 2 Uhr bis 3 Uhr	I Writing. II Reading. III Writing.	I II } Geography. III Reading.	I II } Drawing. III Reading.	I Writing. II Reading. III Writing.	I II } Geography. III Reading.
Von 3 Uhr bis 4 Uhr	I II } Spelling. III Arithmetic.	I II } Singen. III	I II } U.S History. Drawing. III	I II } Spelling. III Arithmetic.	I II } Singen. III

Figure 8.1 Proposed bilingual *Stundenplan*, 1893

best schools imaginable (and the German schools of the time *were* the best bilingual schools then imaginable) the force of American linguistic culture was simply too strong.

8.4.4.2 Producing balanced bilinguals

The work by Lambert and his colleagues at McGill University (Peal and Lambert 1962; Lambert and Tucker 1972; Lambert 1977) indicates that effective methods of producing balanced bilinguals exist, that is, persons able to function in two languages and at home in both cultures. These methods were of course not known or not applied in the German-American schools during their heyday in the nineteenth century however – so the linguistic policy of these schools may have been not only ineffective, but may in fact have unwittingly *contributed* to eventual linguistic assimilation in America. I have tried to justify this claim in my 1987 study: if it can be substantiated, it would have far-reaching implications, both for our understanding of linguistic assimilation in the history of the United States, and for future policy-planning in the area of bilingual education.

8.4.4.3 Facts and fiction

In my earlier study of the language policies of the German-American schools, I focused on both fact and fiction. By 'fiction' I refer to the *official* policies of the various churches, which I contend were often not in line with the actual day-to-day policies in schools and churches. The later *de facto* policies are often not explicitly reflected in the official historical records, although it is possible to discover them in other historical materials, or to extrapolate them from other evidence. In particular I examined the policies of two important German-American denominations, the so-called Missouri Lutheran Church (*Evangelisch-Lutherische Synode von Missouri, Ohio und Anderen Staaten*) and the Evangelical and Reformed Church (especially one of its forerunners, the *Evangelische Synode des Westens*). These two denominations differed in important ways in their theological bases, and I earlier contended that these differences in theology not only had a differential effect on the language policy of the two churches, but contributed to differential rates of assimilation that have been largely ignored by the attention paid only to the *official* change in policy of the two around the time of World War I.

In my earlier study of the German-American Church I examined problems related to the question of what kind of language policies, both covert and overt, those denominations practised, the outcomes they expected, and the outcomes they actually got.[30] I was interested in establishing the following points:

1 Whether it is theoretically possible for there to be a society whose citizenry is to a large extent functionally bilingual.
2 Whether the methodology and expertise existed that would have allowed a minority such as Germans to devise a curriculum for their bilingual schools that would have accomplished their goal.
3 Whether, given the best efforts of the German minority in America, American culture would have been tolerant of their goal, and their schools would have succeeded in turning out functional English-German bilinguals, thereby succeeding in maintaining the German language up to the present.
4 Whether the overt policy of the German-American Church was in fact counter-productive, unwittingly aiding language shift in the children in its schools.
5 Whether assimilation of German-Americans was brought about by the overt repression of 1917–23, or whether it was caused by covert policies that were gaining ground throughout the nineteenth century.

In short, what I was trying to establish in that study was whether there was anything German-Americans could have done differently to affect the eventual outcome – the defeat of their school policy and the loss of the German language. Given what we have seen of attempts at restrictive legislation, xenophobic intolerance, and other unpleasantness, combined with the German-American conception of the possibility of balanced bilingualism with compartmentalized subject-matter, there was probably little that could be done differently. The Germans also failed to see that factionalism, denominationalism and internal squabbling led to lack of co-operation on the whole issue of German bilingual schools. They were also blind to the gradual grass-roots changeover to English amongst the American-born *Nachkömm-linge*.

And, though attacks like the legislation of 1889–90 were beaten back, even one year's interruption in the previous German-only curriculum meant that it was impossible to return to exclusive use of German when the bans were lifted. A 'compromise' repartition of classes as suggested in the *Stundenplan* may have seemed like an acceptable way to handle the problem – it still kept German for religious subjects (and satisfied the church elders that German was indeed the language of the schools), but admitted that American-born children needed to have English-language skills in 'practical' subjects.

The German-American churches coasted along for another 35 years before World War I presented them with their final challenge. The German-American children who were the products of these schools were effectively English-dominant bilinguals, and this was the covert pattern evident from the records of Synodical requests beginning in the 1880s. From this I must conclude that the policy of the German-American Church, though overtly German-retentive, was covertly *assimilationist*, since its schools, for better or worse, produced English-dominant bilinguals.

8.4.5 Development of overt policy, covert policy and an American linguistic culture

The crucial question we now have to deal with concerns developments during the nineteenth century which affected linguistic minorities in various ways. Almost all researchers of the issue of language loyalty, language maintenance, and immigration history focus on this period, since it was simultaneously the period of greatest immigration, and the time during which an explicit policy of sorts began to be constructed. Many researchers have focused on the details of various groups – their attempts to create an ethnic space for themselves in America, and the attempts of local and state governments to restrict linguistic rights in various ways. Much of the significant writing on this issue can be found in Fishman (1966), Glazer (1966), and Kloss (1977a).

My goal is not to replicate what these authorities have said, but to place the issue in a different perspective. My claim is that what was constructed during the nineteenth century was a coherent *covert* policy, rooted in American linguistic culture, and that this covert policy is what we need to concentrate our attention on, rather than trying to figure out why – with the apparent tolerance of American overt policy, lack of federal intervention, etc. – linguistic assimilation still took place at an apparently irresistible pace. I discern seven factors that evolved and interacted to form a coherent covert policy by the time America entered World War I.

1 Westward expansion and absorption of non-English-speaking groups (Louisiana Purchase, Mexican War, etc.).
2 Development of public schools and a mission for those schools to Americanize immigrants.

3 Increased power and centralization of federal government (development of strong Supreme Court, the Civil War, Antitrust Law, World War I).
4 Rise of nativism and xenophobia (the 'Know-Nothing' Party, the Ku-Klux-Klan, attacks on Roman Catholicism, etc.).
5 Increased immigration. From 1820 onward, large numbers of Germans; at end of nineteenth century up to World War I, other groups from southern and eastern Europe.
6 Increased secularization of society: decline of religiosity, increase 'separation of church and state'.
7 Decline of tolerance toward non-English speaking groups.

I have listed 'decline of tolerance' as a separate factor: in some sense this is the overall summation of the others, though in another sense it could be subsumed under 'rise of nativism': there are some aspects of it that should be treated independently however. What I would like to show is that these factors underlay various attempts to overtly define a policy and directly control and limit non-English language-speaking groups, so that even when overt policies were thwarted, the cultural value underlying it still supported the outcome (suppression) – even though the legality of it may have been overturned.

Let us examine these factors one by one.

8.4.6 Increased power of central government

As many researchers have noted, federal policy in the USA is not explicit about language and language rights; they are not mentioned in the Constitution or in the Bill of Rights, and attempts to define a federal policy or to officialize English were in fact turned aside. Similarly, however, attempts to officialize or semi-officialize other languages were also turned down (Kloss 1977a; Heath 1977; Ferguson and Heath 1981) despite some pragmatic use of languages like German to recruit soldiers during the Civil War, etc. However there were some policies that developed with regard to the naturalization of immigrants, none of which was actually promulgated by the federal government, though the laws in question were federal laws. Rather, as Mertz has pointed out (Mertz 1982), the idea gradually grew during the nineteenth century that American ideas could not be expressed in a language other than English, and various court cases involving the naturalization of foreign-born persons who did not have proficiency in English were decided negatively, because – as those writing the decision put it – they could not know the true meaning of 'truth, freedom, justice', etc. if they did not know English. Mertz calls this a 'folk-Whorfian' notion, meaning that the decision-makers seemed to believe ideas similar to those articulated decades later by Benjamin Lee Whorf, according to which 'language determines thought'. Mertz traces the development of this idea, which culminates in the Nationality Act of 1906 – requiring (oral) knowledge of English. This was codified in 1940, with a requirement of English *literacy* in the Internal Security Act of 1950. It is obvious that this notion arose from ideas prevalent in American linguistic culture, rather than from any overt federal-level law-making.[31]

8.4.6.1 State initiatives

The same ideas – namely that in order to be an American one had to have the English language firmly embedded in one's psyche in early childhood and throughout elementary school – took root at the state level, as has been documented by Kloss (1977a). After early tolerance of German and other languages in the development of public schools, there were later attempts to ban 'foreign' language from elementary schools.

- Separation of church schools and state schools. With development of public schooling, some religious schools were secularized (New York, 1842), or salaries taken on by state or local public authorities, but with clashes over whether religion could continue to be taught. Gradual removal of religion and prayer from schools (Supreme Court, 1948).

- 1889 Bennett Act in Wisconsin (Edwards Act in Illinois) passed but rescinded in 1990. Would have banned non-English languages in schools until Eighth grade.

- State Councils of Defense in 1917–18 (World War I): ban on languages other than English (aimed at German) in schools, churches, on the telephone, in the press, etc.

- Gubernatorial edicts in World War I: depended on state (Nebraska, Iowa, Oregon were most severe).

- Federal requirement: non-English language presses must print English summaries during World War I.

- Oregon attempt to ban parochial schools, overturned in *Society of Sisters* v. *Pierce* (1922).

- State bans on non-English languages overturned in *Meyer* v. *Nebraska* (US Supreme Court) in 1923.

Kloss calls *Meyer* v. *Nebraska* the 'Magna Carta of the non-English School' in the USA: the right to a language other than English was tolerated, but *only for adults* (Kloss 1977a: 284); children did not have the *right* to be raised bilingually. Curiously, Kloss wonders why, with this definitive stamp of tolerance pronounced by the Supreme Court, Americans of non-English speech continued to give up their language in favour of English. This seems to stem from Kloss's belief that an overt Supreme Court decision ought to have as great an impact, or greater, as the unofficial 'absorbing power' of American society. I would conclude however that the power of linguistic culture is and has been much stronger than any Supreme Court ruling.

8.4.6.2 Covert policy reflected at state level

What constituted the covert policy that resulted in the above-mentioned restrictive measures might be stated explicitly as follows:

1 'Children have a 'right' to education in English.' This notion is strongly held by teachers of the 'good schools' movement and can still be heard.
2 English is the language of liberty, freedom, justice and American ideals.
3 Non-English languages are the languages of tyranny, oppression, injustice and un-Americanness.
4 Children cannot learn American ideas through non-English languages (a 'folk-Whorfian' idea, see Mertz 1982).
5 Bilingualism is *bad* for children and should be discouraged in schools.

8.4.7 Increasing immigration

After 1820, as is well known, immigration ceased to be primarily from Britain and increasingly came from northern Europe (Ireland, Norway, Germany), and by the end of the nineteenth century, from southern and eastern Europe. At first the northern Europeans did not threaten the *status quo* very much because of their cultural similarity to (Protestant) Anglo-Americans; the presence of large numbers of (Catholic) Irish and very large numbers of Germans of various backgrounds began to be perceived as a threat by xenophobic groups in the last half of the century. But it was probably the influx of southern and eastern Europeans in the late nineteenth century that resulted in the greatest xenophobia. These immigrants were poorer, less educated, more likely to be Catholic, Eastern Orthodox or Jewish, and therefore much less culturally similar to Anglo-Americans than the previous groups.[32]

- The Germans were able to create their own cultural space in some places, with schools, churches, newspapers, and even theatre and musical associations in many midwestern cities. But as Kloss points out, their numerical superiority was often perceived as a threat.

- The ability of late settlers to create cultural institutions the way the Germans had, and to compete with strong 'American' schools was greatly reduced. As Kloss points out, late settlers had to contend with higher-quality American institutions (schools, etc.) than the earlier ones; and they were *a priori* less able to cope with this because of their lower literacy etc. But they were perceived as a threat because of their differentness and/or 'indifference' to education.

8.4.8 Westward expansion

We do not need to document the great westward expansion into what had been French, Spanish, Russian and other territories during the nineteenth century. The expansion fits neatly into the frame of the nineteenth century: between the Louisiana Purchase in 1803 and the final annexation of Hawaii and Spanish territories in the Pacific in 1898. What is important to see is that tolerance was first extended to formerly official languages in those territories, but quickly begins to expire. (My treatment of this factor in California can be seen in the next chapter.) The Civil War also undermined some tolerance policies – such as that of Louisiana, whose first Constitution guaranteed rights to French: after secession, and readmission after the Civil War, that tolerance was gone. Here the metaphor of English as a steam-roller seems apt, as American linguistic culture overwhelmed and overpowered languages in the rush to the Pacific. The notion of Manifest Destiny seemed to also imply linguistic destiny – the growth of a predominantly English-using state.

8.4.9 Outcome: American linguistic culture in 1920 and thereafter

- Non-English schools crippled by restrictive legislation.

- 'A loss to English is never regained.'

- School philosophy, sociology, educational psychology: 'Bilingualism is a *burden* for children.'[33]

- Keep 'foreign' languages out of elementary schools: become high-school subjects only, and then mostly taught only as dead languages.

- After 1920: isolationism, xenophobia, rise of nativism (resurgence of Ku-Klux-Klan); 'America for the Americans, America First'. Senate rejects American involvement in League of Nations; election of conservative presidents (Harding, Coolidge, Hoover); restriction of immigration to pre-1890 proportions.

- All the knowledge an educated person needs can be obtained through English: only adults might need to know, or have the right to know a 'foreign' language (*Meyer* v. *Nebraska*).

- English is not a foreign language: all others are.

8.5 WORLD WAR I: THE HOUSE OF CARDS COLLAPSES

8.5.1 Details of attempts to circumscribe language-tolerance policy

After holding out as long as it could, America entered World War I in April, 1917. Almost instantaneously, attempts to prohibit the use of German were called for, with a virulence that no one had predicted. Congress had created a National Council of Defense on 29 August, 1916 – even before the declaration of hostilities – which promoted the formation of local bodies, state Councils of Defense, in many areas. These state councils in many cases issued edicts on various matters as if they had the force of law, but did not in fact have statutory validity. Kloss (1963: 65–83) lists many acts of state councils that abrogated tolerance for German and/or other languages.[34]

These mini-attacks had no effect on the general law, but had a dampening effect, spreading suspicion and fear, so that German, which was actually on the wane anyway, was dealt a fatal blow.

Schools that had to stop using German were unable to start up again with English after the Supreme Court struck down the restrictions.

8.6 AFTERMATH OF WORLD WAR I

8.6.1 *Meyer* v. *Nebraska*, 1923

The German Lutherans filed suit against the state of Nebraska in *Meyer* v. *Nebraska*. Nebraska and other states had legislated the exclusive use of English, even in private parochial schools: Meyer was a teacher in such a school. He had tutored children in German *after hours*, but was accused of breaking the law anyway. The Supreme Court ruled in June, 1923 that 'forbidding teaching languages other than English until the eighth grade violated the 14th amendment'. The Court also struck down Ohio and Iowa laws. Kloss calls this a 'Magna Carta for the private nationality school' (1977a: 73).

However, the decision did *not* justify or rule on the grounds of:

The rights of group: claim of national minority to a native language.
The rights of an individual (parent or child) to maintain or use their native language.

A European court in Kloss's opinion, would have ruled on the above grounds. The ruling protected only:

1 The right of a child to learn any desired 'foreign language'.
2 The rights of parents to have their child learn any subject-matter that was not a 'threat' to the state.
3 The right of language teachers to exercise their profession.

By this it defined instruction *in* the mother tongue as 'Foreign language instruction'. Protection granted in the Constitution extends to all – to those who speak English as well as those who speak another tongue. Therefore, *language rights were individually protected* but, as Kloss notes, only for adults. Children do not have a right to language maintenance, only second-language learning. And, it is a *personal* right, not the right of a group or a group confined to a *territory*.

However, again, due to a four- or five-year period when language teaching was forbidden, there was a loss to English in all these schools. And, as Kloss puts it, losses (to English) are never regained. Schools continued to teach most subjects in English, but some resumed using German etc. for religious instruction only. Some schools and churches (e.g. Evangelical Synod) saw the writing on the wall and went completely English, converting completely even before *Meyer*.

8.7 THE TWENTIETH CENTURY: THE COVERT POLICY VICTORIOUS

If we look at American minority-language policy from the 1920s on, we see that the covert policy that had been coalescing during the nineteenth century is now ascendant. Whatever condition language-minority schools were in on the eve of World War I, the six or seven years in which they were unable to function because of restrictive state regulations such as those of Nebraska and other states, now means that these schools are English-language schools, and their children are monolingual in English. Many German-Americans who had spoken German at home before the war now use English as a home language. German as a religious language was further restricted, being reduced to an auxiliary *Gottesdienstsprache* in special services for older worshippers only. The main German church denominations moved during the 1920s to change their language officially to English, though even at this point the 'old guard' did not give up without a fight, and the battle was often a bitter one.[35]

Simultaneously, the educational establishment – including social psychology – concluded that bilingualism is not only un-American, it is bad for children.[36] America turned inward-looking and isolationist. The Senate failed to achieve a two-thirds majority to ratify the treaty establishing the League of Nations (March, 1920); immigration was severely curtailed to 1890 proportions. 'Foreign' language was banned from public elementary schools, and despite Supreme Court 'victory', remained only a high-school subject for four decades.

This post-1920 picture prevailed until the 1960s, when certain changes began to appear. It prevailed before and during World War II, when the USA found itself disastrously unprepared in terms of knowledge of languages such as Chinese and Japanese, to say nothing of German. Schools continued to be operated by various ethnically affiliated religious bodies, but the amount of non-English language they taught was minimal.

8.7.0.1 *Ethnically-affiliated All-Day Schools*

Fishman and Nahirny (1966) have studied the ethnically affiliated All-Day Schools and have shown that they are today the most Americanized of all ethnic schools, offering the least amount of language of any other ethnic instruction. 'By every available index the All-Day School is far less embedded in ethnicity, and, therefore, far less concerned with language maintenance, than any other type of ethnically affiliated school' (1966: 95). It is not hard to see how such schools became so de-ethnicized, since the policy of gradually introducing compartmentalized bilingualism is, as I hope to have shown, a covertly (or perhaps unwittingly) assimilationist policy, contributory to eventual monolingualism. That this would be the case was probably furthest from the minds of the policy-makers. But one can easily see why certain groups (some German-American groups among them) had insisted on monolingual ethnic-language schools (e.g. the clergy in Québec insisting on French only) as a bulwark against both Anglicization and Anglo-American mainstream religious thought and practice. The implication is that, unless more attention is paid to what 'partial' bilingual programmes actually do, the battle for language maintenance may be lost in the very arena in which it is appearing to succeed. This is the tragic irony in the failure of bilingual German-English schools to preserve the German language – an irony that the church policy-makers never comprehended, even if the final tragedy of it was clear to them.

8.8 US LANGUAGE POLICY IN THE LATE TWENTIETH CENTURY

We will examine the rise of movements to officialize English in a subsequent chapter – that devoted to the study of language policy in California. But the decade beginning with the election of John F. Kennedy in 1960 also coincided with a rise in ethnic awareness, the so-called 'new ethnicity'. There were civil rights demonstrations, the passage of a Civil Rights Act, and a new focus on language issues. One was sparked by the launching in 1958 of a space satellite known as *sputnik* by the Soviet Union; this prompted investigations into the Soviet educational system. It was discovered that, lo and behold, the Soviets spent a lot of time learning languages. Congress then passed the National Defense Education Act (1958), which appropriated money for the study of specific areas of the world ('Area Studies'); it also appropriated funds for the study of non-Western languages, many of which had never been taught anywhere in the USA. The Peace Corps dispatched young Americans to all corners of the globe, and many of the volunteers learned languages they had previously never even heard of.

In 1959 a revolution in Cuba resulted in a wave of immigration to the USA, and south Florida was suddenly awash with Spanish-speaking refugees, many of them from the more 'bourgeois' segments of society, whose attitude toward the maintenance of Spanish was very different to the many previous waves of Spanish-speaking immigrants. Dade County initiated special programmes for mother-tongue Spanish-speaking children, and the Coral Way Elementary School began a programme of bilingual education for both Spanish-speaking and English-speaking children. By 1967 there was a new attitude about second languages, and the stage was set for some different approaches.

8.8.1 The Bilingual Education Act (BEA) of 1967–8

The Bilingual Education Act of 1967–8 (Public Law 90–247) was proposed by Senator Ralph Yarborough of Texas, where the high drop-out rate of Mexican-American children had attracted the attention of educational authorities throughout the decade; it drew its political support from the successes in South Florida however. It was added to, amended, amalgamated with other Acts, and expanded from an emphasis on just the Spanish-speaking population to other languages, and appropriations were finally approved in 1968.[37]

Yarborough was at great pains to point out that the BEA was not intended as a language-maintenance measure, nor was it intended to create or maintain language islands, or to create Spanish- (or other-language) dominant bilinguals, but neither was it intended to be a 'replacive bilingual' approach either. It was mainly intended as a way to achieve childhood literate *in English* (Kloss 1977a: 37). Many different interpretations of what the term 'bilingual education' meant were allowed by this Act, so that many different approaches, from ESL to full, balanced dual-medium bilingual teaching were and could be funded. In fact the intent of the programme was as a research and demonstration programme, to test a number of hypotheses about the effectiveness of various approaches, and this aspect was reiterated in the authorizations of 1974 and 1978 (Leibowitz 1980: 43). Further, the reauthorizations stipulated *evaluation* criteria, since the pilot programmes the BEA was funding tended to lack clear outcomes; the BEA was intended to *test* the idea that bilingual education might be effective in helping limited English proficiency (LEP) pupils better their achievement – but proof of this was often lacking.

The failure to make it clear whether the goal was language *maintenance, balanced bilingualism,* or *transition-to-English* has bedeviled the bilingual 'movement' ever since. In the minds of some, the BEA established a *right* to bilingual education, or at least mandated bilingual education as a solution to certain problems.[38] In fact, the intent to test a hypothesis is the only clear intention provided in the texts of the laws. In the backlash of the 1980s and 1990s against the 'new ethnicity', bilingual education is perceived by the American public at large as still not having proven itself. In the reauthorization of 1987–8, the effectiveness of bilingual education was much questioned. Indeed, the secretary of education, William Bennett, described it as a 'failed path' and a 'bankrupt course' (Mulhauser 1990: 108) and many Americans appeared to agree with him.

8.8.2 *Lau* v. *Nichols*, 1974

Another landmark legal case of this period is one that came before the Supreme Court case in 1974. Since this is a case that involves California, we discuss it in more detail in the next chapter. But as with many issues that originate in California, *Lau* v. *Nichols* had repercussions for the USA as a whole, especially issues affecting education and equality of educational opportunities for children.

8.8.3 The *Ann Arbor* decision

Meanwhile another issue that has plagued American language policy for many centuries emerged in a court case known as the '*Ann Arbor* decision'. In that case, African-American parents living in a neighbourhood known as Green Road, whose children attended the Martin Luther King School in Ann Arbor, Michigan, brought a suit against the King School, the Ann Arbor School District, and the Michigan Board of Education for '"the authorities" failure to take into account the cultural, social and economic factors that would prevent them from making normal progress in the school' (Labov 1982: 168). The children in question, a small minority of African-Americans in the school, which was predominantly white, had been classified as learning disabled or mentally handicapped; some had been held back, others had been passed into junior high school without adequate preparation. The plaintiffs argued that this had been done without adequate attention to the children's racial and linguistic backgrounds.

The judge in the case dismissed the allegations of cultural, social and economic deprivation, stating that nothing in the US Constitution guarantees the rights of anyone to special services to remedy poor school performance because of cultural, social or economic background. But he recognized that the *linguistic* background might be significant, and that the school authorities might have failed to take action under Title 20 of the US Code, section 1703(f), which specifically mentions linguistic barriers.

The case then rested on whether the Green Road children spoke a vernacular known as 'Black English', whether Black English was significantly *different* enough as a variety of English to warrant special intervention, and whether the school authorities had failed to provide intervention to specifically address this issue. It must be noted that students with limited English proficiency and with linguistic differences (such as being mother-tongue speakers of another language or dialect) have often been treated in American schools as if they were either physically handicapped, linguistically (and therefore intellectually) 'deprived' or had some kind of 'deficit', spoke a 'reduced' ('inferior', 'restricted') code, or exhibited some kind of pathology that interfered with their ability to learn. Such pupils were then usually sent to a speech therapist, or at best, received 'special education', in order to deal with their 'disability'. This in fact had been the School District's response to the problems of the Green Road children.

The judge therefore retained one of the complaints, quoting section 1703(f) of Title 20 which rests on the 'failure by an educational agency to take appropriate action to overcome linguistic barriers that impede equal participation by its students in its instructional programs'. For the first time, a judge ruled that *linguistic barriers* did not have to be foreign languages, and that a language barrier arising from dialect differences between the speech of White and Black children might be a cause for difficulty, if these differences could be shown to arise from conditions of racial segregation. The task of the plaintiffs was therefore to show that:

- There exist radical differences between Black English Vernacular (BEV), as spoken by the Green Road children, and 'Standard' American English (SAE).

- These differences were not taken account of by the School District, leading to impediments to equal participation by the plaintiffs in the instructional programmes of the school.

From about the mid-1960s on there had been extensive research on BEV.[39] Before this period the general idea among educationalists about this linguistic variety was that it was defective, and constituted evidence of Black 'inferiority', but could perhaps be corrected by compensatory education. Linguists, dialectologists and anthropologists were more interested in discovering what the code of BEV was like, but there was no agreement at this time about *how* different it was from SAE.[40] Research into Gullah dialect, creoles and pidgins, and inner-city Black speech led many to conclude that BEV, while internally logical and in no way defective as a code, was in fact different enough from SAE to constitute a barrier to communication between pupils and their teachers, many of whom were White and, given their training and upbringing, would share the 'deficit' point of view.

Labov shows that by the time of the trial in 1979, there was more consensus among the linguists who were called as expert witnesses, and the notion that language was inherently variable (and could not therefore be easily quantified) was widely accepted among them. The variability of the copula *be* in BEV, and its complex aspectual character, was crucial in the formation of this consensus – in particular the focus on the variability of contraction and deletion of forms of the copula *be* in BEV. Though these phenomena are related to similar phenomena in an overall grammar of English,[41] other conditions affecting contraction and deletion (morphological and phonological) are complex, and not easily understood. This complexity (and apparent inconsistency) has led many teachers to think of the deletion of *be* as laziness, mental defectiveness, an inability to think clearly, or proof of the inherent decrepitude of African-American English, rather than as being a coherent, though variable, system.

Labov depicts the emergence of consensus in this area as a long and complicated process, interesting in its own right as a kind of intellectual process. Certainly it was very important in this process that Black linguists and educators themselves became interested in the possibility that the decreolization of BEV was responsible for a lot of the variability, and were able to participate in the historical 'reconstruction' of this process; as native speakers of BEV, they were also to provide a richer understanding of the semantic complexities of the aspectual character of the system.[42] The judge's opinion, finding for the plaintiffs, was delivered on 12 July, 1979. The Ann Arbor School

Board was directed to identify children who spoke Black English and to use knowledge about BEV to teach such students to read standard English.

Some mythology has arisen about this case, just as we have seen in a number of other similar court cases about language. One is that the Ann Arbor decision somehow ordered schools to *teach students Black English* or *ordered teachers to learn Black English* or to *use BEV as a medium of instruction*. Another is that the case was a landmark and has the force of a Supreme Court decision. Neither of these myths are true of course. There were no expectations that BEV should ever be used as a language of instruction, only that teachers must help students whose dialect is BEV to acquire standard English, that is, it seems to recommend that teachers need to know something about BEV and how it works, and how to teach SAE without recourse to theories of deprivation, deficit, or therapy. Second, because this case was decided in a federal district court in Michigan, and was not appealed, it does not apply in other jurisdictions, though the findings in the case have since been used in other districts that desired to deal with these issues. What they have done is to attempt to remove the negative stereotyping some teachers seemed to apply to their pupils, and replace it with a systematic attempt to deal with the linguistic differences as linguistic differences – not as evidence of 'deprivation', 'reduced code', 'mental incapacity', or whatever.

Despite Judge Joiner's eloquent summation of the issues and the recommended solutions (Labov 1982: 192), the mythology (perhaps due to inadequate press reporting), has spread far and wide that what the court ordered was the opposite of what was actually decided. Perhaps the American people are used to court *orders* and expect that if the court found for the plaintiffs, the solution must have been radical. In a sense this solution is radical, because it requires teachers to look at language in a different way.

8.8.4 Officializing English

We deal with the issue of officializing English in some detail in the next chapter – devoted to language policy in California. In some sense, the issue has always been with us, as we have seen, but it has surfaced again in recent decades as the result of liberalized immigration, and with the kinds of legislation – such as those dealt with in this section – that seem to allow new latitude for languages other than English.[43] Because of a decline in support for the old notion of the 'melting pot' in some quarters, especially among educationists, polarization of attitudes is now very strong, and a middle ground may be difficult to find.

It is difficult to give a history of the origin and rise of the US English movement[44] without descending into a morass of claims and counter-claims involving xenophobia, eugenics, racism and 'politics-as-usual'. Nunberg (1989) gives a sober overview of its history, aims, and intellectual merits. The organization known as 'US English' was founded in 1983 by the late US senator S. I. Hayakawa and John Tanton, founder of an organization known as FAIR (Federation for American Immigration Reform). Its main goals were the officialization of English in the USA and opposition to bilingual education and to bilingual services. Using direct-mail campaigns it raised considerable amounts of money; originally the organization hoped to get an amendment to the US Constitution on officialization of English, but lacking success in this area, it then turned to the financing of state initiatives and referenda, where it has had considerable success[45] in such states as California, Arizona, Florida and Colorado, all with large Spanish-speaking populations.

Despite pressure on public agencies and private firms to abandon use of bilingual forms, menus, ATM machines, etc., it is, as Nunberg points out, too early to assess their substantive effects. As we will see and have seen in other areas, while the courts have not expanded the definition of fundamental rights to include linguistic rights, neither have they stood by and allowed groups or classes of citizens (including linguistic groups) to be singled out for the denial of rights. None of the recent restrictive laws (referenda, initiatives, etc.) has been tested in anything but local courts, but many observers feel that if and when they are, the higher courts will strike them down. In some sense the passage of such legislation has tended to satisfy large numbers of people in a symbolic way (though perhaps not the more passionate devotees of officialization): support for even more restrictive regulations does not seem to exist, except in an abstract way. In many states and localities, support for multilingualism, expressed by the term 'English-Plus' has been firm, and has been translated into legal support of one kind of another.

8.8.5 Native American Languages Act

In 1990, in a move that can only be described as 'locking the barn door after the horse is stolen', the US Congress passed a Native American Languages Act.[46] The text of this act is too long to include in its entirety, but it emphasizes the uniqueness and the value of the languages, the responsibility of the USA to work together to preserve the languages, the special status of Native Americans, the wrongness of acts of suppression and extermination, etc. The act states (104), that:

> It is the policy of the United States to preserve, protect, and promote the rights and freedom of Native Americans [previously defined] to use, practice and develop Native American languages.

The text goes on to emphasize language survival, educational opportunity, the right to use Native-American languages in all Bureau of Indian Affairs schools, in all tribal deliberations and all other social and cultural activities of Native-American people, and directs all heads of federal departments, agencies and instrumentalities to re-evaluate their policies in light of the above-mentioned policies. It can be argued that this act is the most explicit statement on *language* ever to have issued from the US Congress in all its history. In none of the other deliberations, Supreme Court cases, Civil Rights Legislation, Bilingual Education Acts, Lau guidelines, or any other official documents, decisions, rulings, or interpretations do we have such explicit language about language. Coming as it does on the heels of English Only legislation and referenda in states such as California, we are clearly in for some heated discussions. I can only conclude that some people will see it as a 'Magna Carta' for language rights, and will try to use this legislation and its text as a precedent for establishing other language rights, but I predict that these attempts will *not* be successful. With the stipulation of the uniqueness and special status of Native-American cultures and languages, probably we have here only an example of Kloss's 'Pioneer Status' writ large. That is, now that Native-American languages are practically extinct, and pose no threat to anyone anywhere, we can grant them special status.

8.8.6 Summary

Though the last 30 years have witnessed a number of statutory laws, initiatives, and Supreme Court cases, a coherent and explicit policy about language and language rights has not emerged, despite the high hopes of some and the fears of others. Language rights have not been seen as *central* by American courts: they are viewed as rights allied with other more fundamental rights, such as religion, due process, educational equity – or they are seen as rights possessed by individual adults (as in *Meyer* v. *Nebraska*) but not as a group right (Coulombe 1993), or as rights possessed by or necessary for, children. On the other hand, the courts are not willing to allow states to restrict the rights of specific groups when language is the defining issue, nor to ignore legal situations where language differences might lead to the exclusion of a group. But the courts have stopped short of interpreting the US Constitution to mean that language rights are a fundamental American right.

Meanwhile, the consensus about covert policy that held sway from the 1920s until about 1960 has not been fundamentally changed, though it has occasionally been challenged. The 'melting pot' hypothesis is still assumed to be valid by many school administrators and emerges in popular journalistic discussions of issues such as officialization of English (Imhoff 1990: 59). Opposed to it are theories of cultural pluralism ('multicultural education') that deny that the melting pot ever had any validity, or that it has lost its validity or was only true for white immigrants to this country. Some schools may offer foreign-language instruction in the elementary schools (so-called FLES) programmes, some may offer bilingual programmes or immersion programmes as 'magnets' to attract certain populations into certain schools – and many state and local jurisdictions allow the use of 'foreign' languages where it helps their constituents to obtain a drivers' licence or whatever. But antipathy to any expanded role for 'foreign' language in American life is strong, and allied perhaps to xenophobia, racism and other unsavoury attitudes, it does not wish to tolerate something that it sees as dangerous, untrustworthy, expensive, perhaps even un-American. When 'foreign' languages are perceived to be too much of a drain on the public purse, for example when schools face budget cuts, they are eliminated. I interpret this to mean that knowledge of a language other than English is not an essential component of an American public education, so it is no surprise that it is difficult to convince college students that the K/12 view of the utility of other languages is not applicable at the level of higher education. Thus American college students have to be dragged kicking and screaming to fulfil their 'foreign' language requirements. Public-policy-makers may decry this attitude: they may point out how important trade with Japan is, and how we need to learn Japanese or Chinese or whatever, but the American public is not convinced of the necessity of paying for this with public monies.[47]

9 Language policy in California

9.1 CALIFORNIA: TREND-SETTER OR OFF THE WALL?

The state of California is known for its superlatives – its natural beauty, its magnificent redwoods, its pleasant climate, its heretofore excellent public educational system, including universities with Nobel prize-winning faculties. It has the largest population of any US state, the most automobiles, the worst air pollution, the highest rate of in-migration from other American states, the largest number of foreign-born, and is often thought of as a trend-setter – things happen first in California. The free-speech movement, the anti-war movement, the hippy movement of the 1960s, the election of a movie actor as governor in 1966 – all appeared first in California. It is the birthplace of the tax revolt, the drive-by shooting, the urban forest fire, and if this is not enough, California is also the first state to pass an English-only ballot initiative (Proposition 63, in 1986).[1] Add to this the ever-present threat of earthquakes and the fantasy-land 'lifestyle' provided by the entertainment 'industry', with its fabulously wealthy stars, executives and quirky personalities of various sorts, whose ideas about fashion, child-rearing,[2] marriage, divorce, the family, etc. are publicized in the media and imitated by consumers of entertainment commodities everywhere. I am not the first to note that with California, one is truly dealing not just with a state, but also with a 'state of mind'.

When Spanish and other explorers reached California's shores they also had something in mind – this was the period when conquistadors marched thousands of miles in search of fabled cities of gold. The Spanish, of course, did not find gold, and none was found until the famous discovery at Sutter's Mill in 1848, after California had already been ceded to the United States. Critics of the California scene are quick to point out how it long remained a mecca for disgruntled elements from other parts of the United States, and even now continues to be thought of as the pot of gold at the end of the rainbow by immigrants from other countries, though no longer by other Americans, who are reported to be leaving in droves.

9.1.1 California and language regulation

California is also in the 'forefront', as it were, in attempting to legislate what languages can be used in education, on street signage,[3] or in any way that involves the expenditure of public funding.[4] The passage of Proposition 63 in 1986 raised the spectre of officialization of English in other states and localities,[5] and provides us with an excellent textbook example of language-policy formulation in the American context. It shows quite clearly how an issue like language policy can become tied up with other political issues (immigration, class, race, haves versus have-nots, etc.), and be obfuscated to the point of fatal confusion.

9.2 THE NATIVE-AMERICAN HERITAGE

California is, of course, a state that was previously a colony of Spain, and for twelve years after Mexico gained independence from Spain, California remained a Spanish colony (actually under the administration of the Franciscans until 1834); thereafter it was ceded to Mexico by Spain. But before Spanish missionaries and conquistadors arrived, there were Native-American populations in residence, speaking a large variety of languages belonging to a wide spectrum of language families, not thought to be closely related to each other.[6]

9.2.0.1 California as a 'cultural area'

With the arrival of the Spaniards,[7] Native Americans became the object of the missionizing friars. The missions were established along the California coast as far north as Sonoma, and not until later did the Spaniards come into contact with Indians of the interior. The area now known as California was, of course, at that time not so bounded; its present-day boundaries result from the divisions following the Treaty of Guadalupe-Hidalgo. Nor can we say that California as presently bounded constitutes a coherent cultural area, such that the Native-American tribes domiciled there shared characteristics with each other that were not shared with groups to the north, east or south. In fact if boundaries are drawn on the basis of shared cultural or linguistic characteristics, there is overlap into southern Oregon, western Arizona and northern Baja California, while portions of the eastern part of the state along the Nevada border would be excluded.[8] Estimates of the original population of Native Americans in California vary widely; from Thernstrom *et al.* (1980) one would get the impression that the population of Native Americans was in the vicinity of less than 13,000, while the first US census that contained Californian data, that of 1850,[9] gives the impression of less than 2,000.

9.2.1 Historical demography

It is clear however that we cannot rely on mid-nineteenth-century figures as indicative of pre-Columbian population statistics, since we also know that epidemics of smallpox and even malaria decimated the native population after the earliest contact with Whites. The archaeological record and the benign climatic and ecological conditions also point to much higher figures – in fact estimates as high as 1 million have been made (Cook 1978: 91), though a re-evaluation by Cook taking into account many diverse factors estimates that the pre-Columbian population of California must have been in the neighbourhood of 310,000, declining to about about 100,000 by 1850, 50,000 by 1855, and to 20,000 by 1900. In any event, the low mid-nineteenth-century estimates (1850 Census, etc.) are at best indicative of poor and inaccurate returns, chronic underreporting of linguistic and other minorities, and of the decimating effects of epidemics which arrived even before the influx of Anglo-Americans, diseases to which the Native Americans had no resistance.[10] On the other hand, one must bear in mind that though California is now a region that supports a huge population, it does this by importing vast quantities of water, and currently depends heavily on large-scale irrigation – water is not only brought from other states (via the Colorado River, etc.), it is transported hundreds of miles from north to south as well. Pre-irrigation California, in contrast, did not support a native population as large as the present-day multitudes.[11]

The Spanish did not undertake complex linguistic or anthropological field studies among the Native-American populations of California, because as Heizer puts it (1966) 'these facts were considered unimportant as contributing to the knowledge of mankind'. During the entire 300-year Spanish/Mexican period of colonization, 'no person ever attempted to write a general ethnographic sketch of the California Indians who were known, or to place the names and locations of known tribal groups on a map of the territory' (Heizer 1966: 1). This is not to say that there were not individual studies and observations here and there, but only that there was no overall comprehensive survey. In fact the very multiplicity of languages was a factor in the lack of any systematic approach to recording or learning any language – there were just too many of them, and no one language predominated or could serve as a *lingua franca*. The Yokuts alone seemed to exhibit at least 50 different dialects, which was equivalent to one-third of all the different speech forms in California.

Also, though the missions throve, and the Native Americans seemed to take to the irrigation and grazing agriculture, large numbers died from introduced diseases, while survivors either entered the ranks of Hispanic society at the yeoman level, or escaped to join the as yet unconverted inland tribes (Thernstrom *et al.* 1980: 952). What resistance there was to missionization and colonization was often fierce, but it would have involved the spilling of Native-American blood, not that of the conquistadors, and they were in any case outnumbered. Fugitivism, or escape to the interior, was the only way out, but ironically, the fugitive may have also carried disease with him to as yet unaffected areas, resulting in further spread of epidemic. The well-known Friar Junipero Serra, whose champions are now seeking to canonize him as a saint of the Roman Catholic Church, was not beloved of the Native Americans, and there are many reports of brutal treatment by Serra and other friar/conquistadors.[12] Unlike Mexico,[13] where language policy was often ambivalent (alternating between using Nahuatl and other languages, and then attempting to annihilate the languages) Californian languages and peoples were not considered to be worth saving.[14]

In Mexico there were clearly 'noble' peoples, even royalty, and they even had a kind of writing system. No such 'high' civilization was perceived by the Spanish to be in existence in California. The net result of this is that nothing systematic in the way of linguistic research or language maintenance dates from the period of first contact with Europeans[15] and most of what we know about Native-American populations is fairly recent.

9.2.2 Early ethnographic and linguistic research

In the American context, it is impossible to separate the notions of linguistic research and ethnographic research, since the latter often rests on results of the former. Since California has so many different linguistic groups, with a large genetic diversity, it may appear that other cultural traits might also be very divergent, but in fact this is not the case. As is often the case, cultural habits are easier to borrow (or lend) than linguistic habits. Also, because of the tendency of Anglo-American settlers to marginalize native populations, rather than incorporate them as the Spanish and Mexicans did (albeit at the lowest socioeconomic level), the American period was characterized more by policies of extermination, both overt and covert (i.e. by epidemic). The first systematic research on Native Americans in California was begun by Powers in 1871–2, but was mainly ethnographic, not linguistic. In the same decade Albert S. Gatschet attempted some linguistic analyses and comparative vocabularies. Then John W. Powell, the first linguist with systematic training to address the question of Native-American languages in the American west, began, with his Smithsonian-funded assistants, to attempt to classify the languages (Powell 1966, first published 1891). Since nineteenth-century linguistics was heavily weighted toward historical and genetic classification, Powell's task was not rendered easier by the great diversity of genetic groupings among California Native-American languages. After the turn of the century the name of Alfred Kroeber finally appears: Kroeber was an influential figure who placed his mark not only on anthropology but on Native-American linguistics, and on the whole enterprise of ethnography and linguistics in the state of California and its flagship university at Berkeley.

Kroeber and other researchers notwithstanding, the history of Indian/White relations in California is a sorry one. The California legislature managed to veto the establishment of reservations and recognition of treaties with the Indians by the US government, and all attempts to settle land claims and establish which groups had which rights were blocked, botched, jinxed and left unsettled for over a century.

9.2.2.1 Sapir and Native-American pre-history

The linguist Edward Sapir, thought by some to be the American scholar who was most influential in helping develop an American school of linguistics, did much work on Native-American languages. One of his articles, 'Time perspective in aboriginal American culture: a study in method' (Sapir 1949 [1916]) used data from Native-American languages in California and elsewhere to evaluate evidence about which tribes were of longer settlement in various areas. He developed a number of techniques to do this kind of 'linguistic

archaeology' – using internal evidence from the languages themselves to determine what place names, such as Mt *Shasta,* actually
meant, and whether the 'transparency' of a place name could be used
as evidence for prior settlement of one group or another.

9.2.3 Language rights

As we have seen previously in this study, language *rights* are poorly
defined in almost all of the legal traditions that contributed to the
make up of the American nation; indeed linguistic rights are poorly
defined in most polities before the modern period. Most Native
Americans would have probably found the issue of language rights
inseparable from the right to fish, hunt, breathe the air and drink the
water. So, as with subjected peoples everywhere, they have often
found their language rights denied as part of a covert policy of the
subjugating powers, usually after all other God-given rights had been
denied.

As we have already seen, language rights seem to be an easy target
because it is theoretically possible to switch languages, to give up
one's language for another. Populations do undergo language shift; it
has happened since the beginning of time. Unlike giving up one's
skin colour or one's biological gender, language shift is theoretically
quite harmless (though psychosocially, it can be devastating). As we
have already noted, conquering armies often arrive with language
shift as a goal, especially when cultural resistance to the conqueror's
hegemony manifests itself.

Very little has been written from a Native-American point of view
on issues of language rights and language use in pre-Columbian
California, but a study by Deloria (1992)[16] of two recent Supreme
Court cases concerning religious rights of Native Americans provides
us with some idea of how Europeans viewed Native Americans'
rights to land, to their religion, and their languages. *Lyng* v. *North-
West Indian Cemetery Protective Association* (108 Sup. Ct. 1319
(1988)) and *Employment Division, Department of Human Resources
of Oregon* v. *Smith* (110 Sup. Ct. 1595 (1990)), retrace the conceptual
and legal apparatus with which European powers approached the
lands they occupied, and reveals attitudes about Native-American
languages and their speakers that quickly put to rest any illusions
one might have about the value placed on Native-American language
maintenance by the colonial powers. One of these cases (*Lyng*)
concerns Indian land and religious rights in northern California, so
it is particularly pertinent here.

Deloria's analysis of *Lyng* focuses on the conflict of rights between Native Americans in the Six Rivers National Forest area and the federal government, represented by the US Forest Service, which manages the land in question. The issue, essentially, is whether Native-American religious rights, that is, the right to have religious sites and shrines remain inviolate, are rights that transcend the *property* rights of the owners of the land in question. In this case, the federal government holds the land in trust for the American people, and the Forest Service manages the land, that is, allows private individuals to harvest forest products for a fee.

We should note at the outset that the case of *Lyng* does not mention language rights in any way – since language rights are nowhere specified in the US Constitution, this is true in general in the United States. Most cases involving language, whether Native-American languages, the English language, or immigrant languages, must be decided on other grounds. Argumentation (as we have seen in *Meyer* v. *Nebraska* and others) has to resort to questions of other kinds of rights, rights indeed guaranteed by the US Constitution, such as religious freedom, freedom of speech, and others. What Deloria seeks to establish in the *Lyng* case is what philosophy of law underlay US treatment of Indian rights historically. What emerges is a picture of the kind of linguistic culture that was embedded in the ideas that the colonial powers – whether Spanish, French, Dutch or British – brought with them regarding the land they colonized and the people who lived on it.

The notion the Spanish seemed to be operating under was that the pope was the vicar of Christ, and if colonial operations were done in Christ's name and in a Christian manner, any actions were justified. (The actual implementation of this policy cannot help but have its origins in the Spanish Catholic kings' successful attempt to expel the Moors from Spain, and reclaim it for Spanish Catholicism.) The Protestant colonial powers, such as Britain and the Netherlands, did not use the pope's argument; they simply saw Native-American peoples as pagans, and felt justified in doing whatever they wanted.

The case of *Lyng* brings up a number of constitutional issues, which are too complex to evaluate here. But there are a number of approaches to constitutional interpretation that are of broader scope, and which apply not only to religious rights, but also to language. One is the Treaty relationship; a second is the Trust Doctrine; a third is the issue of property ownership.

9.2.3.1 The Treaty relationship

As is well known, early explorers set out from Europe to develop alternate trade routes to the spices and other riches of the Orient. Because their way was blocked by Arab and other traders in the eastern Mediterranean, the Arabian Sea and the Indian Ocean they sought other routes that would avoid these obstacles. Curiously, though they did not at first establish colonies in India and southeast Asia, they did, upon arrival in the New World, claim various territories for their own. The difference seemed to rest upon the following:

- The lands reached in India and east of India were already *occupied* and there was a sovereign presence there. The trade rights were controlled by Arabs or others, and were not up for grabs.[17]

- Though the kingdoms of the East were not headed by Christian sovereigns, there was a recognition that their rule and rulers were legitimate and legal.[18]

- Land claims in the New World were only legitimate if unchallenged: when European conquerors were repulsed from one area or another by Native Americans, the colonial claims were seen as invalid.[19]

- When a toehold was gained in one area but not in adjacent areas, some of the powers enacted *treaties* with the Native Americans: this was especially the case with the British, the French and the Russians, whereas the Spanish seemed to be operating on the notion that the right of discovery gave sovereignty. The Spanish *conquered*, other colonial powers negotiated.

In the United States, treaties were enacted by both the British before 1776 and by the Americans after 1776: after 1778 formal written treaties, rather than oral agreements were recorded. Treaties enacted before the ratification of the US Constitution in 1779 were mentioned in the US Constitution as being equivalent to treaties with foreign nations. However, this equivalence has been attacked repeatedly by those who find Native-American rights inconvenient, and in case after case, the validity of such treaties has been defended only weakly. When California became a state, for example, the USA intended to establish treaties with California Indians, and work was actually carried out, resulting in 18 separate treaties being negotiated. The California legislature objected however, and the US Senate (led by its California senators) blocked this move, so the treaties were never ratified, and all records were sealed until 1905 (Heizer 1978c: 702).

9.2.3.2 Grants of rights

As Deloria has pointed out, in *United States* v. *Winans* (1905) such treaties with Indians were a grant of rights *to* the United States, not a grant of rights *from* the United States to the Indians, and therefore rights not granted (to the United States) are reserved – just as rights not granted by the people or the states to the federal government, such as matters involving education, *language*, and others, are reserved by the people and the states. This notion has been eroded and attacked constantly, as Deloria notes (1992: 270), as the federal government moved into what is perceived as a legal vacuum, in effect usurping the rights originally reserved by Native Americans.[20]

One might also note, on the issue of recorded treaties, a cultural conflict over what constitutes a verbal agreement. Deloria shows that the French, in their treaty negotiation, treated the discussions and arguments leading up to the agreement as part of the whole picture, and recorded them almost verbatim. Other powers, in particular the Anglo-Americans, saw only the finished agreement as being worth recording, so that the lines of reasoning, the thought process, the intent of certain statements, the whole *discourse*, in fact, were not recorded. For the Native Americans, the French process seems to have been more satisfying, so as encroachments began to build and they had to deal with the United States, total disagreement then resulted as to what the treaty actually *meant*. For members of a pre-literate culture, recording only the summary of the negotiations was a mockery of the process, but in many cases they did not know what they were left with because they could not read the document. Since they had no other record themselves except perhaps a memory of the total process – even if it was verbatim – they ended up empty-handed.

9.2.3.3 Negotiated settlements

In recent years tribe after tribe has brought up old claims, and the solution that has evolved is the so-called negotiated settlement, an agreement hammered out between the descendents of the original Native-American signatories and the US Congress, usually for a cash payment, but sometimes involving title to land itself. And recall, of course, that there are some Native Americans who do not have treaty status, that is are not recognized as having any claim to reservation land anywhere. Such tribes are treated as if they do not exist. In the *Lyng* case, the US government did not suggest a negotiated settlement, so litigation resulted instead.

9.2.3.4 The Trust Doctrine

Another issue that enters the picture here is the notion of a Trust Doctrine, according to which the federal government holds certain lands in trust for the people (of the United States), and acts to defend the best use of those lands against other claimants. In the *Lyng* case the federal government claimed to hold the Six Rivers National Forest in trust, and that its interests overrode any claims to religious sites by Native-American tribes.

Deloria's characterization of the doctrine is worth quoting in full:

> The so-called Trust Doctrine is a strange creature composed of long-standing themes prevalent during the first century of 'discovery' of the 'New World': the need to find some operative principle to describe the internal location of Indian nations within the area claimed by the United States and for a practical guideline for the administration of services promised to the Indians in treaties and agreements. No single source can be found for the Trust Doctrine outside of the historical and political situations in which it has been invoked as a measure of federal performance. Consequently, it stands outside the constitutional framework as a moral presence much as does the idea of freedom with respect to American citizenship.
>
> (Deloria 1992: 271)

In other words, there is no constitutional guarantee or licence spelt out for the principle that the US government holds certain lands and other goods *in trust* for Native Americans or for the Forest Service, the National Park Service, or even for all Americans. We only measure how this is working by asking whether the federal government is performing its duties well; presumably the courts must decide this, and revoke the 'trust' if it has been violated. But when a small Native-American tribe is pitted against the resources of the Forest Service, or the federal courts, the intangible rights of the Native Americans, nowhere spelt out in the Constitution, are likely to receive short shrift.

This is an important point for the issue of language rights in general I think. They are not granted to the federal government, so they are presumably reserved for the states, or to the people, as citizens of these states. But the history of conflict between the federal and state governments on the one hand, and individual citizens on the other, especially those who claim the right to hold a certain religious tenet, and to also *act* upon that belief, is not a glorious one. As for the right to language, it is not mentioned in the US Constitution or specified in any way in early legislation, nor, as Heath points out (Heath 1992) were any specific recommendations, such as establishing English or other languages, ever agreed to, or stipulated. Many colonists came to America for religious freedom – the colonies of Plymouth, Massachusetts Bay, Pennsylvania, Maryland and others were founded as safe havens for religious refugees, but nobody came to the colonies for *linguistic freedom* or because of *linguistic oppression*.

9.2.3.5 Language: inalienable or inconsequential?

The founders of the United States seem to have acted as if language was either so inconsequential that it was not worth mentioning, or was inalienable, and therefore did not need protection. They seem to have acted as if language was irrelevant for their purposes, and that therefore all languages were on the same plane of equality. Yet we know that the latter was not part of their belief systems. Language *was* an important issue in the Protestant Reformation, and the turmoil of the Reformation led to the empowerment of vernacular languages that had previously had little status. An important tenet in all brands of Protestantism seemed to be direct access of each believer to the gospels without the intermediary of priests – this meant that all Christians had to be able to read the Bible themselves, in whatever language they spoke. The Bible instructed all Christians to go out into all lands and preach the gospel, and after the Reformation, this meant in whatever languages the heathen spoke. In America, one of the earliest printing efforts was a version of the Bible in Massachusett, a member of the Algonkin family, and other translations followed for certain other languages.

Yet the notion that these languages were somehow *equal* to English or other 'Christian' tongues does not seem to have been current, either. If translation was necessary, it was necessary only up to a point – the conversion of the heathen. After that, a linguistic conversion was in order. That, after all, was the beauty of language – it can be abandoned in favour of other ones. People could not change their skin colour or their sex (at least in those days) but they could adopt a new religion and could learn a new language. The two seemed to go hand in hand.

But for all the defence of religious belief in the US Constitution, certain kinds of religious belief are not in fact protected. Citizens whose religious beliefs involve a strong opposition to war, and whose beliefs compel them to refuse to bear arms and serve in the armed forces, have not had a happy time. The federal government has seemed to take the tack that one may have a right to conscientious objection to war, but this does not give one the right to put this belief into *action*, because such action endangers the welfare of the state.[21] Quakers and members of other historic peace churches went willingly to prison rather than violate these principles, until the principle of conscientious objection, and alternative service to war, was recognized as a valid right.

Other religious beliefs held by Native Americans and others have not fared as well. In the *Lyng* case, and in cases involving the ceremonial use of peyote (an hallucinogenic substance derived from the peyote cactus), the courts have taken the tack that to allow these beliefs for some people but not for others, is tantamount to giving preferential treatment to some people, and is a kind of *establishment of religion*, which of course is forbidden by the US Constitution. Since certain things are spelt out in the US Constitution, and other things are not (in particular the rights not granted to the federal government), it tends to be the case that explicit rights take precedence over implicit rights in US constitutional history. I might add that this is perhaps the way of the world, at least as far as the history of language rights are concerned – wherever linguistic rights are not spelt out explicitly, and guaranteed in all their complexity in constitutions, laws and regulations, they are weakly defended.

9.2.3.6 Paternalism

Where the Trust Doctrine does operate is in guaranteeing a kind of paternalism – the Bureau of Indian Affairs (BIA) will take care of this or that, because it has been established to take care of health and Indian education; the Forest Service will take care of forests, because that is its responsibility. One sees a conflict, of course, in the notion of *whose* trust – is the (commercial) value of the land held in trust more important than the Native-American right to use the land for particular purposes? The courts' tendency has been to rule on behalf of the BIA and other federal agencies, rather than on behalf of Native Americans, and we will find the same principle with regard to language – the rights of *all* Americans (to English) are viewed as more important than the rights of any subgroup of Americans to a language other than English. Here we see the argument that since everyone has religious rights, no small group's religious rights can take precedence over anyone else's, or what would result would be *establishment* of religion. Thus, one may conclude, since everyone has linguistic rights, no one group's right to a language can be recognized, since that would *establish* that language. This despite the fact that the right to *any* language at all is not within federal competence to judge, since rights not granted to the federal government are reserved by the people and the states under the Tenth Amendment.

Deloria sees the Trust Doctrine arising out of the discovery claims inherited from Great Britain after the Treaty of Paris. I would add that for some other territories, such as the Louisiana Purchase, Florida, Alaska, and some others (e.g. the Gadsden Purchase), the operative word is *purchase*. The territories in question were bought by the American government from other governments, whose claims were valid by discovery. Some other territories, for example California, Puerto Rico, Arizona–New Mexico, etc., were the spoils of war, but these followed upon the great purchases and were treated in the same way. That is, by purchasing the land, the US government owned it, and held it *in trust* for its citizens. The fact that Indians may have occupied the land was largely irrelevant. A way to deal with Native-American land claims did not evolve until the late twentieth century, and then it was fraught with the complexities of native people's oil rights in Alaska. Before that many usurpations of Native-American land were upheld by the courts, the most famous cases being those having to do with the invalidation of Cherokee claims in Georgia. Since the Cherokee lands had been granted by treaty, the US courts had to redefine the 'ward' and 'guardian' relationships as constituting part of the 'Trust' Doctrine.

Perhaps the best summary of the courts' view of Native-American land rights is the following quote, from the Supreme Court's ruling in *Johnson* v. *McIntosh* in 1823:

[T]he Indian inhabitants are to be considered as merely occupants, to be protected, indeed, while in peace, in the possession of their lands, but to be deemed incapable of transferring the absolute title to others.

(quoted in Delorian 1992: 272)

9.2.3.7 The issue of property ownership

Sixty years later, another issue led to further abrogation of Indian rights over their own lands. In a dispute having nothing to do with either language or religion, the question arose as to whether Indians were subject to federal and state laws such as those applying to murder. At first the Supreme Court affirmed that federal and state laws did not apply when powers were reserved by treaty. But then a case from California in 1886, *United States* v. *Kagama*, involving the murder conviction of two Indians on the Hoopa Reservation brought things to a head. The Supreme Court decided that whatever powers it did have to regulate commerce and raise taxes were not enough to allow it to enact criminal codes that would apply to reservations; instead it argued that territories that are under the geographical control of the US government are in fact under its political control, and since Indian reservations and territories, unlike states, are not self-governing, rules and regulations applying to them derive from its *ownership* of the country, which gives the right of exclusive sovereignty to the US government.

Thus Indian reservations are declared to be owned by the United States, unlike public domain lands, which are not a competitive type of land ownership. Be this as it may, we see that little by little, Indian treaty lands are reduced from the status of sovereign nations to lands held in trust, and then to lands *owned* by the federal government.

By the time we get to the *Lyng* case, the cards are stacked. Indian treaty rights protecting religious sites are now subordinate to the rights of the Forest Service, which represents the US government, as *owner* of the land. Since there were other, non-Indian groups such as conservationists and environmentalists who wished to keep the Six Rivers National Forest pristine and free of logging and other depredations, the case aroused much interest, and there were more plaintiffs and *amici curiae* than just the Yuroks, Karuks and Tolowas. The complaint was based on Forest Service violation of the First Amendment (religion), the Indian Religious Freedom Act, and many other environmental, historical, and administrative acts. The Indians had three possible approaches to this problem: to invoke the treaty relationship, invoke the trust relationship, or invoke the property relationship. The treaty route would have required prior action by the tribes when the Forest Service first made its proposal, asking for the Six Rivers area to be set aside. When 'trust' is invoked, it turns out to have validity only as one of many factors, and is not sacrosanct. And as is so often the case in the United States, those bodies set up to regulate various activities eventually end up being regulated by the people and interests they are supposed to be regulating. Acting in trust then becomes acting in self-interest for forest products companies, road-builders, polluters, ranchers, and so on.

To make a long story short, the Supreme Court eventually found for the Forest Service, even though the Forest Service then decided not to build the road. But the line of reasoning adopted by the majority of the court pounced on the First Amendment argument as too dangerous to protect here, since to privilege Indian religious rights over the territory would empower anybody to declare any site sacred, and bring the functioning of the federal government to its knees. The environmental arguments (based on the California Wilderness Act) were dismissed, since they had in fact been dealt with in the Ninth Circuit Court ruling, and unfortunately for the Forest Service, they would have lent weight to the religious arguments. The court held that the prerogatives of *landowners* were always more important than those of members of a religious group, since protecting one group's beliefs would be tantamount to *establishing* that religion. The California Wilderness Act had in fact already barred logging in the area, so if the Forest Service gave in and gave up their road, they would be perceived as caving in to the religious beliefs of Native-American groups.

The Supreme Court decided in *Lyng* that the Forest Service could build its road, though it would not be used for logging. Then the Forest Service proceeded to abandon the idea of building a road. But the decision in *Lyng* severely undermined Native Americans' ability to bring suits to protect or regain use of sacred lands, and secondly, it weakened the government's trust responsibility toward Native Americans, and placed its own property-ownership issues (or perception of its own property ownership) above them. Native Americans are now left with only one avenue, the negotiated settlement.

I have dwelt on this religious rights issue at some length in order to illustrate how even a right that is guaranteed by the US Constitution may be limited and whittled away. When the issue is that of language, mentioned nowhere in the US Constitution and guaranteed by no statutes, and in fact increasingly abrogated by statutes such as Proposition 63, there seems to be little more that can be said about Native-American language maintenance efforts. By the end of the twentieth century, they would appear to be, in California at least, moot, were it not for the sudden appearance in 1990, like a *deus ex machina*, of the Native American Languages Act.

9.3 POSTSCRIPT: THE NATIVE AMERICAN LANGUAGES ACT

In many a western 'genre' movie made on the back lots of Studio City, the train leaves the station with some of its passengers still standing on the platform, and for better or for worse, they decide to try to run after and catch the train. In a similar vein, almost a century and a half after most of the damage has been done to Native-American languages in California and elsewhere, in 1990 the US Congress passed a Native American Languages Act.[22] The text of this Act is too long to include in its entirety, but it emphasizes the uniqueness and the value of the languages, the responsibility of the USA to work together to preserve the languages, the special status of Native Americans, the wrongness of acts of suppression and extermination, etc. The text of the Act states that:

> It is the policy of the United States to preserve, protect, and promote the rights and freedom of Native Americans [previously defined] to use, practice and develop Native American languages[.]

(s. 104)

The text goes on to emphasize language survival, educational opportunity, the right to use Native-American languages in all BIA schools, in all tribal deliberations and all other social and cultural activities of Native-American people, and directs all heads of federal departments, agencies and instrumentalities to re-evaluate their policies in light of the above-mentioned policies.

It can be argued that this act is the most explicit statement on *language* ever to have issued from the US Congress in all its history. In none of the other deliberations, Supreme Court cases, Civil Rights legislation, Bilingual Education acts, Lau guidelines, or any other official documents, decisions, rulings, or interpretations do we have such explicit language about language.

Coming as it does on the heels of English Only legislation and referenda in states such as California, we are clearly in for some heated discussion. I can imagine that some people will see it as a 'Magna Carta' for language rights, and will try to use this legislation and its text as a precedent for establishing other language rights, but I predict that these attempts will not be successful. With the stipulation of the uniqueness and special status of Native-American cultures and languages, we have here probably only an example of Kloss's 'Pioneer' status writ large. That is, now that Native-American languages are now practically extinct, and pose no threat to anyone anywhere, we can grant them special status.

9.4 THE SPANISH HERITAGE

Adding to California's fantastic allure is the fact that it is also perhaps the only state to be named before it was discovered – the name derives from a story by Garci Ordoñez de Montalvo, *Las Sergas de Esplandián* (1510), of Black Amazons who inhabited an island with this name[23] thought to lie somewhere east of the Indies. Since Baja California was discovered first, the name was given to it around 1533, but soon it extended, in the plural (*las Californias*) to everything north of Cabo San Lucas. In 1542 Juan Rodrigues Cabrillo (with help from a successor, since Cabrillo died in the attempt) explored the entire coast of the current state; in 1579 Sir Francis Drake spent more than a month anchored at Drake's Bay[24] and had some 'commerce' with the Indians there. There was regular trade between Acapulco and the Philippines across the Pacific, and given the currents and winds, the galleons usually sailed along part of the coast: in the early 1600s Sebastián Vizcaíno discovered Monterey Bay and reported on his exploration of the coast. Jesuits entered Baja California in 1697 but were expelled 70 years later. Spain did not make any claims on the territory until Russian incursions into Alaska and then as far south as the Russian River convinced them that some settlements must be made. Those in San Diego and Monterey were among the first, with Franciscan and Dominican missions, 21 in all, extending from San Diego to Sonoma.

As we have already noted, despite the early explorations of Cabrillo and others, the Spanish impact on California is light. Perhaps because gold was not discovered, perhaps because California was an outpost of Mexico, perhaps because what lay between temperate and balmy Upper California and Mexico was the long peninsula now known as Baja California, a definitely inhospitable and arid territory, reachable only by water, and perhaps because of the difficulty of managing agricultural enterprises without large-scale irrigation, Spain did little to settle, colonize or missionize until the pressure of competing Russian exploration spurred the creation of the missions and the *camino real* linking them. This dates from about 1770.

The upshot of this is that in terms of overt language regulation, schooling would have been exclusively in Spanish. We have seen that the Spanish did not attempt a systematic and thorough study of any native language,[25] nor did they utilize any California language for any but pragmatic purposes, and that the mission system would have preferred to use Spanish as a catechistic language, Latin as a liturgical language, and Spanish as medium of instruction. As Kloss points out (1977a: 180) the administration of Upper California was in the hands of the missions until 1823 (both Cook and Heizer say 1834), so there would have been no school language policy other than the mission policy.[26] Native-American languages, as we have seen, were too diverse and there were too many of them to come to grips with, and none emerged as an obvious *lingua franca*.

Population estimates for the end of the Spanish/Mexican period, as we have seen, range from as low as 13,000 'Spanish Californios and inland Indian tribes' taken together, at the point when the Gold Rush brought 87,000 (mostly English-speaking) immigrants (Thernstrom *et al.* 1980) to a high of 100,000 (Cook 1978). As we have seen, the figure of 13,000 is now thought to be much too low, so estimates vary between this low and a high of 100,000, having declined from a pre-Columbian high of 310,000.

9.5 THE ARRIVAL OF ANGLO-AMERICANS

English-speaking Americans began to arrive overland and to settle in California while it was still a Mexican colony, bringing with them the idea that it was America's 'Manifest Destiny' to extend from sea to shining sea. Since the population of California in the early part of the nineteenth century probably did not exceed 13,000 Spanish speakers,[27] the presence of Anglo-Americans began to be felt while California was still a Mexican colony. Some sources report that from the very first, Americans agitated for California to secede from Mexico, become a separate republic, and/or join the United States. When war broke out with Mexico in 1846, this was used as a pretext to press for advantage, and military incursions and occupations of various settlements, for example Monterey, seem now to have been premeditated. Congress had begun to discuss the issue of statehood for California even before the terms of the Treaty of Guadalupe-Hidalgo in 1848, but were stymied by the issue of slavery – northern states wanted no new states where slavery was permitted, and southern states wanted no new states where slavery was banned.

In 1848, the war with Mexico ended with the signing of the Treaty of Guadalupe-Hidalgo, under the terms of which Mexico ceded what is now Texas, New Mexico, Arizona, California and portions of other states to the United States. In the same year, gold was discovered at Sutter's Mill on the American River, near Sacramento, and the resultant flood of immigrants tipped the balance of the population strongly in favour of the Anglo-Americans.[28] A perception developed that any rights Spanish speakers may have had pre-1848 were rendered moot by the fact that, without immigration to replenish their numbers, the percentage of the population knowing Spanish was gradually decreasing. Thus the right to 'Pioneer' status that Kloss (1977a) recognizes as a part of implied American tolerance was seen to belong only to original Spanish settlers. When immigration resumed from Latin America after World War I, and boomed after World War II, no tolerance for the rights of new Spanish speakers was left. 'Pioneer' status tolerance, it seems, is a finite commodity, and when it is exhausted it cannot be replenished or reinvigorated. In fact one could almost say that linguistic tolerance *expires*, and latter-day demands for it seem to trigger the opposite reaction – intolerance. The fact that Spanish speakers who remained in California were members of the 'enemy' defeated in the war that transferred the sovereignty of the territory seems to have tainted relations between Anglo-Americans and Hispanics to this day.

9.6 TREATY OF GUADALUPE-HIDALGO

Under the Treaty of Guadalupe-Hidalgo, certain guarantees of the rights of Spanish speakers to their customs and religion and language were spelt out. But as with much language legislation of this sort, the language was either not explicit enough or assumed certain other conditions, so that almost from the beginning these rights were not upheld, or were whittled away by various statutes and *ad hoc* regulations.

A useful summary of early California language legislation is to be found in Kloss (1977a: 180–5). The 1849 Constitution states that:

> All laws, decrees, regulations and provisions which from their nature require publication shall be published in English and Spanish.
>
> (Art XI (21), quoted in Kloss 1977a: 181)

This language sounds unambiguous – if things need to be published, it shall be done in the two languages. However, the requirement that things be published in Spanish was not stated to be a *right* of Hispanic Californians; it was not connected to their persons, as a personal right, nor to them as a group, nor to the territory of California. It was as if the requirement to publish in Spanish was just a favour, to be extended as long as the Anglo-American majority wished to do so. It is not surprising that erosion of the requirement that laws, decrees, regulations and provisions be published in Spanish began almost immediately. As Kloss shows, it is in the *implementation* of this provision that things begin to fall apart, mainly by the following:

- The fact that the State Translator was elected by the Legislature, which made it a political appointment.

- By the fact that translation into Spanish often was delayed by seeking the lowest bidder to do the job.

- By waiting until one year's accumulation of material had accrued.

- By restricting the availability of translations to certain counties only (mainly coastal southern California).

Thus, regulations that narrowed the scope of this provision were enacted in 1852 and 1863, and finally, when a new constitution was worked out in 1879, the provision for publication of laws, decrees, regulations and provisions in Spanish was almost totally gone. Similarly, in 1851, 1857 and 1863 regulations were adopted as to how much Spanish was to be allowed in oral court proceedings, how much of the written record had to be in Spanish, and in which counties.

9.6.1 Language and education

Furthermore, laws relating to the language of the medium of instruction in public schools were non-existent at the time of Guadalupe-Hidalgo, since public education was not established until later in this raw new territory.[29] When school laws were enacted, it was with other populations in mind, such as German and French speakers in San Francisco, who were given the same kind of tolerance as Germans enjoyed for a time in the Midwest, with so-called 'Cosmopolitan Schools' established in 1867[30] – featuring instruction in German or French for 1½ hours per day in the elementary grades, rising to 50 per cent time in either language in the upper grades. After 1900 this was extended to southern California, and Italian was added, with a 1913 amendment adding Spanish. These 'Cosmopolitan Schools' continued in existence even after the restrictive post-1918 laws in the Midwest, and were strengthened by a 1929 statute, which was not repealed until 1965. In 1967 and after the Bilingual Education Act (1968), the scene shifted from essentially élite bilingual schools to the attempt to deal with disadvantaged children, and new languages entered the picture.[31]

9.6.2 The Constitution of 1879

As we have already seen, restrictions on and erosions of the translation provision began almost immediately. By 1879, when a new State Constitution was written, tolerance was almost gone.

Crawford (1992) provides a number of documents illustrative of conflict over language in California: especially cogent is the excerpt of the constitutional debate of 1879 (Crawford 1992: 51–8) on a provision for guarantees for Spanish, which lost, resulting in complete abrogation of the provisions of Guadalupe-Hidalgo, and making California, in Crawford's words, the first 'English-only' state, a condition that lasted until 1966.

As Crawford points out, this was a period of strong 'nativist' inclinations, of 'Know-Nothingism', of populist laws and protection of the working-man's rights against the incursions not only of Spanish speakers, but Chinese immigrants and other threatening groups. The kinds of arguments adduced for the abrogation of rights for Spanish speakers are of the following sort:

- Thirty years (since 1848) is enough time for people to have learned English.

- Spanish documents are available by the ton, but are not being read.

- 'This is an English-speaking Government' and people who cannot speak English should not participate in public activities.[32]

- Granting rights to Spanish is 'demagogism that panders to the foreign element' and many of the Spanish speakers are 'bandits, cut-throats and robbers'.

- The Spanish speakers 'sold us their country, and we have paid them the money'. (Language rights, if any, were 'sold', too.)[33]

Even after the vote was passed on a provision to make English the only constitutionally protected language of the state, an amendment by a delegate from San Bernardino to allow, but not require, discretionary legislative use of Spanish, in areas where needed, failed to pass (by 27 to 55 votes).

9.6.3 Erosion of residual linguistic rights

Certain things seem clear from this: it seems to be the understanding in California that there are limits to language rights. We might paraphrase these 'limits' as follows:

- Language rights, even when supposedly guaranteed by an international treaty, can be abrogated by state provisions.

- Language rights are time-limited and can therefore expire; once expired, they cannot be renewed.

- Language rights are granted with the 'understanding' that people will learn English. If they do not manage to learn English in the interim, it is too bad.

- Other 'immigrants' and 'foreigners' learn English – why can't Spanish speakers?

- Failure to learn English is a failure of the individual, and weakens his or her right to participate in public life. If you want to be an American, and vote, and hold office, and serve on juries, learn English.

- English is the language of the most powerful and successful countries in the world; failure to learn it is to 'choose powerlessness'.

9.7 *LAU* V. *NICHOLS*, 1974

As we have noted, between 1879 and 1913, there were no rights for Spanish speakers in California, though speakers of German, French and eventually Italian enjoyed a kind of bilingual school option, the 'Cosmopolitan School', extended finally to include Spanish in 1913, renewed by statute in 1929, and only discontinued in 1965.

But European language speakers were not the only settlers in California; after early attempts to restrict Chinese and other East Asian immigration, settlement from East Asia did proceed, but with restrictions: Asians born in other countries could not become naturalized citizens. There were also some instances of segregated schools for Asians, though the use of their own languages would have been limited to Saturday schools or other supplemental programmes, not paid for by tax-payers.

It is then perhaps no surprise that California's antipathy to Asian settlers should come back to haunt it, in the form of an important

Supreme Court case, *Lau* v. *Nichols*, 1974.[34] In that case, parents of Chinese-speaking children whose understanding of English was limited sued the San Francisco Unified School District for providing unequal educational opportunities to their children, supposedly in violation of the Fourteenth Amendment. The Supreme Court ruled that simply providing equal facilities without providing access to an education conducted wholly in English, especially in the large numbers alleged in the *Lau* case, was not equal education. On the basis of section 601 of the Civil Rights Act of 1964 the California Court of Appeals was reversed.

But the *Lau* decision did not specify any remedies for this inequality; it noted that bilingual education was already an option under California law, and remanded the case 'for appropriate relief'. Since appropriate relief was not defined, it fell to respondents of various sorts to come up with some. Bilingual education (whatever and however that was to be defined) was obviously one form; ESL programmes were another. Since the Office of Civil Rights (established in the wake of the Civil Rights Act of 1964) had already begun to amass data on possible discrimination against 'national origin-minority' children, the US Commissioner of Education acted to establish what came to be known as 'Lau Remedies', informal guidelines that were never published in the Federal Register (Jiminez 1992: 246), such that their ability to be enforced was severely weakened. Later, under President Carter (1976–80), the Department of Education developed *Lau Regulations* that spelt out what steps would be appropriate to remedy linguistic inequity. But under the Reagan administration (1980–8), *Lau Regulations* were again challenged, and never became law.

Unlike the outcome of *Brown* v. *Board of Education*, which mandated that schools be desegregated 'with all deliberate speed', the *Lau* decision never resulted in a definition of 'appropriate action to overcome language barriers', a requirement of the Equal Educational Opportunities Act (20 USC sections 1701–20) which was passed soon after *Lau*. But the EEOA also failed to define appropriate action, so school districts continue to muddle along; states continue to pass English-only legislation, and a confused picture persists in all quarters.

9.8 PROPOSITION 63

In 1986 California (preceding Florida and Colorado by two years) approved a referendum on language known as Proposition 63; it was part of the efforts of an organization known as US English, which was bankrolling English-only initiatives both at the federal and state level.[35] Clearly US English taps into concerns about immigration, eugenics, welfare reform, population and environment control, and political movements that wish to preserve America as a White English-speaking nation. Its direct mailings constantly assail us with 'statistics' about birth rates, the refusal of immigrants to learn English, the dangers of multilingualism (French Canada, Bosnia, etc.) and the death of civilization as we know it. Such misinformation appeals to voters afraid for their jobs and tired of welfare abuse and inner-city crime; teachers feel threatened that they will have to teach something other than 'standard English', and older immigrants feel cheated that they and their parents had to learn English, but modern immigrants and illegal aliens do not.

One of the things that happens when an issue like Proposition 63 is proposed is that public debate of all sorts begins to appear in the media, and though the understanding of the issues at stake is often fraught with confusion and outright ignorance, not to mention misinformation, this public debate is useful and healthy. The public begins to discuss such things as:

1 What is bilingual education and what examples do we have of effective bilingual education programmes?
2 What rights do we as American citizens (or California citizens) have to language(s)?
3 What is actually the legal policy on language in the USA or in any specific state?
4 What attempts have been made in the past to officialize one language or another, and what legal precedents are there for bilingualism?

Unfortunately the public discussion of language rights tends to shed more heat than light; both proponents and opponents of Proposition 63 believe strongly that language is a common bond in our society, that it expresses our only link to ethnicity, that it represents access and opportunity to its citizens. Curiously then, both proponents and opponents seem to be able to use these arguments for their own position. As MacKaye puts it:

Language is seen as the *only* common bond among Americans, as the *only* factor in the attainment of the American dream, as the *only* cue to ethnicity. Enormous power is ascribed to language, making it the great equalizer, without considering any of the other societal and cultural factors in play. In each of these beliefs there is truth and error, symbol and substance, history and myth, and the weight of tradition, both real and invented. Consequently, legislation concerning language issues is not the simple matter it may appear to be.

(MacKaye 1990: 146, emphasis added)

Nowhere in the discussion surrounding Proposition 63 was it mentioned that California's own history is one of perfidy and abrogation of previously guaranteed rights, nor that California rode roughshod over the provisions of the Treaty of Guadalupe-Hidalgo. Nobody mentioned that 'Cosmopolitan Schools' using German, French and Italian were a legality for many years, but not for Spanish, nor that Spanish-speaking Californians are desperate to learn English, and will stand in line all night to sign up for ESL classes. Californians, in what is unfortunately the 'true' spirit of American thinking on language issues, are quick to point the finger and short on memory. In all these discussions the following facts are typically ignored, or rejected with spurious or insufficiently documented arguments:

1 Learning to read in one's own language first seems to facilitate literacy in another language, such as English.[36]
2 English as a Second Language (ESL) classes regularly turn away large numbers of potential students because of inadequate funding.
3 Recent immigrants follow the same path to assimilation that our grandparents' generation followed, that is bilingualism in the first generation, monolingualism in English by the second.
4 The attainment of true (balanced) bilingualism is probably extremely rare, and what we actually get out of 'bilingual' programmes is simply ease of transition to English.
5 The sink-or-swim immersion programmes of the past (our grandparents' experience) meant that many in fact sank; they dropped out and became unskilled labourers. The demand for unskilled labourers today is, of course, extremely low.

9.9 AFTER PROPOSITION 63

And yet; *and yet*. Now that Proposition 63 and many other state statutes of this sort have been in effect for a few years, the net result and the visible impact seem to be minimal. We are informed (Crawford 1992: 303) that California State statutes already on the books to do with language services for LEP Californians continue to be available. Shigekane (1992) provide a list of services that must be provided in various languages other than English, in over 44 different state agencies, from health to employment to motor-vehicle licensing. This is summarized in one source as follows:

> California . . . has originated some of the most extensive governmental programs to serve the needs of non-English speakers. Its most sweeping declaration of policy is contained in the Dymally-Alatorre Bilingual Services Act, CAL. GOV'T CODE §7290 which declares:
>
>> Every state agency . . . directly involved in the furnishing of information of the rendering of services to the public whereby contact is made with a substantial number of non-English-speaking people, shall employ a sufficient number of qualified bilingual persons in public contact positions to ensure provision of information and services to the public, in the language of the non-English-speaking person.
>
> ID. §7292. Moreover all written materials explaining governmental services must be made available in a language other than English when that language is spoken by more than five percent of the people served by a local office. *See* ID. §§7292.5, 7296.2. Specifically '911' emergency services must be made available on a multilingual basis, *see* Warren-911-Emergency Assistance Act, CAL. GOV'T CODE §53,112; information regarding unemployment insurance must be made available in Spanish, *see* CAL. UNEMP. INS. CODE §316; and a synopsis of the laws regulating the operation of vehicles must be published in Spanish in sufficient numbers to meet demand, *see* CAL. VEH. CODE para. 1656(b).
>
> (*Harvard Law Review* 100(6): 1345)

As this source points out, officialization of a language may have no effect on bilingual services already mandated by state law; but Proposition 63 does explicitly permit citizens to mount a legal challenge to certain bilingual programmes. As the *HLR Note* puts it:

> The question therefore arises: to what extent should a state's official-English declaration require or permit a court to dismantle state programs designed to meet the needs of non-English speakers?
>
> (*HLR Note* 100(6): 1347)

the *Note* goes on to argue that:

> the legal force of state declaration of an official language is narrowly circumscribed by federal statutory provisions and by

the equal protection clause of the fourteenth amendment.

(HLR Note 100(6): 1347)

In other words, state regulations , no matter how they arise, through whatever process, whether the referendum, the initiative, or administrative code, cannot violate the US Constitution, since denial of equal protection to language minorities might impermissibly single out 'quasi-suspect classes' for discriminatory treatment: the Supreme Court has struck down many laws that it found to be discriminatory in this way.

At the time of writing, no such challenges have appeared, and if they were to appear, would surely be brought to the Supreme Court for adjudication, where, it is predicted, official-English pronouncements would not be allowed to undermine existing bilingual programmes.

What is clear here is that when laws and rulings are made in a number of different ways, from the top down (the legislature), or the outside in (through initiatives) and from the bottom up (as a response by one or another agency to the problem of delivery of social services) conflicts will arise, and the policy will not be settled until all legal differences are reconciled.

Since this is, as I have claimed throughout, typical in the United States – and indeed is seen as one of the strengths of our system – language policy in California, as elsewhere, will continue to lack coherence, and some parts of it will act at cross-purposes with others.

9.10 SUMMATION

We began this chapter with a somewhat tongue-in-cheek question – is California 'off the wall?' In our review of language policy in that state, we have seen that from the arrival of Europeans to the present, language policy has been a hyper-acute version of Anglo-American policy – just as California is just like the rest of the country, only more so. California's language policy (both official and unofficial) is more of the same, only worse. In its treatment of aboriginal Native-American populations, of original Spanish speakers, of present-day speakers of languages other than English, California has from Day One ridden roughshod over all concepts of decency and civilized behaviour. Especially in the Anglo-American period, language policy has been as rough and ready as the miners who raped the valleys for their gold. California attempted from the very first to thwart stipulations made in the Treaty of Guadalupe-Hidalgo about the rights of *Hispanos*, it bottled-up legislation designed to protect Native Americans and their right to Indian land, and therefore their right to protect their religion, culture and language. It forced Asian immigrants to live in specific ghettoes, and attempted to restrict immigration from Asia. From its earliest days as a state, California has been in violation of many of the common ideals and courtesies supposedly cherished by Americans of good will. In retrospect it seems quite clear that the failure to require California to remain a territory for a trial period prior to statehood – until it could prove itself capable of self-government – was a grievous mistake. The question of whether any of this can be rectified today, by judicial or statutory means, is one that will require commitment, courage and vision in the time to come.

10 Conclusion

As we have seen from the examples of language policy treated in the previous chapters, language policy is primarily a social construct. It may consist of various elements of an explicit nature – juridical, judicial, administrative, constitutional and/or legal language may be extant in some jurisdictions, but whether or not a polity has such explicit *text*, policy as a cultural construct rests primarily on other conceptual elements – belief systems, attitudes, myths – the whole complex that we are referring to as *linguistic culture*, which is the sum totality of ideas, values, beliefs, attitudes, prejudices, religious strictures, and all the other cultural 'baggage' that speakers bring to their dealings with language from their background. Linguistic culture also is concerned with the transmission and codification of language and also has bearing on the culture's notions of the value of literacy and the sanctity of texts. This also involves the role of language as the main vehicle for the replication, construction and transmission of culture itself.

And of course language itself is a cultural construct – no one is genetically predisposed to learn any particular language,[1] so children of any racial or genetic background will learn any language they are exposed to, if given enough social encouragement. However, having said that language is a construct, this does not imply that it can be deconstructed, changed, or radically altered by the application of particular political scrutinies of one sort or another. That is, the post-modern project of skewering all social constructs and hanging them up to dry does not, in the case of language, alter the structure of particular languages in any significant way. Some attention to racism or sexism may result in linguistic *avoidance*, perhaps, but the avoidance of sexist language, or of gender-laden pronouns has not altered the fundamental structure of English in any but the most trivial way.

Nor has it, to my knowledge, changed the power structure of the English-speaking world.

We have also seen that though speakers may unequivocally identify themselves as speakers of one particular language or another, there are also speech forms that cannot be unambiguously classified as one so-called language rather than another. That is, the boundaries between what is one language and what is another (e.g. what is German and what is Dutch; or Serbian or Croatian; or Hindi, Urdu and Panjabi), though they seem clear to speakers at the centre or focal area of each 'language', are at certain transitional zones[2] not clear. Thus the linguist who is called in to classify something as either A or B must throw up his hands when the speakers of A or B use political or social or religious criteria to decide what they speak, and not linguistic behaviour. Conversely, speakers who themselves identify their various dialects as one language may find that political structures identify them as separate languages, in order to divide and conquer – Maithili is a 'dialect' of Hindi when spoken within Nepal, but contested by some as a separate 'language' across the border in India. The various Turkic languages of central Asia were once thought of as part of a great Turkic/Turkish complex, but under Soviet hegemony had to develop separately. In the post-Soviet era, more *rapprochement*, especially with Anatolian Turkish, is again observable.

Earlier we also discussed problems with *conceptions* of language – what are we talking about when we formulate a policy about language? Linguists see it as *the code* – a set of grammatical rules plus the lexicon which allows us to specify (generate) all the sentences of the language. For others, language is the code plus all the sentences of the language, or at least all of the 'best' sentences, the important texts, the literature. For some it is the language spoken by the 'best' or most important or most powerful people in the society. Still other analysts would have their own definitions, combining the above with questions of blood, race, soil, territory, with aspects of culture that are officially despised under the United Nations charter, yet may still inspire a Bosnian Serb to kill a Bosnian Muslim: both are by the linguist's definition speakers of the same language. Thus it is possible for some analysts to label the English language 'imperialistic' because some behaviours exhibited somewhere by some English speakers appear to result in the subjugation of other languages (or their speakers).[3] We have seen in France the widespread notion that English (as a language) is the enemy, rolling across territory and exterminating, or at least threatening to annihilate, French language and culture. Yet the 'brilliance' and 'radiation' of French, especially in its heyday in the seventeenth and eighteenth centuries, was seen as salutary – after all, French is (or was thought to be) the language of culture, the highest expression of Western civilization. No parallels can be seen between these two situations by the defenders of the illumination of the French language.

As if these definitional problems were not enough, we also see that language policies, rooted as they are in murky and ill-specified beliefs about language, are often vaguely defined. The French Revolution decreed the teaching of French in every commune where French was not in force, but then the policy bogged down in definitional problems, unable to say whether something was a *patois*, an *idiome*, a *langue*, or a dialect – because to do so might legitimize the claim of non-French speakers to linguistic and even political autonomy. Ironically, as we have seen, the French Revolution was a victory for *monarchist* language policy, and this centralized and unyielding policy stands on its own even today, unaided by any legislation or legal statute.[4] The social construct that is French language policy, thought by the French to be rooted in its legal tradition, is largely a matter of habit and custom. It works because the French appear to think it works. The French model illustrates how corpus policy and status policy can be confused, or at least not kept separate.

In polities such as India, however, traditional multilingualism is in conflict with foreign models that have been shown to be bankrupt in their home countries. The Soviet model of language policy was borrowed lock, stock and barrel in post-Independence India, but it has failed (as it failed in the former USSR), and the natural multilingualism, code-switching, diglossia and other long-standing complex linguistic behaviours of the region have reasserted themselves. Indeed more people are now said to be studying English in India than before Independence, while the legal status of English has had the pins knocked out from under it. With very little status support, English continues to survive and flourish in India. In the Tamil area, much heat and very little light are generated over language issues. The great hope that purification of Tamil would return Tamilnāḍu to the halcyon Sangam period of milk and honey has been dashed.

In the USA we are presented with perhaps the murkiest of language policies – one that is (or at least used to be characterized as) superficially tolerant of linguistic diversity, and that does not explicitly enshrine English or any other language as *primus inter pares*. Yet attempts to stretch this 'tolerance' policy are met with increasing intolerance, and nowhere more vehemently than among the vast majority of Anglo-Americans who may themselves be the products of the powerful but covert assimilationism inherent in American policy. Attempts to treat language rights as a civil rights issue, or as a freedom of speech issue, or any of the other rights protected explicitly in the US Constitution and the Bill of Rights have been consistently rebuffed. Simultaneously, the courts have not allowed laws to be passed that single out any particular *group*, whether it be religious, linguistic or ethnic, for exclusionary or punitive actions. US language policy remains in limbo, therefore – the courts deny it explicitness, but the people (both the monolingualists and the multilingualists) demand explicit guarantees. It has evolved from its original *laissez-faire* tolerance: the arrival of millions of German-speaking, Spanish-speaking and other language groups has tested it and led to inflexibility in certain areas (e.g. citizenship), but several factors inhibit radical change at the federal level.

One is that education and most of the other areas where linguistic rights are demanded remain non-federal rights: states and other jurisdictions are therefore free to pass legislation of various sorts, so long as it does not single out specific groups, and deny them their constitutional rights. The other is that language rights are not among those guaranteed explicitly in the original Constitution, because no linguistic group came to America for linguistic freedom. It was not one of the crucial issues leading to the American Revolution, and to a strict constructionist, is not one of the rallying points of our revolution.

A third factor may be the eternal one – that language shift *can* take place with very little personal disruption, if conditions are right. Children will learn the language of their environment, and most Americans do after two generations learn English. The primordialists who demand the protection of their language, who see its loss as personally and culturally devastating do not represent the majority view in any US immigrant group. They may speak the loudest, or the most eloquently, and may appear to be advocating demands that speak for everyone in their group, but do nothing but enrage the Anglocentrists; but their children hedge their bets and learn English. English Only and similar movements are therefore beating a dead horse. There is no danger that any group will not learn English, so the politics of Anglocentricity must be seen as an attack on something else – race, power, class or demographics.

In the end, every language policy is culture-specific, and it is in the study of linguistic culture that we will come to understand why language policies evolve the way they do, why they work (or do not work) the way they are planned to work, and how peoples' lives are affected by them. The real challenge in the study of language policy is that there are so many variables to be dealt with, and that simplistic notions or one-note theories cannot hope to capture the complexity that is language and linguistic culture.

Notes

1 INTRODUCTION: LANGUAGE POLICY AND LINGUISTIC CULTURE

1 In the state of Washington, for example, one can take the written driver's licence test in a number of languages besides English, but such an option is not available for the examination for a pilot's licence on the state ferry system.
2 Despite caveats to the contrary, such as the following:

> [I]t should be evident that no rational talk about language policy or planning can begin until the actual language situation, or sociolinguistic profile, of the particular country has been determined in some detail, never to be lost sight of while taking any measures to act on it. (Bugarski 1992: 11)

For examples of attempts to deal with the complexity of the problem, see Falch 1973, Kloss 1966a and Stewart 1968.
3 The most immediate effect of widespread diglossia is that people acquire literacy in a form of their language that is widely different from the variety they learn as children at home; this puts a heavy burden on the educational system, and is a strong factor in the high drop-out rate, the low rates of functional literacy, and so forth.
4 Though typically in these societies, the belief is that only the H-variety is under control, while the L-variety or varieties are devoid of any rule-governance.
5 If diglossia is ignored, the ability of millions of pre-literate citizens to communicate adequately is blocked. Diglossia, in other words, has policy implications for *literacy* in such societies, and the failure to deal with it is in effect a policy *failure*.
6 The only way to change such policy would be to change the way the culture 'thinks' about language, perhaps by some consensus-building process, rather than by fiat or by legislative decree. In the few South Asian linguistic cultures that have attempted to elevate the lower variety, such as Bengali and Telugu, it took the intervention of prestigious writers and educators who deliberately published in those varieties to bring about a change.

7 This notion was first proposed in Schiffman 1993.

8 See, for example, Mertz 1982 for an analysis of US language law as being based on a Whorfian folk theory about language, in particular the notion that since language 'determines' thought, the goal of US language policy was to ensure that the first language locked in Americans' heads would be English.

9 Fasold calls it 'the approach to the sociolinguistics of language in which the use of language in general is related to social and cultural values' (Fasold 1984: 39).

10 What is nature and what is nurture here is problematical; we know there is a human capacity, both mental and physiological, for speech, and for language acquisition; but without input from society during certain crucial years, language acquisition does not take place.

11 Subsequent to Hoenigswald's research, perhaps as a result of it, there has developed an interest in research on language attitudes, as exemplified by Lambert *et al.* (1972).

12 The bibliography accompanying Hoenigswald's article is illustrative of work already done on this topic.

13 I borrow this distinction from Benjamin Lee Whorf (1964: 131), who used it to describe distinctions between overt and covert classes or categories in the grammar of a language; but I refrain here from psychologizing about 'world-views' or the role of language in 'defining experience'. There is also a parallel in the notions of 'latent' and 'manifest' culture proposed by Becker and Geer 1960, in the notions of overt and covert prestige promulgated by Labov 1972 and elaborated in Trudgill 1983: 89–90. Tollefson (1988) has also referred to covert aspects of US language policy toward refugees.

14 The German text is as follows:

> Die engere und weitere Bedeutung des Begriffs Sprachpolitik sollte aber nicht vermischt werden, denn sie unterscheiden sich in einem wesentlichen Punkt: Sprachpolitik im engeren Verständnis – ich nenne sie *explizite* Sprachpolitik – ist gesellschaftliches Handeln, das *unmittelbar* auf die sprachlich vermittelten Lebenszusammenhänge der Sprecher gerichtet ist, während *strukturelle* Sprachpolitik dasjenige Handeln gesellschaftlicher Gruppen oder staatlicher Administrationen bezeichnet, das nachweislich sprachlich vermittelte Lebenszusammenhänge in den Gesamtzusammenhang als allgemeiner politischer Praxis einbezieht. (Gessinger 1980: 22–3)

Gessinger's goal is to show how language policy in Germany in the eighteenth century, and especially in Prussia, had not only explicit aspects but had built into it assumptions about language and its role in the transmission of culture, and in particular the expansion of German *Kultur* into the areas of Poland recently acquired by the partition of that nation, assumptions that are tacit in the policy but built into the culture.

15 Veltman (1983: 211) refers to the 'power of the English language in the USA to subordinate and eradicate the languages of immigrants to that country'. Saer *et al.* (1924: 609) characterize English as the 'powerful and penetrating English tongue, which in every part of the world has proved itself to be all-conquering among the languages of the earth'.

16 Despite the claims of such movements as *US English* and *English First*.

17 For example, the requests for support of English-speaking congregations, indicative of the existence already by that time of many English-dominant members that began in the 1880s from the Indiana and other synods, but were not acted upon until much later.

18 Trudgill 1983: 101–6.

19 I borrow this term from Prague School linguistics, where it was used to refer to the fact that a minor distinction such as phonemic contrast between English [ð] and [z] (which is probably used only to distinguish 'then' and 'Zen'), and [θ] and [s] (which would distinguish a few more pairs, such as 'sink' and 'think'), that is, dental fricatives contrasting with alveolar fricatives are not used to distinguish very many words, but where the phonemic contrast is used – in deictics and demonstratives such as 'the, this, that, there, then' – its functional load is high. For further discussion see Matesius 1961 [1931].

20 See Krishnamurti 1988 for some discussion of standardization problems in Indian languages.

21 Even in France many scientists and technologists publish their results in English *in French journals*, in order to be more widely read.

22 As I have tried to show (Schiffman 1987) such policies as those employed for the German-American Church are actually but unwittingly covertly assimilationist; Kloss (1977a) states that it is an 'axiom' of the American linguistic scene that a loss to English (by or from another language) is never regained. We must see this axiom as a part of American linguistic culture, since it is not a part of US overt language policy.

23 Nathan Glazer calls this the 'enormous assimilative power of American civilization' (Glazer 1966: 360).

24 In Paraguay, for example, there is little or no recognition of the proficiency and status that Paraguayans have in Guaraní despite the great compartmentalization of domains described in Rubin 1972.

25 The German text is as follows:
Das Deutsche, Französische, Italienische und Rätoromanische sind die Nationalsprachen der Schweiz.
Als Amtssprachen des Bundes werden das Deutsche, Französische und Italienische erklärt.

26 See also Weinreich 1968 [1953] for a description of language use and language contact in the Confederation, especially in the Romansch/German diglossia.

27 See for example the cantonal examples enumerated in Falch 1973: 38–40:

> Les écoles communales ne sont pas obligées de donner un enseignement à des enfants qui proviennent d'autres cantons et qui parlent une autre langue. Cela provient du fait que la langue de l'administration et de l'école est fixée une fois pour toutes. Ce principe non écrit a été consacré par un jugement du Tribunal fédéral de 1931: les frontières linguistiques du pays doivent être considérées comme intangibles.

28 See also McRae 1983 for other examples of how linguistic rights are managed cantonally.

29 Banakar (1982), simultaneously polemicizes against certain linguistic minorities (for which read 'Tamils') who demand too many rights, while at the same time pointing a finger at certain states (read 'Tamilnāḍu') where 'linguistic minorities . . . are uncared for and their legitimate interests have been suppressed and safeguards enshrined in the constitution itself have not been provided' (Banakar 1982: iv).

30 For a summary of India's language policy as expressed in the 1950 Constitution, see Watts 1970: 152–4. The Eighth Schedule (§§ 344(1) and 351) is the section that lists the legitimized languages, whose rights are mentioned elsewhere. A careful reading of these portions of the constitution reveals that although many clauses protect various languages and the rights of their speakers to *promote* their own languages, and prohibit restrictions on individual initiatives, very little is stated about domains that are reserved for languages, except to mention Hindi, or the right of a speaker to use his or her language in certain situations. Article 347, for example, allows for minority linguistic groups 'with a substantial proportion of the population' that have a grievance in a particular state to petition the president, who, if satisfied that they have a grievance, may direct the state to recognize that language. What a 'substantial proportion' is, is left up to the president to decide, as is the decision whether to issue orders to a state. And Article 350A encourages every state to provide adequate facilities for instruction in the mother tongue at the primary stage of education to children belonging to linguistic minority groups, and the president may issue instructions to any state that is not doing so; but as we shall see in our later review of this subject in the chapter on language policy in India, nothing here is required or guaranteed.

31 It is no surprise that this policy is satisfactory only to Hindi speakers, and a source of disaffection for non-Hindi speakers.

32 Tadadjeu does not cite this in the text but his bibliography lists Welmers 1971, its probable source.

33 It should be noted, however, that for Ferguson, all of the attitudes and beliefs that we are subsuming under the rubric of linguistic culture are dealt with as *myth*, whereas I am distinguishing between myth and other aspects of linguistic culture.

34 In the text, Miller refers to the Japanese language by its Japanese name, *Nihongo*.

35 In fact, when wholesale borrowing of foreign models does happen, as I will argue was the case with post-independence language policy in India, the result was disastrous.

36 Gessinger's work (1980) also focuses strongly on the 'structural' language-policy effects of the penetration of High German and its strong identification with Lutheranism into Low German, Polish, Kashubian, and Lithuanian-speaking areas acquired by Prussia through the partition of Poland.

2 TYPOLOGIES OF MULTILINGUALISM AND TYPOLOGIES OF LANGUAGE POLICY

1 Typologies and taxonomies are commonly used by linguists and anthropologists to analyse and/or sort out different kinds of things; one can use a branching tree-diagram, a flow-chart, a feature-analysis, or some other kind of symbolic structure. The main idea is that the *value* of variables in question, as they apply to the thing being analysed or pigeon-holed, are binary and/or bipolar – if the thing being analysed is a pronominal system, the pronouns are either singular or plural (category of number), first person, second person, or third person (category of person), and if there is gender, the variables are masculine, feminine, neuter, etc.. If the system being analysed is a folk taxonomy of medicinal plants, the variables are different. The main problem that arises is when categories *overlap*. Then these analytical frameworks can fail to deliver the goods.

2 The work of Fasold, Ferguson, Fishman, Kloss and Stewart come immediately to mind.

3 In many polities, this is seen as a threat; in France, speakers of Alsatian and Corsican dialects have at times been seen as a kind of German (or Italian) speaker, and were not accorded the same treatment as speakers of dialects spoken only in France, for example, Breton. Tamil speakers in Sri Lanka are seen as an invasionary force of the Tamil population of mainland India.

4 In many analyses, the *why not* is treated as a vexatious or trivial issue, not germane to any critique of the policy in question, for example Hindi has failed to be accepted because of the recalcitrance of the non-Hindi population, not because the proposal to use Hindi was lacking in merit.

5 In the United States, different agencies such as the Bureau of Indian Affairs, Department of Agriculture, Social Security Administration, Military, CIA, Treasury, Bureau of the Census, may use certain languages for their own purposes.

6 There are some other studies, such as Falch 1973, which present a rather laconic and dispassionate categorization of language laws in Europe. Falch's is an extreme example of an emphasis on *de jure* policies without any attention to how individual policies actually work when confronted with the facts of multilingualism. On the bright side, Falch does list details of statutes of various sorts, that is, where statutory provisions are located

7 NCCs of types A2–4 are monolingual only in childhood/home language: 'monopaedoglossic'.

8 We need a cover term for differences between 2 and 3/4: *endo-diglossic* versus *exo-diglossic*?

9 Although the word 'policy' appears in the text, it is clear from the discussion that follows that what is meant is *polity*.

10 I borrow the term 'functional load' from Prague School phonemics, where it is used to deal with the factor of a particular phonemic contrast not having a wide distribution in a language in terms of distinguishing certain words, but by virtue of its occurrence in certain words that occur frequently, is functionally loaded. In particular the voiced phoneme /ð/ (spelled 'th' like its voiceless counterpart /θ/), occurs infrequently in

English, but its occurrence in such words as 'the, this, that, then, there', etc. means that this sound has a high functional load, and cannot be treated as an insignificant contrast simply beeause so few words have it. The parallel with the status of English in India may be apt.

11   The wide diversity in the continuum of Hindi dialects, Urdu dialects, and Panjabi in the Indian subcontinent would be one of these.

12   In fairness to Kloss, Ferguson and Stewart, a careful reading of their proposals indicates they were quite aware of these problems and deficiencies.

13   At the time Ferguson wrote, only Castilian was official in Spain, but since the death of Franco, changes in the status of both Catalan and Basque have come about.

14   Roberge (1992) shows how the origin myths that underlay the development and maintenance of Afrikaans will no longer be viable in post-apartheid South Africa, so the whole notion of who is a speaker of Afrikaans, and who is an Afrikaner, will change; independently, official language policy in South Africa's new constitution supposedly makes eight languages official and co-equal, so languages like Xhosa, Zulu and others are now being learned by White South Africans, instead of the other way around.

15   When I say 'registers prefer' etc. I mean, of course, that decision-makers who control the standards of the register prefer or disprefer, and may explicitly state these preferences in style-manuals for various journals, etc. Some researchers have noted that register is related to *uses* rather than *users*. Scherer and Giles (1979: 51–3) devote two pages to a description of both differences in lexicon and the 'complex, unusual semantic relations amongst perfectly commonplace words' found in certain registers.

16   I use this example because of a situation that arose during my observation of a Toḍa ritual in the Nilgiris District, Tamilnāḍu, India. A shaman went into a trance and began divining the future. Although I did not understand any Toḍa, the speech of the shaman while in a trance was to me impressionistically quite different from samples of Toḍa I had heard up to that point. One frequent sentence-final utterance, delivered with rising intonation [ariyo:↑] sounded like a possible borrowing from Malayalam, with the probable meaning 'do you know?' I asked the Toḍa informant guiding us what the utterances meant, and he explained them without hesitation. But when I asked him to repeat some of the words, he said that he couldn't *say* those words *unless he was in a trance*. Toḍa also has a register for songs that is phonologically so different from spoken Toḍa as to be unrecognizable to someone who only knows spoken Toḍa (Emeneau, personal communication). This illustrates how even a numerically small and pre-literate language like Toḍa may have three registers that are so different linguistically that they constitute separate and mutually unintelligible codes, that is, the existence of complex registers is not just a characteristic of post-industrial Western languages.

17   This would be the case for the Toḍas, where all adult males are expected to understand trance language but are not expected to speak it, or for language situations where men's and women's language differs drama-

tically, or for 'bilingual' communities where groups understand each other's language but would never produce specimens of the other's speech, except to mock them, make jokes, or whatever.

18 For example, a Pakistani doctor trained in her own country may be very fluent in an English medical/technical register, but may lack communicative competence in a 'bedside manner' register for speaking to patients in English; she might be more likely to possess the latter in Urdu, but not the former.

19 The only exception would be someone who attends an English-medium school from an early age, in which case acquisition of H-variety Tamil may be minimal, and if nothing is done to change this, the control of this domain will be passive at best.

20 That is if one register is replaced or displaced by another, perhaps as a result of a conscious policy decision.

21 Singapore's bilingual education policy recognizes that different proficiencies in English and mother tongue are natural, and requires less bilingual proficiency from those who will leave school at an early age than those who take Cambridge A-level exams.

22 In Singapore, for example, there is little or no recognition of the proficiency that Singaporeans have in Chinese dialects (Hokkien, Hakka, Teochew, Cantonese), spoken Tamil, and other languages, despite the official use of exonormic Mandarin, RP English, Literary Tamil, and standard *Bahasa Malayu*. In fact the educational system sees these mother tongues as a problem that needs to be eradicated, rather than a resource.

23 For a summary of India's language policy as expressed in the 1950 Constitution, see Watts 1970: 152–4. The Eighth Schedule (§§ 344(1) and 351) lists the legitimized languages, whose rights are mentioned elsewhere. A careful reading of these portions of the Constitution reveals that although many clauses protect various languages and the rights of their speakers to *promote* their own languages, and prohibit restrictions on individual initiatives, very little is stated about domains that are reserved for languages, except to mention Hindi, or the right of a speaker to use her/his language in certain situations. Para. 347, for example, allows for minority linguistic groups 'with a substantial proportion of the population', that have a grievance in a particular state to petition the president, who, if satisfied that they have a grievance, may direct the state to recognize that language. What a 'substantial proportion' is, is left up to the president to decide, as is the decision whether to issue orders to a state. And § 350A encourages every state to provide adequate facilities for instruction in the mother tongue at the primary stage of education to children belonging to linguistic minority groups, and the president may issue instructions to any state that is not doing so; but nothing here is required or guaranteed.

24 It is no surprise that this policy is satisfactory only to Hindi speakers, and a source of disaffection for non-Hindi speakers.

25 The German text is as follows:

> Das Deutsche, Französische, Italienische und Rätoromanische sind die Nationalsprachen der Schweiz.

Als Amtssprachen des Bundes werden das Deutsche, Französische und Italienische erklärt.

26 In actuality, this blank is filled by 'German', since that is the reality (though not the policy) in the Romansch-speaking areas.

3 RELIGION, MYTH AND LINGUISTIC CULTURE

1 A partial but not exhaustive list might mention Hebrew for Judaism, Latin in the Roman Catholic Church, Church Slavonic in Eastern Orthodoxy, Sanskrit in Hinduism, Qur'anic Arabic in Islam, Pali in Buddhism, Amerindian languages in Native-American religious tradition, etc.

2 'Es que el guaraní, por la riqueza du su léxico, por la perfección de su estructura gramatical, por la superabundancia de palabras que posee para la expresión de conceptos abstractos y por la belleza y diversidad de sus formas de dicción, tiene la alcurnia de los languajes de los paises de elevada cultura' (Rona 1966: 278, quoting Bertoni 1950: 87).

3 Whorf 1964. An immense literature has grown up that attempts to test this hypothesis, often with tests that use colour terminology, but because of the need to go *through* language to test it, the proof remains unconvincing. This notion is nevertheless seductive to many when they first start thinking about language, its structure and its meaning.

4 This notion, that of lists of names for animals and birds, that is, only things that can be seen and have real referents in the world, is a fairly primitive idea of what constitutes language. More complex, abstract nouns, or verbs or adjectives are not mentioned.

5 The linguistic diversity created by God as a punishment for man is temporarily (or, for Pentecostals, periodically) wiped away in the New Testament at Pentecost, when the presence of the Holy Spirit enabled people to speak in any known or unknown language, and still be understood by everyone present.

6 I will never forget reviewing this notion one day in class and hearing a gasp from a young woman in the first row. When I looked at her, she was staring at the floor, her mouth agape. She seemed to be grasping my idea, but at the same time part of her belief system seemed to be crumbling before her eyes.

7 There is inadequate space here to deal with these issues as they arise in Judaism, Sikhism and Buddhism, three other 'religions of the Book', but language policy in Israel, in Panjab State in India and in Sri Lanka (a polity where devotion to Buddhism is state-sponsored) are all fraught with cultural baggage deriving from older hieratic traditions.

8 Excellent studies of purism can be found in Wexler 1974, Annamalai 1979b and Jernudd 1989.

9 Gessinger's work (1980) also focuses strongly on the 'structural' language policy effects of the penetration of High German and its strong identification with Lutheranism into Low German, Polish, Kashubian and Lithuanian-speaking areas acquired by Prussia through the partition of Poland.

10 The progress of the recognition of Afrikaans seems to be as follows: founding of the first newspaper, 1875; first spelling and reading book for

children, 1878; rise of Afrikaner national feeling, war of 1899 (Boer War); foundation of various language associations, 1905, 1906; foundation of SA Akademie, 1909; recognition of Afrikaans by provincial councils, 1914 (with introduction into schools); acceptance by Church, 1916–19; recognition by parliament, 1925; appearance of Afrikaans Bible, 1933 (Haarhoff and Van Den Heever, 1946: 17–26). Of course Dutch itself had to struggle for equal rights in South Africa after the Boer War, winning equal recognition with English in the Act of Union in 1910; but Afrikaans was already on the ascendant and simply inherited this right from Dutch, since many speakers interpreted Dutch in South Africa to mean Afrikaans (Lockwood 1976: 207).

11 It should be noted, however, that for Ferguson, all of the attitudes and beliefs that we are subsuming under the rubric of linguistic culture are dealt with as *myth*, whereas I am distinguishing between myth, attitude, and other aspects of linguistic culture.

12 It is interesting to see how Islam, which incorporates a great deal of ancient Near-Eastern sacred writings into its tradition, such as the story of Cain and Abel and all the other patriarchs of the Hebrew tradition, manages to consider the Qur'an, which was only revealed (to Muhammad) in the seventh century, as *anterior* to Cain and Abel. That is, since Cain, meanings of words have been less direct, and obscure, but the Arabic of the Qur'an was not affected by this. It thus has a timeless quality.

13 In the text, Miller refers to the Japanese language by its Japanese name, *Nihongo*.

14 In fact, when this does happen, as I will argue was the case with post-independence language policy in India, the result was disastrous.

4 LANGUAGE POLICY AND LINGUISTIC CULTURE IN FRANCE

1 Two hundred years before, the revolutionary calendar that replaced the Gregorian date of 27 January, 1794 was in effect, and the date was the eighth of the month of *pluviose*, in the second year (*an II*) of the Revolution. French laws are often referred to by the date of their adoption, rather than by a name, though many laws and decrees subsequently acquire the name of their most vociferous sponsor: the decree of *8 pluviose an II* is now often referred to as the 'Decree Barère', after its most ardent champion. This calendar was officially abandoned in 1805, but had earlier fallen into disuse. Many of the milestones of the Revolution are still referred to by their revolutionary calendar dates. The actual bicentennial of this policy passed without mention in the French press.

2 In fact it requires much much less than what Balibar (1987: 9) thinks it requires.

3 As Balibar has noted, most French citizens are not troubled by the effects of their official language policy: what they *are* troubled by are attempts to 'democratize' access to the language by reforming spelling, as we shall see later.

4 The French word for the power of French to disseminate itself far and

wide is *rayonnement*, meaning 'radiance' or 'brilliance' of the French language and French culture. In this section we confront a number of French terms and metaphors that are best used in the original, rather than translated, as translation obscures their meaning and takes them out of the context (some people might say discourse) of talking about language as it is carried on in French. Many of the terms used to talk about the French language use the vocabulary of light – the brilliance, the radiation, the illumination and the *illustration* or 'inwardly-lighted-ness' of French. Another term we will not try to translate is *francisation*, or 'frenchification', that is the process of making French speakers out of speakers of other languages, or the process of making the territory, institutions, morals and customs of non-French-speaking regions French. We will leave without translation the word *patois*, which is variously used, but mostly as a non-standard, low-prestige form of French – less than a dialect, but not quite as low as a jargon or argot. As we will see, policy toward *les patois* was different from policy toward dialects and other 'languages', for which the term *idiomes* was more common. But note that in the eighteenth century, when serious policy-making about language began, there was little agreement on terms such as *patois, dialecte, langue*, etc. (Tabouret-Keller 1986).

5 Weinstein says that '[b]laming the laziness and carelessness of the masses is a theme that recurs in France and in Quebec' (1989: 56).

6 This is exactly where Balibar (1987) begins, referring to the *Serment* as 'the text which gave birth to the French language' [*le texte qui a donné naissance à la langue française*].

7 Weinstein (1989) describes *la francophonie*, which he calls an international movement, as having both corpus and status goals. For some of the most militant supporters, the two goals are inseparable, but for others, the puristic (status) goals are not important.

8 *La langue est un facteur puissant de la conscience nationale, le véhicule par excellence de cet héritage national dont l'école ne peut pas ne pas être le principal organe de transmission. Nous ne sommes pas d'accord avec ceux qui se résignent à la déchéance de la langue française, à la présentation d'un tableau superficiel et appauvri de sa grammaire, de son lexique, de sa stylistique ou à l'élimination de l'enseignement de la littérature nationale.*

9 I shall not debate whether French linguistic culture is 'constructed' (in the sense that it can then be deconstructed) or is somehow inherent (Guilhaumou 1989) in the language, unless if by 'language' is meant French linguistic culture in its totality. I have dealt with such confusions of what is meant by 'language' in a previous chapter. Neither do I believe that it has been consciously elaborated, although one can trace the progress of its elaboration; the French call this the institutionalization (*l'institution*) of the language (Balibar 1985). I do not view French linguistic culture as having the kind of coherence that would imply that it is a system elaborated to justify French expansionism, the French colonial empire, patriarchalism, syndicalism, or any other overt policy.

10 Or, Latin *was corrupted* into French, etc.

11 For the French version of their history, I rely on *Petit Larousse* 1962: 1368.

12 Balibar (1985) contends that Charles was *not* a speaker of (Old) French, and that his brother just mouthed the words composed for him by the clerics. If this is so, then *neither* of the brothers was a French speaker, curious indeed if the claim is that the French language was born under these circumstances. I am unable to evaluate the evidence for this contention. But the important point was to use the language of the other realm – to legitimize the reciprocal use of the language of each other's kingdom, which, beginning with this moment, seems to have started the process of gradual elaboration and legitimization of two national languages, German and French.

13 Note that when we speak of language shift we do not need to consider any movement of population – the language can move like a wave through the population through a stage of bilingualism to eventual monolingualism. Where the language boundary would have been before it began to move is difficult to say, since accurate linguistic censuses did not exist: before that time, records were kept in Latin, so there was little evidence even of a change from Latin to 'French'. Most authorities believe that the *berceau*, 'cradle', of this new Romance language is undeniably the Ile de France region, dominated of course by Paris and its court.

14 Even today dialects of German spoken west of the Rhine and in the Moselle region are known as *Fränkisch*, while the French names for these same Germanic dialects is *francique*, for example, *bas francique* for *Nieder-Fränkisch*, 'Lower Franconian'. Note that the name of the dialect of Ile de France is officially known as *le francien*, yet another logonym with the *franc-* root in it. Curiously, this name has also spread east as far as India and into Southeast Asia, where the first Europeans were known as *firangi/farangi* and the name is still used to refer to foreign (Western) things and people.

15 Balibar (1985: 12) ascribes the use of two vernaculars rather than one classical language to the wish of the clerical bureaucratic apparatus to legitimize languages they wished to see become better established.

16 Britto (1986) refers to spoken languages in a diglossic relationship as the 'authentic' level; this is the language used for authentic communication, so the use of two vernacular languages here would be for the purpose of authenticity.

17 Balibar (1985) refers to this as *colinguisme*, by which she means something like reciprocal or equal bilingualism.

18 It is worth noting that a stamp commemorating the *ordonnance* of *Villers-Cotterêts* was issued on 14 December, 1989, in a *séance solonelle* of the francophile organization *Défense de la Langue Française*.

19 Since Brunot is in many ways like an encyclopaedia, references will be to the publication year of the reprinted edition (1967) plus volume number and page. In many cases the actual volume may have been written by someone else.

20 Most discussions of French language policy assume that there is on the one hand a standard French language and on the other hand a large number of non-standard speech forms: some of these are simply subsumed under French as dialects of it, but there is a recognition also of an

old linguistic boundary between the northern French dialects (*langue d'oil*, where *oui oil* is the word for 'yes') and *langue d'oc*, where *oc* is the word for 'yes'. The boundary between these two regions is approximately a line running from the Atlantic southeast along the Gironde river, then turning northeast to circle above Limoges and the Massif Central, then southeast again to run south of Lyon, then east to the point where French dialects end and Italian begins. Scholars distinguish three main focal areas: *Gascon* (southwestern), *Occitan Moyen* (central and southeastern), and *Nord Occitan* (north-central and northeastern). Bec (1970–1) gives various maps with dialect and language boundaries. One should also note that philologists of French distinguish another *langue* in the southeast of France – *Franco-Provençal*, centred around Lyon, but extending east into southern French Switzerland until it meets the German and Italian language/dialect areas. We must bear in mind that these boundaries are approximate, and reflect at best bundles of major dialect isoglosses. Only in the southwest of France does the Gironde river act as a clear boundary between *langue d'oil* and *langue d'oc*. *Occitan Moyen* had a literary language during the Middle Ages known as *Provençal*, but it began to decline as it was progressively abandoned, starting in the late Middle Ages, first by the nobility, then the middle classes, then urban speakers, and finally rural speakers in the nineteenth and twentieth centuries (Roland Breton, personal communication). The *langue d'oc* area is thought by some to represent an older, more Latin or Roman stratum, with no admixtures or substrata (of Germanic or Celtic) such as is the case with *langue d'oil*. But there were other languages on the fringes of the territory of *langue d'oc*, such as Catalan, from the old county of Toulouse, and the Béarn dialect (which was used as a written language for court records, etc.), as well as other speech forms (e.g. Basque) all spoken on the periphery of the region – the Spanish, Swiss and Italian borders. Then there were the German dialects used in Alsace and parts of Lorraine: Bas-Breton (or just Breton) used in lower Brittany, and Flemish used in French Flanders. Brunot and others make a distinction between these last as *idiomes*, or languages (probably what Kloss (1967) would call *Abstand* languages, if not *Ausbau* languages), dialects, which may have at some point been written (such as Roussillon or Béarnais) and *patois*, which are merely 'corrupt' forms of French. Others, especially anyone opposed to the use of languages other than French, tend to denigrate all *idiomes* and *dialectes* to the status of *patois*.

21   Much of Alsace had fallen to France by the Treaty of Westphalia in 1648 (conclusion of the Thirty Years War), but German Hapsburg princes retained some rights in the area (they were *possessionées* even up until the French Revolution, so Strasbourg still considered itself a free city in 1685, though it had been 'annexed' in 1681).

22   The most southwesterly province of Béarn, though it joined France in 1607, had a Protestant queen who welcomed Protestant refugees.

23   This consensus eventually was perceived to be a 'fixing' of the spelling system, which we will see, it was not and could not be.

24   In modern 'popular' French, for example, *ses*, 'their: his/her (pl.)'; *ces*, 'these'; *sais*, '(I) know'; *sait* '(he) knows' and *c'est* 'it is', are all pronounced [se], and therefore ought, by phonetic principles, to be

written the same. (In an older, more 'correct' style, the first two, *ses* and *ces*, are pronounced [se] while the last three are pronounced with a lower vowel: [sɛ].)

Similarly, *parlez, parler, parlé, parlée, parlés* and *parlées*, all forms of the verb 'to speak', are pronounced identically, [parle], but cannot be used interchangeably. One must know enough grammar to recognize that the first is the second person plural/polite, the second the infinitive, and the rest are participles marked for varying degrees of gender and number.

25 I use the angled braces < > to enclose written letters, square brackets [ ] to enclose phonetic material, and slashes / / to enclose phonemic transcriptions.

26 See Tabouret-Keller 1986 for an analysis of usage by the *Encyclopédistes*, which reveals that 'usage' meant the usage of an élite (and still does), and that diglossia was problematical in French even then. She also attributes the slow development of the sociology of language in France to the problem of defining these terms two centuries ago.

27 '*On prononce une langue, on en écrit une autre; et l'on s'accoutume tellement pendant le reste de sa vie à cette bizarrerie qui a fait verser tant de larmes dans l'enfance, que si l'on renonçait à sa mauvaise orthographe pour une plus voisine de la prononciation, on ne reconnaîtrait plus la langue parlée sous cette nouvelle combinaison de caractères.*'

28 The priests and the Church probably understood that they would be better off retaining *patois*, because if they did not, French would replace it, and then perhaps French would replace Latin.

29 Not colleges in the American or British sense, but at the level of British public schools or American private preparatory schools: the term has been revived to refer to a type of secondary school whose graduates are not destined for university study.

30 He argued that a French book is as good as a Latin book. Perhaps the hostility to Latin was for utilitarian reasons: the ideas of Locke and the Port-Royal grammarians were gaining ground.

31 '*Aucune pensée directrice, aucune ordonnance générale n'avait consacré les changements, ne les a imposés. La monarchie n'avait point de système pédagogique. Le pouvoir royal assistait a la lutte; il ne s'y mêlait point.*'

32 Principally, the distinctions of masculine and feminine, certain tenses not used in the spoken language, conjugation of verbs, formation of noun plurals etc. could not (and still cannot) be written properly without at least some low-level knowledge of grammar.

33 Under the *ancien régime, les pays d'élection* were administered directly by the crown, whereas *les pays d'Etats* were administered by provincial authorities, *les Etats provinciaux.*

34 Essentially this was a reiteration of the *ordonnance* of *Villers-Cotterêts*, but in this case it was accompanied by some delegated power and responsibility.

35 That is dialectalized French.

36 '*L'édit de 1787 qui accordait aux provinces une sort de consécration officielle, donna lieu à un mouvement particulariste. Il est extrêmement remarquable que dans les revendications des provinciaux qui ont alors*

fouillé les titres des archives, constaté les coutumes et les traditions, il ne se trouve pour ainsi dire jamais une réclamation fondée sur les particularités de langage. L'idée qu'on peut appuyer le groupement politique ou administratif qui doit se constituer sur cette parenté d'idiome ne vient à personne.

On convoque les Etats-Généraux: Les 'Cahiers' des pays de langue romane sont à peu près tous en français' (Brunot, vol. 7(4): 187).

37 One might even say that it is 'politically correct' to hold this view.

38 The *Etats-Généraux* were a representative system that had fallen into disuse, but the monarch was in desperate financial straits and needed to get the members of the First Estate (the nobles), the Second Estate (the Church) and the Third Estate (the common people) to vote him more money to finance war with England. Instead the *Etats-Généraux* began to talk about their grievances.

39 French book titles, and names of various things are capitalized only at the beginning, so if we refer to the *Assemblée nationale* in French, only the first word is capitalized: if we refer to it in English, for example National Assembly, both will be capitalized.

40 '*ainsi disparaîtront insensiblement les jargons locaux,* les patois *de 6 millions de français qui ne parlent pas la langue nationale. Car . . . il est plus important qu'on ne pense en politique d'extirper cette diversité d'idiomes grossiers, qui prolongent l'enfance de la raison et la vieillesse des préjugées'.*

41 Grégoire's 'sociolinguistic survey' is described in complete detail in de Certeau *et al.* 1975. Grégoire pulled no punches: his report to the *Convention* on the *16 prairial*/4 June, 1794 is entitled 'Report on the necessity and the means of annihilating the *patois* and of universalizing the use of the French language'.

42 '*la force des choses la commande'.* Note here Brunot's idea that a language policy is something that comes from above, promulgated by 'great men', that is, is the result of the overt and relentless pursuit of the goals and actions of a Talleyrand or a Grégoire, but not of lesser mortals.

43 By a decree of 14 January, 1790 translation of all decrees is authorized: the people demanded it, and they want more use of their languages and *idiomes.*

44 1 Their language was different: some people even used German to try to get Germans (in Germany) to join the revolution (after all this was a universal revolution of all people against their tyrants).

    2 German was a language with its own 'florescence', good writers and poets.

    3 Religion linked Alsace with German Protestantism.

    4 There were few ties with France; the Vosges Mountains constituted a geographical barrier.

45 And this is the picture we get in the nineteenth century also, when dialectologists began the great dialect surveys that accompanied the development of historical and comparative linguistics. French dialects did not group themselves into larger units the way German dialects did, for instance. The French dialectologists espoused the notion that *chaque mot a sa propre histoire,* and already by the nineteenth century the strong attraction of the centre made each dialect orient itself toward

Paris, rather than its neighbours. What this does not explain is the existence of named dialects such as *le picard, le lorrain, le dauphinois, le francien,* etc.

46 Whenever *francisation* is effective, this is *progress* for Brunot, and whenever *francisation* is hindered, this is lamentable.

47 *'En somme, le fédéralisme et la superstition parlent bas-breton; l'émigration et la haine de la République parlent allemand; la contre-revolution parle italien et le fanatisme parle basque. Brisons ces instruments de dommage et d'erreur. Il vaut mieux instruire que faire traduire, comme si c'était à nous à maintenir ces jargons barbares et ces idiomes grossiers qui ne peuvent plus servir que les fanatiques et les contre-révolutionnaires.'*

48 Brunot displays his admiration for Grégoire as follows: 'Nevertheless there was one man, at least, who never ceased, almost from the beginning of the Revolution, to think about making French the national language. This is the Abbé Grégoire, the famous priest from Embermesnil.' Grégoire had served in parishes in Lorraine and was familiar with the effect of the German dialects spoken there, and had also pronounced himself as opposed to the dialect spoken by the Jews of Strasbourg. He defrocked himself early in the Revolution and was elected to various bodies.

49 The answers to these questions and letters expressing views of all sorts kept coming back to Grégoire for years after he began the survey, and constitute an important historical source of information about language and how people viewed language at the time.

50 Most analyses of French language policy are in agreement that one should not speak of the monarchy as having a language policy, since its policy was totally *lassaiz-faire*, as Brunot has shown. But I would contend that the *implicit* policy of pre-revolutionary France was a centralizing one, with the French language in all its glory having no rival on earth. Since this idea seems to still persist in certain circles, I would venture to call it a tenet of French linguistic culture.

51 This is described quite graphically in the autobiography of Pierre-Jakez Hélias, a Breton speaker whose family was *rouge* ('red'). The schoolmaster came to his house to impress upon him the necessity of learning French:

> *Si seulement il n'y avait pas tout ce français à apprendre, je pourrais commencer tout de suite. Mais l'école, qui est à la République, parle français tandis que l'Eglise, qui est blanche, parle breton.*
>
> 'If only there wasn't all that French to learn, I could start [school] right away. But the school, which belongs to the Republic, speaks French whereas the Church, which is white [that is, not 'red'] speaks Breton.'

Hélias's grandfather goes on to explain why French is useful:

> *Avec le français on peut aller partout. Avec le breton seulement, on est attaché de cour comme la vache à son pieu. Il faut toujours brouter autour de la longe. Et l'herbe du pré n'est jamais grasse.*

'With French you can go everywhere. With just Breton, you're like a cow tethered to a stake. You can only graze in a circle around it. And the grass there is never as green' (Hélias 1975: 192–3)

52 Ironically, some spellings of the period are more 'modern' (i.e. phonetic) than present-day spellings, for example the spelling *tems* for *temps* 'time, weather'. Many 'silent' letters no longer written in 1789 have subsequently been reintroduced, perhaps to show the connection with *temporale*, 'temporal', where the <p> is actually pronounced. This is not to say that other languages, such as English, have done a better job of modernizing their spelling. But if revolutionary changes were going to be made, the Revolution of 1789 was a perfect time to do it. In effect, it left the corpus of the language alone, and only tried to change its status.

53 *'il sera crée et organisé instruction publique, commune à tous les citoyens, gratuite'*.

54 We assume he wanted French, but he did not state this. But the door was not closed on *patois* or *idiomes*.

55 'Wherever communications are disrupted by particular *idiomes,* which have no *illumination,* and are only a residue of the barbarism of past centuries, one should make haste to take all necessary measures to make them disappear as soon as possible' (Title III, articles 1–7, quoted in Brunot 1967(9): 163–7).

56 Note that the king (Louis XVI) was tried and condemned in late 1792 and executed in early 1793, *before* the creation of the Committee of Public Safety: his trip to the guillotine was not a product of the Terror of Robespierre and the Committee of Public Safety.

57 There were, of course, pre-revolutionary *grammaires raisonnées* prepared during the *Académie française* period but they were not suitable for children or pedagogy.

58 It is evident here that various committees of the *Convention* were beginning to make rules in the same area, that is have turf wars: the Committee of Public Safety was impatient with the *Convention* and its policy of translation, and began to *arrêter,* 'decide, fix or decree' various things that may or may not have jurisdictionally been its right to decide. Since they were all making up the rules as they went along, it was not at all clear who had the right to decree what. Brunot 1967(9) refers to this as a 'decree' (p. 163) but wonders whether it was actually carried out, and admits that further research is required to determine whether it ever was.

59 Rousseville proposed to deport enemies of the republic from these areas, and repopulate them with French patriots from the 'interior' of France. These proposals were of course heard in Alsace and elsewhere, which may have excused Alsatians from feeling a little jumpy about their rights, though not, apparently, to Brunot.

60 Note again the light metaphors, how illuminated and 'illustrious' the French language is, how dark other languages are: German is referred to as having its own 'illumination'; French must be defended and 'illustrated' (brightened, burnished?).

61 Barère uses the term *ancien,* which can mean either former or old: he probably wants people to consider them *no longer useful.*

62 Articles 1–6 are given in Brunot 1967(9): 184.

63 '*de manière à ce que le français devient*'.

64 Brunot 1967 (9): 319.

65 Elementary school-teachers have as their school 'district' their *département*; secondary school-teachers have as their 'district' all of France. Recall, for instance, that the French existentialist writers Simone de Beauvoir and Jean-Paul Sartre began their teaching careers in *lycées* in various provincial locations, and gradually worked their way back to Paris.

66 The laws that created the educational system that implemented the language regulations are known as the *Lois Ferry*, after Jules Ferry, who is responsible for the development of the primary-school system (Slone 1989).

67 Note that Balibar (1985: 9) begins her work with a lament about the rigidity of French language policy, and how it is the oldest formal policy in the world. And recall her observation that most French citizens are not troubled by the effects of their official language policy: what they *are* troubled by are attempts to 'democratize' access to the language by reforming spelling.

68 The report on the spelling changes was made by Maurice Druon, permanent secretary of the *Académie française*, and president of the working group, on 19 June, 1990, to the *Conseil supérieur de la langue française*. It is addressed to the prime minister (of the republic). It appears as No. 100/1990 of the *Journal officiel de la république française*, which is published as part of a series of *documents administratifs*.

69 This word is a crucial one for our thesis. The French word *permanence* means a number of things: it can be the same as English 'permanence', that is something permanent; it can mean something like 'care-taking', for example, having a *permanence* in an office means having the office 'covered', always having someone 'on duty', 'minding the store,' etc. M. Druon is noting that when you take on French spelling, you encounter the *permanence* of the system: you do not tangle with it without getting a few scratches. There is also a huge quasi-burocracy that guards the edifice, which consists of people at all levels of society. French spelling is serious business, and French spelling reform is serious business.

70
> [*En installant, en octobre dernier, le Conseil supérieur ici assemblé, vous le chargiez, entre autres missions, de] formuler des* proposi-tions claires et précises *sur l'orthographe du français, d'y apporter des* rectifications utiles *et des* ajustements *afin de résoudre, autant qu'il se peut, les problèmes graphiques, déliminer les incertitudes ou contradictions, et de permettre aussi une formation correcte aux mots nouveaux que réclament les sciences et les techniques.*
>
> *Qu'on veuille bien ne voir dans ma remarque aucune assimilation hâtive ou gênante.*
>
> *Je voulais simplement souligner qu'une permanence apparaît et s'impose dès lors qu'on entreprend d'agir sur les structures du français, et que cette permanence s'exprime par les termes de certitude, clarté, précision, pureté, toutes qualités qui font notre langue suprême dans les domaines de l'ethique, du droit, des*

*accords et conventions, et plus généralement, dans l'art de l'exposé
ou de la définition.*
*Perdrait-elle ces caractères qui l'ont faite universelle, notre
langue verrait son audience et son emploi se réduire dans le monde.*

71 A metaphor involving architecture is often used by defenders of the
system – French spelling is like a medieval cathedral – it is the product
of many great minds, but like a gothic cathedral, has inconsistencies.
Should we then tear down and rebuild the great cathedrals to straighten
out these gothic eccentricities?

72 Part of the motivation for this reform comes from the kinds of mistakes
students typically make on their exams, the idea being that if 90 per cent
or more of the population spells a word a certain way, why not accept
this as a fact of the genius of the language, as expressed by its users.

73 In fact in French, as in other languages with many homophones (e.g.
English and Chinese), speakers often spell out words that might be
ambiguous, for example *Il lui faut la mer – m . . . e . . . r –* 'he needs
the sea' instead of 'he needs his mother'; or 'he was cited (c . . . i . . . t
. . . e) by the police' (to avoid confusion with 'sighted', or even 'sited').

74 Even a team of the *Centre national de la recherche scientifique* that
attempted to study the impact of the proposed reforms found itself the
object of revulsion: some of its questionnaires were returned defaced
with right-wing slogans or soiled with excrement by people who found
even the idea of *discussing* spelling reform to be a left-wing attack on
the sanctity of the language.

75 See Petitjean and Tournier 1991: 128–9 for a fairly extensive list of
milestones in French spelling policy formulation. Most efforts since
1835 have in fact been unsuccessful: that of 1835 in fact *restored* /t/s
previously deleted, as in *enfan(t)s* 'child(ren)'.

76 School-teachers have often been in the forefront of proposals to simplify
things, since they find that they spend a disproportionate amount of their
time teaching a system that is so full of inconsistencies that neither they
nor their students can respect it. But they are then usually reviled by the
public for their 'treasonous disregard' for the French language – since
they are expected by the general public to defend the system, not
dismantle it.

77 French scientists often complain that scientists in other countries will not
publish in French because it is too daunting: a reform that would
normalize spelling would make French more competitive, goes this
line of reasoning.

78 As we have seen, the *Académie* did not ultimately succeed in standardiz-
ing spelling because its own members refused to abide by its rules;
spelling reform has remained a bugaboo, and will continue to be one
into the twenty-first century.

5 FRENCH IN THE MARGINAL AREAS: ALSACE AND THE OTHER REGIONS

1 They are inconsistent not only in what they call them but in how they deal with the whole question of centre/periphery, core/margin, or whatever kind of polarity is established.

As for what to call different speech forms, Brunot and others distinguish between *langues hétérogénes* (or *idiomes*) such as German, and dialects of French. Brunot does not use *patois* as part of his definition but he does use the term *patois* extensively. German, he says, is a real language, possessing its own *illumination*, and capable of expressing everything that French could. Alsace, therefore, is and always has been a special case where *francisation* moved very slowly.

As we have seen in the last chapter, the French wish to avoid the notion that marginal areas have a right to be different, or are different because they really belong elsewhere. It is not that the *aires marginales* are not French, it is that they are *insufficiently* French, and need help to become more so.

2 Gordon quotes Calvet's reference to it as a *rouleau compresseur*, 'steam-roller' (Gordon 1978: 31).

3 Technically, we ought perhaps to be considering Lorraine as well but much of what we will say applies to both. The boundaries of Alsace have varied over the centuries, and after the French Revolution ceased to exist as an administrative territory, having been replaced by the *départements* of Haut-Rhin, Bas-Rhin and (for Lorraine) Moselle. But as a cultural entity, citizens of the area certainly recognize something called *Alsace* and what it means to be *Alsaciens* within a larger French nationhood and identity. In French reference works such as *Petit Larousse*, the history of Alsace seems to begin with its annexation by the French Crown under Louis XIV by the Treaty of Westphalia (1648); Strasbourg was '(re)united' with France in 1681; Alsace was ceded to the Germans in 1871 but became French again in 1918, but '*la domination á laquelle furent soumis ses habitants entre 1871 et 1918 n'avait pas affaibli les liens qui les unissaient a la France*': Alsace 're-entered into French unity' ('*rentra dans l'unité française*'). As for Alsace-Lorraine, *Petit Larousse* defines it as a term given by the Germans when they 'tore' ('*arrachées*') Alsace and Lorraine away from France in 1871.

4 The poster is by the artist Henri Royer, and printed by Imprimeries Minot, Paris, n.d.

5 Quoted by Brunot, in Zwilling 1888, *Die Französische Sprache in Strasbourg*, in *Festschrift des protestantischen Gymnasium*.

6 Recall that Goethe was a student in Strasbourg in this period when it was 'under French jurisdiction' but was considered a German university: Goethe's romantic rhapsody about the cathedral in Strasbourg was called 'On German architecture'.

7 Goethe, in his essay *Dichtung und Wahrheit*, and also in *Über Deutsche Baukunst*, mentions the threats made to him about what the Jesuits would do to his French if he went to Strasbourg.

8 *Le peuple Alsacien, lui, se servait de son dialecte francique dans le Nord, alémanique dans le reste de l'Alsace, comme langue de communication*

courante. Les plus illustres de ses fils avaient même réussi à en faire un moyen d'expression littéraire de tout premier ordre. Mais la Réforme et l'invention de l'imprimerie favorisèrent l'implantation et l'extension d'une sorte d'allemand commun dont l'emploi s'imposait de plus en plus aux hommes instruits. Parmi ces hommes, on comptait des Alsaciens, parfaitement à l'aise en dialecte et maniant tout aussi parfaitement la nouvelle forme d'allemand, qui avaient également une connaissance suffisante du français pour s'ouvrir à la culture française.

9 One of the terms various people use without embarrassment, though it betrays a double standard of sorts, is referring to the core areas of France, those that were French from earliest times, as the 'interior' of France. This seems to me a euphemism for territories that are 'really' French, or as some say, *français-français*. This is to avoid validating the notion that the territories on the fringes where other languages are spoken are not really French, but the subtext seems to me to be clear. During certain times in its history governmental representatives have talked about deporting people into the 'interior' of France, and bringing in new settlers from the 'interior' of France, etc. Another term used to refer to the periphery is 'marginal areas' (*aires marginales*), that is not part of the core of France, not in the interior. This is also an attempt to avoid saying that they are not really French, because that would be an admission of their right to claim they are different. Rather, the reproach made to them is that they are *inadequately* French, and that they need to rectify this inadequacy. In these peripheral or marginal areas, various language competencies are referred to by a verb, for example *bretonnant*, that is speaks (passable) Breton, or *francisant*, speaks French, or *patoisant*, speaks *patois*. If a person speaks French influenced by *patois*, it is called *français patoisé* or dialectalized French.

10 See Hélias 1975 for an autobiographical account of growing up bilingual in Breton and French.

11 Brunot attributes this quote to Grégoire.

12 The University of Strasbourg, along with many other French universities, was closed during the Revolution. The Germans reopened it in 1871, re-established a faculty of theology, and when Alsace returned to France in 1918, it retained the right to continue its divinity school, the only university in France to have such a right. This is because it was established by papal concord, the *Concordat*, an agreement made between Napoleon and Pope Pius VII in 1801 (and continued under German hegemony after 1871), whereas the rest of France is ruled by the *Loi de séparation de l'église et de l'Etat* of 1905, which superceded the *Concordat*. Since Alsace was a part of the German Empire in 1905, the law of 1905 could not apply, nor did it abrogate or supersede the *Concordat* after Alsace returned to France in 1918.

13 My favourite is the term *ci-devant*, 'heretofore, up to now, previous, ex-', as in *le roi ci-devant*, 'the previous king, the ex-king' (lit. 'the person who was king up until recently'), which was used to characterize so many things that had previously had a certain kind of status, but had lost this because of the Revolution. It became a kind of political correctness to accurately preface old terms with *ci-devant*, such that overuse of the

term became known as *ci-devantisme*, that is, being politically correct but not much else.

14 The French, as do many other linguistic cultures, have a *horreur* of mixed language. *Le franglais* is a terrible example of this kind of linguistic degradation, so code-switching involving French and something like Alsatian is just another attempt to destroy French.

15 *All right then, I won't keep you any longer.* Kiss everyone for me and see you Saturday then.
   See you Saturday then, and have a good afternoon, in spite of the weather.
   Thank you, *let's hope we have nice weather then.*
   Yes, yes, it would be nicer *if it didn't rain.*
   Yes, yes.
   Well it doesn't matter, *we have to take what comes.*
   In the original, Alsatian material is in italics, French in roman letters.

16 To use the historical-linguistic term, which has been used also to refer to the process of reducing differences between dialects.

17 During a recent stay in Alsace during which I was closely observing code-switching of various kinds, I was always addressed first in French unless it was assumed I was a German tourist, in which case I was addressed in *Hochdeutsch* or dialectalized *Hochdeutsch*, with two exceptions. Once I was addressed in Alsatian dialect by a vendor in a street market who overheard me explaining to my son what the French and German words for 'apple' were, and once by an elderly woman who understood no French but had also apparently lost control of what *Hochdeutsch* she had once commanded. That she was a native of the area, however, was evidenced by the fact that she was able to give me detailed directions on how to reach the railroad station, all in dialectalized *Hochdeutsch*.

18 The complete text of the law can be found in Falch 1973: Article 1 states: '*Le Conseil supérieur de l'Education nationale sera chargé, dans le cadre et dès la promulgation de la présente loi, de rechercher les meilleurs moyens de favoriser l'étude des langues et dialectes locaux dans les régions où ils sont en usage*' (1973: 215).

19 An attempt was made by deputies Zeller, Caro, Ferretti, Fuchs, Klein and Koehl in the legislative session of 1979–80, to propose a law No. 1612, *tendant à introduire l'enseignement de la langue régionale dans les établissements scolaires des départements du Rhin et de la Moselle et à y assurer le développement du bilinguisme.* Needless to say, these and other attempts fail to capture the support of a majority.

20 Actually not a unified dialect, but a continuum, in fact a broken continuum ranging from dialects of Lower Franconian in the Moselle region to Swiss-like Alemannic dialects in the Sundgau. Lötscher (1983: 149–50) gives a map that demonstrates the lack of congruity of the major isoglosses with the political borders, and confirms that '[*i*]*n einem konkreten Sinn faßt überhaupt die Mundartforschung die Dialekte in Südwestdeutschland, in der Schweiz und im Elsaß in einen größeren länderübergreifenden Dialektraum des Alemannischen zusammen*'.

21 '*La culture alsacienne est la culture que l*'Alsacien d'aujourd'hui *peut et doit pouvoir acquérir par la combinaison des éléments français, alle-*

mands et alsaciens qui, ensemble, *donnent à la culture* vécue *dans le milieu alsacien sa marque spécifiquement alsacienne.'*

22 *'L'administration et le public ne sauraient se désintéresser de suivre l'évolution de plus en plus* satisfaisante *de l'assimilation linguistique des trois départements depuis leur retour à la mère patrie'* (Forward by R. Dumas, INSEE 1956, emphasis added)

23 See for example Philipps 1975, 1978, 1982; Hell 1986.

24 Strasbourg newspapers list not only the programmes for three German networks, but for Swiss and Belgian networks as well, which can be received on cable (the Swiss programmes come in three flavours – German, French and Italian).

25 This daily paper also appears in a German edition (also daily), but readership has declined to the point where fewer than 25 per cent of subscribers prefer the German edition.

26 Recall that even nursery schools, *écoles maternelles* are provided free for French children beginning at about age 3, so it is not just a small élite group of children that might benefit from this.

6 INDIAN LINGUISTIC CULTURE AND THE GENESIS OF LANGUAGE POLICY IN THE SUBCONTINENT

1 There is a concern with being 'fair' to everyone, not to impose categories or hierarchies, or patriarchal systems, or 'white culture' etc. on subaltern populations.

2 As Das Gupta points out, policy-planners in pre-Independence India did not concern themselves with distinctions between 'common language', 'official language' and 'national language'. 'However, when assuming the official responsibility of formulating a national language for an independent nation it was necessary to use these categories with greater caution' (Das Gupta 1969: 580).

3 See for example Das Gupta 1969: 579.

4 On the other hand, Tsarist policy varied from region to region: in Finland, for example, Swedish and Finnish were also accorded some rights, while in Poland no rights existed for Polish. The tolerance for Finnish and Swedish was covert and probably based on trying to avoid offending Sweden, from whom the Grand Duchy of Finland had been taken. The lack of tolerance for Polish was based on some notion of Pan-Slavism, according to which Polish Slavs should welcome the opportunity to allow themselves to be Russified. The same subversive policy was true for Catalonia in Franco-Spain.

5 The subject of language and culture and diversity in India is one with an extensive bibliography. I cite for starters Ferguson and Gumperz 1960 (*Linguistic Diversity in South Asia*) and Shapiro and Schiffman 1981 (*Language and Society in South Asia*).

6 Again, the literature on this topic is extensive: the best modern overview is Deshpande 1979 (*Sociolinguistic Attitudes in India: An Historical Reconstruction*).

7 For our purposes here, in dealing with ancient Indian culture I will treat South Asia and India as the same thing.

8 The question of exactly when Europeans first encountered Sanskrit depends on whether one attributes to this to Sir William Jones or to predecessors of various sorts who were aware of Sanskrit but had only limited access to it. Whatever the case may be, it was Jones's encounter with Sanskrit that was published and had an impact on Western scholarship and which led to the development of the whole enterprise of Orientalism, or at least Indian Orientalism.

9 There is some question in the minds of scholars whose expertise lies in areas of inquiry not related to the subcontinent whether oral transmission can have been primary, and whether perhaps there has not always been some use of written records to reinforce the oral. Emeneau gives some examples of recourse to written texts to correct spoken errors, but in fact more often the opposite seems to be true. Salomon has reviewed this issue (Salomon n.d.) and found the attacks on orality unconvincing. Those aligning themselves against orality follow the lead of Goody (1986), while Staal (1986), Graham (1987) and Coulmas (1989), having first-hand contact with Indic civilization, are more aware that the oral tradition is real and deeply rooted in the culture. Staal also points out that the question of whether the oral preservation really does the job is verified by the historical-phonological evidence – the texts contain accurate reflexes of what one would expect on the basis of historical and comparative reconstruction: were error to have been introduced, the forms would have been affected, and not usable as phonological data.

10 Only male members of the priestly caste may receive the long training involved in the learning, by rote, of the texts.

11 The Gospel of Matthew begins with the text 'In the beginning was the word, and the word was with God, and the word *was* God'.

12 Even in the non-Brahman movement in Tamilnādu, the successful displacement of Brahmans from the power-élite of the state did not result in the fall of literary Tamil from its dominant position controlling powerful linguistic domains in the society. On the contrary, Brahmans were thought to have corrupted Tamil by introducing Sanskrit loan words and sounds into it, and it needed to be restored to its former state of purity by the Non-Brahman movement.

13 I consider diglossia to be one of the most fundamental facets of Indian linguistic culture: in attributing anthropomorphic characteristics to it, I am really attributing these traits to Indian linguistic culture. Such is the power of such features of a linguistic culture, I claim, that they begin to operate independently without overt agents in the culture.

14 One might well characterize Indian bilingualism as 'additive bilingualism', a term used to define situations where individuals (usually) add languages to their repertoires, rather than replacing existing ones with new languages ('replacive bilingualism').

15 Princely states and the Madras Presidency in the south were largely untouched by Grierson's survey.

16 There were also many Germans, and miscellaneous Italian and other nationalities, all of whom would have had strong linguistic backgrounds.

17 Many of these were produced for the convenience of missionaries and teachers, but many were also translated and reshaped indigenous gram-

mars, such as Kittel's (1903) *Grammar of the Kannaḍa Language* based on Kēśava's Śabdamaṇidarpaṇa, a thirteenth-century work.

18 Or at least a stage of Tamil culture that showed little Aryan influence.

19 British India comprised perhaps two-thirds of the territory of present-day India and Pakistan: the rest was governed by traditional rulers, all of whom had been forced into a kind of feudal relationship with the 'Empress' of India, Victoria, and her successors. The princes in the princely states governed their territories internally, and Britain did not interfere in their self-governance except in extreme cases. Language policy was not one of these.

20 One commissioner, S. K. Chatterjee, dissented and wrote a minority report.

21 For a review of Soviet language policy and its evolution through various periods, see Lewis 1972: 67–90.

22 This was similar to the use of vernacular languages for the spread of the Reformation under Luther, or the spread of Buddhism under Aśoka.

23 That Stalin, a non-Russian, should resort to Russification as a language policy is often found curious. But Russification as a *covert* or underlying strategy in Russian and Soviet policy was obviously recognized by Stalin as a powerful centralizing force.

24 By 1947, of course, Leninist policy had been Stalinized, and the role of Russian expanded again, with intensified Russification: India unfortunately borrowed this element of the policy as well.

25   There has always been a tendency, and not only in India, to give a serious literary medium an enhanced air of respectability by approximating it to and buttressing it with forms taken from more prestigeful classical languages. An extreme example of this is the so-called Buddhist Hybrid Sanskrit, a MIA language so Sanskritized as to disguise its identity.

(Masica 1991: 57)

26 Gandhi is one of those who seems to have been under the erroneous impression that Hindi was widely used in South India (Nayar 1969: 59, quoting Gandhi's *Thoughts on National Language* [M. K. Gandhi 1956: 3–7, 147]).

27 Nayar accuses the opponents of Hindi of confusing 'the requirements of administration with literary appreciation, apart from ignoring the developments since independence' (1969: 63). In this Nayar fails to give weight to the literary prestige factor as a *prerequisite* in Indian linguistic culture to other instrumental factors. The fact is that Gandhi's stricture against both Sanskritized and Persianized Hindi as a basis for Hindi was an impossible one, given the linguistic culture. Gandhi's assumptions were wrong on two counts, but his preferences were nevertheless given strong credence, and wishful thinking carried the day.

28 Yamuna Kachru refers to 'the emergence of a classical "diglossic" situation' for Hindi (1986: 400).

29 At least some language speakers find this more difficult: speakers of other languages, such as Malayalam, with heavy borrowing from Sanskrit, rather than later stages of Indo-Aryan (Prakrits, etc.) might find this easier to master, and in fact Malayalis seem to be among those southerners who do quite well with modern Hindi. But witness the

famous complaint of Nehru, who failed to recognize his own speeches
when their Sanskritized form was broadcast on All-India Radio.

30 The question of 'Which Hindi?' did of course arise.

31 It was unfortunate that the rivalry between Hindus and Muslims had to
develop into a battle between Hindi and Urdu, but it is even more
unfortunate that this rivalry led to the development of a kind of Hindi,
and attitudes about the appropriateness of Hindi which then made it
impossible for the rest of India to stomach the policy. It is possible that
some form of Hindi or Urdu might have sufficed as a link-language in
post-Independence India, but only without the exaggerated claims that
went along with it. Hindi extremists shot themselves in the foot on this
issue, charging it with all kinds of emotional baggage that was simply
counter-productive to its acceptance by the rest of India. In fact most of
that rhetoric is simply irrelevant for Bengalis and Tamils, for example,
who care not a wit whether the vocabulary is Sanskritized or Persianized. What seems to have happened in this issue is that various factions
took positions that they could (or would) not back down from, and
ignored the fact that new issues had arisen since the nineteenth century
that make the maintenance of a polarity between Hindi and Urdu
counter-productive for the rest of India. Advocates of Hindi are blind
to the effect of their purism on the rest of India: they in effect are
focused only on the rivalry with Urdu, and see all other contestants as
despoilers of Hindi purity.

32 One could argue that if goals for language policy are defined somewhat
differently, the Hindi-only policy has been a success in Hindi areas of
north India (i.e. in Grierson's Inner Ring) and even a modified success in
non-Hindi areas of north India (i.e. Grierson's Outer Ring). Khari Boli
Hindi has become the language of instruction in many schools where
formerly Urdu, Panjabi, or non-standard dialects of Hindi were formerly
in use. Corpus planning for Hindi has been a success and much neolo-
gistic vocabulary that was thought odd a generation ago has now been
accepted. But in the non-Hindi areas of the south, and in Bengal, the
policy has not been a success.

33 That is, as Tamil becomes symbolic, its purity, antiquity and immutability are emphasized, and it ceases to function as an instrument
suitable for modern education, etc.

34 Lewis (1972: 195) describes schools in multilingual areas such as
Daghestan, where children from up to 25 different nationalities all
attend Russian-medium schools, because of the difficulty of setting up
separate schools for all of them.

35 The simplest way to observe this is to visit a Sanskrit college where
Sanskrit is taught in the old pandit tradition: observers will see (and
hear) in operation techniques devised to enhance the commitment to
memory of long and complicated texts. (Staal 1986: 17–18 provides a
detailed description of this system.) The final product of these colleges is
a novice pandit, capable of repeating at will any portion of any text he
has learned.

7 LANGUAGE POLICY AND LINGUISTIC CULTURE IN TAMILNĀḌU

1 In addition to approximately 60 million speakers in India, Tamil is, of course, spoken also in Sri Lanka by approximately four million speakers, and in Malaysia and Singapore by more than a million. Tamils emigrated to Fiji, South Africa and other British and French colonial possessions during the nineteenth century, and many now live in North America and in Europe, where they have not been able to maintain their language beyond the first generation. My transliteration of Tamil follows that of Burrow and Emeneau; some sources I quote use other transliterations, which I have followed only when directly quoting them. In general, the word Tamil will appear in its Western spelling (with a final 'l'), even though the final frictionless continuant (symbolized ழ in Tamil orthography) would be (and ought to be) transliterated by Burrow and Emeneau (1984) as 'ṛ'. This continues a tradition begun by Pope (1900: xcvii).

2 As we have seen in previous chapters, so do many others in South and Southeast Asia, France, Japan, etc.

3 Establishing the exact dates for anything in ancient India is notoriously difficult. Some scholars declare *Tolkāppiyam* to be contemporary with, or even later than Sangam literature (see below) rather than earlier than it; arguments can be adduced to support both claims. Hart (1975: 10), citing epigraphical and paleographic evidence, shows that parts of the *Tolkāppiyam* may be later than the Sangam period.

4 For example, the number of nominal cases is exactly seven, just as in Sanskrit, despite Tolkāppiyanār's discomfort with such a system, since it does not do justice to the Tamil case system, which requires a different analysis. This seven-case analysis was also eventually applied to the other Dravidian languages, with the same unfortunate effects. When confronted with this evidence that the grammatical tradition is borrowed from Sanskrit, Tamil apologists usually reply that Sanskrit borrowed it from *Tolkāppiyam*. This of course fails to explain why it does not fit the Dravidian languages as well as it fits Sanskrit.

5 I would only change the word 'know' to 'believe' in what I wrote then.

6 For example, see Srinivas Iyengar 1929.

7 Even then the Madras Presidency was separated physically from large parts of British India by intervening princely states. The only word for 'India' in Tamil, for instance, is *indiyaa*, borrowed from English.

8 It is true, of course, that some pandits do not apply all of Pavanandi's rules, so in fact nobody really writes thirteenth-century Tamil. But post-Pavanandi innovations, if covertly tolerated, would not be overtly allowed.

9 Some Tamils would say that it is corrupt and debased, and spoken *only* by illiterates, children, women, etc., and therefore not worthy of any attention.

10 This calls to mind an anecdote about the purity of the Ganges. A student of bacteriology from a Western country wished to do a study of water pollution in the Ganges River. Her Indian superviser informed her that this was not a useful topic, because the water of the Ganges was pure. The student persisted, and brought back samples of water to show the

pollution. The superviser continued to refuse to accept the evidence. Finally the student returned with a report that the Ganges water was indeed pure, but that impurities had been *introduced into it* by human agency. The superviser accepted the report.

11 There is a myth currently being propounded by a Japanese scholar that Tamil and Japanese are directly related; when I argued in a letter to the editor of the *Newsletter of the International Journal of Dravidian Linguistics* that this had not been proven, counter-arguments were raised that claimed that Indo-European languages changed at a different rate than did other languages, and that my arguments had little or no bearing on the subject.

12 Beschi (1728) wrote the first grammar of Tamil in a Western language (Latin).

13 Known generally in Tamil as the *taṇit tamir̤ iyakkam*, though the proponents who used this term represent only part of the picture.

14 This was a dynasty of Telugu-speaking kings who were highly Indo-Aryanized.

15 Historical linguists are usually very careful to cite the source for loan words, but in the Tamil case it is extremely difficult to determine whether the donor language here was actually Sanskrit or some other form of Indo-Aryan such as Prakrits, Pali, or even another Dravidian language acting as the intermediary. As Tamil orthography does not represent voicing or aspiration contrasts, it is frequently impossible to tell what the source of a loan was. I shall use the term Indo-Aryan to cover for all sources such as Sanskrit, Prakrits, and even modern Hindi, Marathi, etc.

16 All of the missionary-grammarians built on the work of their predecessors, so that a modern grammar of Tamil such as Arden (1942) is an accretion of the work of many others; so, too, the dictionary of Fabricius, begun in 1779 by that German missionary but added to and carried on by many others.

17 Ramanujan calls him 'the most influential and probably the most thoroughgoing of nineteenth and early twentieth century Tamil scholars' (1970: 68), but this is partly an example of an attempt to counter anti-Brahman bias; there were other reformers, such as C. W. Dhamodaram Pillai who played as important a role in the rediscovery, editing, and publication of the Old Tamil manuscripts (Ramaswamy 1993: 138).

18 The conflict between the northerners and southerners went on for centuries, and in some cases has only led to stalemate, as at the Śrī Pārtasārati Svāmi temple in Triplicane (Madras City), where to this day both factions claim control, and have been reduced to sharing different services of the day, rather than relinquish control to the other side.

19 I think we dare not underestimate the power of any movement in the subcontinent in which any goal (or indeed even the means toward that goal) is seen as salvific or redemptive. Too much latter-day scholarship fails to understand religious movements in India (or elsewhere) because we are products of a secular culture where religious motivations are seen as nefarious, or at best politically incorrect.

20 Tamiḻtāy means Tamil as mother; in much of this movement Tamil is seen as a feminine, motherly, even divine entity.

21 One way to mobilize this power is to turn to literary resources, what S. Ramaswamy calls the 'Poetics of praise'. The outlines of this are: Tamiltaay is incomparable, higher than all other deities; most glorious, most compassionate; the language she embodies is the most excellent in the world. A new religion emerges: anti-colonial, anti-Brahman, anti-Aryan, but monotheistic, pro-Shiva, Tamil-Dravidian. Maraimalai Adigal and K. Subramania Pillai call for break with 'Hinduism'; abolition of caste, betterment of women, vegetarianism/teetotalism, re-establishment of Tamil forms of worship based on Tamil scriptures, performed by Tamil priests (non-Brahman) with Tamil as liturgical medium. These developments occurred in contrast to two other formulations of Indian culture: colonial and Neo-Hindu nationalist. Colonial: Orientalism, spiritual, fudamentally religious – other-worldly fanatical, ritualistic. Meanwhile Neo-Hinduism/nationalism sought to equate the decline of Hindu society with the aboriginal *dasyus*, who were equated with Dravidians (and Muslims). Thus Aryan civilization was pristine and glorious but had become corrupted by contact with Dravidians. South Indians therefore saw Neo-Hindu nationalism as anti-Southern, and saw the possibility that Brahmans would hijack the nation and turn it into a Sanskritic, Hindu, Aryan/Brahman domain. Non-Brahman Tamilians would be denegrated. The British, meanwhile, divided and conquered.

22 To save space, I will sometimes refer to these as CmC and CnC, respectively.

23 Tamils love to be known by initials, rather than by names. Just as the most famous American political figures are known by FDR, LBJ, JFK, etc., the highest form of political flattery in Tamilnādu is to be known by one's initials. In the Tamil naming practice, initials are never spelled out, since they stand for one's father's name and one's ancestral home, and are not technically part of one's name. Forced by other naming conventions (e.g. North Indian, British, North American) to spell them out, Tamils will do so, but at the cost of distorting their own system. Instead an E. V. Ramaswamy Naikker will aspire to be known simply as EVR.

24 Usually spelled 'Dravida Kazhagam' in English.

25 Usually spelled 'Dravida Munnetra Kazhagam' in English.

26 The 1993 dissertation of Sumathi Ramaswamy is a notable exception; it is both a complete sourcebook of material both in English and in Tamil, as well as an incisive critique of the whole enterprise of Tamil revivalism. I have drawn on it for much of my own analysis.

27 Tamils are perceived as fanatical and even demented on the issue of language.

28 I use the terms 'communalism' and 'cast(e)ism' to refer, in the former case, to differences between Hindus, Muslims and/or Sikhs, and in the latter case to intra-community disagreements (usually Hindu, since the other religious groups supposedly have no caste differences).

29 The rise of the DK and the DMK have been chronicled by Irschick 1969 and Hardgrave 1965. One ought also to mention the breakaway AIDMK 'All-India DMK' of Karunanidhi, which developed in opposition to the dominance of the DMK by M. G. Ramachandran (MGR).

30 Actually, the myth feeds not only on the rediscovery of the 'lost' material but also on the reasons for its loss – the perfidy of 'Northerners'. Zvelebil (1992) reminds us of the real reason for the loss of so much of the early literature: simple neglect, ignorant neglect (such as the sectarian habit of immersing old texts in water or consecrating it to fire, without also making new copies) and destroying or adulterating texts of heterodox writers. Some of this was the work of Brahmans, but some would have occurred when earliest Shaivism was eclipsed by Jainism and Buddhism, and again when Jain and Buddhist texts were rejected as 'Hinduism' triumphed again in the medieval period. The myth also allows Tamil to claim whatever it wants as an ancient state – if philologists discover ancient borrowings from Sanskrit or wherever that seem to contradict the myth of ancient purity, one simply appropriates those words to ancient Tamil, claiming instead that Sanskrit (or whatever) borrowed them from Tamil. Thus the word *aracaṇ* 'king', found in ancient Tamil texts, is most probably derived from Sanskrit, *rāj*. To admit this would be an embarrassment, however, so one simply declares *rāj* to be borrowed from Tamil *aracaṇ*, and the problem is resolved.

31 As we have already seen with Japanese and Arabic, similar notions are found in those linguistic cultures. What is ironic about such Tamil ideas is that many of the features of Tamil they consider most distinctive, such as the retroflex frictionless continuant [ṛ], the last sound of the name of the language ([tamiṛ]), are also found in Malayalam, Tamil's sister language to the west. But then, to many Tamils, Malayalam is only a dialect of Tamil anyway.

32 By 'foreigner' is meant any non-native speaker of Tamil who does not look like a native of the subcontinent. The criterion is essentially based on appearances – skin colour, clothing, body language. When this writer speaks Tamil on the telephone, for example, no one ever fails to understand, or attempts to use another language.

33 There is an extensive literature both on diglossia in general (Ferguson 1959a) and in Tamil in particular (for the latter, see Shanmugam Pillai 1960, 1965; Schiffman 1978, 1979; Britto 1986, etc.).

34 This is a matter of some debate among certain segments of the population. This writer attended a conference of Tamil studies recently where some people in attendance protested the use of English for a panel on computer applications; the paper presenters were forced on the spur of the moment to paraphrase their papers in Tamil rather than give them in English. This was not a 'natural' situation, but rather forced upon them by politically more powerful elements of society. Once back in their computer labs, those same scientists continued their discussions in English, not in Tamil.

35 To speak of a particular language as diglossic or not is at best imprecise, since a language (e.g. English) as spoken in one part of the world may exhibit no diglossia, while the same language (again using English as an example) as used in a creole community (or Black English speech in the USA) would have to be considered diglossic.

36 Some writers on the subject claim that the existence of diglossia depends on there being high percentages of illiteracy in the linguistic culture, but

there are counter-examples to this, such as German Switzerland (Schiffman 1991). Literacy is rising in Tamil every decade, but diglossia shows no signs of diminishing.

37 Especially if it is a case of Fishman's type (d), where there is a written/formal-spoken norm.

38 Even in America one sees a style shift in these same genres of broadcasting, for example when an anchorperson finishes reading a prepared news story and turns to someone in the field for an on-the-spot report, or at least a more relaxed discussion of something: 'We're *gonna* go now to Tom Brokaw, who's on the floor of the Convention . . . '.

39 Perhaps it is the case that L-varieties can more successfully colonize new domains (opened by new technology) than invade old ones.

40 Some researchers would claim that *all* languages are diglossic to some extent, so that diglossia would in effect never be eliminated; perhaps at best we can speak of the *perception* (or to use Fishman's term, the *consensus*) that diglossia does not exist.

41 In what appears to be the opposite sort of case, but is actually illustrative of the same phenomena, my distant German relatives, whose L-variety is an Alemannic dialect, begin to lapse into that dialect soon after I arrive for a visit, and seem to expect that I will understand it; when I remind them that I understand it only with difficulty, they reply that they expect me to understand it because I am 'one of them'. This happens sooner and more frequently with one of the relatives with whom I exchange the T pronoun (*Du*) than with those with whom I am on a *Sie* basis.

42 The kind of behaviour that is typically encountered, and my proposed ways to deal with it are:

1 *Selective refusal/reluctance to speak target language* The principal feature of the 'roadblock' is the reluctance or outright refusal of the target language speaker (TLS) to carry on a conversation with the language learner in the target language. This can either take the form of outright refusal (by TLS) to speak *any* language if the learner has not attained some *minimal* level of competence in the TL, or simply the refusal of the TLS to speak the TL except with other native speakers, or other (usually socioeconomically *lower*) persons deemed to be appropriate interlocutors, resorting instead to some other *lingua franca*, or international high-prestige language.

An example of the first case, refusal to speak unless minimal competency has been attained, has often been reported anecdotally for French, and can be verified by this writer, with some qualifications.

2 *Reasons for outright refusal*
   (a) Lack of a tradition of foreigners learning Tamil, especially light-skinned ones, or foreign-looking ones.
   (b) Existence of diglossia
   (c) Prestige of English among educated Tamils.
   (d) Fact of Tamil as identity-marker among Tamils (solidarity, T vs. V).
   (e) Use of language to *prevent* communication in South Asia.
   (f) Inappropriateness of Tamil for a particular *topic* (part of diglossia?).

(g) Code-switching of English-knowing élites is natural.

(h) Xenophobia?

(i) Myths of separateness and antiquity. Tamils will accept H-variety from foreigners they do not *know*; negotiation of the 'right' to use H or L is negotiation to assign an in-group place to the foreigner.

43 Ramaswamy (1993) describes the poetic rhapsodizing that went on on the floor of the Tamilnāḍu legislature during the debate over the official language.

44 In English orthography, Tamil Nadu or Tamilnadu.

45 The Western metaphor, of course would be David and Goliath, with Tamil as David and Sanskrit/Hindi as Goliath.

8 LANGUAGE POLICY IN THE UNITED STATES

1 ©1966

2 Ferguson and Heath (1981); Fishman (1966); Heath (1977); Kloss (1977a); Glazer (1966), etc..

3 The beginning date coincided with the entry of the USA into World War II on 16 April, 1917 and the ending date marks the Supreme Court decision in *Meyer* v. *Nebraska* that has been called the 'Magna Carta' of American linguistic policy (Kloss 1977a).

4 We shall examine these and other legal decisions at a later point.

5 Veltman (1983: 211) refers to the 'power of the English language in the United States to subordinate and eradicate the languages of immigrants to that country'. Saer *et al.* (1924: 13) characterize English as the 'powerful and penetrating English tongue, which in every part of the world has proved itself to be all-conquering among the languages of the earth'.

6 Today's advocates of multiculturalism may disagree, but I do not see that this goal will be realized any day soon.

7 In the discussion of linguistic rights, the First Amendment right to free speech is often cited, especially when it is the case that American-born citizens do not happen to speak English; in the struggles of the German-American Church the right to freedom of religion was also invoked, but the Supreme Court has usually responded in terms of Fourteenth Amendment rights, but not First Amendment rights.

8 Despite the claims of such movements as US English and English First.

9 My own focus has been on linguistic assimilation in the schools of the German-American Church (Schiffman 1987).

10 For example, the requests for support from English-speaking congregations, indicative of the existence already by that time of many English-dominant members that began in the 1880s from the Indiana and other synods, but were not acted upon until much later.

11 The great danger here, of course, is that if one assumes that the code contains ideology, one is adopting a strong Whorfian bent, which takes us into uncharted waters which would also allow anyone to claim that some languages are better suited for certain purposes than others, which most analysts would want to avoid.

12 An overview of English linguistic culture since the Norman conquest may be found in Grillo 1989.

13 Sources for the linguistic situation before European contact are diverse; the best overall statement is Sturtevant (1983–95, and in progress), a multivolume encyclopaedic study focusing on the facts of individual languages, the historical relatedness of various languages, and other issues such as treaties, that have repercussions to this day in the relationships between Native Americans and the dominant culture. As I write, the Clinton administration is hosting a conference with leaders of all tribes, and promising a new approach. A concise and fairly recent study of Native-American languages can be found in Ferguson and Heath 1981, chapters 6–8.

14 See Coulombe 1993 for a discussion of the concept of language rights in the Canadian and other contexts.

15 But neither can we ignore folk notions about what languages are official, such as the widely-accepted notion that English is the official language of the USA, and is guaranteed in the Constitution. Despite reiterated denials of the officiality of English in the USA, the cherished belief that it *is* comes back to bedevil us when issues such as bilingual education are contested.

16 Contrast this with France, where, with the lifting of the Edict of Nantes, French Huguenots were forced to emigrate to *non*-French territory, since they were not to be tolerated in any French colony either. And note that in Spanish and French colonies, the rights to claim the souls of the inhabitants, old or new, were often granted in advance to one or another Catholic order; this was not so pre-ordained in English colonial policy.

17 DeCamp says (DeCamp 1971: 20) that plantation owners went one step further and chose to purchase slaves with the intention of having the greatest possible variety of linguistic backgrounds, to further reduce the possibilities of communication and the danger of insurrection.

18 Questions about language did not appear on the US Census until the mid-nineteenth century: speakers of Native American and other languages would therefore not be inferrable from the early censuses, and African languages brought by slaves would by this point have been replaced by English or creolized English.

19 By shunting aside the real Native Americans, American-born English speakers could claim 'native' status.

20 Kloss quotes a report of the Missouri Supervisor of Public Education for 1887–8, according to which:

> In a large number of districts of the State the German element of the population greatly preponderates and as a consequence the schools are mainly taught in the German language and sometimes entirely so. Hence if an American family lives in such a district the children must either be deprived of school privileges or else be taught in the German language. (Handschin [1913], quoted in Kloss 1977a: 89–90)

Kloss also quotes the next year's report, in which the Superintendent states that this condition exists without any legal basis, and that this 'injustice' could cease to be tolerated at any time.

21 Kloss 1977: 62–3. Different states tried different variations on the funding formula, but attempts to get state funding for the non-religious

portion of parochial school education (e.g. school lunches, funding for secular subjects, for busing) continued into the twentieth century.

22 More details are available in Kloss 1977a. Kloss cites Cubberley 1934 as a source for the claim that 9 April, 1842 was a kind of watershed for all state public school laws. Before 1842, says Cubberley, (1934: 178–9) many states entertained applications to the state school fund for support, even if they were private or parochial schools, and in 1840, Governor Seward of New York 'urged the establishment of schools in the cities of the state in which the teachers should be of the same language and religion as the foreign patrons' (op. cit.: 178). When the New York legislature acted in 1842, however, it was to create a City Board of Education for New York City, and to declare that no school funds were to be given to schools in which 'any religious sectarian doctrine or tenet should be taught, inculcated, or practiced' (op. cit.: 178). Other states were facing similar demands, but after this decisive act in New York, no other demand was sucessful, and with the rise of Know-Nothingness and increased immigration from Catholics, (e.g. from Ireland) the lines were drawn. Eventually almost all states included this kind of ban in their constitutions, and Cubberley lists 38 states that eventually included such provisions, either as constitutional amendments or in their original constitutions at the time of admission to statehood (Cubberley 1934: 180).

23 In the issue of language and religion, the attacks began first on the religious issue and the parochial school system.

- Ohio 1853: Bill introduced to require *all* children to attend public schools three months out of the year – rejected.

- 1873: Cincinnati attempts to tax Roman Catholic schools – the original Ohio law had allowed teaching of German in German if parents requested it. Local option choice of subjects and language. From 1834 on growth of German (bilingual) schools. Louisiana copied this for French.

- Minnesota: parochial schools had no legal status for years until 1911, when Germans and Scandinavians got it passed.

- Nebraska 1911: attempt parallel to Ohio 1853 – also rejected

- Oregon 1922: starting 1920, harsh law against non-English language press required bilingual editions.

- Oregon 1922: law requiring all children aged 8–15, from 1926 onward, to attend public school only. 1924: Florida, California, Ohio, Michigan, Montana, Washington followed suit.

- Oregon 1925: case of *Society of Sisters* v. *Pierce*. Supreme Court ruled against Oregon law of 1922 (and all others) that tried to ban parochial schools. enumerate

24 I conclude this from the relative status of the 'foreign' language teacher and the athletic coach in the typical American school. When there are budget cuts, it is the language teacher who gets cut first, not the PE teacher.

25 Unless otherwise noted, details are from Kloss 1977a.

26   The Republican party controlled legislatures in Wisconsin and Illinois, and tried to stamp out German Protestant schools. German Protestants had been Republican but went over *en masse* to the Democratic party (joining Catholics, Scandinavians, Poles, and German Catholics and *Freidenker*). The Republicans were defeated, and the Democrats changed the laws back in 1890. Democrats also won federally in the House of Representatives in 1890, and Grover Cleveland was re-elected in 1892.

27   Let us also note that as soon as German immigration peaked, assimilation of the earlier generation of German-American children began to increase (or, people began to notice that assimilation was happening). The proposed *Stundenplan* is probably a response to the attempts at restrictive legislation.

28   A longer version of this section has appeared with the title 'Losing the battle for balanced bilingualism: the German-American case' in *Language Problems and Language Planning* (1987). Research reported therein was supported in part by a grant from the University of Washington Graduate School Research Fund.

29   In my 1987 article I concentrated on what one might call the internal weaknesses of the policy of the German-American Church, focusing on such questions as what kinds of schools produce balanced bilingualism; what motives underlie policies furthering compartmentalized bilingualism; whether those who implement bilingual programmes know if their policies will result in specific goals; and what strategies a bilingual school must follow to compensate for factors in the dominant linguistic culture that mitigate against balanced bilingualism.

30   For a discussion of definitional problems, especially in typologizing bilingual education, see Fishman 1974: 40–6, 118–23; Mackey 1970: 603; 1972; Kloss 1966a; Shapiro and Schiffman 1981; Weinreich 1968.

31   It is interesting to note that in the present decade there has emerged a kind of mass swearing-in ceremony in many parts of the country, at which large numbers of new citizens are sworn in at the same time, accompanied by speechifying, music and other ceremonial behaviour. In one area of the country the language of the ceremony has been Spanish because of the large number of Spanish speakers who would otherwise not understand the proceedings. Though there is no legal sanction for these ceremonies (in Seattle, for example, they are sponsored by the Northwest Ethnic Heritage Society, a private group) there have been public denunciations of the Spanish-language ceremonies, and demands that they be conducted in English.

32   One perception was that their religious services were conducted in mysterious ritual languages (Greek, Church Slavonic, Latin, or Hebrew) accompanied by 'mumbo-jumbo', 'hocus-pocus' and lots of smoke and incense.

33   Haugen (1956: 80–2) reviews these arguments.

34   Victoria County Council of Defense (Texas) asked people to give up German in public and private; Findlay, Ohio fined people $25 for use of German on streets; Turner County, South Dakota forbade German on the street; Philadelphia Select and Common Council petitioned Congress on 19 May, 1917 to pass a law forbidding the use of German in public gatherings; May, 1918, Iowa Governor forbade the use of non-English in

a public place, on telephone, on railroads – public conversations were permitted only in English, and church services in non-English were to be held in private homes. Schools were also forbidden: in Scott County Iowa four women had to make contributions to the Red Cross because they had spoken German (*Plattdeutsch*) on the telephone; Nebraska 1919, public meetings in English only, but churches and lodges excepted; New York passed a law against use of non-English in business signs and notices, but this was thrown out by New York courts. German was prohibited in many states for all educational institutions. Some states prohibited German, others prohibited German for 'regular subjects', or all non-English instruction; some prohibited non-English in elementary schools only. In Iowa the edict was by proclamation of the governor; in South Dakota by the state council of defense; in Nebraska, by resolution of the legislature.

35 A pastor of the Evangelical Church reported the following story to me. At a meeting of the General Synod of the Evangelical Church in Pittsburgh 1922, the German language was demoted as official language of the Evangelical Church, and English was voted in. Theodore Mayer, an official of the Synod, sent a telegram to a like-minded colleague in the St Louis Synodical office saying 'The German dogs have been licked'. Unbeknownst to Mayer, the telegraph clerk who took his telegram was a member of a German-loyal Evangelical church congregation in Pittsburgh, who reported the text of the telegram to his German-loyal pastor, and the next day there was hell to pay. Mayer was Christian Education Director of the Synod and a crusader to get rid of German.

36 Haugen (1956: secs 4.6ff.) lists a number of 'research' studies that show that bilingual education was *harmful* for children. Unfortunately, research was done using only samples of children who were socioeconomically disadvantaged, and furthermore they were tested in the language they were weakest in, English. This view nevertheless dominated for four decades.

37 The BEA was amended again in 1974 and in 1978; *Rules and Regulations* were issued in 1974 and in 1980.

38 Secada shows how again and again analysts interpreted certain legal 'enticements' as if they were equivalent to legal mandates, even though 'there is no direct, legal basis on which to mandate bilingual education on a federal scale. Rather, legal mandates for bilingual education have been fashioned by the courts as remedies for the denial of equal educational opportunity to minority-language students' (Secada 1990: 84).

39 Also known as 'Negro Dialect', 'Black English' and 'African-American Vernacular English'.

40 As Labov shows, traditional dialectology tried to show that BEV contained no features not found in the speech of any other American group, though they were more common in the speech of rural, southern working-class Whites. Many middle-class, educated Blacks themselves opposed the notion of extreme difference, calling it another kind of racism.

41 That is, where other dialects can *contract* forms of the copula, BEV can delete *or* contract it; where other dialects cannot contract forms of the copula, BEV can neither delete *nor* contract it. Thus in SAE, *is* may be

contracted – as in '*He's* comin' tomorrow' but not in 'I don't know where *he is* (*he's) right now', in BEV the first example would allow deletion ('*he* comin' tomorrow') but the second would not.

42 Labov summarizes the consensus the linguists arrived at in four areas (1982: 192).

43 The literature on this subject is fairly extensive, and also includes much of a polemical nature. See for example Smitherman 1994; Adams and Brink 1990; Cazden and Snow 1990.

44 This is referred to by some as the English Only movement, but this sobriquet is considered misleading by defenders of US English (Imhoff 1990: 61).

45 But see the discussion on the effects of officialization in California as a result of the passing of Proposition 63.

46 *Congressional Record* § 15024–30, 11 Oct., 1990.

47 Or the school district may attempt to pay for it by sending the driver-education teacher for retraining as a Japanese teacher, as happened in one school district in Washington State.

9 LANGUAGE POLICY IN CALIFORNIA

1 Other states had English-only legislation at other periods, but not arrived at by the Initiative process.

2 One only need recall the flap that ensued during the 1992 presidential election campaign, when then Vice-President Quayle castigated a character in a television sitcom, *Murphy Brown*, for her decision to have a child out of wedlock. 'Ms Brown' was attacked for being a bad role-model for teenage girls. In the next episode, the programme used the opportunity to attack Vice-President Quayle for his violation of 'Ms Brown's' privacy.

3 Monterey Park, located just east of Los Angeles in suburban San Gabriel Valley, has struggled with the issue of how to deal with its large Asian minority, specifically merchants who want to attract business by displaying advertisements in Chinese on publicly visible signs. For a short time, Monterey Park actually had its own official municipal language policy (English only), but this has since changed. The case is discussed in some detail in Horton and Calderon (1992: 186–94).

4 There were, of course, nineteenth-century attempts elsewhere, as we saw in the previous chapter, though most of these were overturned by *Meyer* v. *Nebraska* in 1923, or rendered innocuous.

5 Colorado, Arizona and Florida voted in English-only amendments to their state constitutions in 1988, and other states are considering legislative measures.

6 Powell (1966 [1891]) is a fair summation of late nineteenth-century classificatory schemes of Native-American language families. He gives 58 separate families of Native-American languages north of Mexico; Boas (1966 [1908]) reduces these to 55. Of these, 14, or almost exactly 25 per cent of all Native-American language families, are found in California. (This is not in terms of absolute numbers of speakers, of course, but of then-known families.) The great task of American lin-

guists interested in the historical relatedness of Native-American languages has been to discover principles for grouping them into families
and megafamilies. Gradually in the twentieth century the number of
groupings has been reduced, for example Miwok, Costanoan, Yokuts,
Maidu and Wintun were grouped together into a 'Penutian' family, a
hypothesis only some support.

7 The Gaspar de Portolá/Junipero Serra expedition entered Alta California
in 1769, and established the first mission at San Diego.

8 The figure given in Heizer 1978a illustrates a number of different
attempts; none of them is totally congruent with the artificial boundaries
of the current state.

9 In the 1850 US Census, figures for California, which attained statehood
in that year, are rather sketchy, and it is admitted that many returns were
lost, burned, or unaccounted for. The 'White' population of California in
that census is given as 91,635, and the percentage of White to total as
98.9 per cent; the total population is therefore in excess of 93,000,
although this is based on estimates. In 1852, perhaps because of the
inadequacy of the 1850 count, a state census was conducted, with much
higher figures: 171,841 Whites; 1,678 Blacks; 528 Coloureds; 31,266
'Indians domesticated', and 54,803 foreign residents, for a total of
255,122 – almost three times the 1850 figure. It is interesting to note
that Indians are counted in this census, though no figures for Spanish
speakers are given in either one: given the very high percentage of
Whites in the 1850 Census, Spanish speakers would of course have
been included automatically in that rubric. The 31,266 figure for
Indians is much higher than the estimate of Thernstrom *et al.* The
number of public schools in California is given as two, with two
teachers and 49 pupils; there are six public schools, with five teachers
and 170 students.

10 Cook's succinct statement of this bears being quoted at least in part:

> Consideration of these factors and of the apparently tremendous
> increase in population of the California Indians throughout the
> twentieth century leads one to hypothesize that all the estimates,
> counts, and censuses from 1861 to 1930 yield values that are much
> too low. Natural increase plus immigration from the east . . . cannot
> account for a rise from 25,000 in 1930 to an enrollment figure of
> 70,000 in 1970 or a doubling of the census count in the single
> decade 1960 to 1970. The only reasonable explanation must be
> that both the Bureau of Indian Affairs and the Bureau of the Census
> failed to notice thousands of Indians who had withdrawn physically
> and emotionally from American civilization after the debacle of the
> 1850s and whose descendants have only recently been emerging
> under the influence of a new social climate and of possible material
> benefits. (Cook 1978: 94)

11 Large portions of California before irrigation were in fact desert –
perhaps some portions, such as San Diego, were balmy deserts with a
mild climate, but nevertheless existing water supplies were minimal;
Native-American populations naturally congregated where there were
reliable supplies of water. This is quite obvious in many settlements near

the border: lush green golf courses and private lawns on the American side (irrigated with northern California water) and desert on the Mexican side.

12 The few attempts to utilize or preserve Native-American languages that date from the Spanish period are summarized by Heizer (1966: 9–10) with the maps of Kroeber and Powell (ibid.: 15–16). Some of this map-making, which was based on the testimony of the Native Americans themselves, was later used to try to determine land claims.

13 For a review of language policy in Mexico, see Heath 1972.

14 The account in the *Encyclopaedia Britannica* puts it like this:

> As for the intellectual development of the Indians the mission system accomplished nothing; save the care of their souls they received little instruction, they were virtually slaves, and were trained into a fatal dependency, so that once coercion was removed they relapsed at once into native customs. (*Encylopaedia Britannica*, 10th edn, 1968: 633–4)

15 Heizer lists some of the sporadic attempts, such as those of Fr Felipe Arroyo de la Cuesta, Sitjar, and Tac, but as he notes, 'the ethnological gleanings from these sources are usually slim and often in error' (1978a: 6). There were also sporadic contacts by Russians, errant Chinese, German, French and British explorers some of whom laid claim perhaps to small areas but never attempted to establish their hegemony over the area.

16 This study contains an excellent bibliography on law, colonization practice, Indian treaties, and critiques of all of these. See also the contribution of Jon Reyhner in Crawford 1992.

17 Later, of course, the colonial powers gained footholds, but at first the object seemed to be mainly trade.

18 Not until much later did various colonial powers encroach upon the sovereignty of territories in India, Malacca, Java, etc. and actually claim territory there. In British India the principle was to take territory away from rulers whose ruling style was found to be in conflict with certain British principles.

19 See for example the explorations of Juan de Fuca, sailing for the Spanish crown in the late sixteenth century. His explorations in Puget Sound resulted in some place names, but since he left behind no settlement, his land claims were not honoured when Vancouver dropped anchor two centuries later.

20 The same issue was fought constantly as slavery came to a head, then later over desegregation – what were 'States Rights' and what were federal rights?

21 Similarly, a religious group that believes that antibiotics and inocula-tions are against God's will may find their children forced to be inocu-lated, because of the health hazard of having portions of the school-age population unprotected in time of epidemics, etc. Worse scenarios than this often surface with particularly 'apocalyptic' groups, such as the Jonestown group or the Branch Davidians at Waco, Texas.

22 *Congressional Record* para 15024–30, 11 Oct., 1990.

23 I take this account from the entry on California in *Encyclopaedia Britannica*, 10th edn, 1968, pp. 633–4.

24 There is some uncertainty about where exactly Drake anchored, since it could have been any one of a number of bays, from San Francisco Bay to Point Reyes. Interestingly, Heizer 1947 uses linguistic evidence, based on what we now know about Native-American groups resident in the area, to declare for Drake's Bay, though Bodega Bay is another likely candidate.

25 Some missions may occasionally have used Native-American languages along with Spanish and Latin; Cook and Marino (1988: 477) give an illustration of a prayer board from San Antonio de Padua Mission in 1817, with 'prayers and songs in Salinan, Latin and Spanish languages'. But no systematic descriptions of Native-American languages from the Spanish period exist.

26 About the only evidence we have about language use in the missions comes from the result of a questionnaire sent to the various mission-aries in 1811 (Cook 1976: 142) which requested a report on linguistic 'progress', which meant progress in learning Castilian. Answers are brief and sometimes vague, indicating that some Native Americans spoke or understood Castilian to some degree. But as Cook points out,

> It must be remembered that the missionaries undoubtedly made out as good a case as possible. In conformity with traditional Spanish colonial policy, every effort was to be made to introduce Castilian among the natives, and in so far as possible to suppress the local idiom. This policy had, indeed, been reaffirmed in a royal decree transmitted by Borica in 1795 (Prov. Rec., 6:143). (Cook 1976 [1990]: 143, fn. 10)

The Borica Cook refers to was Governor Diega de Borica, resident in Monterey.

27 Perhaps we can accept the figure of 13,000 Spanish *Californios*, with perhaps 85,000 or more Native-Americans.

28 Cook minces no words in his description of the situation:

> When the gold rush and Mexican War brought into California thousands of ordinary Anglo-Americans plus an enormous criminal element recruited from the scum of the earth, conditions changed greatly. (Cook 1976 [1990]: 308)

In actuality, the discovery at Sutter's Mill was not the first discovery of gold; there was an earlier find at Placerito in Los Angeles County, but it did not attract wide attention and precipitate a rush (W. Bright, personal communication).

29 California, unlike most other states that were not ratifiers of the original US Constitution, never passed through the phrase of being a 'territory' but proceeded directly to statehood after Guadalupe-Hidalgo. This fact is also often used to explain why California is politically immature, whacky, volatile and spaced out.

30 Kloss 1977a: 183.

31 The effect of the Bilingual Education Act of 1968 was at first minimal, because its programmes were offered as an option, not as a mandate;

when later developments were interpreted in terms of it, became a watershed. As one writer puts it,

> The Bilingual Education Act, contrary to its name, did not require school districts to implement programs of bilingual education for LEP [Limited English Proficiency] children. What it did do was signal a national commitment of political will and financial resources to serving the needs of these students. It was enacted in 1968, at a time of growing concern about the educational neglect of Mexican American children in the southwest. ... [It] created a competitive grants program to help train teachers and administrators, finance research on effective teaching methods, and support educational projects. It mandated no special treatment for LEP children. ... Over the years most of these Title VII grants have been reserved for school programs that use LEP children's native language. This became a source of controversy during the 1980s, leading to charges of federal intrusiveness on decisions previously left to local educators. (Jiminez 1992: 44)

32 By which is presumably meant serve on juries, vote, manage taxes on their land, etc.
33 Another misinterpretation of the Treaty of Guadalupe-Hidalgo – Mexico *ceded* the territory to the USA, it did not *sell* it.
34 The text of the *Lau* ruling, without attribution of source, is given in Crawford 1992: 251–5. (The case number is 414 US 563, 565, 1974.)
35 For background on Proposition 63 and US English, see MacKaye 1990.
36 As early as 1880, Dakota children in the American Mission boarding school were taught first in Dakota, with elementary schoolbooks and the Bible in Dakota as reading material. It was reported that first teaching

> children to read and write in their own language enables them to master English with more ease when they take up that study . . . [A] child beginning a four years' course with the study of Dakota would be further advanced in English at the end of the term than one who had not been instructed in Dakota. (quoted in Reyhner 1992: 44)

Though this was not 'official' policy in BIA schools (in fact it was officially discouraged) many teachers of the time report developing their own effective methodologies that utilized children's native languages. A century later, the weight of evidence still seems to be in favour of *some* use of students' native language, though what is actually meant by 'bilingual education' is often confused and confusing. Some researchers prefer early and rapid transition to English (Porter 1990), while others advocate teaching all subjects in the mother tongue as a language-maintenance strategy. There seem to be no serious advocates any more for 'sink-or-swim' immersion, as was the pattern a century ago. See Secada (1990: 82, fn. 1) for a concise review of 'effectiveness' studies, especially Willig (ibid.: 93).

10 CONCLUSION

1 Though the Chomskian paradigm of language and cognition would hold that humans are predisposed to learn language, and to acquire it *in a particular way* that results necessarily in the construction and acquisition of grammars consisting of the elements that the paradigm specifies.

2 This may be both geographical, e.g. at the political borders of countries, or socially, that is some speakers are sure of their linguistic identity, and others are not so sure.

3 It is difficult to believe that under this model the English language, that is, its *code* or structure have imperialistic tendencies, or that there are specifically English *ideas* embodied in the English language that are imperialistic, but this is the interpretation that forces itself on us. Otherwise we would see as imperialistic only the *behaviour* of certain people who happen to be English-speaking.

4 The few efforts to defend French passed since 1975 are mainly directed at English and at attacks on the status of French, not its corpus.

Bibliography

Abel, Stephen (1976) Tamil in the twentieth century: its development as a political medium and a political issue. Master's thesis, University of Washington.

Adams, Karen L. and Brink, Daniel T. (eds.) (1990) *Perspectives on Official English: The Campaign for English as the Official Language of the USA*, vol. 57 of *Contributions to the Sociology of Language*. Mouton de Gruyter, Berlin and New York.

Adigal, Maraimalai (1972a) Taṇit-t tamiṟum kalappu-t tamiṟum. In *Uraimaṇi-kkōvai*, South India Saiva-Siddhanta Publishing Society, Madras, pp. 61–77.

Adigal, Maraimalai (1972b) *Uraimaṇi-kkōvai*. South India Saiva-Siddhanta Publishing Society, Madras.

Adler, Max K. (1980) *Marxist Linguistic Theory and Communist Practice: A Sociolinguistic Study*. Buske, Hamburg.

Ager, Dennis, E. (1990) *Sociolinguistics and Contemporary French*. Cambridge University Press, Cambridge.

Alisjahbana, S. Takdir (1976) *Language Planning for Modernization: the Case of Indonesian and Malaysian*, vol. 14 of *Contributions to the Sociology of Language*, Mouton, The Hague.

All India Language Conference Report (1958) *Modern India Rejects Hindi*. Association for the Advancement of the National Languages of India, Calcutta.

Amorose, Thomas (1989) The official-language movement in the United States: contexts, issues and activities. *Language Problems and Language Planning*, 13(3): 264–79.

Andhra Pradesh, Government of (1989) *Brochure on Safeguards and Facilities for the Linguistic Minorities of Andhra Pradesh*. Technical report, Andhra Pradesh Director of Printing. General Administration (Political-B) Department, Hyderabad.

Ândronov, M. S. (1962) *Razgovorny Tamil'skij Jazik i ego Dialekty*. Izdatel'stvo Vostočnoj Literatury, Moscow.

Ândronov, M. S. (1975) Problems of the national language in Tamilnad. *Anthropos*, 70: 180–93.

Annamalai, E. (1968) Changing society and modern Tamil literature. *Mahfil, a Quarterly of South Asian Literature*, 4 (3, 4): 21–36.

Annamalai, E. (ed.) (1979a) *Language Movements in India*, vol. 5 of *CIIL Conferences and Seminars Series*. Central Institute of Indian Languages, Mysore.

Annamalai, E. (1979b) *Movement for Linguistic Purism: the Case of Tamil*. Central Institute of Indian Languages, Mysore.

Annamalai, E. (1989) *The Linguistic and Social Dimensions of Purism*, vol. 54 of *Contributions to the Sociology of Language*. Mouton de Gruyter, Berlin.

Annamalai, E. (1990) Dimensions of bilingual education in India. *New Language Planning Newsletter*, 4(4).

Annamalai, E., Jernudd, B. and Rubin, J. (eds) (1985) *Language Planning: Proceedings of an Institute*. Central Institute of Indian Languages and Institute of Culture and Communication, East-West Center, Mysore and Honolulu.

Appadurai, Arjun (1981) *Worship and Conflict under Colonial Rule. A South Indian Case*. Cambridge University Press, Cambridge, London and New York.

Apte, M. (1975) Language controversies in the Indian parliament: 1952–60. In W. O'Barr and J. O'Barr (eds) *Language and Politics*. Mouton, The Hague.

Arden, A. H. (1942) *A Progressive Grammar of Common Tamil* (5th edn). Christian Literature Society, Madras.

Asher, R. E. (1969) The Tamil renaissance and the beginnings of the Tamil novel. *Journal of the Royal Asiatic Society*, 1: 14–28.

Babiniotis, G. (1979) A linguistic approach to the 'language question' in Greece. *Byzantine and Modern Greek Studies*, 5: 1–16.

Balbir, Nicole (1983) La modernisation du hindi. In F. István and C. Hagège (eds) *Language Reform: History and Future*. Buske, Hamburg, pp. 101–7.

Balibar, Renée (1985) *L'Institution du français: Essai sur le colinguisme des Carolingiens a la république*. Presses Universitaires de France, Paris.

Balibar, Renée and LaPorte, Dominique (1974) *Le Français national: Politique et pratiques de la langue nationale sous la Révolution française*. Hachette Littérature, Paris.

Banakar, Mahadev (1982) *Safeguards for Linguistic Minorities in India. Karnataka sets a Model*. Smt. Parwatamma Mahadev Banakar, Bangalore.

Bankwitz, Philip C. (1978) *Alsation Autonomist Leaders, 1919–1947*. University Press of Kansas, Lawrence.

Barnett, Marguerite Ross (1976) *The Politics of Cultural Nationalism in South India*. Princeton University Press, Princeton, NJ.

Baron, Dennis, E. (1990) *The English-Only Question: An Official Language for Americans?* Yale University Press, New Haven.

Barve, S. G. (1957) [1956] *A Note by the Secretary, Official Language Commission, of his Observations during his Short Visit of Deputation to the USSR for a Study of the Language Problem*. Government of India Press, New Delhi.

Bec, Pierre (1970–1) *Manual pratique de philologie romane*. A. & J. Picard, Paris.

Beck, Walter H. (1939) *Lutheran Elementary Schools in the United States*. Concordia Publishing House, St Louis.

Becker, Howard S. and Geer, Blanche (1960) Latent culture: a note on the theory of latent social roles. *Administrative Science Quarterly*, 5: 304–13.

Beer, William R. (1980) *The Unexpected Rebellion: Ethnic Activism in Contemporary France*. New York University Press, New York.

Beer, William R. (1985) *Language Policy and National Unity*. Rowman & Allanheld, Totowa, NJ.

Bernauer, Ludwig (1967) Die Statistik als Spiegel der französischen Assimilationspolitik im Elsaß und in Deutschlothringen. In Franz Hieronymus Riedl (ed.) *Humanitas Ethnica: Festschrift für Theodor Veitner*. Wilhelm Braumüller, Vienna and Stuttgart, pp. 183–97.

Beschi, Constantine (1728) *A Grammar of the High Dialect of the Tamil Language, termed Shen-Tamil: to which is added an Introduction to Tamil Poetry*, trans. (from Latin) Benjamin Guy Babington (1822). The College Press, Madras.

Boas, Franz (1966) Introduction. In Preston Holder (ed.) *Introduction to Handbook of American Indian Languages and Indian Linguistic Families of America North of Mexico*. University of Nebraska Press, Lincoln, pp. 1–79.

Boisgontier, Jacques, Michel, Louis and Petit, Jean-Marie (1981) *Atlas linguistique et ethnographique du Languedoc oriental*, vols 1–3. Editions du Centre national de la recherche scientifique, Paris.

Brabec, Ivan, Hraste, Make and Živković, Sreten (1954) *Gramatika Hrvakskoga ili Srpskog Jezika*. Školska knjiga, Zagreb.

Breton, Roland J.-L. (1991) *Geolinguistics: Language Dynamics and Ethnolinguistic Geography*. Presses de l'Université d'Ottawa, Ottawa.

Bright, William O. (ed.) (1966) *Sociolinguistics. Proceedings of the UCLA Sociolinguistics Conference, 1964*. Mouton, The Hague and Paris.

Britto, F. (1986) *Diglossia: A Study of the Theory with Application to Tamil*. Georgetown University Press, Washington, DC.

Brown, R. and Gilman, A. (1972) [1968] The pronouns of power and solidarity. In Joshua Fishman (ed.) *Readings in the Sociology of Language*. Mouton, The Hague, pp. 252–75.

Brunot, Ferdinand (1967) [1905–53] *Histoire de la langue française des origines à nos jours*, vols 1–13. Librairie Armand Colin, Paris.

Bugarski, Ranko (1992) Language situation and general policy. In Ranko Bugarski and C. Hawkesworth (eds) *Language Planning in Yugoslavia*. Slavica, Columbus, OH, pp. 10–26.

Burrow, T. and Emeneau, M. B. (eds) (1984) *A Dravidian Etymological Dictionary* (2nd edn). Clarendon, Oxford.

Caldwell, Robert (1961) [1856] *A Comparative Grammar of the Dravidian or South-Indian Family of Languages*. University of Madras, Madras.

Caro, Jean-Marie, Ferretti, Henri, Fuchs, Jean-Paul, Klein, Georges, Koehl, Emile and Zeller, Adrien (1980) *Proposition de loi tendant à introduire l'enseignement de la langue régionale dans les établissements scolaires des départements du Rhin et de la Moselle et à assurer le développement du bilinguisme*. Technical report 1612. Assemblée Nationale, Paris.

Cassidy, Frederic, G. (1971) Tracing the pidgin element in Jamaican creole. In Dell Hymes (ed.) *Pidginization and Creolization of Languages*. Cambridge University Press, Cambridge, pp. 203–21.

Castillo, Edward D. (1978) The impact of Euro-American exploration and settlement. In Robert F. Heizer (ed.) *Handbook of North American Indians*, vol. 8: *California*. Smithsonian Institution and Government Printer, Washington, DC, pp. 99–107.

Catach, Nina (1991) *L'Orthographe en débat: dossiers pour un changement*. Editions Nathan, Paris.

Catach, Nina (1992) *Recherche et réforme*. Technical report 19–20. CNRS series Liaisons-HESO, Ivry-sur-Seine.

Cazden, Courtney, B. and Snow, Catherine E. (eds) (1990) *English Plus: Issues in Bilingual Education*, vol. 508 in *The Annals of the American Academy of Political and Social Science*.

Chambers, John W. (ed.) (1983) *Black English: Educational Equity and the Law*. Karoma Publishers, Ann Arbor.

Chomsky, Noam (1965) *Aspects of the Theory of Syntax*. MIT Press, Cambridge, MA.

Citrin, Jack, Reingold, Beth, Walters, Evelyn and Green, Donald P. (1990) The 'Official English' movement and the symbolic politics of language in the United States. *The Western Political Quarterly*, 43(3): 534–59.

Cloonan, J. D. and Strine, J. M. (1991) Federalism and the development of language policy: preliminary investigations. *Language Problems and Language Planning*, 15(3): 268–81.

Cobarrubias, Juan and Fishman, Joshua (1983) *Progress in Language Planning: International Perspectives*, vol. 31 of *Contributions to the Sociology of Language*. Mouton, Berlin, New York and Amsterdam.

Concordia Publishing House (1865–1920), *Evangelisches–Lutherisches Schulblatt*, vols 1–55. St Louis. (A journal for teachers in the schools of the Lutheran Church, Missouri Synod.)

Cook, Sherburne F. (1976) [1900] *The Conflict Between the Californian Indian and White Civilization*. University of California Press, Berkeley and Los Angeles.

Cook, Sherburne F. (1978) Historical demography. In Robert F. Heizer (ed.) *Handbook of North American Indians*, vol. 8: *California*. Smithsonian Institution and Government Printer, Washington, DC, pp. 91–99.

Cook, Sherburne F. (1978) Historical demography. In Robert F. Heizer (ed.) *Handbook of North American Indians*, vol. 8: *California*. Smithsonian Institution and Government Printer, Washington, DC, pp. 91–8.

Cook, Sherburne F. and Marino, Cesare (1988) Roman Catholic missions in California and the southwest. In Wilcomb E. Washburn (ed.) *Handbook of North American Indians*, vol. 4: *History of Indian–White Relations*. Smithsonian Institution and Government Printer, Washington, DC, pp. 472–80.

Cooper, Robert L. (1989) *Language Planning and Social Change*. Cambridge University Press, Cambridge.

Coulmas, Florian (1989) *The Writing Systems of the World*. Blackwell, Oxford.

Coulombe, Pierre (1993) Language rights, individual and communal. *Language Problems and Language Planning*, 17(3): 140–52.

Crawford, James (ed.) (1992) *Language Loyalties: A Source Book on the Official English Controversy*. University of Chicago Press, Chicago and London.

Cubberley, Ellwood (1934) *Public Education in the United States*. Houghton Mifflin, Boston, New York and Chicago.

Curie, Eve (1937) *Madame Curie, a Biography*. Doubleday, Garden City, NJ.

Cuvāminātaiyar, U. Ve. (1949) *Cankattamirum Pirkālattamirum*. Madras.

Das Gupta, Jyotirindra (1969) *Official Language Problems and Policies in South Asia*, vol. 5 of *Current Trends in Linguistics*. Mouton, The Hague.

Das Gupta, Jyotirindra (1970) *Language Conflict and National Development: Group Politics and National Language Policy in India*. University of California Press, Berkeley.

de Bary, Wm. Theodore (ed.) (1958) *Sources of Indian Tradition*, vol. 2. Columbia University Press, New York.

DeCamp, David (1971) Introduction: the study of pidgin and creole languages. In Dell Hymes (ed.) *Pidginization and Creolization of languages*. Cambridge University Press, Cambridge, pp. 13–39.

de Certeau, Julia D., Revel, Jacques and Revel, Michel (1975) *Une politique de la langue. La Révolution française et les patois: l'enquête de Grégoire*. Gallimard, Paris.

Delesalle, Simone and Chevalier, Jean-Claude (1986) *La Linguistique, la grammaire et l'école, 1750–1914*. Armand Colin, Paris.

Deloria, Vine Jr. (1992) Trouble in high places: erosion of American Indian rights to religious freedom in the United States. In M. Annette Jaimes (ed.) *The State of Native America: Genocide, Colonization, and Resistance*. South End Press, Boston, pp. 267–90.

Deshpande, Madhav M. (1979) *Sociolinguistic Attitudes in India: An Historical Reconstruction*. Karoma, Ann Arbor.

Deshpande, Madhav M. (1986) Sanskrit grammarians on diglossia. In Bh. Krishnamurti (ed.) *South Asian Languages: Structure, Convergence and Diglossia*, vol. III of *MLBD Series in Linguistics*. Matilal Banarsidass, Delhi, pp. 312–21.

DeStefano, Johanna S. (1973) *Language, Society and Education: A Profile of Black English*. C. A. Jones, Worthington, OH.

Dēvanēyan, G. (1949) *Collaaraaycci-K Katturaikaḷ*. South India Saiva-Siddhantha Works Publishing Society, Madras.

Dēvanēyan, G. (1967) *Tamir Varalaaru*. Nēcamaṇi Patippakam, Katpadi.

de Vaugelas, Claude Favre (1984) *La Préface des 'Remarques sur la langue françoise'*, no. 37 in *Recueil de travaux publiés par la faculté des lettres*. Faculté des lettres, Neuchâtel, and Librairie Droz, Neuchâtel, Geneva.

Dietz, Paul T. (1949) The transition from German to English in the Missouri Synod from 1910 to 1947. *Concordia Historical Institute Quarterly*, October: 97–127.

Director of Languages and Development of Kannaḍa (1976). *Official Language Problems Analysed*. Papers read in the Southern States Official Language Seminar, Mysore, Bangalore.

Druon, Maurice (1990) *Les Rectifications de l'orthographie*, no. 100 of *Journal official de la république française*.

Dua, Hans R. (1985) *Language Planning in India*. Harnam Publications, New Delhi.

Dupuy, Andre, Carriere, Marcel and Nouvel, Alain (1976) *Historique de l'Occitanie*. A. Nouvel, Montpellier.

Emeneau, Murray B. (1956) India as a linguistic area. *Language*, 32(1): 3–16.

Emeneau, Murray B. (1964) Oral poets of South India – the Toḍas. In Dell Hymes (ed.) *Language in Culture and Society*. Harper & Row, New York, pp. 330–43.

Emeneau, Murray B. (1974) *Ritual Structure and Language Structure of the Toḍas*, vol. 64(6) of *Transactions of the American Philosophical Society, New Series*.

Ervin-Tripp, S. (1969) Advances in experimental social psychology. *Sociolinguistics*, 4(3): 91–165.

Falch, J. (1973) *Contribution à l'étude du statut des langues en Europe*, no. 3. Centre international de recherches sur le bilinguisme, Québec.

Fasold, Ralph (1984) *Introduction to Sociolingustics*, vol. I: *The Sociolinguistics of Society*. Blackwell, Oxford.

Ferguson, Charles A. (1966) National sociolinguistic profile formulas. In William O. Bright (ed.) *Sociolonguistics. Proceedings of the UCLA Sociolinguistics Conference, 1964*. Mouton, The Hague and Paris, pp. 309–15.

Ferguson, Charles A. (1959a) Diglossia. *WORD*, 15(2): 325–40.

Ferguson, Charles A. (1959b) Myths about Arabic. In Joshua Fishman (ed.) (1972) [1968] *Readings in the Sociology of Language*. Mouton, The Hague, pp. 375–81.

Ferguson, Charles A. and Gumperz, John J. (eds) (1960) *Linguistic Diversity in South Asia: Studies in Regional, Social and Functional Variation*, vol. 26(3): part 2 of *International Journal of American Linguistics*.

Ferguson, C. and Heath, S. B. (eds) (1981) *Language in the USA*. Cambridge University Press, Cambridge.

Fernandez, Mauro (1993) *Diglossia. A Comprehensive Bibliography, 1960–1990, and Supplements. With an Introduction by W. F. Mackey*. John Benjamins, Amsterdam and Philadelphia.

Fishman, Joshua (ed.) (1966) *Language Loyalty in the United States*. Mouton, The Hague.

Fishman, Joshua (1967) Bilingualism with and without diglossia; diglossia with and without bilingualism. *Journal of Social Issues*, 23(2): 29–38.

Fishman, Joshua (ed.) (1972) [1968] *Readings in the Sociology of Language*. Mouton, The Hague.

Fishman, Joshua (ed.) (1974) *Advances in Language Planning*, vol. 5 in *Contributions to the Sociology of Language*. Mouton, The Hague.

Fishman, Joshua (1977) *The Spread of English as a New Perspective for the Study of 'Language Maintenance and Language Shift'*. Newbury House, Rowley, MA.

Fishman, Joshua (1980) Bilingualism and biculturism as individual and societal phenomena. *Journal of Multilingual and Multicultural Developments*, 1(1): 3–15.

Fishman, Joshua (ed.) (1986) *The Fergusonian Impact: Sociolinguistics and the Sociology of Language*, vol. 2. Mouton de Gruyter, Berlin.

Fishman, Joshua (1989) *Language and Ethnicity in Minority Sociolinguistic Perspective*. Multilingual Matters, Clevedon and Philadelphia.

Fishman, Joshua and Lovas, John (1970) Bilingual education in sociolinguistic perspective. *TESOL Quarterly*, 4: 215–22.

Fishman, Joshua and Nahirny, Vladimir (1966) The ethnic group school and mother tongue maintenance. In Joshua Fishman (ed.) *Language Loyalty in the United States*. Mouton, The Hague, pp. 92–126.

Fishman, Joshua, Cooper, R. and Conrad, A. (1977) *The Spread of English*. Newbury House, Rowley, MA.

Fishman, Joshua, Ferguson, Charles and Das Gupta, Jyotirindra (eds) (1968) *Language Problems in Developing Nations*. Wiley, New York.

Flaitz, Jeffra (ed.) (1988) *The Ideology of English: French Perceptions of English as a World Language*, vol. 49 of *Contributions to the Sociology of Language*. Mouton de Gruyter, Berlin, New York.

Gardner-Chloros, Penelope (1985) Language selection and switching among Strasbourg shoppers. *International Journal of the Sociology of Language*, 54: 117–35.

Gardner-Chloros, Penelope (1991) *Language Selection and Switching in Strasbourg*. Clarendon Press, Oxford.

Gessinger, Joachim (1980) *Sprache und Bürgertum: Zur Socialgeschichte sprachlicher Verkehrsformen in Deutschland des 18. Jahrhunderts*. Metzler, Stuttgart.

Glassé, Cyril (ed.) (1989) *A Concise Encyclopedia of Islam*. Stacey International, London.

Glazer, Nathan (1966) The process and problems of language maintenance: an integrative review. In Joshua Fishman. (ed.) *Language Loyalty in the United States*. Mouton, The Hague, pp. 358–68.

Glazer, Nathan (1981) Pluralism and ethnicity. In Martin Ridge (ed.) *The New Bilingualism: An American Dilemma*. Univerisity of Southern California Press, Los Angeles, CA, pp. 55–70.

Goody, Jack (1986) *The Interface between the Written and the Oral*. Oxford University Press, New York.

Goossens, Jan (1969) *Strukturelle Sprachgeographie: Eine Einführung in Methodik and Ergebnisse*. Carl Winter Universitätsverlag, Heidelberg.

Gordon, David (1978) *The French Language and National Identity 1930–1975*, vol. 22 of *Contributions to the Sociology of Language*. Mouton, The Hague, Paris, New York.

Graebner, Alan H. (1965) The acculturation of an immigrant Lutheran Church: the Lutheran Church–Missouri Synod, 1917–29. PhD thesis, Columbia University.

Graham, William (1987) *Beyond the Written Word: Oral Aspects of Scripture in the History of Religion*. Cambridge University Press, Cambridge.

Grierson, George A. (1967) [1903–28] *Linguistic Survey of India*, vols 1–11. Motilal Banarsidass, Delhi.

Grillo, R. D. (1989) *Dominant Languages: Language and Hierarchy in Britain and France*. Cambridge University Press, Cambridge.

Guilhaumou, Jacques (1989) *La Langue politique et la Révolution française*. Méridiens Klincksieck, Paris.

Gumperz, John (1964) Linguistic and social interaction in two communities. *American Anthropologist*, 66(6), part II: 137–54.

Gumperz, John and Hymes, Dell (1972) Introduction. In John Gumperz and Dell Hymes (eds) *Directions in Sociolinguistics: The Ethnography of Communication*. Holt, Rinehart & Winston, New York.

Haarhoff, T. J. and Van Den Heever, C. M. (1946) *The Achievement of Afrikaans*. Central News Agency, South Africa.

HCLF (Haut commissariat de la langue français) (1975) *La Loi relative à l'emploide de la langue française*. Technical report. La Documentation Française, Paris.

Hagège, Claude (1987) *Le Français et les siècles*. Editions Odile Jacob, Paris.

Halliday, M. A. K., McIntosh, Angus and Strevens, Peter (1964) *The Linguistic Sciences and Language Teaching*. Longmans, London.

Hamers, Josiane and Blanc, Michael H. A. (1989) *Bilinguality and Bilingualism*. Cambridge University Press, Cambridge.

Hardgrave, Robet (1965) *The Dravidian Movement*. Popular Prakasan, Bombay.

Harmer, L. C. (1979) *Uncertainties in French Grammar*. Cambridge University Press, Cambridge.

Harris, Roy (1981) *The Language Myth*. Duckworth, London.

Harris, Roy and Taylor, Talbot (1989) *Landmarks in Linguistic Thought: the Western Tradition from Socrates to Saussure*. Routledge, London.

Hart, George L. (1975) *The Poems of Ancient Tamil. Their Milieu and their Sanskrit Counterparts*. University of California Press, Berkeley and Los Angeles.

Hartweg, Frédéric (1980) Le dialecte Alsacien: domaines d'utilisation. *Zeitschift für Dialektologie und Linguistik*, 32: 75–82.

Hartweg, Frédéric (1981) Sprachkonkakt und Sprachkonflikt im Elsaß. In Wolfgang Meid and K. Heller (eds) *Sprachkontakt als Ursache von Veränderungen der Sprach- und Bewusstseinsstruktur: eine Sammlung von Studien zur sprachlichen Interferenz*, vol. 34 of *Innsbrucken Beiträge zur Sprachwissenschaft*. Institut für Sprachwissenschaft, Innsbruck.

Hartweg, Frédéric (1983) Tendenzen in der Domänenverteilung zwischen Dialekt und nicht-Deutscher Standardsprache am Beispiel des Elsaß. In Werner Besch, Ulrich Knoop, Wolfgang Putschke and Herbert Ernst Wiegand (eds) *Dialektologie: ein Handbuch der deutschen und allgemeinen Dialektforschung. Handbücher zur Sprach- und Kommunikationswissenschaft*, II (81): 1325–31.

Hartweg, Frédéric (1986) *Die Entwicklung des Verhältnisses von Mundart, deutscher und französischer Standardsprache im Elsaß seit dem 16. Jahrhundert*. Walter de Gruyter, New York and Berlin, pp. 1949–77.

Haugen, Einar (1956) *Bilingualism in the Americas: A Bibliography and Research Guide*. Alabama University Press, Montgomery.

Haugen, Einar (1957) The semantics of Icelandic orientation. *WORD*, 13: 447–60.

Haugen, Einar, McClure, J. D. and Thomson, D. (eds) (1981) *Minority Languages Today*. University Press, Edinburgh.

Hauptfleisch, T. (1977) *Language Loyalty in South Africa*, vol. 1: *Bilingual Policy in South Africa – Opinions of White Adults in Urban Areas*. South African Human Sciences Research Council; Institute for Languages, Literature and Arts, Pretoria.

Hazen, Charles D. (1917) *Alsace-Lorraine under German Rule*. Henry Holt & Co., New York.

Heath, Shirley Brice (1972) *Telling Tongues; Language Policy in Mexico, Colony to Nation*. Columbia University, Center for Education in Latin America Publications. Teachers College Press, New York.

Heath, Shirley Brice (1976) A national language academy? Debate in the new nation. *International Journal of the Sociology of Language*, 11: 9–43.

Heath, Shirley Brice (1977) *Language and Politics in the United States*, no. 28 in *Georgetown University Round Table on Languages and Linguistics*. Georgetown University Press, Washington, DC, pp. 267–98.

Heath, Shirley Brice and Laprade, Richard (1982) Castilian colonization and indigenous languages: the cases of Quechua and Aymara. In Robert Cooper (ed.) *Language Spread*. Indiana University Press and Center for Applied Linguistics, Bloomington, pp. 118–47.

Health, Shirley Brice (1992) Why no official tongue? In James Crawford (ed.) *Language Loyalties: A Source Book on the Official English Controversy*. University of Chicago Press, Chicago and London, pp. 20–31.

Heizer, Robert F. (1947) *Francis Drake and the California Indians, 1579*. University of California Press, Berkeley and Los Angeles.

Heizer, Robert F. (1966) *Languages, Territories and Names of California Indian Tribes*. University of California Press, Berkeley.

Heizer, Robert F. (1976a) *The California Indians vs the United States of America (HR4497): Evidence Offered in Support of Occupancy, Possession and Use of Land in California by the Ancestors of Enrolled Indians of California*. Ballena Press, Socorrow, NM.

Heizer, Robert F. (1976b) *The Indians of California: A Critical Bibliography*. Indiana University Press, Bloomington.

Heizer, Robert F. (1978a) History of research. In Robert F. Heizer (ed.) *Handbook of North American Indians*, vol. 8: *California*. Smithsonian Institution and Government Printer, Washington, DC, pp. 6–15.

Heizer, Robert F. (1978b) Introduction. In Robert F. Heizer (ed.) *Handbook of North American Indians*, vol. 8: *California*. Smithsonian Institution and Government Printer. Washington, DC, pp. 1–5.

Heizer, Robert F. (1978c) Treaties. In Robert F. Heizer (ed.) *Handbook of North American Indians*, vol. 8. *California*. Smithsonian Institute and Government Printer, Washington, DC, pp. 701–4.

Heizer, Robert F. (1978d) *Some Last Century Accounts of the Indians of Southern California*. Ballena Press, Ramona, CA.

Heizer, Robert F., Nissen, Karen M. and Castillo, Edward D. (1975) *California Indian History: A Classified and Annotated Guide to Source Materials*. Ballena Press, Ramona, CA.

Hélias, Pierre-Jakez (1975) *Le Cheval d'orgueil: Mémoires d'un Breton du pays bigouden*. Plon, Paris.

Hell, Victor (1986) *Pour une culture sans frontières: L'Alsace, une autre histoire franco-allemande*. BF éditions, Strasbourg.

Herbert, Robert K. (ed.) (1975) *Patterns in Language, Culture and Society: Sub-Saharan Africa*, no. 19 in *Working Papers in Linguistics*, Ohio State University. Department of Linguistics, Columbus.

Hinton, Leanne and Montijo, Yolanda (1993–94). In our own words: how much is really left of California's native languages? *News from Native California*, 7(4): 4–9.

Hoenigswald, Henry (1966) A proposal for the study of folk-linguistics. In William O. Bright (ed.) *Sociolinguistics. Proceedings of the UCLA Sociolinguistics Conference, 1964*. Mouton, The Hague and Paris, pp. 16–26.

Hoffmann, F. (1981) Triglossia in Luxemburg. In Einar Haugen, J. D.

McClure and D. Thomson (eds) *Minority Languages Today.* Edinburgh University Press, Edinburgh.

Hofman, John E. (1966) Mother tongue retentiveness in ethnic parishes. In Joshua Fishman (ed.) *Language Loyalty in the United States.* Mouton, The Hague pp. 139–50.

Hofman, John E. (1972) [1968] The language transition in some Lutheran denominations. In Joshua Fishman (ed.) *Readings in the Sociology of Language.* Mouton, The Hague, pp. 620–38.

Hornby, Peter A. (1977) *Bilingualism. Psychological, Social and Educational Implications.* Academic Press, New York.

Horton, John and Caldéron, José (1992) What happens when English only comes to town? A case study of Lowell, Massachusetts. In James Crawford (ed.) *Language Loyalties: A Source Book on the Official English Controversy.* University of Chicago Press, Chicago and London, pp. 186–94.

Hudson, Alan (ed.) (1991a) *Studies in Diglossia.* Linguistic Association of the Southwest, Denton, TX.

Hudson, Alan (1991b) Toward the systematic study of Diglossia. *Southwest Journal of Linguistics,* 10(1): 1–22.

Hudson, Alan (1992) Diglossia: a bibliographic review. *Language in Society,* 21(4): 611–74.

Hughes, Christopher (1954) *The Federal Constitution of Switzerland.* Clarendon Press, Oxford.

Hymes, Dell (ed.) (1964) *Language in Culture and Society.* Harper & Row, New York.

Ihde, Thomas W. (ed.) (1994) *The Irish Language in the United States: A Historical, Sociolinguistic, and Applied Linguistic Survey.* Bergin & Garvey, Westport, CT and London.

Imhoff, Gary (1990) The position of US English on bilingual education. *The Annals of the American Academy of Political and Social Science,* 508: 48–61.

Inoue, Kyoko (1991) *MacArthur's Japanese Constitution: A Linguistic and Cultural Study of its Making.* University of Chicago Press, Chicago.

INSEE (Institut National de la Statistique et des Etudes Economiques) (1956) *Aspects particuliers des populations alsacienne et mosellane. Langues – personnes déplacées – religions,* no. 7 of *Etudes et documents démographiques.*

Irschick, Eugene F. (1969) *Politics and Social Conflict in South India. The Non-Brahman Movement and Tamil Separatism, 1916–1929.* University of California Press, Berkeley and Los Angeles.

Ivič, Pavle (1958) *Die Serbokroatischen Dialekte. Ihre Struktur und Entwicklung. Allgemeines und die Štokavische Dialektegruppe,* vol. I. Mouton, The Hague.

Jacob, James E. (1990) Language policy and political development in France. In Brian Weinstein (ed.) *Language Policy and Political Development.* Ablex Publishing Corporation, Norwood, NJ.

Jernudd, Björn (1989) *The Texture of Language Purism: an Introduction,* vol. 54 of *Contributions to the Sociology of Language.* Mouton de Gruyter, Berlin.

Jeyakanthan (1972) *munnāōṭṭam.* Talaignan Patippakam, Madras.

Jiminez, Martha (1992) The educational rights of language minority children.

In James Crawford (ed.) *Language Loyalties: A Source Book on the Official English Controversy*. University of Chicago Press, Chicago and London, pp. 243–55.

Kachru, Yamuna (1986) Expanding domains and changing roles of a standard language: Hindi in multilingual India. In Bh. Krishnamurti (ed.) *South Asian Languages: Structure, Convergence and Diglossia*, vol. III of *MLBD Series in Linguistics*. Matilal Banarsidass, Delhi, pp. 400–17.

Keyes, Charles F. (1977) *The Golden Peninsula. Culture and Adaptation in mainland Southeast Asia*. MacMillan, New York.

Khubchandani, Lachman M. (1983) *Plural Languages, Plural Cultures. Communication, Identity, and Sociopolitical Change in Contemporary India*. University of Hawaii Press, Honolulu.

Khubchandani, Lachman, M. (1988) *Language in a Plural Society*. Indian Institute of Advanced Study, Shimla.

Kittel, F. (1903) *A Grammar of the Kannaḍa Language, in English*. Basel Mission Book and Tract Depository, Mangalore.

Kloss, Heinz (1940) *Das Volksgruppenrecht in den Vereinigten Staaten von Amerika*, vol. 1. Essener Verlagsanstalt, Essen.

Kloss, Heinz (1963) *Das Nationalitätenrecht der Vereinigten Staaten von Amerika*. Braumuller, Vienna.

Kloss, Heinz (1966a) Types of multilingual communities: a discussion of ten variables. *Sociological Inquiry*, 36(2): 7–17.

Kloss, Heinz (1966b) German-American language maintenance efforts. In Joshua Fishman (ed.) *Language Loyalty in the United States*. Mouton, The Hague, pp. 206–52.

Kloss, Heinz (1967) *Abstand* languages and *Ausbau* languages. *Anthropological Linguistics*, 9(7): 29–41.

Kloss, Heinz (1969) *Research Possibilities on Group Bilingualism: a Report*. Technical report. International Center for Research on Bilingualism, Québec.

Kloss, Heinz (1977a) *The American Bilingual Tradition*. Newbury House, Rowley, MA.

Kloss, Heinz (1977b) *Les Droits linguistiques des Franco-Americains*. Les Presses de l'Université Laval, Québec.

Kohn, H. (1960) *Die Welt der Slawen*, vol. 1. Fischer, Frankfurt.

Krishnamurti, Bh. (1988) Standardization of Indian languages. In Lachman A. Khubchandani (ed.) *Language in a Plural Society*. Indian Institute of Advanced Study, Shimla.

Krishnamurti, Bh., Masica, Colin and Sinha, Anjani (1986) *South Asian Languages: Structure, Convergence and Diglossia*, vol. III of *MLBD Series in Linguistics*. Matilal Banarsidass, Delhi.

Labov, William (1972) *Sociolinguistic Patterns*. University of Pennsylvania Press, Philadelphia.

Labov, William (1982) Objectivity and commitment in linguistic science: the case of the Black English trial in Ann Arbor. *Language in Society*, 11(2): 165–201.

Laitin, David D. (1993) Migration and language shift in urban India. In Carol M. Eastman (ed.) *Language in Power*, special issue, *International Journal of the Sociology of Language*, 103: 57–72.

Lambert, W. E. (1977) The effects of bilingualism on the individual:

cognitive and sociocultural consequences. In Peter A. Hornby (ed.) *Bilingualism. Psychological, Social and Educational Implications.* Academic Press, New York, pp. 15–28.

Lambert, W. E. and Tucker, G. R. (1972) *Bilingual Education of Children: The St Lambert Experiment.* Newbury House, Rowley, MA.

Lambert, W. E., Gardner, R. C., Olton, R. and Tunstall, K. (1972) [1968] A study of the roles and attitudes and motivation in second-language learning. In Joshua Fishman (ed.) *Readings in The Sociology of Language.* Mouton, The Hague.

Laponce, Jean A. (1984) *Langue et territoire.* Les Presses de l'Université Laval, Québec.

Leibowitz, Arnold (1976) Language and the law: the exercise of power through official designation of language. In W. M. O'Barr and J. F. O'Barr (eds) *Language and Politics.* Mouton, The Hague.

Leibowitz, Arnold (1980) *The Bilingual Education Act: A Legislative Analysis.* InterAmerica Research Associates, Rosslyn, VA.

Lelyveld, David (1991) *Zuban-i urdu-i mu'alla*: vernacular language and the Mughal Court. Paper delivered to S. Asia conference, Wisconsin.

Lenin, V. I. (1950) *O prave Nacij na samoopredelenie.* Gosudarstvennoe Izdatel'stvo Političeskoi Literatury, Leningrad.

Lévy, Paul (1929) *Histoire linguistique d'Alsace et de Lorraine.* Société d'Edition Les Belles Lettres, Paris.

Lewis, E. Glyn (1972) *Multilingualism in the Soviet Union.* Mouton, The Hague.

Lockwood, W. B. (1976) *An Informal History of the German Language, with Dutch and Afrikaans, Frisian and Yiddish.* André Deutsch, London.

Lötscher, A. (1983) *Schweizerdeutsch. Geschichte, Dialekt, Gebrouch.* Huber, Fravenfeld.

Lowenberg, Peter H. (1988) *Language Spread and Language Policy. Issues, Implications, and Case Studies.* Georgetown University Press, Washington, DC.

MacKaye, Susannah D. A. (1987) California Proposition 63 and Public Perceptions of Language. Master's thesis, Stanford University.

MacKaye, Susannah D. A. (1990) California Proposition 63: Language attitudes reflected in the public debate. *Annals of the American Academy of Political and Social Science*, 508: 135–46.

Mackey, William (1970) A typology of bilingual education. *Foreign Language Annals*, 3: 596–608.

Mackey, William (1972) The description of bilingualism. In Joshua Fishman (ed.) *Advances in the Sociology of Language*, vol. II. Mouton de Gruyter, The Hague and Paris, pp. 413–32.

McRae, Kenneth D. (1983) *Conflict and Compromise in Multilingual Societies*, vol. 1: *Switzerland.* Wilfred Delaurier University Press, Waterloo.

McRae, Kenneth D. (1986) *Conflict and Compromise in Multilingual Societies*, vol. 2: *Belgium.* Wilfred Laurier University Press, Waterloo.

Maier, Everette and Mayer, Herbert T. (1964) The process of Americanization. In Carl S. Meyer (ed.) *Moving Frontiers: Readings in the History of the Lutheran Church–Missouri Synod.* Concordia Publishing House, St Louis.

Mandelbaum, David G. (ed.) (1949) *Selected Writings of Edward Sapir in*

Language, Culture and Personality. University of California Press, Berkeley.

Marr, John Ralston (1985) *The Eight Anthologies. A Study in Early Tamil Literature.* Institute of Asian Studies, Tiruvanmiyur, Madras.

Martinet, André (1985) The dynamics of plurilingual situations. In Joshua Fishman (ed.) *The Fergusonian Impact: Sociolinguistics and the Sociology of Language,* vol. 2. Mouton de Gruyter, Berlin, pp. 245–52.

Masica, Colin P. (1991) *The Indo-Aryan Languages.* Cambridge University Press, Cambridge.

Matesius, Vilém (1961) [1931] Zum Problem der Belastungs- und Kombinationsfähigkeiten der Phoneme. *Traveaux du Cercle Linguistique de Prague,* IV: 148–52.

Mead, Richard (1988) *Malaysia's National Language Policy and the Legal System.* Technical report 30. Yale Center for International and Area Studies, New Haven.

Mertz, Elizabeth (1982) *Language and Mind: A 'Whorfian' Folk Theory in United States Language Law,* no. 93 in *Working Papers in Sociolinguistics.* Southwest Educational Development Laboratory, Austin.

Mertz, Elizabeth and Weissbourd, Bernard (1985) Legal ideology and linguistic theory. In Elizabeth Mertz and Richard Parmentier (eds) *Semiotic Mediation: Sociocultural and Psychological Perspectives.* Orlando Academic Press, Orlando, FL.

Meyer, Carl S. (ed.) (1964) *Moving Frontiers: Readings in the History of the Lutheran Church–Missouri Synod.* Concordia Publishing House, St Louis.

Mezger, G. (ed.) (1922) *Denkstein zum 75. Jubiläum der Missourisynode.* Concordia Publishing House, St Louis.

Michel, J. (1967) Tentative guidelines for a bilingual curriculum. *Florida FL Reporter,* 5(3): 13–16.

Miller, Roy Andrew (1982) *Japan's Modern Myth: The Language and Beyond.* Weatherhill, New York and Tokyo.

Mulhauser, Frederick (1990) Reviewing bilingual-education research for congress. *Annals of the American Academy of Political and Social Science,* 508: 107–18.

Nader, Laura (1972) [1968] A note on attitudes and the use of language. In Joshua Fishman (ed.) *Readings in the Sociology of Language.* Mouton, The Hague, pp. 276–81.

Nayar, Baldev Raj (1969) *National Communication and Language Policy in India.* F. A. Prager, New York.

Note (1987) 'Official English': federal limits on efforts to curtail bilingual services in the states. *Harvard Law Review,* 100(6): 1345–62.

Nunberg, Geoffrey (1989) Linguists and the official language movement. *Language,* 65: 579–87.

Pachori, Satya S. (1990) The language policy of the East India Company and the Asiatic Society of Bengal. *Language Problems and Language Planning,* 14(2): 104–18.

Pädagogische Zeitschrift (1891–98) A journal of the *Evangelische Synode des Westens.* St Louis.

Panikkar, G. K. (1985) The minority language situation in Kerala. *International Journal of Dravidian Linguistics,* 14(2): 286–97.

Peal, E. and Lambert, W. E. (1962) The relation of bilingualism to intelligence. *Psychological Monographs*, 76: 1–23.

Petit Larousse (1962) (12th edn). Librairie Larousse, Paris.

Petitjean, Luce and Tournier, Maurice (1991) Bibliographie sur les réformes de l'orthographe. *Orthographe et Société*, special issue, *Mots*, 28: 128–9.

Philipp, Marthe (1978) Abschliessende Bemerkungen zum Thema Dialekt. In A. Finck, R. Matzen and M. Philipp (eds) *Mundart und Mundartdichtung im Alemannischen Sprachraum*. Institut de dialectologie alsacienne, Université des Sciences Humaines de Strasbourg, pp. 71–81.

Philipps, Eugène (1975) *Les luttes linguistiques en Alsace jusqu'en 1945.* Culture Alsacienne, Strasbourg.

Philipps, Eugène (1978) *L'Alsace face à son destin: la crise d'identité.* Société d'Edition de la Basse-Alsace, Strasbourg.

Philipps, Eugène (1982) *Le Défi Alsacien.* Société d'Edition de la Basse-Alsace, Strasbourg.

Phillipson, Robert (1992) *Linguistic Imperialism.* Oxford University Press, Oxford.

Piatt, Bill (1990) *Only English? Law and Language Policy in the United States.* University of New Mexico Press, Albuquerque.

Pool, Jonathan (1987) *Linguistic Equality*, special issue, *Language Problems and Language Planning*, 11(1).

Pool, Jonathan (1991) The world language problem. *Rationality and Society*, 3: 78–105.

Pope, George U. (1990) *The* Tiruvāçagam, *or Sacred Utterances of the Tamil Poet, Saint, and Sage Maṇikka-vāçagar.* Clarendon Press, Oxford.

Porter, Rosalie Pedalino (1990) The Newton alternative to bilingual education. *Annals of the American Academy of Political and Social Science*, 508: 147–59.

Powell, J. W. (1966) [1891] Indian linguistic families of America north of Mexico. In Preston Holder (ed.) *Introduction to Handbook of American Indian Languages and Indian Linguistic Families of America North of Mexico.* University of Nebraska Press, Lincoln, pp. 83–218.

Queneau, Raymond (1959) *Zazie dans le Métro.* Gallimard, Paris.

Rai, Amrit (1984) *A House Divided: The Origin and Development of Hindi/ Hindavi.* Oxford University Press, Delhi.

Ramanujan, A. K. (1970) Language and social change. In R. I. Crane (ed.) *Transition in South Asia: Problems in Modernization.* Duke University Press, Chapel Hill, NC.

Ramaswany, N. (1979) Formal and informal Tamil. PhD thesis, Kerala University, Trivandrum.

Ramswamy, Sumathi (1993) En/gendering language: the poetics of Tamil identity. *Comparative Studies in Society and History*, 35(4): 683–725.

Reyhner, Jon (1992) Policies towards American Indian languages: a historical sketch. In James Crawford (ed.) *Language Loyalties: A Source Book on the Official English Controversy.* University of Chicago Press, Chicago and London, pp. 41–7.

Renou, Louis (1956) *Histoire de la langue sanskrite. Collection Les langues de monde.* Editions IAC, Lyon.

Republic of India, Government of (1956) *Report of the Official Language Commission.* Technical report. Official Language Commission, Delhi.

Republic of India, Government of (1971) *The Twelfth Report of the Commission for Linguistic Minorities in India*. Technical report. Ministry of Home Affairs, Delhi.

Rhodes, Nancy C. (1980) Attitudes toward Guarani and Spanish: a survey. *The Linguistic Reporter*, 22(7): 4–5.

Rhodes, Susan and Thompson, Norman (1990) Anatomy of a positivist language policy: writing for the APA. Term paper for Linguistics 433.

Richelet, Pierre. (1680) *Dictionnaire française contenant les mots et les choses*. Widerhold, Geneva.

Roberge, Paul T. (1992) Afrikaans and the ontogenetic myth. *Language and Communication*, 12(1): 31–52.

Robertson, D. M. (1910) *A History of the French Academy*. Dillingham, New York.

Rona, J. P. (1966) The social and cultural status of Guaraní in Paraguay. In William O. Bright (ed.) *Sociolinguistics. Proceedings of the UCLA Sociolinguistics Conference, 1964*. Mouton, The Hague and Paris, pp. 277–98.

Rubin, J. (1972) [1968] Bilingual usuage in Paraguay. In Joshua Fishman (ed.) *Readings in the Sociology of Language*. Mouton, The Hague, 512–30.

Sadasivam, A. (1968) The Dravidian origin of Sumerian writing. In Xavier S. Thani Nayagam, V. I. Subramoniam, L. P. Kr. Ramanathan, S. Arasaratnam, R. E. Asher, Rama Subbiah and S. Singaravelu (eds) *Proceedings of the First IATR Conference*. Universiti Malaya, Kuala Lumpur.

Saer, D. J. Smith, Frank and Hughes, John (1924) *The Bilingual Program: A Study Based upon Experiments and Observations in Wales*. University College of Wales, Aberystwyth. Hughes & Son, Wrexham.

Salomon, Richard (n.d.) Orality, literacy and the shaping of religious tradition. Unpublished paper.

Sapir, Edward (1949) [1916] Time perspective in aboriginal American culture: a study in method. In David G. Mandelbaum (ed.) *Selected Writings of Edward Sapir in Language, Culture and Personality*. University of California Press, Berkeley.

Scherer, K. and Giles, Howard (1979) *Social Markers in Speech. European Studies in Social Psychology Series*. Cambridge University Press and Editions de la Maison des Sciences de l'Homme, Cambridge, London and Paris.

Schiffman, Harold F. (1974) Language, linguistics, and politics in Tamilnad. In Edwin Gerow and Margery D. Lang (eds) *Studies in the Language and Culture of South Asia*, no. 23 in *Publications on Asia of the Institute for Comparative and Foreign Area Studies*. University of Washington Press, Seattle, pp. 125–34.

Schiffman, Harold F. (1978) Diglossia and purity/pollution in Tamil. In Clarence Maloney (ed.) *Contributions to Asian Studies*, vol. II: *Language and Civilization Change in South Asia*. E. J. Brill, Leiden. pp. 98–110.

Schiffman, Harold F. (1987) Losing the battle for balanced bilingualism: the German-American case. *Language Problems and Language Planning*, 11(1): 66–81.

Schiffman, Harold F. (1989) Language loyalty in South Asia: some problems and approaches. *Berliner Indologische Studien*, IV: 225–8.

Schiffman, Harold F. (1991) Swiss-German Diglossia. *Southwest Journal of Linguistics*, 10(1): 173–88.

Schiffman, Harold F. (1992) 'Resisting arrest' in status planning: structural and covert impediments to status change implementation. *Language and Communication*, 12(1): 1–15.

Schiffman, Harold F. (1993) The balance of power in multiglossic languages: implications for language shift. In Carol M. Eastman (ed.) *Language in Power*, special issue, *International Journal of the Sociology of Language*, 103: 115–148.

Schneider, Carl E. (1939) *The German Church on the American Frontier.* Eden Publishing House, St Louis.

Schneider, Susan G. (1976) *Revolution, Reaction or Reform: The 1974 Bilingual Education Act.* LA Publishing Co., New York.

Schweitzer, Albert (1931) *Aus meinem Leben und Denken.* P. Haupt, Bern.

Secada, Walter G. (1990) Research, politics, and bilingual education. *Annals of the American Academy of Political and Social Science*, 508: 81–106.

Seligmann, N. (1979) Connaissance déclarée du dialecte et de l'allemand. *Chiffres pour l'Alsace*, 26(4): 21–30.

Shanmugam Pillai, M. (1960) Tamil – literary and colloquial. *International Journal of American Linguistics*, 26(3): 27–42.

Shanmugam Pillai, M. (1965) Merger of literary and colloquial Tamil. *Anthropological Linguistics*, 7(4): 98–103.

Shapiro, Michael C. and Schiffman, Harold F. (1981) *Language and Society in South Asia.* Motilal Banarsidass, Delhi.

Shigekane, R. (1992) Bilingual public services in California. In James Crawford (ed.) *Language Loyalties: a Source Book on the Official English Controversy.* University of Chicago Press, Chicago and London, pp. 303–11.

Shipek, Florence C. (1978) History of Southern California mission Indians. In Robert F. Heizer (ed.) *Handbook of North American Indians*, vol. 8: *California.* Smithsonian Institution and Government Printer, Washington, DC, pp. 610–18.

Shulman, David D. (1980) *Tamil Temple Myths.* Princeton University Press, Princeton.

Shuy, Roger W. and Fasold, Ralph W. (eds.) (1973) *Language Attitudes: Current Trends and Prospects.* Georgetown University Press, Washington, DC.

Silverman, Dan P. (1972) *Reluctant Union: Alsace-Lorraine and Imperial Germany, 1871–1918.* Pennsylvannia State University Press, State College.

Simpson, Paul (1993) *Language, Ideology and Point of View.* Routledge, London.

Sivattambi, K. (1979) *Taṇittamiṟ Iyakkattiṉ Araciyar Piṉṉaṇi.* Madras Book House, Madras.

Slone, G. Todd (1989) Language revival in France: the regional idioms. *Language Problems and Language Planning*, 13(3): 224–42.

Smith, David M. (1988) Language, speech and ideology: a conceptual framework. In Jeffra Flaitz (ed.) *The Ideology of English.* Mouton de Gruyter, Berlin, New York.

Smitherman, Geneva (1994) *Black Talk.* Houghton Mifflin: Boston.

Smolicz, J. J. (1979) *Culture and Education in a Plural Society.* Curriculum Development Center, Canberra.

Sommer, Martin S. (1922) Die Englische Arbeit in unserer Synode. In G. Mezger (ed.) *Denkstein zum 75. Jubiläum der Missourisynode.* Concordia Publishing House, St Louis.

Sonntag, Selma and Pool, Jonathan (1987) Linguistic denial and linguistic self-denial: American ideologies of language. *Language Problems and Language Planning,* 13(3): 46–65.

Sotiropoulos, Dimitri (1977) Diglossia and the national language question in modern Greece. *Linguistics,* 197: 5–31.

Spear, Percival (ed.) (1958) *The Oxford History of India* (3rd edn). Clarendon Press, Oxford.

Sreedhar, M. V. (1974) *Naga Pidgin: A Sociolinguistic Study of Interlingual Communication Pattern in Nagaland.* Central Institute for Indian Languages, Mysore.

Srinivas Iyengar, P. T. (1929) *History of the Tamils from the Earliest Times to 600 AD.* Naidu & Sons, Madras.

Staal, Frits (1986) *The Fidelity of Oral Tradition and the Origins of Science,* vol. 49(8) of *Mededelingen der koninklijke Nederlandse Akademie van Wetenschappen, afd. Letterkunde, Nieuwe Reeks.* North-Holland Publishing Company, Amsterdam.

Stach, J. F. (1942) A history of the Lutheran schools of the Missouri Synod in Michigan, 1845–1940. PhD thesis, University of Michigan, Ann Arbor.

Stellhorn, August C. (1963) *Schools of the Lutheran Church–Missouri Synod.* Concordia Publishing House, St Louis.

Stewart, Omer (1978) Litigation and its effects. In Robert F. Heizer (ed.) *Handbook of North American Indians,* vol. 8: *California.* Smithsonian Institution and Government Printer, Washington, DC, pp. 705–12.

Stewart, W. A. (1972) [1968] A sociolinguistic typology for describing national multilingualism. In Joshua Fishman (ed.) *Readings in the Sociology of Language.* Mouton, The Hague, 531–45.

Sturtevant, W. (ed.) (1983–95) *Handbook of North American Indians.* Smithsonian Institution Press and Government Printing Office, Washington, DC.

Tabouret-Keller, Andrée (1972) [1968] A contribution to the sociological study of language maintenance and language shift. In Joshua Fishman (ed.) *Readings in the Sociology of Language.* Mouton, The Hague. pp. 365–76.

Tabouret-Keller, Andrée (1986) Le bon et le mauvais usage selon la 'grande encyclopédie': une chimère diglossique au xviième siècle. *International Journal of the Sociology of Language,* 62: 129–56.

Tabouret-Keller, Andrée and Luckel, Frédéric (1981) La dynamique sociale du changement linguistique: quelques aspects de la situation rurale en Alsace. *International Journal of the Sociology of Language,* 29: 51–70.

Tadadjeu, Maurice (1975) Language planning in Cameroon: towards a trilingual education system. In Robert K. Herbert (ed.) *Patterns in Language, Culture and Society: Sub-Saharan Africa,* no. 19 in *Working Papers in Linguistics,* Ohio State University Department of Linguistics, Columbus, pp. 53–75.

Thernstrom, Stephan, Orlov, Ann and Handlin, Oscar (eds) (1980) *Harvard Encyclopedia of American Ethnic Groups.* Belknap Press, Harvard University Press, Cambridge, MA.

Tollefson, James (1981) Centralized and decentralized language planning. *Language Problems and Language Planning,* 5(2): 175–86.

Tollefson, James (1988) Covert policy in the United States refugee program in Southeast Asia. *Language Problems and Language Planning*, 12(1): 30–43.

Trudgill, Peter (1983) *Sociolinguistics: An Introduction to Language and Society*. Penguin, Harmondsworth.

US Government (1990) *Tribally Controlled Community Colleges Bill, s. 2167. Volume S 15024–15030*. Congressional Record, Washington, DC.

Vachek, J. (1964) *A Prague School Reader in Linguistics*. Indiania University Press, Bloomington.

Vassberg, Liliane M. (1993) *Alsation Acts of Identity: Language Use and Language Attitudes in Alsace*. Multilingual Matters, Clevedon, Avon.

Veltman, Calvin (1982) La régression du dialecte. *Chiffres pour l'Alsace*, 3: 65–72.

Veltman, Calvin (1983) *Language Shift in the United States*, vol. 34 of *Contributions to the Sociology of Language*. Mouton, Berlin.

Veltman, Calvin and Denis, M.-N. (1988) Usages linguistiques en Alsace: présentation d'une enquête et premiers résultats. *International Journal of the Sociology of Language*, 74: 71–89.

Verdoodt, Albert (1972) The differential impact of immigrant French speakers on indigenous German speakers: a case study in the light of two theories. In Joshua Fishman (ed.) *Advances in the Sociology of Language*, vol. II. Mouton de Gruyter, The Hague and Paris, pp. 377–85.

Vermes, Genevieve and Boutet, Josiane (eds) (1987) *France, pays multilingue*, vols I and II. L'Harmattan, Paris.

von Steinmeyer, Elias (1963) [1916] *Die kleineren Altochdeutschen Sprachdenkmäler. Deutsche Neudrücke: Reihe Texte des Mittelalters*. Weidmann, Berlin.

Wackernagel, Jacob (1896) *Altindische Grammatik*, vols I and II. Vendenhoeck & Ruprecht, Göttingen.

Wardhaugh, Ronald (1983) *Language and Nationhood: The Canadian Experience*. New Star Books, Vancouver.

Washbrook, D. A. (1976) *The Emergence of Provincial Politics: The Madras Presidency, 1870–1920*. Cambridge University Press, Cambridge and New York.

Washburn, Wilcomb E. (ed.) (1988) *Handbook of North American Indians*, vol. 4: *History of Indian–White Relations*. Smithsonian Institution and Government Printers, Washington, DC.

Watts, Ronald I. (1970) *Multicultural Societies and Federalism*, no. 8 in *Studies of the Royal Commission on Bilingualism and Biculturalism*. Information Canada, Ottawa.

Weckmann, André (1975) *schàng d sunn schint schun làng. Petite Anthologie de la Poésie Alsacienne*. L'Association Jean-Baptiste Weckerlin: Strasbourg.

Weinreich, Uriel (1968) [1953] *Languages in Contact*. Mouton, The Hague.

Weinstein, Brian (1989) *Francophonie: Purism at the International Level*, vol. 54 of *Contributions to the Sociology of Language*. Mouton de Gruyter, Berlin.

Welmers, William E. (1971) Christian missions and language policies. In T. Seboek (ed.) *Current Trends in Linguistics*, vol. 7. Mouton, The Hague.

West Bengal, Government of (1958) *Debates on the Non-Official Resolution on State Language*. Technical report, Proceedings, Legislative Council, Government of West Bengal.

Wexler, Paul (1971) Diglossia, language standardization and purism: parameters for a typology of literary languages. *Lingua*, 27: 346–54.

Wexler, Paul (1974) *Purism and Language. A Case Study in Modern Ukrainian and Belorussian Nationalism (1840–1967).* Indiana University Press, Bloomington.

Wexler, Paul (1989) *Hieratic Components in Soviet Dictionaries of Yiddish, Dungan, and Belorussian,* vol. 54 of *Contributions to the Sociology of Language.* Mouton de Gruyter, Berlin.

Whorf, Benjamin Lee (1964) A linguistic consideration of thinking in primitive communities. In Dell Hymes (ed.) *Language in Culture and Society.* Harper & Row, New York, 129–41.

Witherspoon, Gary (1977) *Language and Art in the Navajo Universe.* University of Michigan Press, Ann Arbor.

Zvelebil, Kamil (1991) *Tamil Traditions on Subrahmanya-Murugan.* Institute of Asian Studies, Madras.

Zvelebil, Kamil (1992) *Companion Studies to the History of Tamil Literature.* E. J. Brill, Leiden.

Index